new dimensions

new

dimensions

An Introduction to Human Communication

Linda Costigan Lederman
Rutgers University

wcb

Wm. C. Brown Company Publishers
Dubuque, Iowa

P90
L37

Book Team

Ed Bowers, Jr. Publisher/Editor
Jeannine Carlson Permissions Editor
David Corona Designer
Bill Evans Design Layout Assistant
Gloria Godenich Production Editor
Mary Heller Photograph Researcher
Ruth Richard Manager, Production-Editorial Department

Wm. C. Brown Company Publishers

Wm. C. Brown President
Larry W. Brown Executive Vice President
Ann Bradley Director of Marketing Strategy
Jim Buell Director of Information Management
John Carlisle Assistant Vice President, Production Division
Robert Chesterman Comptroller
David Corona Design Director
Lawrence E. Cremer Vice President, Product Development
Richard C. Crews Publisher
John Graham National Marketing Manager
Chuck Grantham National College Sales Manager
Linda Judge Director of Personnel/Public Relations
Roger Meyer Assistant Plant Superintendent
Paul Miller Vice President/Director, University Services
Roy Mills Assistant Vice President/Plant Superintendent
Ed O'Neill Vice President, Manufacturing
Dennis Powers Director of Information Services

Credits appear on page 390.

Copyright © 1977 by Wm. C. Brown Company Publishers

Library of Congress Catalog Card Number: 76–19473

ISBN 0–697–04118–2

Printed in the United States of America

To M. E. and the L. C. D.

This text, **New Dimensions: An Introduction to Human Communication,** is accompanied by the following learning aid:

Instructor's Manual to Accompany
New Dimensions: An Introduction to Human Communication

Contents

**Communication
Experiences**

The human being is a social animal and, as such, spends a great deal of time in some form of social interaction. An integral part of any human interaction is communication. *Communication* is a term that refers to the very broad range of behaviors from an infant's first cries of hunger, thirst, or boredom to the adult's most profound attempts at understanding and being understood. One's successes and failures at coping with his environment and the individuals peopling it are directly related to his abilities to communicate and to be communicated with.

Scholars in academic disciplines as diverse as biology,[1] anthropology,[2] psychology,[3] linguistics,[4] and zoology[5] concern themselves, in varying degrees, with communicative processes. The biologist views the human organism as composed of communicating systems of cells; the anthropologist is concerned with cultural patterns of communication; the linguist with language structures; and the zoologist with the communicative behavior of all animals, including the human animal. The vantage point from which the *process of communication* is viewed largely determines the defining characteristics of communication and the operative facets of the process.

This text is primarily concerned with the communication that occurs between people in face-to-face oral communication situations. Communication is defined as message-related behavior.[6] It is that process involving people, their messages, and their attempts to share meaning through the exchange of those messages. Our explorations encompass those elements and dynamics present in face-to-face verbal/nonverbal encounters.

The reader should be cognizant of three important features of this text. First, the text uses a two-pronged approach to communication: conceptual and experiential. Experiences related to communication concepts are integrated throughout the text. I believe that the student of communication is benefited by learning communication theory and at the same time exploring its applications to personal communicative behavior. Just as the student of dance must learn theories of movement and ways to translate that theory into improvement of bodily movement, the student of communication is shortchanged if the concepts of communication cannot be translated into improved communicative behavior.

The second feature of the text is its organization. The text focuses on interpersonal communication. Part one provides the student with an overview of the process and its interrelated elements. Part two dissects each of the elements, as defined in part one, revisiting the dynamics related to and affecting the particular element being explored. Part three builds on the understanding of interpersonal communication by exploring other contexts of human communication situations (the small group, public speaking, and public media). By introducing other communication situations in this last section of the text the student's understanding of the underlying similarities and differences in different human communication contexts is enhanced.

The third feature of the text is the replacement of the traditional third person pronoun, *he,* by a variation in which masculine (he), feminine (she), and neuter (one) are used interchangeably. This substitution has been made for two reasons. (1) There is a growing concern in our culture about the preponderance of racism and sexism in our language and (2) many nonracist and nonsexist words have been introduced into the language. This method of interchangeability has been selected as the least cumbersome way of dealing with the problem. The second and most important reason for this change has to do with sensitivity to language. In a text that spends a great deal of time analyzing meaning and where meanings lie, it would be inconsistent not to recognize the concern for sexism in language.

It is my position that words are arbitrary symbols used as vehicles of meaning. When a symbol such as *he* begins to take on discriminating connotations, new symbols need to be invented. But until that point is reached, an interchange of *he, she,* and *one* seems best for indicating that the pronouns used are not meant to carry any sex role significance. Meanings lie in people, not in words. Our behavior, however, often indicates that the meanings are in the words rather than in the people using them. It is for this reason that I have felt it necessary to explain the use of pronouns and what they mean in the writing of this text.

Notes

1. J. Z. Young, *Doubt and Certainty in Science: A Biologist's Reflection on the Brain* (New York: Oxford University Press, 1950).

2. Ray L. Birdwhistle, *Kinesics and Context* (Philadelphia: University of Pennsylvania Press, 1970).

3. Roger Brown, *Social Psychology* (New York: The Free Press, 1965).

4. Charles E. Osgood, George J. Suci, and Percy H. Tannenbaum, *The Measurement of Meaning* (Urbana, Ill.: University of Illinois Press, 1957).

5. H. Frings and M. Frings, *Animal Communication* (New York: Blaisdell, 1964).

6. Brent Ruben, "Communication, Communication Systems, and Conflict," a paper presented at the annual convention of the ECA, Philadelphia, 1976.

Acknowledgments

The approach used in this text grew out of experimentation with the basic course in communication while I was a member of the faculty at Nassau Community College. My colleagues, especially Pat Stack, and students at Nassau must be credited for creating the kind of learning environment in which such a project could begin.

In the course of writing and revising the manuscript, I relied on the help and moral support of colleagues and friends. My expressions of gratitude must begin with Sandy Landa, whose generosity and friendship cannot really be fully repaid. His help in the physical preparation of the manuscript was one of the factors that made it possible for me to complete an otherwise insurmountable task. I thank him and the many members of his staff whose services he generously allowed me to use over the course of the preparation of the manuscript.

I am grateful to the students and faculty at Rutgers University with whom I worked while preparing the final revision. I thank Richard Budd for his encouragement, Nancy Harper for her suggestions, and Brent Ruben for his advice as consultant on the communication concepts to be illustrated. Many students in the department of human communication also provided me with data and insights for the text. I am especially indebted to Mona Plummer for her assistance in gathering materials to illustrate the concepts.

Finally, I wish to express my appreciation to those people who have contributed directly to the final revision of the manuscript. I am indebted to colleagues who served as reviewers of the materials, especially Michael Moore and Brenda Burchett, and also Keith Miller, Patricia Stack, Ronald Subeck, and Darlyn Wolvin. Their insights and suggestions provided an invaluable vantage point from which to rethink the project. I am grateful to Dick Crews with whom the project was initiated, and to my editor for his expertise, encouragement, support, and sense of humor.

Many other people have contributed indirectly to the text in the course of my interactions with them. Among them I must single out Jim Barnhill who introduced me to speech fundamentals and public address, Franklin Haiman with whom I first studied group dynamics, and Mel Fishman from whom I have learned much that I know about interpersonal interaction. Most of all, I am indebted to Irv Lederman whose understanding and encouragement is a central force in my life; Joshua Lederman who has taught me more about communication in the five years since his birth than I realized I needed to learn; Wyn and Fritz Costigan; and my extended family, Florence, Paolo, Marco, Anthony and Michael Cucchi who endured with Irv and Josh the demands that this project has made on my time, energy, and sense of humor.

Part

1

Interpersonal Communication: An Overview of the Process

Basic Elements in the Process of Interpersonal Communication

1

Introduction

Communication is a word used to refer to a multitude of activities in which people engage, such as talking, touching, writing, looking, etc. Viewed differently, however, the word refers not to an activity itself but to a process basic to any life activity. This text focuses on communication as a set of activities in which people engage, while addressing some of the implications of communication as a basic life process.

As a process in which people engage with one another, **human communication** is a cycle involving at least four basic elements: (1) the sender–source, (2) the message, (3) the receiver–destination, and (4) the feedback–response. The *sender* has an idea or feeling to convey to someone; he initiates the communication. The idea or feeling that the sender transmits is the *message*. The *receiver* is that person to whom the sender directs his message. And, *feedback* is any response by the receiver to the message. The reason communication is referred to as a cycle is essentially due to feedback.

If we were to conclude our definition at this point we would be using the term *human communication* to refer to *any* message exchange between people. It could be oral (the sender talks to the receiver), written (the sender writes to the receiver), verbal (words), nonverbal (anything other than words). It could involve one person, two or more people, or a multitude. For our purposes we will be using the term *human communication* (or, communication) more narrowly, concerning ourselves primarily with those verbal and/or nonverbal exchanges between two or more people in face-to-face oral communication situations.

By limiting our definition of human communication, we are focusing on **interpersonal** communication. Our explorations will encompass those elements and dynamics present in the face-to-face verbal/nonverbal encounter. This and the following chapter, comprising part one, present an overview of the interpersonal communication process wherein all the elements and dynamics are named and explained.

Communication Goals

This chapter introduces a theoretical and experiential approach to the process of communication. It is written to enable you to begin your understanding of the process by:

1. Recognizing and defining the process of interpersonal communication.
2. Being more conscious than before of the role(s) you play in that process.
3. Distinguishing between verbal and nonverbal messages, and understanding the inseparable nature of the two.
4. Being more aware of the broad range of nonverbal behavior in your daily interactions.
5. Being more conscious of the channels through which communication occurs.
6. Understanding the kinds of interference that can take place in communication.

3

Communication Is a Cycle

Human communication in the interpersonal context has at least four
elements: sender, message, receiver, and feedback. It is the element of
feedback that makes the process circular. A simple model to illustrate this
description of communication is presented in figure 1.1. In elaborating
on our basic definition of communication, we will discuss each of the
elements presented in the model, and the circular nature of the entire
process in the interpersonal communication situation.

Figure 1.1
The Interpersonal
Communication Cycle.

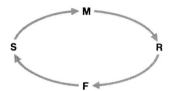

Sender, Message, Receiver, and Feedback
The first element depicted in the model is the **sender** or **source** of the
message(s). The sender is the initiating communicator, with an urge or need
to convey a thought, feeling, or wish. In interpersonal communication,
the sender can also be referred to as the *speaker,* or *encoder:* speaker,
because he expresses himself, at least partially, in spoken words; encoder,
because in effect he translates or encodes the inner workings of himself
into words.

There are further implications of acknowledging the sender as an
encoder, rather than limiting our description solely to speaker. In the oral
communication situation, words are only one of the possible **codes** (sets of
symbols) into which the sender can translate her inner experiences. Other
codes are **nonverbal.** Nonverbal communication codes cover the entire
range of communicative behavior exclusive of the verbal. Nonverbal codes
can be classified as performance (nonverbal signs arising out of bodily
action, such as gestures, smiles, or handshakes), artifactual (nonverbal
signs arising through the use of cosmetics, dress, furnishings, etc.),
mediational (nonverbal signs arising out of the selection and arrangement
of things in the media, such as where something is placed), and contextual
(nonverbal signs arising out of the use of time and space, such as sitting
closer to someone, or constantly being late).[1]

The sender, then, is the communicator who initiates the interpersonal
exchange. He may do it verbally ("It's snowing hard, so I'm not going to
work today"), nonverbally (pointing out the window; walking out the door
and right back in) or a combination of the two (walking out the door, right
back in, and saying as he takes off his coat, "It's snowing hard, so I'm
not going to work today.")

The **message** (M), the second element included in the communication model, is the thought, feeling, or wish that the sender has encoded in an attempt to communicate with the intended receiver. It is the content of the interpersonal exchange and may be encoded verbally and/or nonverbally, as shown by the example in the previous paragraph—the reaction to the heavy snowfall. In actuality, the message is not easily divisible into verbal and nonverbal components; rather, it consists of elements of both, which are often inseparable. The words and the actions of the sender are conveyed by his reaction to the snow. This dualism is exemplified by the words in an old song, "your lips tell me no, no, but there's yes, yes in your eyes." Ray L. Birdwhistle,[2] an anthropologist who has contributed extensively to research in nonverbal communication, puts it more scientifically. He argues that when the communication is properly understood, it is a multichannel phenomenon that must incorporate nonverbal as well as verbal activity. Using the words *verbal* and *nonverbal* together is as redundant, to Birdwhistle, as referring to someone as a loving lover.

The message(s) being sent between sender and receiver must travel along some pathway. **Channel,** or **medium,** is the term used to refer to any pathway through which a message is transmitted. Some of the channels used in interpersonal communication are visual, vocal/auditory, tactile, gustatory, and olfactory. In other words, the senses and the ways in which they are used serve as channels of communication. If we conceive of communication as *multichanneled,* we are acknowledging that more than one channel is conveying the message at a time. A person can taste as well as smell that food is rotten; hear fear in a friend's voice in addition to seeing it in his eyes; and see, feel, and taste snow.

The third element in the interpersonal communication cycle as represented in our model is the **receiver** (R)—the one who receives the message. In interpersonal communication, we can also refer to the receiver as the *listener, decoder,* or *responding communicator.* She is a *listener* because one of the channels used in interpersonal communication is the spoken verbal channel; *decoder* because she must reverse the process used by the sender and decode the message in order to understand what the sender is trying to convey; or *responding communicator* because her response or feedback indicates an understanding or misunderstanding of the sender's message. When the initiating communicator takes his coat off while saying, "It's snowing hard, I'm not going to work today," the receiver listens to the words, decodes their meaning, and responds, "Oh yeah?" Her response is the feedback to the initial message.

Feedback (F) is the fourth and final element in the model of communication. It refers to any response by the receiver to the sender's message, such as a nod, a wink, a smile, or a responding statement. Even what appears as a failure to respond is feedback. Feedback is not only a response, it is a message; it is the receiver's message. In traditional interpersonal communication theory, feedback is viewed as the information that flows from the receiver and is used by the initial sender of the message to measure his own effectiveness. In this framework communication is viewed as a cycle, as depicted in figure 1.1, with messages flowing from sender to receiver and back again.

Communication as Mutually Causal Cycles

While the foregoing view of interpersonal communication is a vital basis for understanding the process, it is a simplification. To make it a more consequential representation of the process, we must elaborate on the role of the receiver. In so doing we will expand our overall understanding of the workings of the interpersonal communication process.

Rather than viewing communication as the simple sender–message–receiver–feedback cycle, the role of the receiver must be realized as instrumental in determining meaning. Interpersonal communication must be depicted as **mutually causal cycles**[3]—all communicators interchangeably playing the parts of sender/receiver, and encoder/decoder. Figure 1.2 is our model of interpersonal communication as a mutually causal encounter.

This model presents an elaboration of the sender–message–receiver–feedback model by designating the dimension of sending and receiving as facets of the role of each communicator in the communication process. Consequently in figure 1.2, the initiator of the message is referred to as S/R rather than S to indicate that he is S (sender) when initiating

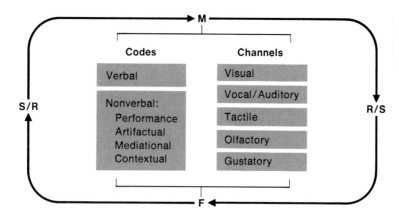

Figure 1.2
An Expanded Model of the
Interpersonal Communication
Cycle.

messages and R (receiver) when receiving them. In the model, the messages S/R receives are feedback from his initial receiver. The receiver is represented as R/S. She is receiver (R) when she is the destination for messages emanating from the sender, and the sender (S) when she encodes and transmits her response (F).

Let us refer once more to the message exchange regarding the heavy snowfall. If we were to use the *mutually causal* framework to analyze it, we would see that both the initiating communicator and his receiver are communicating simultaneously. After the initial words, the responder says something, thereby becoming the sender. The initial sender is then in the position of receiver of the responder's message, to which he in turn responds. If they were to communicate only by words, it might be realistic to assume that one person spoke while the other listened. The second person would then take her turn, and they would alternate. Making these assumptions would be safe even though we know that in the heat of a discussion verbal exchanges can overlap as the communicators vie for the "floor."

Once we understand communication as a multichanneled phenomenon, both people in the interpersonal communication situation can be seen as sending and receiving messages at once. However, in terms of the verbal code, only one of them usually speaks at a time and is therefore termed the sender, but both have available facial expressions, bodily actions, and sounds other than words (grunts, groans, ahha, umms, etc.) that also communicate. In any given interchange, all the verbal and nonverbal responses of the receiver affect the initial communicator. This is why we view the cycle as mutually causal. Each participant causes responses in the other.

Furthermore, this model incorporates more of the details about the process of communication (codes; channels) discussed earlier in the chapter. The result is a model that more realistically represents the communication process than the model presented in figure 1.1. It shows communication as a sending/receiving multichanneled and multimessage sending process.

A Working Definition of Interpersonal Communication

We have used the models of communication and the explanation of the various elements of the models as a way of indicating some of the complexities of the seemingly simple interchange of words between two people. Messages, encoded verbally and nonverbally, are sent rapidly and often in tandem with one another. Each participant in the interchange plays the roles of sender/receiver, encoder/decoder. Each switches from one role to the other almost imperceptibly; the communicator may not even be conscious of the role change. Communication experience 1.1 is designed to illustrate the dual roles people play while communicating with one another.

Communication Experience 1.1

Principle

All communicators act as senders and receivers of messages simultaneously.

Procedure

1. Select a partner.
2. Arrange to telephone one another later that day to discuss a preselected topic.
3. Designate who will be the initiator of the conversation.
4. At some point in the conversation, the person who has taken the role of receiver is to begin to inject *only* monosyllabic feedback (e.g., "ummm," "uh-huh," "oh," "ah," etc.). After two-to-three minutes of this, the person acting as receiver is to give *no* feedback for at least ninety seconds.

Discussion

What is the difference, to you, between talking to your partner in person or on the telephone? Does your partner agree with this difference? Who was the sender, who was the receiver, and how were you able to distinguish the difference? Would this have been easier or harder to do in person? What role did feedback play in this experience? What were the effects of the monosyllabic feedback? Of the silence? What other aspects of communication theory can be discussed as a result of your experience with this exercise?

As illustrated by communication experience 1.1, interpersonal communication can be defined as the transaction in which two or more people in a face-to-face communication situation act as senders and receivers of messages. These messages are encoded and transmitted through the verbal and nonverbal channels. This process is circular and mutually causal and contains the elements of sender, message, receiver, and feedback, which are present in any kind of human communication. In amplifying the basic explanation of the interpersonal communication process and its elements, let us take a more detailed look at the verbal and nonverbal codes as well as the channels available for their transmission. Communication experience 1.2 is designed to illustrate the interplay between the verbal and nonverbal codes.

Communication Experience 1.2

Principle

Verbal communication is affected by the nonverbal cues accompanying it. The absence of nonverbal cues interferes with message clarity.

Procedure

1. Work in dyads (pairs).
2. You and your partner sit in chairs that are positioned back to back.
3. You both have five minutes to discuss any given topic.
4. Do not look at one another until the experience has been completed.

Discussion

What did you discuss? Would the topic make any difference? What affects did your inability to see your partner have on your conversation? What affects did tone of voice or vocal cues have on the conversation? Was there use of gesture despite the arrangement of the chairs? How, if at all, does this exercise differ from communication experience 1.1 (the phone call)?

As illustrated by communication experience 1.2, interpersonal communication is composed of both verbal and nonverbal codes. In many respects these codes are so inseparable that it is hard to distinguish between them. But the distinction can be made for purposes of analysis. By dividing communication into verbal and nonverbal codes, we can examine and discuss how each contributes to the whole process of communication.

The Verbal Code: Words Are Symbols

The **verbal code** in interpersonal communication is made up of words. It is the set of verbal, or word, symbols into which communicators encode their thoughts and feelings. A person's stomach growls; he says, "I'm hungry." The words themselves are the symbols representing those nonverbal inner experiences referred to as feelings or thoughts (hunger, for example). To understand the role of words in interpersonal communication demands some understanding of the entire word-making process.

All words are symbols that stand for the objects and/or ideas to which one wants to refer. The objects and ideas are the **referents.** Words used to stand for or replace referents, words like *book, pew, candy,* and *coat* stand for, or name, physical objects. One can tell someone else about an object by using the word that stands for it.

All words have referents. Referents are divided into three classes: *object, concept,* and *process* referents. Object referents are persons, places or things, such as the physical objects previously cited. These are the easiest referents to distinguish. Concept referents are thoughts or ideas. Such words as *beauty, love,* and *charity* are symbols standing for concepts. They are concept referents. Process referents have to do with the ways in which something is or happens. Words like *is, going,* and *thinking* stand for process referents.

The verbal code, then, is composed of symbols that stand for objects, ideas, and processes. A language is a verbal code. The English language has rules (grammar) for the ways in which symbols are constructed and used in relation to one another. French, Italian, Spanish, German, and Swahili are examples of other verbal languages or verbal code systems. Each relies on verbal symbols to stand for objects, ideas, and processes. The rules for symbol making and usage differ from one verbal language to another. However, the basic process of a word standing for its referent is the same.

To understand the process of interpersonal communication, one must know something about these kinds of verbal codes. The messages that pass between people in interpersonal communication are often verbal. The verbal code is one of the ways in which people share their inner worlds with one another. In part two of the text we will analyze, in detail, the elements of the interpersonal process. The chapters dealing with the element of the message are devoted to an analysis of verbal codes. Communication experience 1.3 is designed to provide a basic understanding of the symbolic nature of the verbal code in interpersonal communication.

Communication Experience 1.3

Principle

In interpersonal communication, the verbal code is a set of symbols that stand for objects, ideas, and processes.

Procedure

1. Work individually.
2. Select a word that identifies some object that you frequently use.
3. For forty-eight hours you may not use that word.
4. During that time span, carry around with you the object for which the word stands.
5. Whenever it is necessary to refer to the object, show the object rather than use the word that stands for it.

Discussion

Was it possible to keep from using the word during the forty-eight hours? Did the direct use of the object instead of the verbal symbol affect communication? How? What are the benefits for having word symbols? What are the implications of this experience? How does it illustrate the symbolic nature of words?

As illustrated by communication experience 1.3, words are symbols They form the verbal code, which is one of the languages by which messages travel between senders and receivers in the interpersonal communication process. Nonverbal codes, representative of nonverbal behavior, are other languages we use to encode messages. They form the second facet of message making in the process by which people share thoughts, ideas, and feelings with one another.

Nonverbal Codes: Word-Related Behaviors

Generally, when one hears the term **nonverbal communication,** what comes to mind is silence—communication without words. But the nonverbal component of interpersonal communication consists of any meaning-carrying code other than words. A smile is as potentially communicative as the words, *I am happy;* a wink is as communicative as the word, *hello;* an "uggh" can show as much dissatisfaction, or even more, than a verbal explanation of one's dislike of something. Since humans are capable of attaching some sort of symbolic meaning to almost

anything, nonverbal communication encompasses a vast range of communicative behaviors. Earlier in the chapter, we divided nonverbal communication into four codes: performance, artifactual, mediational, and contextual. Another schema used to analyze nonverbal behavior divides it into three areas: kinesics, paralanguage, and proxemics.

The most obvious nonverbal communication stems from the use of the body and is referred to as **kinesics.** Gestures, facial expressions, and bodily movements or postures are all in the realm of kinesics. All are potential avenues for nonverbal meanings. Many of the kinesic cues emitted by the sender may be so unconscious that she is unaware that she is communicating something. Even such unconscious movement as changes in body position (shifting in a chair, slumping, or tensing) can provide significant cues that either reinforce or contradict the verbal message they accompany. A man, in the lobby of a hotel, who sits lighting one cigarette from another while glancing at a clock "says" nothing verbally, but he communicates nonverbally. Communication experience 1.4 is designed to illustrate kinesics in the process of interpersonal communication.

Communication Experience 1.4

Principle

A richness of meaning is available to communicators even when verbal cues are limited. Our bodily actions or behaviors are as expressive as the word symbols we use to communicate.

Procedure

1. Work in groups of four.
2. Each group must decide
   a. where they are; for example, in a taxi, at a party, or in a classroom.
   b. who they are in relation to one another; for example, a driver and three passengers, host and hostess and party crashers, or teacher and students.
3. Each group has ten minutes for its members to communicate with one another.
4. Group members may use only the words *rutebager, rutebager, cabbages and kings.*
5. The object is to convey to those observing the group their identities and relationships.

Discussion

How can those acting as the observers tell anything about the groups and their interrelationships? How did group members attempt to communicate? What, if anything, interfered? How did the verbal symbols sound by the end of the experience? What was the interface between verbal and vocal cues? Verbal and visual? How much did things other than what the group did affect the audience's perception of the meaning of the exercise?

As illustrated by communication experience 1.4, body codes carry meanings. So, too, do one's tone of voice and vocal utterances (sounds other than words). A second major nonverbal code is **paralanguage,** which consists of any kind of vocal, but not verbal, communication. Grunts, groans, and laughs all qualify as paralanguage or vocal nonverbal communication. Another aspect of vocal communication is tone of voice: how one says the words he uses. Perhaps tone of voice is a good example of the interrelationship between verbal and nonverbal communication. While **verbal communication** is made up of the *words* the sender uses, **vocal communication** is the *sound* of those words, plus any other accompanying sounds. In oral communication, the verbal and vocal messages are often so overlapping as to be indivisible. Spoken words are never uttered without vocal communication. The word *yes* can carry as many meanings as the tones of voice by which it can be uttered (Yes, Yes? Yes! y-e-s?).

The third area of nonverbal communication is concerned with the use of time and space in communication and is called **proxemics.** Proxemics is the study of the ways in which people communicate by their use of time and space in dealing with other people. The way an executive places the furniture in her office is an example of space being used to mean something. The distance between her desk and a chair in which a visitor may sit can be interpreted as saying something about the formal nature of the relationships between people using that office. It also denotes power. So, too, does the use of time. That same executive can keep a potential employee waiting for almost any length of time for an appointment, communicating her authority or power. The job applicant, however, cannot come two hours late for his interview—the exception being the applicant who is so outstanding that he may be able to assert power by his use of time.

We have discussed the verbal and nonverbal components of the interpersonal communication situation. The verbal and nonverbal codes and the interplay between them account for the complexity of meaning in any one given exchange. While the words say "yes," the tone may say, "if I have to," and the bodily tensions and physical distancing may convey other implications. Let us now briefly survey the channels through which these encoded messages are transmitted.

Channels of Communication: Pathways for Messages
Since communication codes are verbal and nonverbal, the messages they carry are encoded verbally, visually, and/or vocally. In fact, the five senses play a vital role in communication. The senses are the channels by which messages are sent and received; they are the pathways through which

verbal and nonverbal messages are transmitted. You can communicate or be communicated with by use of your sense of sight (visual), sound (vocal/auditory), touch (tactile), and taste and smell (gustatory and olfactory), or any combination of these. If as someone walks into his house, he *sees* a fur coat on the couch, *hears* his aunt's voice in the kitchen, *touches* the coat and *feels* fresh raindrops still clinging to it, *smells* coffee brewing, and goes into the kitchen to join them in *tasting* his mother's brownies and coffee, all of his senses would be used in decoding messages. Communication experience 1.5 is designed to illustrate that all the senses are used in interpersonal communication.

Communication Experience 1.5

Principle

Interpersonal communication relies on the use of all of one's senses as pathways for verbal and nonverbal messages.

Procedure

1. Work with a partner.
2. Sit facing your partner, at least three feet away.
3. The partners close their eyes, keeping them closed until the experience is completed.
4. Partners touch hands and try to send messages, without using words.
5. After five minutes, stop, open your eyes, and use words to tell each other the messages sent. Discuss what messages each thought the other was trying to convey.

Discussion

Was communication possible? How? Why or why not? How did you and your partner feel about doing this exercise? What effect did keeping your eyes closed have on the experience? Did the distance between you and your partner have any effect? How well did the two of you know each other before the exercise and did that have any bearing on your feelings? In what ways did tone of voice and body language affect the discussion of the first part of the exercise?

As illustrated by experience 1.5, the channels of communication are merely pathways. The messages traveling along them may be verbal or nonverbal: one can *see* words (*written*-verbal) or gestures (nonverbal); one can *hear* words (*oral*-verbal) or tones (nonverbal); the other senses would seem to be designated more for detecting nonverbal messages: one can touch, smell, or taste something, and from it derive meaning.

The pathways for messages in interpersonal communication are the senses of the communicator. She uses them for hearing, seeing, touching, smelling and/or tasting. The meanings derived by use of the senses are the products of the people interacting with one another.

Interference with Intentional Communication

In the contemporary study of human communication, three points of view have emerged on the ability of humans to communicate with one another: (1) we *can* communicate, (2) we *cannot* communicate, and (3) we *cannot not* communicate.[4] The differences rest on two fundamental questions concerning the meaning of the word *communicate*. The first question asks, does the word *communication* include in its meaning "understanding"? That is, in order for communication to take place must the communicators understand one another? Second, does *communication* include the concept of "intent"? That is, in order for one to communicate, must he have intended the meaning derived by his receiver? The ways in which these questions are answered determine one's point of view on the question of whether or not we can communicate with one another interpersonally.

Both the first and second positions rest on the assumptions that communication includes both understanding and intention. To communicate therefore means to be understood; if there is no understanding, there is no communication. We often hear about a daughter's inability to "communicate" with her mother, or a husband and wife in divorce court claiming they no longer "communicate" with one another. (I just don't understand him any more. He's not the man I married.) To communicate would also include intent. (I'm not communicating. That's not what I meant.) If there is understanding and intended meaning, then the communicators can communicate; if one or the other is absent, they cannot communicate.

The third position, we *cannot not* communicate, rests on the assumption that intent and understanding are extraneous to the concept of communication. Proponents of this position argue that communication exists regardless of the sharing of meaning or the intention of the initiator of the communication. These people contend that when someone says "I'm not communicating," what he's really saying is that he is not communicating what he *intended* to communicate; but nonetheless, he's communicating something. Everything, whether or not it is intended or understood as intended, has meaning and therefore communicates. The

Mr. Joe B., Vice President
XYY Company
Ann Arbor, Michigan

Dear Joe:
 I know you believe you understood what you
think I said,
 But I am not sure you realize what you heard
is not what I meant.
 What I meant was we really do make good
tires.

                    Warm regards,
                    Sandy L.

child may not get his mother to understand him, but he does communicate with her; a husband and wife in divorce court haven't stopped communicating, they just don't like what they communicate to one another.

Since I believe that we cannot not communicate, I see "interference" with communication as interference with *intended* meaning.
In the earlier part of the chapter, I described the process of communication and how it works. Another approach is to look at what, if anything, can interfere with the process. If factors interfere with the desired communication it does not mean that communication has not occurred. Instead, they inhibit receipt of the message as it was intended by the sender.

There are factors that can stand in the way of communicating as desired. For example, if two would-be communicators have no common language, verbal or nonverbal, an interference with intentional communication would exist. Other examples of barriers to intentional communication include deafness or extreme hostility toward the speaker. In such instances, obstacles must be overcome before purposive (intended) communication can take place.

The specific interferences central to the process of communication are those forces that explicitly block or inhibit effective shared communication. Inhibiting factors may exist prior to an overt attempt to communicate: one may know someone's reputation as a liar and therefore be closed to letting him communicate with him. Other inhibiting factors occur during the course of the interpersonal exchange. Someone may say something he means one way but his listener interprets it to mean something else; a student may hear only part of the instructions given by his teacher, because of poor acoustics or daydreaming; a friend may take so long in telling a story that his listener's attention drifts. In each instance an interference with shared understanding of a message exists. The sender and the receiver understand the messages being sent between them, but they understand them differently. Certainly everyone has had the experience of getting feedback that indicated that his message was not understood in the way he had intended it. But often, there are different understandings of the meaning of a message with neither person having any idea that the meaning he understands is different from that of the other person. Each just assumes that there is an understanding.

Interpersonal communication is a cycle involving a sender, message, receiver, and feedback, and the codes and channels, into and through which the messages are transmitted. Interference with intentional meaning can occur in the functioning of any one or more of these components. Specific interference involving the speaker, message, or receiver will be discussed in the sections of the text that follow. For the moment, then, it is sufficient to note that shared meaning is impossible if there is any interference with the transmission of the messages between the speaker and listener.

Interpersonal communication is an interpretative process. People use words and actions in an attempt to share their inner thoughts and feelings with one another. Each uses his senses for observing those words and actions. He must then interpret what he observes. This interpretation step is at the "heart" of discovering meaning. Each communicator is equipped with his own set of ways for interpreting or understanding behavior. He enters the interaction in hopes of arriving at shared meaning—similar interpretations of words and actions. But, this is a complex process, it involves people's communication behaviors and people's understanding of one another. Interference with intentional meaning exists when those meanings are not shared. Exploring interpersonal communication is exploring human behavior. It involves analysis of (1) what people say and do and (2) how those words and actions are interpreted by both the person acting and the person observing the actions.

I believe in

Universal Disarmament,

the elimination of all guns.
Guns are an indication
that there has been
a breakdown in communications.
They are the end result
of the failure to communicate.

In this chapter we have presented an overview of the process of communication. We have named and briefly explained the basic elements of the process that will be looked at in detail in part two of this text. These are the important points to understand as a basic starting point in talking about communication: **Summary**

1. Communication can be defined in many ways, depending on the perspective of the person giving the definition.
2. Interpersonal communication is the exchange of messages between a sender and a receiver in an oral face-to-face communication situation.
3. The elements present in interpersonal communication are sender, message, receiver, and feedback. Because of the feedback element, the process is considered a cycle.
4. The cycle of communication in the interpersonal situation is mutually causal. All communicators are senders/receivers and receivers/ senders of messages.
5. Messages in interpersonal communication are verbal, nonverbal and, most often, a combination of the two.
6. One method of categorizing nonverbal messages is through the use of codes: performance, artifactual, mediational, and contextual.
7. The pathways through which messages are sent in interpersonal communication are referred to as channels or media. All five senses are channels.
8. Feedback is any response, or lack of response, to the initiating communicator's message.
9. Verbal communication consists of the verbal, or word, code into which messages may be put.
10. Nonverbal communication can be discussed as kinesics, paralanguage, and proxemics.
11. Interference with intentional meaning between the communicators exists when communicators do not share common meanings for their words and actions.

1. How, if at all, would communication be changed if the process did not include feedback? **Questions for Discussion**
2. If your lips say "yes" while your eyes say "no," to which does the receiver respond?
3. How does nonverbal communication include sexual communication?
4. In which occupations does communication play an important role? What occupations are not affected at all by communication?
5. In any given situation, what might a speaker expect to receive as feedback from his receiver? How does the speaker determine the meaning of the feedback?

6. Discuss the difference between the following statements.
   a. *We don't communicate.*
   b. *We don't communicate what we intend to communicate.*
7. Why is the visual aspect considered part of *oral* interpersonal communication? Elicit as many points of view as possible on the hypothesis that the eyes are a source of interpersonal communication.
8. Differentiate the problems arising from the following situations.
   a. *The speaker is unaware of the feedback from his receiver.*
   b. *The speaker misinterprets feedback from his receiver.*
9. Discuss the barriers to communication that you have experienced as a sender or receiver of a message.
10. Why are the senses of touch and smell considered channels of communication?
11. Discuss the nonverbal messages you use to size up a professor on the first day of class.
12. Note the physical arrangement of a living room, a professor's office, a dentist's office, a dorm lounge or a restaurant. What messages are sent by the arrangement, style of furnishings, colors, and any other visual stimuli?
13. What do you know about your vocal communication, especially your tone of voice? Does it ever get you into trouble?

Notes

1. Randall P. Harrison, "Nonverbal Behavior: An Approach to Human Communication," in *Approaches to Human Communication,* ed. Richard Budd and Brent Ruben (New York: Spartan Books, 1972), p. 257.

2. Ray L. Birdwhistle, *Kinesics and Context* (Philadelphia: University of Pennsylvania Press, 1970); "Communication," in *International Encyclopedia of Social Sciences,* vol. 3, ed. D. Sills (New York: Macmillan, 1968).

3. Brent D. Ruben, "General Systems Theory," in *Approaches to Human Communication,* ed. Richard Budd and Brent Ruben (New York: Spartan Books, 1972), p. 133.

4. I am indebted to my colleague, the late John Kim of Rutgers University, for his articulation of this distinction.

Berlo, David. *The Process of Communication: An Introduction to Theory and Practice.* New York: Holt, Rinehart and Winston, 1960. A basic communication text. It is especially recommended for Berlo's model of communication.

Birdwhistle, Ray L. *Kinesics and Context.* Philadelphia: University of Pennsylvania Press, 1970. Birdwhistle is an anthropologist who has contributed a good deal to the study of nonverbal communication. His book is recommended for his emphasis on context as affecting meaning.

Bosmajian, Haig A. *The Rhetoric of Nonverbal Communication.* Glenview, Ill.: Scott, Foresman and Company, 1971. An anthology devoted to nonverbal communication. Recommended for the student interested in a variety of aspects of nonverbal behavior.

Budd, Richard and Brent D. Ruben. *Approaches to Human Communication.* New York: Spartan Books, 1972. This is an anthology of approaches to communication. It is difficult for the beginning student, but worth the effort for one who has a basic understanding of communication concepts.

Fabun, Don. *Communications: The Transfer of Meaning.* Beverly Hills, Calif.: Glencoe Press, 1968. A short, visual, communication pamphlet. Recommended as a supplement to any basic interpersonal textbook.

Selected Bibliography

New Dimensions: Dynamics Affecting Interpersonal Communication

2

Introduction

The phenomenon of communication is quite familiar to most of us, and generally speaking *communication* is a very popular term these days. This makes it more difficult to talk "sense" about communication, because the more familiar a phenomenon is the more difficult it is to develop a sound, observable, and testable understanding of it.[1] To simplify this task, we approach interpersonal communication by discussing the components of the process—the sender–message–receiver–feedback components. This, like any such classification, presents a scheme for distinguishing classes of processes and elements of a given concept. In choosing a framework in which to classify the elements of interpersonal communication, we have a perspective from which we can discuss the various parts of that process.

Interpersonal communication occurs between people who are the senders/receivers of messages. People are complex beings shaped to a large extent by all their experiences prior to and during any given attempt at communicating interpersonally. As a commuter observed, "The bus driver's wife must have burned his toast this morning, and so he's snarling at all the passengers." In order to analyze any interpersonal attempt at communication, we must look not only at the communication itself, but also at the communicators and the internal and external dynamics that shape them and their communicative behavior. In this chapter we will do this by presenting another model of communication that builds on the models presented in chapter one, by incorporating those dynamics.

Communication Goals

This chapter introduces those dynamics essential to any interpersonal communication and has been written to enable you to continue your understanding of communication by:

1. Noting the limitations of discussing the interpersonal exchange with reference only to the sender–message–receiver–feedback elements.
2. Beginning to be more sensitive to certain dynamics present in the communication situation.
3. Being more aware of the influence of all of your life experiences prior to and during any communication exchange.
4. Taking stock of some of the effects of those experiences, such as encoding and decoding skills; perceptions of self and others; and the influences exerted on you by the groups to which you belong or belonged.
5. Becoming aware of the effects of the environment and role relationships between communicators that shape the ways in which they communicate.
6. Understanding these dynamics as they interrelate with one another and the four basic elements of communication as a frame of reference from which to view the process; and as tools for a more analytical understanding.

Communication Concepts and Experience

Joshua (age 5) and his friends Anthony (7), Marco (8), and Danny (8) sat one day looking at a finger painting that Marco had made in school. Marco explained to his friends that the painting reminded him of the ways in which all forms of animal life had to cooperate and share the gifts of nature. Each of the others elaborated (in 8-year-old terms) on that theme, until it was Joshua's, the youngest's, turn. He looked at them and said, "I was going to say that it looked like a birdie and doggie, but I changed my mind."

Expanding the Communication Model: New Dimensions

We can only begin to analyze the interpersonal interaction that took place in this example if we limit ourselves to the sender–message–receiver–feedback components of the communication process. Joshua's change of heart had to do with the ways in which he perceived himself, his friends, and their expectations of him. It resulted from the messages they were sharing and all the other dynamics of communication present at the moment the boys were sharing their thoughts. Figure 2.1 presents a model of communication designed to incorporate the essential components (S-M-R-F) plus the dynamics that shape or in some way influence the communication in any interpersonal exchange. We will use it and the explanations thereof to focus on the dynamics affecting the S-M-R-F cycle.

Each of us is the product or sum total of all our living experiences, represented in the model as the circle encompassing each sender/ receiver and receiver/sender, and labeled **field of experience**.[2] The boxed-in area in each circle of life experience contains the dynamics of the living experience most central to interpersonal communication,

Figure 2.1
New Dimensions in the
Interpersonal Cycle.

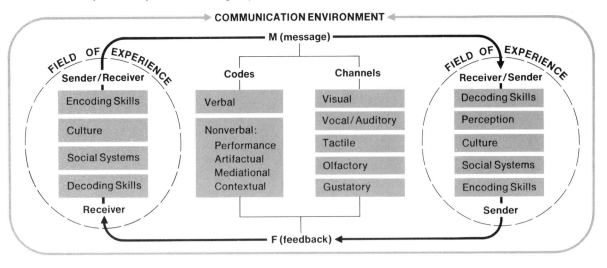

labeled: *encoding/decoding skills, perception* (of self, others, messages), *social systems,* and *culture.* The model is bounded by a square labeled *communication environment,* which represents the specific social and physical reality within which the communication occurs. We will complete our overview of the process of communication by discussing each of these dynamics and then considering the levels of analysis that can be used in a communication situation. Part two of the text uses this overview as a frame of reference for dissecting the components of the communication process.

Field of Experience

Everything is part of the communicator's field of experience, including whether or not she hated green jelly beans as a child. In fact, everything that she has experienced comprises her field of experience: food preferences, schools attended, health, religion, race, sex, nationality, sisters and brothers, allergies, economic status, eye color, weight, and sexual experience, to name a few.

Since the communicator's field of experience includes everything in his life, it also affects his communication. When friends, who share a "private" joke are reminded of it by a third person who "innocently" says something, it is funny to them because of what previously happened to them. This is part of the field of experience. The reverse is true for the innocent third party. He doesn't know what occurred beforehand, so the discussion does not touch on something in his field of experience, and therefore he doesn't share the private meaning of the situation. Communication experience 2.1 is designed to illustrate the effects of one's field of experience on communication.

For intentional communication to occur,[3] there must be an area of overlap in the communicators' fields of experience in relation to the message. A man who speaks only French will not be able to communicate verbally with a woman whose only language is English. Since the cultures from which they come are similar (Western) in terms of nonverbal communication (overlap in field experience), the two would be able to communicate via gestures and facial expressions. But if the countries from which they came were America and country X, rather than England and France, there could be confusion, even nonverbally. The American might smile and offer to shake hands, meaning "Hello; let's be friends." In the other's culture, however, to show teeth (smile) might mean a sign of aggression, and the extended hand might signify a declaration of war.

The field of experience of each communicator encompasses all of his life experiences. Those most crucial to interpersonal communication are

Communication Experience 2.1

Principle

We are all products of our living experiences and the ways in which we perceive things are shaped in part by our previous experiences.

Procedure

1. Work in small groups of six-to-ten people.
2. One person reproduces *exactly* the following sample on a blackboard or screen.

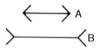

3. Take ten minutes for the group to discuss and come to agreement on which line in the sample is longer than the other. (The person drawing the lines on the blackboard must not participate verbally, or nonverbally.)

Discussion

What conclusions did you reach? On what basis? Did all of the group members agree? How did they arrive at agreement? Had people believed they saw the sample before? In what ways did it affect their answers if they had?[4]

---

divided into five categories in our model: *encoding/decoding skills; perception; culture;* and *social systems.* Each will be defined and explained.

Encoding and Decoding Skills

A central question for communication students is, Where does meaning lie? Behaviorally, we act as if meaning resided in the words themselves, in the message. Children must learn long lists of vocabulary words, yet they are criticized for using "bad words." And we often stereotype or are stereotyped by the words we use (she had the vocabulary of a sailor). "There is no medium, including the human ear or human speech, capable of transmitting or receiving anything but codified data."[5] Language (any system of codifying data verbally or nonverbally) does not carry or

transmit meaning. What it actually does is to present the sender and receiver with tools with which to encode and decode the communicator's meaning. The Morse code has no inherent meaning; its meaningfulness lies in the abilities of the communicators to encode and decode the messages formed by its system of symbols. This holds true for any verbal or nonverbal language, be it the English, Arabic, sign, or body language. Each is a system for coding meanings.

The skills of the communicator to encode outgoing messages and to decode those messages received are basic to communication. An experience for which a person lacks the encoding skill necessary to express himself must go unshared; a message that the receiver is unable to decode is equally uncommunicative. Encoding skills involve making decisions about what to say, how to say it, and how effective the choice will be. Before these decision-making aspects of communication can be dealt with, the communicator must have mastered the codes of the languages into which he can then choose to encode his message. If an American travels to Italy, his skills in English may be of little use to him except during encounters with Italians who speak English. The only way he can communicate nonverbally is with nonverbal symbols shared by both Italians and Americans. Communication experience 2.2 is designed to illustrate the nature of the relationship between symbols and people.

Communication Experience 2.2

Principle

Language codes are sets of symbols. Meanings are in people, not in the symbols themselves.

Procedure

1. Work in groups of five-to-seven people.
2. Discuss with one another any "secret languages," such as "pig latin" or "bop," that group members knew as children, and explain to those unfamiliar with the "language" how it works.
3. Invent a language system similar to any one of those discussed, *except* that it will be known only by the members of this group.
4. After the language system has been perfected, compare it with the language systems developed by the other groups in the class. Experiment with translating sentences into each "language" (e.g., I like this game; I don't; I'm happy; how's the weather; who wants a beer?).

Discussion

Were the members of the group able to come up with a "language?" If not, why not? Have the group members worked together before? If so did this affect accomplishment of the task? Could groups understand each other's codes? Why or why not? What are the implications for intentional communication?

As illustrated by communication experience 2.2, meanings are in people, not in symbols. People attach meanings to symbols. The sender must be able to encode; to find a symbol to carry his meaning. When functioning as the receiver, the communicator must be able to reverse the process and decode the language of the message addressed to him. Many Americans who study a foreign language in high school and then have no opportunity to use it until years later may find that they have retained more skill at decoding than at encoding the foreign language; they can still read a menu in a Spanish restaurant, but have to resort to English to ask the waiter questions.

Encoding and decoding skills do not begin or end with learning and using the language. More sophisticated skills include, as mentioned above, choices about what to say, when to say it, and in what ways. Although all of one's coding skill is part of one's field of experience, choices in how and when to encode and decode are in part shaped by the communicator's perception of the communication situation.

Perception of Self, Others, and Messages

Perception has been defined as a process of extracting information from both the world outside ourselves, as well as the world within.[6] All the channels of communication, our senses, serve to extract such information. An infinite number of possible stimuli are available to anyone at any given time. To perceive every possible stimuli in the environment would be an overwhelming task. Each of us therefore learns to perceive selectively. The student studying for an exam in the library blocks out other potential audiovisual stimuli, paying no attention to those sitting nearby. She has no time or interest in listening to their conversation. The person driving a car has to pay attention to stimuli related to the highway and traffic conditions. He pays less attention to signs in shop windows or the conversation of others in the car. The doctor operating on a patient cannot get involved in her own feelings of hunger or thirst. Communication experience 2.3 is designed to illustrate the effect of perception on communication.

Communication Experience 2.3

Principle

Meaning lies in people. Our perceptions are the product of our observations and interpretations. Those perceptions affect communication.

Procedure

1. Work in dyads (pairs).
2. Have a discussion to learn more about each other.
3. Try to find one prejudice you both have in common that might affect your ability to communicate with another person.
4. Pretend that each of you is someone else. Play the part of that person (role play). Select roles that involve the prejudices of your partner.
5. Discuss a controversial subject while in the roles chosen.

Discussion

Did you and your partner know one another before this experience? Do you "know" each other differently now? Were you able to isolate prejudices that would interfere with communication? Did it get "touchy"? Were the roles selected like or unlike the real people? If unlike, why? What are the implications about perception and communication?

As illustrated by communication experience 2.3, perception affects communication. Each communicator is shaped by the perceptions he has of himself and others, and the messages exchanged. The first effect of perception on communication involves the ways in which the person sees himself; self-perception affects his expectations of others and how they will behave toward him. A person who sees himself as trustworthy will expect to be taken at his word; a person who is self-conscious about some physical deformity will see himself as the potential recipient of ridicule and rejection; a person who sees himself as a good judge of character does not expect to be duped by others. A person, for example, who sees himself as valuable, is more likely to avoid situations of potential danger to himself than one with lower self-esteem.[7] Self-perception has to do with the entirety of how one sees himself. If a person has been obese all his life and loses an enormous amount of weight, he must also change his self-perception from fat to thin.

There are two kinds of overt effects of self-perception on interpersonal communication, the first being the way in which the individual interacts with others. Whether she is sure or tentative, passive or aggressive, open

Rorsach

The ink blot, or Rorsach test, is designed to acquire insight into the ways in which we perceive.

The ink blot, or Rorsach test, is designed to acquire insight into the ways in which we perceive.

or closed is related to her self-perception. Secondly, how she allows others to communicate with her is a product of how she sees herself. A person who feels lovable allows people to be loving toward her. Self-perception may be conveyed to others verbally and/or nonverbally. It affects the ways in which others perceive of and communicate with the communicator, as well as how she interacts with them.

The second effect of perception on communication is the way in which a person sees other people. The perceptions may be based on past experience, the personality of the other communicator at the time of communication, or the perceiver's views of life in general. A person tends to share his innermost thoughts and feelings with those he sees as friends. He acts respectfully toward those he views as deserving respect or who seem powerful enough to demand it. He sees those whose behavior violates the norms and values he holds dear as "deviant." A person who is seen as deviating from the norms and wishes of a group to which he belongs will be the target for communications designed to influence him toward their ways of thinking and behaving.[8]

The third effect of perception is on the meaning attached to messages. Perception is extracting and interpreting information. People take note of some stimuli, attaching meanings to them and responding to those meanings. Two arrows painted on a wall contain a message only for those who notice the arrows and attach some meaning to them. A yellow square sign with a black **S** curve on it has meaning for drivers on a highway if they notice it and if they have learned the language of road signs.

Perception of messages, self, and others is a result of one's observations and interpretations. **Meaning** or significance is that which is attributed to the stimuli by perceivers of those stimuli. A movie is good or bad depending on the perceptions of the moviegoer; a person sees himself as desirable or undesirable depending on his perceptions of himself and of his perceptions of how others see him; a teacher is effective or ineffective depending on how he is perceived by his students.

The ramifications of perception and the effect it has in the communication process are vast and will be dealt with in detail as we dissect each of the elements in the process of communication in part two of the text. Before we can do that, it is important to see the relationships between perceptions and one's culture and social groups, two other elements presented as part of the communicator's field of experience in our model of communication.

Culture

A **culture** is a system of norms and rules that determines to a large extent the ways in which members of that society behave, including their communication behavior. Interpersonal communication occurs in a cultural context. It is the context that in a sense determines the meaning of the behavior that occurs. In San Francisco, to go home and rest for several hours after lunch each day would be grounds for losing one's job; in many European cities it is the norm.

The most significant factor about the influence on communication exerted by culture is that it is often unnoticeable. A person's culture is so familiar and "normal" to her that she may not be aware that there is any other way to behave in a given situation. Anthropologists, who study and compare cultures, know that in Pakistan it is considered good manners to belch after a meal to compliment one's hostess. An American hostess might be anything but flattered. One reason people of the same ethnic (cultural or subcultural) background feel a certain kinship with one another is due to their common cultural conditioning.

Social Systems

Besides the influence of the culture as a whole, every communicator belongs to primary (usually family) and reference (social, economic, educational, intellectual, political, interest) groups. Each of these comprise the individual's **social system membership.** Membership in these groups plays some part in shaping him as a communicator. A person's relationship to various groups affects the ways in which he perceives a message. Whether he accepts, rejects, or distorts the message

Incident

by Countee Cullen

Once riding in old Baltimore,
Heart-filled, head-filled with glee,
I saw a Baltimorean
Keep looking straight at me.

Now I was eight and very small,
And he was no whit bigger,
And so I smiled, but he poked out
His tongue, and called me, "Nigger."

I saw the whole of Baltimore
From May until December;
Of all the things that happened there
That's all that I remember.

is shaped in part by the groups with which he associates and to which he associates himself. A person whose friends are intellectuals might not admit to enjoying soap operas. Or, he might not even enjoy them, because he knows he isn't supposed to.

Everyday life presents itself to us as a reality to be individually interpreted. Our interpretations are subjectively meaningful to us. Our memberships in various groups (family, peer, social, cultural) influence the ways in which we see, experience, and interpret all the experiences of our past and present life. Communication experience 2.4 is designed to illustrate the effects of culture and social systems on one's communication interactions.

Communication Experience 2.4

Principle

Membership in social systems within our culture influence our interpersonal communication interactions.

Procedure

1. Work in groups (any size that seems suitable).
2. Discuss the following story and determine what kind of communication would explain Florence's actions.

Florence's car broke down on the Pennsylvania Turnpike late one night. A truck stopped and two men got out and offered assistance. Florence was hesitant because of stories she had heard about assaults on stranded motorists. She said, "No thanks, but please stop at the next service area and call the AAA for me." The men explained that there was no place to stop for more than twenty miles and that they believed it would be dangerous for her to wait alone in her car. The older of the two men told her that his son had a car like Florence's and he thought it would just need a little work. When he referred to his son he used an Italian nickname. Florence then said to him in Italian that her brother was also referred to as Paulito (little Paul). After a few more minutes of discussion, Florence felt safe to accept the truck drivers' assistance.

Discussion

What were the underlying dynamics in the situation? Why did Florence change her mind? Where did the men take her? Why? How do you know? What would someone else have done? Why? Where do the attitudes evolve that enable us to answer these questions?

These, then, are the essential areas in the communicator's field of experience that affect him and his communication behavior in the interpersonal encounter. The last dynamic presented in the model is the *communication environment*.

Communication Environment

The last concept included in the model in figure 2.1 is the **Communication Environment.** Just as walls offer a physical structure, boundary, within which one must operate, so too does the communication environment shape the communication behavior taking place. The communication environment refers to those physical and/or psychological boundaries within which communication occurs and by which communication is molded. An analogy can be drawn between the communication environment framing an interpersonal interaction and the four walls enclosing a room. When inside a room, the walls limit the space and affect how a person moves from one place in space (inside the room) to another (outside). To exit, it is necessary to go through a door or a window or perhaps make a hole in one of the walls. It would not be probable to walk through the wall or leave through a closed window. Moreover, others seeing a person trying to walk through the wall would certainly have some questions in their minds about such behavior.

The *communication environment* can be defined as the framework within which communication occurs. Just as walls act as the physical structure defining the extent of the space they bound, social, physical, and psychological boundaries exist that shape the structure within which any communication occurs. The communication environment can be divided into two parts: the context (social and physical) in which the communication occurs, and the role relationship between the communicators in that given context.

Whether the context is a supermarket or football stadium, a church or library, a communication environment is supplied for the interpersonal encounter. It defines the kinds of communication behavior that are appropriate and acceptable. In a supermarket or stadium, one may readily shout to a friend. But, to laugh out loud or shout in a church during services would be a serious violation of the communication environment. It is analogous to trying to leave a room by walking through a wall. The boundaries or limits on behavior in the former (often culturally determined) are not as visible as in the latter, but the consequences can be just as painful.

Besides the setting or context in which the communication occurs, the role relationships between the communicators also contribute to the boundaries of acceptable or unacceptable behavior. Mother-daughter,

ONE FLEW OVER THE CUCKOO'S NEST

THE doctor fishes his glasses out again and puts them on and looks to where McMurphy is pointing.

"Right here, Doc. The nurse left this part out while she was *summarizing* my record. Where it says, 'Mr. McMurphy has evidenced *repeated*' — I just want to make sure I'm understood completely, Doc — '*repeated* outbreaks of passion that suggest the possible diagnosis of psychopath.' He told me that 'psychopath' means I fight and fuh — pardon me, ladies — means I am he put it *over*zealous in my sexual relations. Doctor, is that real serious?"

He asks it with such a little-boy look of worry and concern all over his broad, tough face that the doctor can't help bending his head to hide another little snicker in his collar, and his glasses fall from his nose dead center back in his pocket. All of the Acutes are smiling too, now, and even some of the Chronics.

"I mean that overzealousness, Doc, have you ever been troubled by it?"

The doctor wipes his eyes. "No, Mr. McMurphy, I'll admit I haven't. I am interested, however, that the doctor at the work farm added this statement: 'Don't overlook the possibility that this man might be feigning psychosis to escape the drudgery of the work farm.'" He looks up at McMurphy. "And what about that, Mr. McMurphy?"

"Doctor" — he stands up to his full height, wrinkles his forehead, and holds out both arms, open and honest to all the wide world — "do I look like a sane man?"

The doctor is working so hard to keep from giggling again he can't answer.

KEN KESEY

employer-employee, student-teacher, sister-brother, friend-friend relationships, all have culturally determined prescriptions for how one interacts with another. A mother may yell at her daughter, but not at her employer; a sister may badger her brother without end, but not her friend; and a student may rarely express all his feelings to his teacher. These kinds of limits set the boundaries. They determine how and in what directions one can go in the interpersonal communication encounter. The boundaries and boundary-setting process is referred to as the communication environment. It is depicted in figure 2.1 as that square encompassing the other elements of the model and indicates that it is the framework in which the communication occurs. Communication experience 2.5 is designed to illustrate the effects of the communication environment on the communication situation.

Communication Experience 2.5

Principle

The ways in which we communicate are shaped by our physical as well as social environment. The physical environment, or context, provides boundaries within which we communicate.

Procedure

1. Work with a partner.
2. Together, visit at least four different places (movie; library; church; auditorium; restaurant; museum).
3. At each place have the same conversation with one another, regarding any exciting (preferably controversial) subject.
4. Report your experiences back to class; share others' experiences.

Discussion

What, if any, difference did the environment make in your conversation? Were you self-conscious? What conclusions can be drawn?

Communication Model Revisited

When we put together all the concepts discussed in this chapter with those elaborated in chapter one, we arrive at the model presented in figure 2.1. This model can be used as a frame of reference from which to continue our discussion of the communication process. It provides an overview—a picture of the totality of the process with attention to specifics only as

Each of us is a member of many groups (communication networks).

necessary for a basic understanding of that totality. One other element *trust,* not included in the model, is an outgrowth of so many of the other dynamics that it seems important enough to note. Whether or not one person trusts another, and to what extent, is a product of perception, environment, and culture. A feeling of trust and its resultant openness must be measured against the communicator's past experiences, knowledge of self and the other person, the role relationships, culture, and the environment in which the communication takes place. Trust will be discussed throughout part two of the text as each component of the communication process is discussed in detail.

In dissecting the process of interpersonal communication, we focus on the overt messages sent and received between communicators. At the same time, however, we concern ourselves with the inferential communication that often accompanies the overt verbal and nonverbal communication in face-to-face communication situations. **Inferential communication** is implied, or inferred, rather than overtly stated or heard. Buying someone a deodorant for a birthday present may imply that he has body odor, even though such was never overtly stated; "forgetting" someone's birthday may cause him to draw inferences regarding your feelings about him or birthdays in general. Just as we have said that verbal and nonverbal communications are often inseparable, so too are the overt and hidden dimensions of meaning in interpersonal communication. The many dimensions of meaning in messages are the products of people saying and hearing these messages.

Our concerns, therefore, must be with all the messages—verbal and nonverbal, stated and implied—in the face-to-face interpersonal communication situation. In this section of the text, we have presented an overview of the overt messages in the interpersonal exchange. We have looked at the totality of the process and defined or explained its parts in relation to one another. The second part of the text looks in detail at each of the elements of the process.

Interference with Intentional Communication

In this chapter, we have focused on the communicator as a person who enters any communication encounter with an entire life experience (field of experience). We have noted that all people enter the communication encounter with contexual and psychological factors setting the boundaries or limits within which their attempts to communicate will take place. Any potential interference with the meanings intended results from differences in how these dynamics affect the communicators.

The fields of experience of the communicators can present an interference if a lack of common ground or mutuality exists in the experiences of the communicators. This holds true regardless of which aspect of the field of experience we focus upon: encoding/decoding skills, perception, social systems, or cultural background.

When communicators do not share mutual abilities to encode and decode messages, barriers to communication exist. This is true whether they speak different languages (German; Dutch) or at different levels of literacy (the poorly educated man with the vocabulary and verbal skills of the third grader; the nuclear physicist). Communication is not impossible, nor is the intended sharing of meaning. The communicators need be sensitive to their differences and attempt to eliminate the interference by finding some common ground. If the interference is due to a difference in languages spoken, this might be overcome by finding a third language familiar to both, or resorting to common nonverbal codes in an attempt to understand one another. If the difference is due to varying levels of literacy, again some attempt must be made—if the goal is shared understanding—to find a level discernible by both. Language is an attempt to share the experiences of the speaker. He must therefore talk to the experience of his receiver.

Perception of oneself, others, and messages is also part of the field of experience of each communicator. If the perceptions of each

communicator differ, it is not possible to share intended meaning. Many of the interferences with intentional communication can be traced to differing perceptions of the communicators. A compliment is only complimentary if it is perceived as such by both the person offering it and the one for whom it was intended. If a person says, "You look so nice today," meaning how nice he thinks the other looks, but the other person perceives the message to be a way of saying how awful he looked every other day, there is an interference with intentional meaning.

A person's attitude and beliefs, on such subjects as religion, politics, and sex, are the product of socialization in his primary and secondary groups as well as his cultural environment as a whole. What any one woman thinks is meant by the saying, "A woman's place is in the home" is dependent upon her attitudes as shaped by her background and previous experiences. The customary ways of making a guest feel at home is another example. In some families a guest is not permitted to leave without being plied with food. In this kind of household, hospitality is measured by sharing one's food. If a person who is socialized in this pattern visits a home in which he is never even offered a glass of water, he may interpret this behavior as a rejection.

Because the communication environment is the framework within which the communication occurs, differing perceptions of that framework, and understanding of the boundaries implied, can interfere with intentional communication. The communicators must perceive the framework in the same ways in order for each communicator to understand why the other communicates as he does. For example, a rock concert provides a different communication environment from that of a classical music concert. And, acceptable behavior differs in each environment. Two people go together to hear acid rock, but one of them has never been to anything but classical concerts. While his quietness may express the ways he has been taught to appreciate music, the person he accompanies may interpret his behavior as a lack of enthusiasm for the music. An out-of-towner visiting a large metropolitan area may be accustomed to starting conversations with strangers to pass the time of day. To do so in the city may be inviting trouble.

Similar kinds of interference with intended meaning is the result of different understandings of the role relationship between communicators. A doctor may be very reserved in talking to a patient. If the patient does not understand this as part of the nature of the relationship, he may interpret it as indifference on the part of the doctor.

There is much overlapping among the dynamics we have isolated in the communication process. We cannot talk of perception without reference to the experiences that have in some ways shaped those perceptions. We cannot talk of communication realities without referring to the communicators' perceptions of those realities. Any interference with a shared understanding of the communication interaction affects the ability of people to communicate intentionally.

Summary

In this chapter we have completed our overview of the process of communication by naming and discussing the dynamics essential to the interpersonal communication exchange. These dynamics shape and/or affect each of the basic elements of the communication process. Let's review these important dynamics.

1. We only begin to analyze a given interpersonal exchange if we limit our investigation to the sender–message–receiver–feedback elements.
2. A communication model must add to those basics the dimensions of the other essential dynamics present in an interpersonal exchange.
3. The "field of experience"—defined as the sum total of experience of the person before and during any communication encounter—is a broad area encompassing dynamics essential to the ways in which a person is able to communicate and be communicated with. There are four important areas within the field of experience.
    a. *Encoding/decoding skills: The abilities of the sender/receiver of messages to encode inner experiences verbally and/or nonverbally as well as to reverse the process and decode the messages of another receiver/sender.*

b. *Perception: The ways in which one gathers information from the world external to himself as well as from his own inner self.*

c. *Social systems: The primary and secondary reference groups to which any person belongs were discussed as affecting the attitudes, values, and beliefs of the communicator and therefore as essential to the ways in which he communicates and is communicated with.*

d. *Culture: The system or norms and rules that to a large extent determine the ways in which members of that society behave, including their communication behavior.*

4. Besides the field of experience of the individual communicators, the context in which encounter occurs affects interpersonal communication. It is called the communication environment.

5. Communication environment has two dimensions:

a. *Environment—physical and social—in which the communication occurs.*

b. *Role relationships between communicators.*

6. "Trust," an important aspect of communication, is related to many of the dynamics referred to in this chapter.

7. Interpersonal communication involves verbal and nonverbal messages that are implied or explicit.

8. Interference with intended meaning is the product of different perceptions of the dynamics involved in interpersonal communication.

Questions for Discussion

1. What are some of the cultural factors determining communication in our society?

2. What effect does perception have on communication and communication on perception?

3. To what degree do professors reveal themselves so that students may communicate with them?

4. Cite some of the ways a person can discover the field of experience of other members of the class.

5. What are some of the strongest pressures a person feels at a given point in his life, and how, if at all, do they affect his communication?

6. Does your field of experience include your name?

7. What is "trust?" Describe a "trusting person."

8. In what ways do encoding and decoding differ?

9. What attitudes, norms, or values can be traced to one's primary group affiliation?

1. Lee Thayer, "Communication: Sine Qua Non of the Behavioral Sciences," in *Vistas in Science,* ed. D. L. Arm, (Albuquerque, N.M.: University of New Mexico Press, 1968), p. 1.

2. Wilbur Schramm, "How Communication Works," *The Process and Effects of Mass Communication* (Urbana, Ill.: University of Illinois Press, 1955), p. 6.

3. Schramm, "Communication," p. 6.

4. Line B *is* longer than line A. This is different from what the expectations would be, if participants had ever seen the comparison before.

5. Lee Thayer, "On the Mass Media and Mass Communication: Notes Toward a Theory," in *Mass Communication: Dialogue and Alternatives,* ed. Richard Budd and Brent Ruben (Rochelle Park, N.J.: Hayden Press, in preparation), p. 13.

6. R. H. Fergus, *Perception* (New York: McGraw-Hill, 1966), p. 1.

7. Elliot Aronson, *The Social Animal* (San Francisco: W. H. Freeman & Co., 1972), p. 67ff.

8. Leon Festinger, Stanley Schacter, and Kurt Black, *Social Pressures in Informal Groups* (Stanford, Calif.: Stanford University Press, 1963).

Notes

Aronson, Elliot. *The Social Animal.* San Francisco: W. H. Freeman and Company, 1972. This is recommended as an informative introduction to social psychology. It can be read with ease by the beginning student of communication.

Berger, Peter and Thomas Luchmann. *Social Construct of Reality.* New York: Anchor Books, Doubleday & Company, 1967. An in-depth analysis of the sociology of knowledge. Highly relevant to communication students concerned with communication as reality construction. Not recommended as light reading.

Hall, Edward. *The Silent Language.* New York: Doubleday & Company, 1959. Recommended for students interested in an in-depth understanding of proxemics. A good supplemental understanding of nonverbal communication.

Selected Bibliography

2

Elements
in the
Interpersonal
Cycle

The Sender:
Initiating Communicator

3

Introduction

All communicators play the part of senders and receivers of messages. In the interpersonal communication process, the communicator who has a thought or feeling to convey is designated as the *sender, initiating communicator,* or *encoder* of the message. Spoken messages are only one means of encoding available to the sender. Accompanying spoken messages are a range of nonverbal behaviors, all of which are capable of carrying messages. As we investigate the role of the sender in the interpersonal process, our concern will be with both his verbal and nonverbal message making. This chapter highlights the sender, in terms of why and how he sends messages, and the effect "who he is" has on his intended communication. Chapter 4 looks at the role of the sender in the interpersonal process by considering the dynamics present in the communication situation and their impact on the sender. Chapter 5 analyzes the sender as a receiver of messages.

Communication Goals

In this chapter the theoretical and experiential approach is used to explore the role of the sender in the communication process. It has been written to enable you to understand the roles you play as initiator of the communication interaction by:

1. Recognizing and defining the motivation for attempting to communicate with another person.
2. Understanding this need to communicate as a response to some stimulus in your social and/or physical environment.
3. Exploring your encoding skills and ways to maximize them.
4. Increasing your awareness of yourself and others as separate worlds, touching one another in the interpersonal exchange only when the need to do so exists or is promoted.
5. Distinguishing between intended or purposive messages and those that are nonpurposive.
6. Comprehending the impact of the speaker on the message.

Why Communicate?

A story is told of a six-year-old boy whose mother, father, and four older sisters doted on him excessively and worried about him because he had never spoken a word. One morning at the breakfast table, the boy broke his silence and said, "I need some sugar for my cereal." His family, delighted that he could indeed speak, was amazed at his vocabulary, yet puzzled about why it had taken him six years to utter a word. When questioned the boy replied, "Up to now everything's been perfect."

We use this story to illustrate that the act of message making is a response to a need. Every human being has needs for shelter, clothing, food, and the society of others. An attempt to express any such need to another is message making. "I'm cold," "I'm tired," "I'm hungry" are expressions of one's basic physical needs for shelter, food, or clothing. But beyond physical needs are social needs. The human being is a social animal and, like most other forms of animal life, needs contact with other members of his species. There are various ways of explaining these needs or motivations. Contact with other human beings can be a means of avoiding isolation, of sharing, of influencing or being influenced, of exchanging, of growing, of getting or giving, of negotiating, or of making sense of one's reality.

We are motivated by any one or all of these needs at different times during our living experience. There are times when we attempt to communicate with another because we want that other person's company. Or, we communicate to share an experience, thereby making it more meaningful. Many people enjoy good news most when they can share it with others. Sometimes we attempt to communicate for the purpose of influencing. A friend is making a decision and we try to affect his choice. Sometimes, we want to be influenced; another's advice may be helpful in making a decision. Communication can be a means of exchanging information, as when two friends pool their information about movies they have seen; or of growing, trying to learn skills from another who has already mastered them.

Communication can also be a means of getting, giving, or negotiating, for instance, solving the problem of who drives the family car, or whose turn it is to do the dishes. Perhaps most basic of all, communication is a means of understanding one's reality.[1] Often the way we find out what is real and what is not is through the process of communication with others. One thinks he hears a noise and asks, "Did you hear that?" Or, he hears a noise and asks, "What was that?" He then uses the answers he receives to help him interpret the event. A friend's reassurance that the sound was that of a cat's meow, and not a prowler can calm down fears, or reinforce

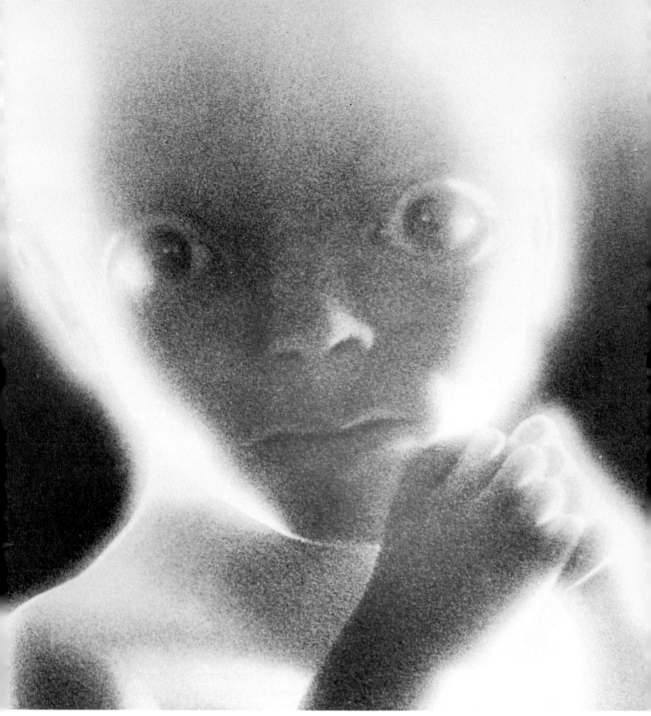

April 12

We come into the world alone.
We go away the same.
We're meant to spend
the interlude between
    in closeness

or so we tell ourselves.
But it's a long way
from the morning
    to the evening.

Rod McKuen

suspicions, and thus affects how he reacts. Communication experience 3.1 is designed to explore the student's own attempts to communicate with others and what motivates these attempts.

Communication Experience 3.1

Principle

Our living experience continually presents us with data that we must interpret and for which we often use others' opinions to help us arrive at our interpretations.

Procedure

1. Each member of the class is to select and bring to class an object (e.g., wearing apparel, jewelry, tool, furnishing, wall object) that she thinks will be unfamiliar to class members.
2. Divide into groups of six-to-ten people.
3. Each member of the group in turn points out the object, names it, and defines its use as he sees it.
4. The person who brought the object may give no clues as to whether or not group members have correctly named or described the use of the object.
5. The activity is continued until each participant is sure of his definition of the object—without help from the others.

Discussion

How was the object selected? Was its name and use known or unknown to group members? How many? How did the participant arrive at his conclusions if the object was unknown to him? If it was known to him, how did he learn about it? Did group members give clues, verbally or nonverbally? How did the participant feel while participating in the experience? How did he feel toward other group members?

Whatever motivates a person to attempt to communicate at a given time is compounded by his need for a response from the person with whom he is trying to interact. One only knows that another is available to him as a companion based on the response he receives as a result of his attempts to communicate. The sender can only be sure that his news is shared by the reaction from his receiver. Attempts at influencing, exchanging, negotiating, or confirming one's reality, as illustrated in communication experience 3.1, are only achieved when the receiver provides some form of feedback. The sender, then, communicates in order

Let every one mind his own business, and endeavor
to be what he was made. Why should we be in such
desperate haste to succeed and in such desperate
enterprises? If a man does not keep pace with his
companions, perhaps it is because he hears a different
drummer. Let him step to the music which he hears,
however measured or far away. It is not important
that he should mature as soon as an apple-tree or an oak.
Shall he turn his spring into summer?

Thoreau

to elicit a response from his receiver. If companionship is what he looks for and his receiver indicates that he is unavailable, the sender has not gotten the response he seeks. If what he needs is to influence and the sender's friend does as he pleases without heeding his advice, the sender has not accomplished his goal. If he looks to another to confirm his reality, and is met with silence, as in communication experience 3.1, he has not succeeded in his intent for communication.

Initiating Communicator: Encoder, Sender, Message Maker

All communicators are potentially senders/receivers of messages. In initiating the message, the communicator plays the role referred to as *message maker, encoder,* or *sender.* Because some need or motivation precedes the attempt to communicate, message making in itself is a response to some stimulus, or felt need. The stimulus may be internal, like a hunger pain that motivates someone to go to the pizza stand to order a snack. It may be external to the communicator, like observing rain clouds and then suggesting to his friends that they head for shelter. Adopting the role of message maker or sender is a consequence of an inner response to a given stimulus. Communication experience 3.2 is designed to illustrate message making as a response to a given stimulus.

Communication Experience 3.2

Principle

A person takes the role of initiator of a message as a consequence of his own response to some stimulus.

Procedure

1. Work in groups of five. Bring a pencil and paper.
2. Sit in a circle with your group.
3. You may either talk or remain silent, as you wish. (Allow at least 5–10 minutes for this phase.)
4. The instructor or a designated student writes on the blackboard or says out loud, "Write down nine items of clothing you see in this room." At the same time he instructs participants not to speak to anyone except their own group members.
5. The instructor (student) turns out all lights immediately following these instructions.
6. The exercise ends when the instructor (student) stops it.

Discussion

Did participants talk to each other? If so, who spoke to whom, and why? If not, why not? What did people talk about? Why? What did they not mention? Why? What effect did the darkness have? Who spoke? To whom did he speak? Why? How aware were participants of the feelings that motivated them to speak or remain silent? What were they? Compare and contrast lists. How and why did they differ?

As illustrated in communication experience 3.2, our environment, both social and physical, presents us with a myriad of potential stimuli, to which we may or may not choose to respond. These stimuli are called **event-data.** Any message is **codified data.**[2] The communicator observes, feels, or thinks something (event data), which she attempts to convey to someone else if she has a code (system of symbols) into which that observation, feeling or thought can be translated. The code may be verbal (words), and the encoder can say, "I have a headache," or nonverbal, putting one's hand on his forehead while grimacing and groaning. In either case, the communicator has translated the inner experience (physical feeling; event data) into a code or language (words, actions) capable of being decoded by another, his intended receiver.

In putting the feeling into a code, two choices have been made. First, a decision has been made to make a message. Second, the encoder has selected the code into which to put the message. Seeing a friend across a crowded room might be stimulus enough to motivate a need to exchange hellos. The circumstance might be such that a wave is more effective than a shouted greeting, or vice versa. The differences in the selection of items listed by participants in communication experience 3.2 also illustrates differences in response to potential stimuli.

A useful pictorial explanation of the concept we are discussing is the Westley-MacLean model[3] presented in figure 3.1.

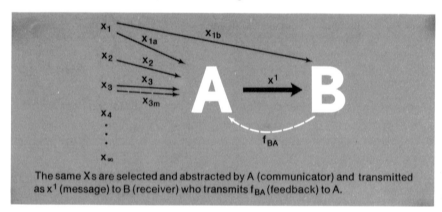

The same Xs are selected and abstracted by A (communicator) and transmitted as x^1 (message) to B (receiver) who transmits f_{BA} (feedback) to A.

Figure 3.1
Westley-MacLean Model.

The Westley-MacLean model illustrates that communication does not begin when one person starts to talk to another. It starts when a person responds selectively to his immediate social and/or physical environment. In the model, the x_1, x_2 . . . x_{00} represents the event data present in the environment that may be perceived and responded to by the encoder (sender), which is represented in the model by A. The receiver in the model is represented by B.

The view from one's window might include a thermometer, the windowsill, the front lawn, the street, trees, grass, a neighbor's lawn across the street, the neighbor's house, the sky, or the clouds. She looks out the window. Of all these potential stimuli (x_1 . . . x_{00}), she notices (selectively perceives) the unmowed lawn in front of her house (x^4). She calls to her husband (B) to get out the lawnmower (x^1; message). She becomes sender (A) of a message to her receiver (B) only after observing and encoding a message about some of the event data (x's) in her immediate environment. She becomes sender if she has a code, verbal or nonverbal, into which she can encode her experiences. In our example, the message is encoded verbally. She calls to her husband. However, if he were standing nearby, she might have chosen a nonverbal code (performance code-gestures).

While we have talked of verbal and nonverbal as distinct and different codes in the daily course of interpersonal communication, we are aware that it is rare for one code to exist without the other. The spoken word is accompanied by *paralanguage* (tone of voice, grunts, groans, etc.), *kinesics* (body language), and *metamessages* (messages about the message). As the woman looked out the window and called to her husband, her message although verbal would have had the nonverbal components of paralanguage (tone of voice, etc.), kinesics (any body language, gestures, facial expression, use of eyes), and metamessages if her husband had been telling her to mow the lawn all weekend. Then her request to get out the mower could carry a message about their past communication on the subject. Communication experience 3.3 is designed to illustrate verbal and nonverbal encoding of messages.

Communication Experience 3.3

Principle

Nonverbal communication is composed of a wide range of behaviors that accompany the spoken word.

Procedure

No. 1

1. Work in small groups, six-to-eight people.
2. Use the sentence, "I am going to Chicago."
3. Compete with the other small groups to see which group can find the greatest number of different meanings the same words can have when said in different ways.

No. 2

1. Work with a partner (dyad).
2. Sit facing one another at least four feet apart.
3. One member of the dyad has five minutes to tell the other where he lives and what it's like there, *without using words* (written and spoken words are taboo).
4. Switch roles. The other partner does the same.
5. When both have had a turn, each tells his partner what he thinks he knows about his home.

Discussion

No. 1

How many different meanings could the words be used for? What determined the meaning? Is this true in other situations?

No. 2

How accurate were the dyad's ideas of what was being described to one another? Why? What ways did each use to convey his message without words? How did each know (or think he knew) if the person to whom he was directing the message understood him? Would words have made a difference?

Communication experience 3.3 illustrates that messages may be encoded verbally or nonverbally. A message is a complex combination of both. Let us now look more specifically at the process of encoding the message.

City girls just seem to find out early
how to open doors with just a smile.
A rich old man, and she won't have to worry;
she'll dress up all in lace and go in style.
Late at night a big old house gets lonely;
I guess ev'ry form of refuge has its price.
And it breaks her heart to think her love is only
given to a man with hands as cold as ice.
So she tells him she must go out for the evening
to comfort an old friend who's feelin' down.
But he knows where she's goin' as she's leavin';
she is headed for the cheatin' side of town.

You can't hide your lyin' eyes,
and your smile is a thin disguise.
I thought by now you'd realize
there ain't no way to hide your lyin' eyes.

On the other side of town a boy is waiting
with fiery eyes and dreams no one could steal.
She drives on through the night anticipating,
'cause he makes her feel the way she used to feel.
She rushes to his arms, they fall together;
she whispers that it's only for a while.
She swears that soon she'll be comin' back forever;
she pulls away and leaves him with a smile.

You can't hide your lyin' eyes,
and your smile is a thin disguise.
I thought by now you'd realize
there ain't no way to hide your lyin' eyes.

She gets up and pours herself a strong one
and stares out at the stars up in the sky.
Another night, it's gonna be a long one;
she draws the shade and hangs her head to cry.
She wonders how it ever got this crazy;
she thinks about a boy she knew in school.
Did she get tired or did she just get lazy?
She's so far gone she feels just like a fool.
My, oh my, you sure know how to arrange things;
you set it up so well, so carefully.
Ain't it funny how your new life didn't change things;
you're still the same old girl you used to be.

You can't hide your lyin' eyes,
and your smile is a thin disguise.
I thought by now you'd realize
there ain't no way to hide your lyin' eyes.
There ain't no way to hide your lyin' eyes.
Honey, you can't hide your lyin' eyes.

Don Henley
Glenn Frey

Encoding the Message

Any communicator can become the sender or initiator of the interpersonal exchange if he can translate his inner experiences into a code(s). All codes, verbal and nonverbal, are learned in a social context. One's culture determines his verbal and nonverbal language. In the course of one's socialization, he is taught these codes. This process begins early in one's life. Some of what is learned is so habitualized that it is only when one meets others with differing codes that he becomes aware of his own. The most obvious comparisons are with people who speak different languages. An example is the French friend who exchanges language lessons with an English-speaking classmate. Another is a new person in town who comes from a different part of the country and has different words for familiar things (in New York, for example, a cola drink is called soda; in Boston, tonic; in Chicago, pop).

Nonverbal languages are determined culturally too. The meaning attached to smiles, handshakes, and kisses are culturally determined; all of which have implications for the encoder of a message. In terms of his verbal and nonverbal language, he must learn to encode his messages differently depending on his expectations of his intended receivers. He must evaluate the most effective way to convey his inner experience to that other person. When looking at the process of communication from the perspective of the sender, one must analyze his encoding skills. Communication experience 3.4 presents an opportunity for the student to evaluate his own encoding skills.

Communication Experience 3.4

Principle

Effective message transmission depends upon the sender's ability to encode his observations into codes that can be interpreted by his intended receivers.

Procedure

1. Have a class member volunteer to describe a diagram to the members of the group who cannot see the diagram and therefore must duplicate it, based on the volunteer's verbal description.
2. Present the volunteer with the diagram that appears in note 7 on page 77. He is to describe it to the group with his back facing them.

3. When he feels he has completed his description, ask him to estimate his success, including those parts of the diagram that he thinks the class has understood correctly.
4. Before showing the original diagram to the class, ask how many think they have it correct; and what part they found was easiest to get right.
5. Compare the original diagram and other versions.

Discussion

Why did the volunteer have his back to the rest of the class? What differences would there have been had he looked at them, and they at him? What percentage of accuracy was achieved, and why? Which parts of the diagram were more difficult than the others to duplicate, and why? What kinds of things did the volunteer do to enhance the ability of the receivers to accomplish the task? What kinds of things did he do that interfered?

Effective Encoding Skills: Some Guidelines

While every human being raised in a given society is socialized into that culture's verbal and nonverbal codes of communication, not everyone learns these codes effectively. Perhaps the most obvious factors that might cause poor learning and consequently drawbacks in the mastery of skills are physical or psychological impairments. Any neurological or sensory defect may decrease one's possibilities for effective encoding of thoughts, feelings, or experiences. Impaired hearing or eyesight or difficulty with the speech organs are physical handicaps that make it more difficult for a person to master the necessary encoding skills.

There are other causes of poor encoding skills. Learning language from adults who set poor models is another possible source of inadequate ability to master language skills. A parent having a severe lisp serves as a model for the child, who then may learn the lisp as if it were supposed to be learned. Parents with limited education and vocabularies may not be able to provide their children with a wide enough range of words into which the child can encode his experiences.

It is quite possible, however, for a communicator to learn to cope with any deficiency in his ability to communicate. The story of Helen Keller, a deaf-mute, is well known. There is also a contemporary Irish author who is a quadruple amputee, but has learned to type by holding a stick in his mouth which he uses to press the keys of his typewriter. Many communicators with less severe impairments find it necessary to deal with encoding handicaps.

When impairment exists, three steps are necessary in developing encoding skills. The first step in dealing with the problem is the recognition that an impairment does exist. Like the person who has a drinking problem and joins Alcoholics Anonymous must learn to say "I am an alcoholic" before he can begin to cure himself, so too the communicator who has an impairment in his encoding skills must recognize (or be helped to recognize) the problem before he can improve himself.

The second step in overcoming encoding impairments is diagnosis of the problem. Is the handicap correctable? Lisps, sound substitutions, and hearing or sight loss, for example, are remedial. Both labeling the problem (recognition) and diagnosing it may need to be done by a professional (medical doctor, speech therapist, or psychologist). If the problem can be corrected, the communicator must then work on that correction—speech lessons for the lisp or sound substitutions, eyeglasses or a hearing aid for sight or hearing loss.

Not all encoding impairments are correctable. When such is the case, the communicator must then take a third step; he must learn to compensate for the problem. Blind people who are unable to encode and decode visual stimuli must learn to make more profound use of their hearing, leading to the bromide that blind people are born with more acute hearing mechanisms. They also learn tactile codes as a means of compensation. Deafness can be compensated for by a greater reliance on visual cues and the learning of sign language. In most cases, with the exception of the most extreme, after an initial phase in which the intended receivers must get used to the sender's problem and the ways he has learned to cope with it, the ability of the sender to communicate with another need not be significantly affected. This is if the sender can be aware enough of himself and his problems to allow his listeners to accommodate to him.

Compensatory Devices: Effective and Ineffective Supplements for Encoders

The awareness of limitations and attempts to cope with them can result in a bonus for the communicator, despite his handicap. It forces him to be aware of not only himself and the person with whom he tries to communicate but also to evaluate whether or not he is being understood. All of us need to learn to evaluate our own sensitivities to others. The frustrated communicator, angered by his receiver's lack of understanding of him, who snaps, "What's the matter, don't you speak English!" fails to evaluate his encoding skills and his receiver's needs.

The kinds of compensatory devices we have been discussing are positive ways of enabling the sender to communicate that which he intends to communicate. But a compensatory device can be used in an ineffective way if it interferes with transmission of intended meaning. The person at a beer party who handles his feelings of uneasiness by being loud and boisterous may be overcompensating and thereby making it impossible for others to understand his feelings and reassure him of his worth. Communication experience 3.5 describes an exercise that can be used to evaluate the student's compensatory behavior.

Communication Experience 3.5

Principle

Knowledge of self enables the sender to evaluate the effectiveness of his attempts to handle himself in a communication situation.

Procedure

1. Work in small groups, six-to-eight people.
2. Each participant takes a turn completing the following statement, "When I first meet new people I usually feel _____. I handle this feeling by behaving _____."
3. After each person has had a turn, compare and contrast differences in experiences.
4. Each participant takes another turn to discuss his interpretation of what the others' behaviors would be like.

Discussion

What were the similarities and differences in the ways members of the group explained their experiences? Can these behaviors be described as "compensatory"? Is "compensatory" behavior effective or ineffective? Should an effective sender make use of compensations or avoid them?

As illustrated in communication experience 3.5, compensatory behavior must be detected and evaluated. This involves the physical and psychological capability of encoding into language comprehendable to the receiver, or compensatory mechanisms for doing so. The second aspect entails making provision for dealing with another person whose private world may be invaded by the sender's attempt to communicate. When two people talk, a good part of what is said is never heard. All of us

Everybody's Talkin'

EVERYBODY'S TALKIN' at me
I don't hear a word they're sayin'
Only the echoes of my mind.
People stoppin' starin'
I can't see the faces
Only the shadows of their eyes

I'm goin' where the sun keeps shinin'
thru the pourin' rain
Goin' where the weather suits my clothes
Bankin' off of the northeast wind
Sailin' on a summer breeze
Skippin' over the ocean like a stone.

And I won't let you leave my love behind   *No,*
    I won't let you leave my love behind   *And,*
    I won't let you leave my love behind.

Fred Neil

forget that we compete with the inner voice of the person we are addressing. According to Blumer,[4] people may be living side by side, but in different worlds. While Blumer's point has to do with how we select and interpret the event-data around us, his statement has significance here in terms of the sender's awareness that his intended receiver has a private world that must be penetrated in order for interpersonal communication to take place.

Everyone has had the experience of being in a conversation during which he was too busy thinking of what he was going to say next to really listen to what the other person was saying; or being at a party and ostensibly in a conversation but really watching the door to see who was arriving, or talking to someone on the telephone without regard to whether or not they were really listening. The problem is that we often fail to behave in accordance with our knowledge. One way to keep this understanding conscious and to make use of it as senders of messages is to remember that communication is "mutually causal." Neither party in an interaction is merely the sounding board for the other. Each is a total human being with likes, dislikes, interests, needs, and private preoccupations, all of which must be penetrated in order for the intended communication to take place. Communication experience 3.6 is designed to sensitize the sender to the inner voice of his intended receiver.

Communication Experience 3.6

Principle

Communication does not take place in a vacuum or in a concise one-way order (sender–message–receiver). Rather, it is the attempt of one to reach another who in and of himself is another world of thoughts, feelings, ideas.

Procedure

1. Work alone on this project outside of class and report its results back to compare and contrast with the experiences of other class members.
2. Select a simple statement that you feel you might be likely to say, e.g., "I'm tired"; "I'm fed up with classes"; "I feel so good"; "What a great day."
3. Over a period of three days, make this same statement twenty-five times, keeping track of to whom the statement was made, where and when, other significant circumstances, and the feedback responses, including a comparison of responses made at different times by the *same* receiver to the statement.
4. Compare and contrast statements and experiences.

Discussion

How did it feel to try this exercise? Would one's feelings affect the results? Did the circumstances have any effect on the people to whom the statement was directed or the way in which it was made? What implications are there for message making?

Communication experience 3.6 illustrates that encoding skills, while essential, do not totally provide for effective communication. They are sufficient only when used together with the communicator's understanding and awareness of himself and others in the process of interpersonal communication.

I'm Nobody! Who are you?
Are you — Nobody — Too?
Then there's a pair of us?
Don't tell! they'd advertise — you know!

How dreary — to be — Somebody!
How public — like a Frog —
To tell one's name — the livelong June —
To an admiring Bog!

Emily Dickinson

The Sender's Awareness of Self and Others

The self has been described as an awareness of one's being and functioning.[5] In other words, to have a concept of self, one has to have an understanding of all her experiences having to do with her "I"ness and "ME"ness. These experiences are products of her interactions with her total environment, including all that she consciously and unconsciously experiences in her inner world, external world, and in the interactions between them. Let us refer back for a moment to the Westley-MacLean model. In the model $x_1, x_2 \ldots$ represents the event-data (internal or external stimulus). A is the interpreter of that data and codifier of its meaning, and B, the recipient of the information. A person's collection of beliefs about himself, which are the basis of his self-concept, are his interpretation of event-data, much of it in this case, internal. This model supported by an example can help clarify what is meant by self-concept.

A person goes to see a film. He is moved to tears, so he cries and says, "I am a sensitive and feeling person." In applying the model to this example, the film and feelings are represented by $x_1, x_2 \ldots$, the person by A, what he says about himself, by x^1, and the recipient of the message, by B. In this example, B can be either the person himself—which would be an instance of **intrapersonal** communication (communication within oneself about oneself in relation to one's environment); or B may be another person to whom A transmits the message x^1. The way in which A interprets $x_1 \ldots$—film, his feelings, his tears, their meaning—is a product of his self-concept. His self-concept defines for him something about who he is. His self-concept is defined for him by the way he already sees himself. Other people having the same set of data to interpret might say very different things about themselves, depending on their interpretation of the behavior. ("I am not manly because men don't cry," "I am too sentimental," etc.)

This perception of self that we call self-concept comes from our interpretations of our experiences. Such experiences are our interactions and reactions with the event-data in our environment. Because we are socialized into our culture, the culture and the whole socialization process plays an important role in our interpretations. How a male defines *manly* and his reaction to interpretation of the behavior he sees as manly, or unmanly, is in part a product of his cultural conditioning. Women, too, are socialized, but somewhat differently than men in our culture. The very same event-data presented in our example could be assessed quite differently if the person having the experience were a female.

Knowledge of self evolves from interactions with the people in one's social environment, how they see him, and what they tell him he is.

Figure 3.2 is the Johari Window, a diagram representing a person's self-knowledge or self-data at any given time.[6]

Figure 3.2
The Johari Window.

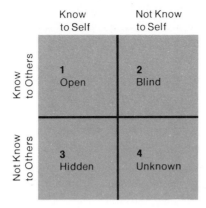

	Know to Self	Not Know to Self
Know to Others	**1** Open	**2** Blind
Not Know to Others	**3** Hidden	**4** Unknown

Quadrant 1 refers to the open feelings and behaviors known to others and to oneself, and is therefore called the **open area.** Quadrant 2, known as the **blind area** refers to feelings and behaviors known to others but not known to oneself. Quadrant 3 refers to those feelings and behaviors that are known to oneself, but unknown to others, and is called the **hidden area.** And Quadrant 4, the **unknown area,** represents the feelings and behaviors unknown to oneself and others.

The Johari Window divides one's personality into four quadrants in order to illustrate the different facets of self-data available to the sender at any given time. Quadrants 1 and 3, the *open* and *hidden* quadrants, are the portions of one's feelings and actions of which he is aware, while quadrants 2 and 4 are those of which he is unaware. Quadrants 1 and 3, which are known to self, provide the basis of one's self-concept. Communication experience 3.6 is based on self-disclosure, or the process of enlarging quadrant 1. It has been used to illustrate compensatory devices, some of which are known to self, and others which are not. The more the sender decreases quadrants 2, 3, and 4, the more he increases quadrant 1, his knowledge of self that he wishes to share with others. Self-data has two other important sets of ramifications for the sender as message maker.

The first set of ramifications has to do with self-knowledge and knowledge of others in the communication process. The more the communicator knows of himself and how he has come to be the person he is, the more he is in touch with his feelings including his needs for communicating and being communicated with. One's knowledge of self derives from his interactions with others, including what they tell him about himself. So too does one know about others based on how well he knows himself.

In the process of communication, one attempts to enter the private world of the person to whom she addresses her message. Her best tool for communicating successfully is her knowledge of self and her use of that self-understanding in an attempt to understand the other. This is not to say that knowing one's own likes and dislikes means that she then knows the likes and dislikes of others. However, by understanding that every person has individual preferences and priorities that determine how receptive he will be to another's attempt at communicating at any given time, one can begin to comprehend the other person. This makes it possible for communication to take place as desired. A student who goes to the library ostensibly to study, but really to see if he can get a date for Saturday night, becomes interested in the woman across from him in the reading room. Because she is cramming for an exam, she pays little attention to his attempts to "break the ice." Her private world differs from his at that moment.

The second set of ramifications has to do with the kinds of messages the initiating communicator can send. Interpersonal communication is a multifaceted process. Verbal and nonverbal messages are conveyed at the same time. Any feeling or behavior the sender is aware of can be translated into an intentional message. But the feelings and behaviors represented in the blind quadrant can also be transmitted without the senders' understanding that he is indeed conveying something.

Message Making and Awareness

At any given time, the sender transmits both **intentional** and **unintentional** messages. The distinction between the two is that *unintentional* messages are those that are unconsciously transmitted by the sender. The young child while rubbing his eyes says, "I'm wide awake," when his mother tells him it is bedtime. The words are the intended message; the yawns and eye rubbing, the unintentional. The substitute teacher stands before the class and tells them she is in charge while her shaking voice implies something quite different. The used car salesperson tries to make a sale but defeats himself by giving information about the car that makes the potential buyer wary.

The communicator's awareness of self and others contributes to the kinds of messages he transmits. When one knows what he is doing, he can then choose whether or not to continue. The person who knows that he has a nervous laugh when he gets frightened has a chance to modify that behavior if he feels it interferes with his intended communication. When he has bad news to relate but finds himself about to laugh, he can try not to because he knows that it acts as an interference with his purpose, or he can in some way compensate for his behavior if he does laugh. ("I laugh sometimes when I'm very nervous" may be just what the listener needs to hear to understand more of the speaker's inner experience, and not be put off by behavior that could otherwise be viewed in a negative light.)

As sender of the message the communicator chooses not only the code, but also the components of that code he employs to translate his message. Awareness of oneself and one's verbal and nonverbal skills and habits are essential to monitoring one's attempts at communicating. Depending upon his intended recipient, the sender might verbalize his attitude toward a particular subject in different ways. Take the issue of abortion as an example. If a person is pro-abortion and feels his listener is in agreement, his language and how much he says may be at variance with what he'd say and how he'd say it to a listener holding extremely different attitudes on the subject. One's self-concept determines much of his behavior—how he thinks he is most effective as a communicator, how he feels he can best elicit the response he wants, and how sure he feels about himself.

The last of these, how one feels about oneself, is most significant in terms of the effect it has on communication. As a person views himself, so he behaves. If he feels inadequate, it shows in what he says and how he says it. These messages tell more about the speaker and his own feelings of self than about the subject to which he is ostensibly addressing himself.

In essence, then, the more one can enlarge the knowledge he has of himself, the understanding of himself as he sees himself (Quadrants 2 and 4 in the Johari Window), the more aware he can be about the ways in which he presents himself as a communicator in the interpersonal process. The speakers actions must be decoded by his intended receiver. The initiating communicator does not have total control over the ways in which the receiver interprets the message. But one's awareness of self and others helps him exert whatever amount of control he has on the receiver's interpretation of the message.

Ethos: The Sender's Impact on the Message

Who the sender is, or at least who he is as perceived by the receiver, affects the receiver's understanding and/or acceptance of the sender's message. Aristotle referred to this phenomenon as *ethos,* the reputation or ethical appeal, of the speaker. In contemporary terms, this concept is called the *credibility* of the speaker. But we cannot talk about the credibility of the speaker without considering the credulity of the receiver. We cannot say a politician is credible, without acknowledging that on some level what this really means is that his constituents believe him.

By indicating that we must take into account the perceptions of the receiver (credulity) while talking of the ethos of the speaker (credibility), we can explain the reasons why a person has high credibility with some

receivers and low credibility with others. Two listeners hearing an authority speak may rate him quite differently in terms of credibility due to individual differences in the ways they perceive him. When a person earns a reputation as a highly credible source, what this indicates is that there are a large number of people who believe him.

The concept **ethos,** or **credibility,** to which we refer goes under a wide variety of names, such as *reputation, prestige, charisma, image, interpersonal trust,* and *attractiveness* or *appeal.* It is probably the single most important element in interpersonal communication. Whatever we label it, it represents the attitude toward the speaker which he arouses in the receiver. Perhaps the attitude is best described as the sender's perceived ethos (whom the receiver perceives the sender to be). Communication experience 3.7 deals with the impact on the message of the message maker as perceived by the receiver of that message.

Communication Experience 3.7

Principle

The complex process of message making is affected by the sender and who he is perceived to be by his intended receiver.

Procedure

1. Work in groups of four-to-six people.
2. Copy the first two paragraphs of the Declaration of Independence on a piece of paper and list numbers and spaces beneath it so that it resembles a petition.
3. Take the "petition" to the student center, a downtown intersection, and a supermarket, and ask people to sign it.
4. One member of the group acts as observer of the members asking for signatures as well as the people who the members approach. The observer questions those who sign the petition. He asks, "What influenced you to sign the petition?"

Discussion

How successful was the group in getting signatures? Did the place affect the willingness of people to sign? What was it about the group members and/or the petition that affected people's willingness to sign? How can this be verified? How can this be translated into other communication transactions?

As can be seen in communication experience 3.7, the sender's perceived ethos affects his receiver. It is his perceived ethos that determines the extent to which the receiver finds him credible.

Interference with Intentional Communication

This chapter has dealt with the communicator who has a need to communicate with another and thereby initiates the communication interaction. We have talked about the encoding skills necessary to do so, and the awareness of self and others essential to purposive communication. Interference with communication results from an absence of any one of these things. Without the need to communicate or to be communicated with, no one takes on the role as initiator of the exchange. Even where that need exists, if the person does not have the codes, verbal and nonverbal, into which to translate his experience, he does not have the necessary tools to satisfy his need. If he has the codes but has not mastered them effectively, here too can be an interference with intended communication, as has already been discussed in this chapter.

There is no greater potential interference with intentional communication than the communicator who, in effect, gets in his own way. A lack of self–awareness results in an inability to understand another person. One who is aware of his own feelings of joy, pain, pleasure, and sorrow can identify with those feelings in another. At the same time he must understand that the stimuli or experiences that elicit particular feelings in him may differ from what triggers these same feelings in another. The communicator who doesn't know himself well enough to know his real feelings or who is blind to his own actions interferes with intentional communication both by his lack of self-understanding and his lack of a tool for understanding, or caring to understand, another.

Essentially, every aspect of the role of the sender that we have discussed in this chapter has potential for enhancing or interfering with the sender's attempt to communicate. One *cannot not* communicate. But the goal of any sender is more than just communicating, where "communicating" is used to mean conveying *any* (intentional or unintentional) message. The goal of the sender is to communicate that which he intends to communicate in the way in which he intends it to be taken. Awareness of himself as sender and the role and functions of the sender in the communication process are basics he must master to accomplish his end.

Summary   In this chapter we have discussed the process of communication from the vantage point of the sender. We have considered the concepts necessary to have a clear understanding of how and why one becomes the intiator of communication. These are the important points to understand:

1. The communicator plays the part of the sender, encoder, or message maker as a result of a felt need to communicate.
2. The need to communicate, itself, is a response to some event-data observed by the communicator in his physical or social environment.
3. The communicator's need for "fidelity," the sought after response, compounds his need to initiate communication.
4. Communication does not begin when one person starts to talk to another, but rather when a person responds selectively to the social or physical environment referred to above.
5. The Westley-MacLean model incorporates the concept of perception of the environment, or event-data, in the process of interpersonal communication.
6. As sender of the message, the communicator encodes his experience verbally and/or nonverbally.
7. Any communicator can become the initiator of the interpersonal exchange if he has the code(s) into which to translate his inner experience.
8. All codes, verbal and nonverbal, are learned in a social context.
9. Effective encoding skills include recognition of any skills impairment, diagnosis of the problem, and correction or compensation thereof.
10. Encoding skills in and of themselves are not sufficient for communication. The sender must also be aware of himself and others in the communication process.
11. The Johari Window presents a representation of the communicator's self-data at any given moment.
12. The sender's reputation, ethos, as perceived by his receiver, colors the reception of his message.
13. Interference with message making relates to ineffective encoding or self-awareness on the part of the sender.

Questions for Discussion

1. What is the primary motivation one can have for attempting to communicate with another?
2. What determines one's choice of verbal or nonverbal codes for the sending of a message? How, if at all, can these codes be separated?
3. What is meant by the "invasion of the private world" of one's intended receiver?
4. Discuss your own assets as an encoder of a message.
5. Compare and contrast purposive and nonpurposive messages. Can nonpurposive messages be eliminated entirely?

6. How does the saying "beauty lies in the eyes of the beholder" relate to the concept of ethos?

7. In what ways can one learn to understand others so as to be better able to communicate with them?

8. List and discuss cultural effects on verbal and nonverbal language.

9. What is event-data?

10. Compare and contrast the "Hidden" and "Unknown" quadrants in the Johari Window.

Notes

1. Peter Berger and Thomas Luckmann, *The Social Construction of Reality* (Garden City, N.Y.: Doubleday, 1960).

2. Lee Thayer, "Mass Media: Notes toward a Theory," in *Mass Communication: Dialogue and Alternatives,* ed. Richard Budd and Brent Ruben (Rochelle Park, N.J.: Hayden Press, in preparation), p. 6.

3. Bruce Westley and Malcolm S. MacLean, Jr., "A Conceptual Model for Communication Research," in *Human Communication: Core Readings,* ed. Nancy L. Harper (New York: MSS Information Corporation, 1974), pp. 336–491. Also found in *Audio-Visual Communication Review,* Winter, 1955, Vol. 3, No. 1, pp. 3–12.

4. Herbert Blumer, "Symbolic Interaction: An Approach to Human Communication," in *Approaches to Human Communication,* ed. Richard Budd and Brent Ruben (New York: Spartan Books, 1972), p. 409.

5. Calvin Hall and Gardner Lindzey, *Theories of Personality* (New York: John Wiley and Sons, 1957), p. 483.

6. Joseph Luft, *Group Processes: An Introduction to Group Dynamics* (Palo Alto, Calif.: National Press, 1963).

7. Diagram for experience on page 62:

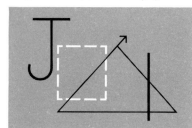

Selected Bibliography

Aronson, Elliot. *The Social Animal.* San Francisco, Calif.: W. H. Freeman and Company, 1972. An introduction to social psychology. Especially readable for the beginning student of communication.

Mortensen, C. David. *Communication: The Study of Human Interaction.* New York: McGraw-Hill Book Company, 1972. A research-oriented communication text. Especially recommended as a survey of the state of the discipline.

Rokeach, Milton. *Beliefs, Attitudes, and Values.* San Francisco, Calif.: Jossey-Bass, Inc., 1972. An in-depth approach to the study of development of attitudes, beliefs, and values. Recommended to the student interested in a philosophical/scientific exploration of these concepts.

Westley, Bruce, and Malcolm S. MacLean, Jr. "A Conceptual Model for Communication Research." In *Human Communication: Core Readings,* edited by Nancy L. Harper. New York: MSS Information Corporation, 1974. An important communication model. The article is recommended for its detailed analysis of the basis of the model.

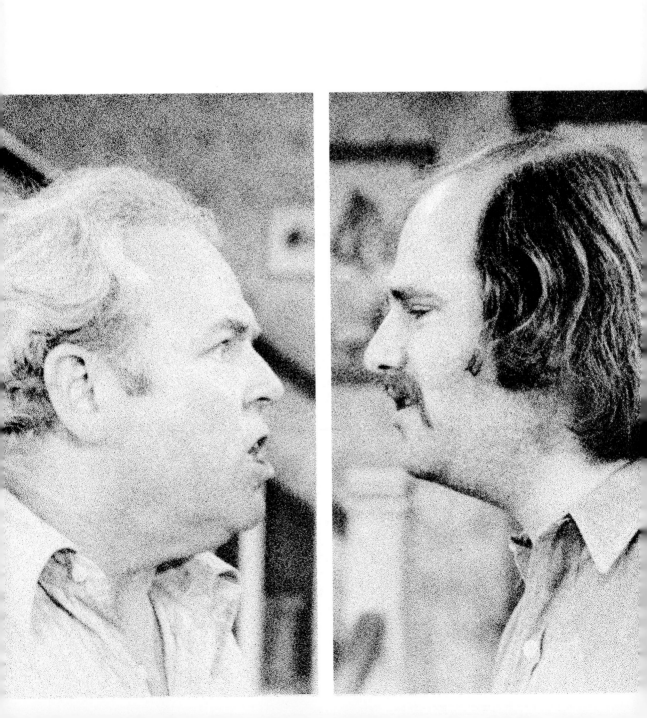

The Sender: Dynamics Affecting the Sender's Message Making

4

Introduction

Communication takes place between people, who play the parts of senders or receivers as one of the multitude of roles they fill in the daily interactions with one another. To really understand message making, we must understand people, the message makers. We must look at people and analyze those things that have shaped or in other ways affected them.

Every communicator is the product of his total life experience (field of experience). In studying the communication process, the most significant aspects of the communicator's experience are the culture and social systems that have helped socialize him, the resultant attitudes and values that he evolves, and the effects of these things in terms of his desires and abilities to communicate. But just as the role of sender cannot be discussed without first analyzing people (senders), the process of interpersonal communication cannot be discussed in a vacuum. Communication takes place in a context—the communication environment. In order to understand any given interpersonal interaction, it is important to consider the communication environment within which it takes place.

This chapter will focus on the dynamics discussed above and the effects they have on the sender and his message making.

Communication Goals

This chapter uses the theoretical and experiential to explore the role of the sender by investigating those significant dynamics that affect her message making. It is written to enable you to understand these dynamics by:

1. Familiarizing yourself with the unique cultural background transmitted to you by those responsible for your socialization.
2. Evaluating the effect of that socialization on your perceptions and behaviors in a communication situation.
3. Defining and recognizing your attitudes and values and the effect they have on your perception and interpretation of self, others, and messages.
4. Understanding the impact of space, setting, and time on message making.
5. Evaluating your coding skills as affected by your field of experience, and the communication environment of the given communication exchange.

Communication Concepts and Experiences

Communication takes place between people who themselves are the products of their living experiences. One of the important dynamics affecting the communicator's message making is the field of experience of which she is a product.

The Sender's Field of Experience

The communicator enters the communication situation not as a blank slate, but crammed full of experiences that affect his ability and desire to communicate, and the ways in which he has learned to do so. All of the communicator's past and present experiences affect the way he perceives himself, the one with whom he attempts to communicate, and the interaction itself. They affect the way he enters any given communication situation. For example, a man says to a woman, "Can you tell me the time?" We can only begin to analyze the interaction by labeling him the *sender,* her the *receiver,* and his statement as the *message.* To understand the exchange more profoundly, we must ask some questions. Some of the relevant questions are "Who is he?" "What does he want to know?" (e.g. the time, or if she might be interested in him), and "What in his past experience has made him believe that this is the way to get what he wants?" In asking these questions, we are looking at the communicator as a product of his experiences. To understand his part in the interaction, we must find out something about those experiences.

Because an individual's field of experience encompasses everything in his life, it must be narrowed down to be discussed meaningfully. The two most important specific aspects of the sender's experiences are first, his culture and the social systems to which he belongs; and second his attitude and value formation.

Culture and Social Systems

All communicators are raised in a culture, a society with its norms, values, and prescriptions for behavior, including communicative behavior. If everyone had the same cultural background, there would be no problem. But culture is transmitted to the individual by the people with whom he has contact, in the various social systems of which he is a member. In terms of communication, then, it is too vague to speak of the sender's "culture." To say that someone is American, raised in this culture, gives only a vague insight into his cultural background. It leads to the kind of stereotyping expressed in statements like, "Once you've seen one, you've seen them all."

The specific transmitters of culture to the individual are social systems, *primary* and *secondary socializers,* through which the individual has been socialized. It is more specific and revealing to describe someone as an American raised in Milwaukee by immigrant parents, thankful to this country for giving them a new start in life, than to describe him as American.

Primary Socialization: Transmission of Culture

The individual is not born a member of a society. He is born with a predisposition toward sociability. **Primary socialization** refers to the early, childhood, social interactions of an individual. It is through these experiences that he becomes a member of society. The infant is hungry and so he cries. The mother (or whoever is in charge) feeds him. The ways in which he is fed, what he is fed, and when and how he is fed are ways that the mothering figure has learned. They are part of the adult's socialization that are passed on to the infant.

In this culture, for example, there have been very different theories regarding the feeding of infants. In the 1940s babies were fed on a rigid four-hour schedule. No matter how much a baby cried for food in between, mothers were taught that to violate the schedule was to spoil the child. In the late 1950s and early 1960s the theory changed and babies were fed on what was called the demand schedule, feedings were determined by the hunger of the child. Part of the socialization of infants in each of these eras depended on the theory that was in use and the adoption of that theory by the parental figures.

From infancy on, the individual learns ways in which to express his needs (hunger, thirst, fear, boredom, love, etc.) and the ways in which those needs will be met. The socializers of the child have also been socialized into the culture. They have their own ways in which to accept and/or reject that culture. The child absorbs not only the norms and values of the culture at large and the subculture of his parents, but also the individual coloration (interpretation) given to that culture.[1]

The food example can be carried along into childhood. Food preference is cultural. The American child is fed milk, vegetables, and snacks that are sweet, etc. The Chinese child is fed rice, pork, kumquats, etc. The American child is encouraged to master use of the spoon, fork, and knife; the Chinese child, chopsticks. Depending on the primary socializers and their attitudes toward feeding, each American child learns different eating patterns. Some are encouraged to eat three meals a day with nothing in between. Some are allowed to eat whenever they wish. When and how each child learns to use silverware depends on the

preference of his socializers. One parent may not be concerned about messiness and will allow the child to eat with his hands until he is four or five. Another may exert pressure on the child to use the eating tools as soon as he is old enough to hold them. Communication experience 4.1 is designed for you to compare and evaluate your own socialization experiences with those of your classmates.

Communication Experience 4.1

Principle

Much of what we know and how we operate on that knowledge is the product of the ways in which we have been socialized into our culture.

Procedure

1. Work in groups of about five people.
2. Each group has thirty minutes to complete the assignment.
3. The U.S. Government has decided that on their next moon shot a time capsule will be placed on the moon for other possible forms of life to know who Americans are.
4. Each group is to decide what that capsule should contain to explain best the culture of America in the late 1960s, early 70s, and late 70s.
5. Each group is to consider the appropriate symbols to represent cultural attitudes toward other people, politics, love, sex, language, and any other significant aspects of American life for that particular period.

Discussion

Compare and contrast group choices. How were the decisions made? How did the group members know about these things? How did they know what to value and how to value it? What does the experience illustrate about the past socialization of the participants? About the ways in which they would socialize others? What implications for message making did you derive from this exercise?

As illustrated in communication experience 4.1, everyone is socialized into their culture and taught how to value the different aspects of that culture. The primary socializers transmit the culture, or their interpretation of that culture, to the child. By this process, the child learns communicative behavior.

We can see the strong interdependence of culture and communication when we realize that all of one's inner experiences can be communicated only when he learns to transmit these experiences in some "meaningful" way. The ways that are meaningful are determined by the culture as translated by the socializers of that child. If an infant has a need for attention and cries but nothing happens, he soon learns other behaviors that are attention-getting. He coos, or gurgles, or smiles. If this behavior is met with a response, he repeatedly engages in it to get what he wants. The culture of the parents, or their interpretation of it, affects which of those behaviors will get the sought after response. The parenting figures who believe that picking up a crying infant is spoiling a child will never respond to the child's cries, but will rush to be with him if he laughs or gurgles.

Nonverbal and eventually verbal behaviors are learned in this way. It is better to say "learned" rather than "taught," because the child may learn more than the parenting figures wish to teach. No one would ever want to teach a child that in order to get what he wants he must have a tantrum. But every time a child's temper tantrum is given into by a worn-down parent, the child "learns" how to get what he wants. The parent says, "Don't interrupt me while I'm talking to someone." If the interrupting behavior results in the sought after attention, the child "learns" to interrupt.

Secondary Socialization: Expanding Circles of Influence
Primary socialization ends when the child has absorbed enough of the culture's norms and values to become an effective member of that society. **Secondary socialization** is any later process that introduces an already socialized individual into new aspects of the society or culture in which he lives. The secondary socializers are those other people with whom the child has contact. Initially they are other family members (relatives other than the immediate family) and neighbors or friends of the family. Eventually secondary socializers include one's peers. By the time children are old enough to play side-by-side, they are socializing one another into language and behavior patterns. The saving grace for a parent whose child uses language that he finds embarrassing is to claim that the child must have learned "those words" from some of the neighborhood children.

Secondary socialization is the acquisition of norms and values of the subcultures to which one belongs. It continues as long as one continues to enter into new groups. Not only does secondary socialization take place for the child entering school, clubs, church, and other peer groups, but for the adult as well. A move from a small town in Kansas to Philadelphia may entail a great deal of secondary socialization regarding the ways in which people's behavior toward one another differ from the

Ever since I was a little kid I didn't want to be me. I wanted to be Billie Widdledon. And Billie Widdledon didn't even like me.

I walked like he walked. I talked like he talked. I signed up for the high school he signed up for —

Which was when Billie Widdledon changed. He began to hang around Herby Vandeman. He walked like Herby Vandeman. He talked like Herby Vandeman.

He mixed me up! I began to walk and talk like Billie Widdledon walking and talking like Herby Vandeman.

And then it dawned on me that Herby Vandeman walked and talked like Joey Haverlin and Joey Haverlin walked and talked like Corky Sabinson.

So here I am walking and talking like Billie Widdledon's imitation of Herby Vandeman's version of Joey Haverlin trying to walk and talk like Corky Sabinson.

And who do you think Corky Sabinson is always walking and talking like? Of all people Dopey Kenny Wellington —

That little pest who walks and talks like me.

Jules Feiffer

patterns of behavior in the person's former environment. Rush hour traffic is a new experience to someone from a town in which there were less than a hundred people, forty of whom were too young to drive cars.

Culture, Social Systems, and the Sender

When one enters a given communication interaction, she takes to it what she has learned in her past experiences and continues using the same modes of communicating. The child who has terrorized her family with her temper tantrums eventually goes off to school, camp, or some other environment different from that of the family setting. Her peers and superiors either continue to reward her behavior or they treat her so differently that she soon learns new ways of coping. The child who needs to be dressed at home is often perfectly able to dress herself at camp where she'll miss swimtime if she can't put on her own swimsuit. The "bully" big sister often learns from her classmates that she cannot bulldoze them as she can her younger brother or sister. It is equally as possible for the secondary socializers to treat the child as her family did and thereby reinforce the ways she has learned to behave.

A problem exists for the communicator if his world and varied experiences expand and change faster than does his learning of ways in which to cope with those changes. One peer group may differ greatly from another. One teacher may be responsive in ways different from all the other teachers a student has had. One employer's expectations may be very different than those of other employers with whom an employee has had contact.

It is important for the communicator to increase his awareness of the ways in which he has been socialized. Such insight gives him an understanding of why he behaves (including communication behavior) as he does. It explains that the ways of expressing his inner experiences have been learned and often need to be relearned. Others having the same inner feelings, or needs, may have been socialized quite differently. As senders they express their inner experiences very differently. As receivers of a message, they interpret them very differently. What constitutes "good manners," for example, is very much a product of socialization. Because of his socialization, a man may believe it is an expression of respect to open a door for a woman. If her socialization has been similar, she may take the gesture to mean just that. But if it differs, she may read his action as an expression of male dominance. Communication experience 4.2 is designed to help you assess your own primary and secondary socialization as relevant to communicative behavior.

Insofar as I can be regarded as
human, it is because I was claimed
at birth as a member of a
communicative network, which
programmed me for participation in
itself. Even such autonomy as
I have developed is not a relic
of some inherent individuality which
has survived socialization but is
itself a product of socialization,
differentiated through social
experience, mediated by
communication.

Geoffrey Vickers

Communication Experience 4.2

Principle

One's socialization is a product of his secondary as well as primary socializers.

Procedure

1. Work in groups of eight-to-ten people.
2. Hold a group discussion on the topic "participants as adolescents."
3. Compare and contrast the ways in which group members dressed during adolescence, their pet expressions, interests and pastimes, and any other significant memories of the ages between thirteen and sixteen.
4. From the discussion, compile a list of experiences descriptive of adolescence and use it to answer the question of whether or not that age group constitutes a "subculture."

Discussion

What were the similarities and differences among group members in terms of adolescent experiences? In what ways do these experiences now affect you and the other members of your group? How, if at all, does the discussion shed light on your socialization? What implications are there for communication?

As illustrated in communication experience 4.2, socialization affects the sender in terms of how he sees himself and others and the ways in which he has learned to attempt to communicate with those others peopling his environment. It affects one's perceptions of self, others, and messages. One of the most specific and observable causes of one's perceptions are the attitudes and values inherent in his culture as transmitted to him by his socializers, or "significant others."[2]

The Sender's Attitudes and Values

An **attitude** is some tendency, predisposition, or approach toward a person, place, idea, or thing. It is an organization of several beliefs focused on a specific object or situation, predisposing one to respond in some preferential manner.[3] An attitude is a package of beliefs. One's attitude toward religion is the sum total of his religious beliefs. One's attitude toward women, or politics, or sex, or the institution of marriage is the totality of his beliefs surrounding all his ideas on the subject.

Values are related to attitudes. They are the worth a person assigns
to something. How much something means to an individual is the degree
to which he values it. Values are personal priorities. They are the order
of importance one attaches to ideas or things. To say that a person has a
"value," is to say that he has a lasting belief that something is preferable
to some other alternative. If he values life and health, he tries to do those
things that will prolong both. If he values his privacy, then he guides his
actions to increase it.

Attitudes and values are important in relation to interpersonal
communication. Each affects the ways in which people perceive and
behave toward one another. Attitudes are basically how one sees things.
Values are the degree of importance one attaches to those things. It is
not the distinction between attitudes and values that is important for human
communication; it is the effects of these preferences on communication.

The sender's attitudes and values are part of his field of experience.
They are learned in the process of his socialization into his culture and
subsequent subcultures. One's attitudes and values determine the ways in

which he perceives and interprets self, subject matter, and intended receivers in the communication process. When speaking of the sender's *perception* of something (self, message, or other), we refer to the way in which he sees or understands and interprets that thing at that given moment. When one's best friend goes to a beer party and gulps down seven beers and begins dancing on tabletops, his attitude toward his friend affects his perception of his friend's behavior and the interpretation he gives it. The friend says, "He's the life of the party." A non-friend observing the behavior perceives the event-data and says, "Drunk; he can't hold his liquor." Both observers begin with the same event-data to interpret. Something regarding the observed behavior differs internally in the encoders of the messages ("life of party;" "drunk"). The internal differences are attitudes and values.

The attitudes and values transmitted in the process of socialization teach us how to evaluate that which we observe. They are the sets of filters through which events are processed or interpreted. One's attitude toward a person drinking seven beers, beer-drinking itself, or party behavior, would shape one's interpretation of the event-data observed. Communication experience 4.3 is designed to illustrate the effects of attitudes and values in a communication situation.

Communication Experience 4.3

Principle

One's attitudes and values structure one's perceptions of his world and the ways in which he makes choices about coping with reality.

Procedure

1. Work in groups of six-to-ten people.
2. Following is a list and description of seven people. Each of them has survived a plane crash in the Andes. Each has injuries that need treatment within twelve hours. A rescue team finds the wreckage. Unfortunately, there is only room enough to transport four people at a time. Since the trip there and back will take a day and a half, those left behind will die. Your group must decide which four are to be transported.

   a. Male, white, 45 years old. Originally from Poland and a very religious Jew. A medical doctor who is semi-retired because of a kidney problem.

   b. Female, black, 18 years old, high school dropout. Recently married to a postman studying at night to be a lawyer. Works as a telephone operator.

c. Female, white, 56 years old, housewife, mother of six and grandmother of two. Although she has never worked outside her home, she is known as a reliable babysitter and homemaker and called Mom by all the neighborhood children.

d. Female, 36, a nun. Member of a nursing order, has lived in primitive cultures as a missionary. Recently blinded by an accident.

e. Male, black, 46 years old. Plumber and handyman. Recently lost his wife and children in a fire. Has had a serious bout with drinking since then.

f. Male, white, 39 years old, attorney. Gave up a very lucrative practice to work for radical causes. Has been arrested for indecent exposure.

g. Female, white, 25 years old, a Ph.D. candidate in sociology financing her studies by prostitution.

3. After reading the list, choose the four people. Explain the rationale for the choices.

4. After making your choices, select a representative to explain your group's decisions to the rest of the class.

5. Representatives from each of the groups sit in a circle surrounded by the rest of the class and explain their group's positions.

Discussion

By what criteria were the choices made? Were any of the candidates selected by all the groups? Were there any not selected by the groups? Were there difficulties in making choices? Are these kinds of decisions ever made outside the classroom exercise? What does this selection process tell you about yourself? What do your values and attitudes have to do with your decision making?

As illustrated in communication experience 4.3 one's attitudes and values affect the ways in which he sees and interprets the event-data presented to him in his living experiences. The ways in which attitudes and values affect the sender can be viewed in two basic ways: (1) in terms of his attitude toward self, others, and messages; and (2), in terms of the metamessages (messages about the message) that he transmits regarding his perceptions of self, others, and messages.

The sender's perception of self—who he thinks he is and how he feels about it—are in large part the result of his attitudes toward himself. If a man's culture values athletic men, then he had better be athletic, or risk a poor self-image. If a woman's culture and those who interpret it for her imply that her place is in the home, but she wants a career as a corporate lawyer, she must either reject her culture's teachings and adopt her own attitudes and values, or see herself as less womanly.

The sender's perception of the subject matter and his intended receiver are also a product of his value system. In our culture, there are taboo subjects that are either left unmentioned or discussed with a tactfulness not necessary when discussing sports, politics, or racing cars. Bodily functions and death are the most obvious examples.

The attitude toward one's intended receiver colors his perception of that person and the ways in which one expects him to respond to one's message. For instance, a person raised to worship authority figures speaks differently to a teacher, minister, or employer than someone with less awe. Communication experience 4.4 is designed to illustrate the relationships between one's field of experience, attitudes, and perceptions.

Communication Experience 4.4

Principle

What we "see" and how we interpret that event-data is a product of our field of experience and the attitudes and values derived therein.

Procedure

1. Work individually, and then compare answers with the rest of the class.
2. Look at the picture presented below and then answer the following questions.

a. The Butter family loves to eat.
   True_____ False_____ Can't answer_____

b. Grandma Butter is a good cook.
   True_____ False_____ Can't answer_____

c. Mr. and Mrs. Butter have two sons and a daughter.
   True_____ False_____ Can't answer_____

d. The Butter's summer home is by the water.
   True_____ False_____ Can't answer_____

e. Bobby and Bill Butter are very neat.
   True_____ False_____ Can't answer_____

f. Mrs. Butter used to be a model.
   True_____ False_____ Can't answer_____

g. It is summertime in the picture.
   True_____ False_____ Can't answer_____

h. Mrs. Butter has a lot of pots to wash.
   True_____ False_____ Can't answer_____

Discussion

What do you know about the Butter family from the picture? If the members of the class arrived at different answers, on what did they base their answers? What implications are there for communication in this game?

As illustrated in communication experience 4.4, perceptions of self, others, and messages are affected by attitudes and values. A second way in which the sender's attitudes and values affect the communication process is in terms of the **metamessages** (messages about the message) that he may transmit regarding how he sees himself, his subject matter, or his intended receiver.

The sender's verbal message is accompanied by a range of nonverbal behaviors that can also serve as messages. The sender's attitudes toward himself, the message he sends, and his receiver may be conveyed verbally by the way he chooses to use his words, and nonverbally by how he looks, how he sounds, and his mannerisms, which together can either enhance or interfere with his intended communication.

In analyzing the role of the communicator as sender, the focus has been on his field of experience, including his socialization and attitude formation. Each affects his ability to act as the initiator of communication. A second important dynamic affecting one's attempts at sending messages is the communication environment and his understanding of it.

I was asleep for 29 years.

Are you sure you're awake while you're reading this?

Maybe you're in the kind of trance I used to be in: get up, go to work, come home. Get up, go to work, come home. You know what I'm talking about:

The 20th Century trance.

If I wanted to do something new and different, I'd think: tomorrow.

Get involved in the community ecology meetings: tomorrow. Go shopping for a portable color TV: tomorrow. Make reservations for a week in the sun: tomorrow.

I used to spend my life going through the motions today, and putting things off until: tomorrow.

Nothing happens in your life unless you make it happen. I started thinking that way once I stepped back and looked at my life.

Self-knowledge is powerful stuff. It can make you throw away a lot of things in your life, and flip the switch to go after the new things you really want.

I have my new color TV now. In fact, a whole living room full of new furniture. I've been away twice this year, not counting long weekends. And not only am I going to community meetings, I'm organizing them.

I woke up to the fact that you have to live your life today, even though you're always planning for tomorrow.

In fact, I feel secure about the future.

But today is where I live.

I live my dreams today, not tomorrow.

Communication Environment: The Message-Making Context

The **communication environment** is the physical, social, and psychological boundaries within which a communication interaction occurs. It serves as the framework (total context) within which the sender attempts to convey his message to his intended receiver. The physical, social, and psychological components of the communication environment can be clarified further by examining the *space, setting,* and *time* in which the sender attempts to communicate.

Space, Setting, and Time

The **space** in which communication takes place is both the physical space (distance and size) and the psychological space (how that physical space is interpreted and used by the communicators). Riders on any rush-hour urban bus or subway, for example, are so crowded together that physical contact is unavoidable. But an elbow in one's side cannot be interpreted the same if the bus were almost empty and one passenger stood there elbowing another. Passengers in an elevator are together in a confined space that may make them feel so physically close to strangers that they keep their distance by looking at the floor numbers, or the light above the elevator door, or reading the inspection card rather than looking one another in the eye. On the other hand, two lovers who want to talk intimately may find a large table in a restaurant too much space (distance) for the kind of feelings they wish to share.

The concept of *space* includes the communicator's personal space. It is the feeling of boundaries or space around one that belongs to him. Our sense of personal space or territory is illustrated by how close we stand or like to be stood next to; our feelings about touching or being touched; one's "place" at the kitchen table; or "seat" (when not officially assigned) in class. The ability to communicate intentionally is increased by an understanding of one's feelings about the space in which the communication takes place and an awareness of the receiver's feelings.

Communication experience 4.5 presents some interesting possibilities for the explorations of the effects of the use of space.

Communication Experience 4.5

Principle

We all have a strong sense of personal space, although we may not always be conscious of our sense of space.

Procedure

1. Work individually outside of class and report back the results.
2. Do all of the following:
   a. Go to a restaurant with another person. While engaging in conversation, move the salt, pepper, etc., to his "side" of the table. Do the same with the water glasses and silverware settings—as casually as possible.
   b. Sit in someone else's favorite chair.
   c. While talking to someone you do not know well at a party, move very close (less than a foot away).
3. Each of these things must be done as unobtrusively as possible, and the reactions of the other person must be observed.

Discussion

What was observed about the other person? Did he change verbally or nonverbally or fail to react? Were the actions of the student participant casual enough so as to get a reaction? Or, were they too obvious? Which was the most successful exercise? Why? What implications are there for the sender of a message?

Every person has a sense of space, including personal space, as illustrated in communication experience 4.5. It is of importance to have an understanding of the meanings of the ways in which that space is used in the communication situation. The use of space is determined by the number of people in it. It is also culturally defined. The same number of people may be found visiting parks as visiting cemeteries, but each place is used differently. Appropriate ways to communicate one's feelings within a given space are determined culturally. Churches, libraries, and schools provide very different communication contexts than do stadiums, dormitories, and amusement parks.

The emphasis is not so much on space itself but the setting it provides for the communication. In terms of the communication environment, the **setting** has both physical and psychological effects on the communication.

Physically, a setting may be conducive to different kinds of communication. A stadium lends itself better to loud noise, shouting, than to intimate conversation. An empty movie theatre may inhibit one's instinct to laugh very loud. Psychologically, the setting provides an atmosphere that either enhances or detracts from one's ability to communicate. The kind of restaurant atmosphere one prefers is determined by whom he is going to be with and the ways in which he wants to communicate. Parents with young children may feel more comfortable in a take-out hamburger place than in a dark, atmospheric French restaurant.

The time of the interaction is another aspect of the communication environment. **Time,** like space, can be considered in its most formal sense to mean the time of day or year. More personally, it refers to what that time means for the communicators. The time of day or year promotes certain kinds of communication, especially in superficial encounters ("Merry Christmas"; "Good night"; "Have a nice weekend"). More personally, it provides a context for what is to be discussed and how it can be said. A husband who needs his wife's undivided attention may have to wait to discuss an important decision until after the children are in bed. A friend who needs advice from another friend who is studying for an exam may have to wait for a more convenient time. The concept of time can also refer to the timing of a message in the relationship between the communicators. Sometimes there is a need to know the other person well before saying certain kinds of things to him. The timing has to be right to air feelings of love or anger.

The communication environment is the space, setting, and time during which an interaction takes place. It provides the context in which the sender attempts to convey his message. Communication always takes place in a context, and the context affects the communication interaction. Understanding the effects of the context helps one understand the interaction in which he is involved. The sender is basically involved in trying to express himself to another human being. By knowing that the ways in which the communicators can attempt to share meaning are affected by the specific context they are in allows each communicator (sender) to evaluate his message-making behaviors. To communicate intentionally the sender must frame his messages so that they are appropriate to the communication environment. To accomplish this, it is necessary for the sender to consider two things in framing his message, (1) the context in which he is trying to communicate, and (2) the relationship in which he is involved. Taking these considerations into account affects what the sender wants to say and the code and channel selections he makes.

The Sender's Code and Channel Selection

The sender learns verbal and nonverbal codes as a part of his field of experience. How and when these codes are learned becomes a product of his unique experience. Words are learned as necessitated by one's experiences. While most children growing up in this country learn English, not all of them learn it as a first or only language. And even those children socialized only in the English language do not all learn the same words or the same feelings about the words they learn. Some words are common to everyone learning a given language. For instance, most infants in our culture begin to learn the word *no* when they get into things that are dangerous (touching the stove) or otherwise taboo (breaking mother's best china). Other words and the order in which they are learned are a product of each child's own unique environment. Words for animals, *dog* and *cat,* may be learned early by children whose parents have a pet, and later (from books or neighborhood experiences) by children in homes without pets. Even though the children from both homes eventually do learn the words for *dog* and *cat,* these words may carry different connotations depending on the feelings about the animals as transmitted by the person giving the word to the child. Parents who own and love a cocker spaniel will transmit those feelings along with the word *dog.* Parents who are afraid of dogs may convey a different feeling.

A person's field of experience may provide him with different words for things than the words learned by someone maturing in a different environment. A child growing up in some parts of New England may refer to the place his family takes dirty clothes as the *cleanser* and the place they take shoes for repair as the *cobbler.* Children in other geographic areas may know these places by the words *cleaner* and *shoemaker,* and others may not know these words at all.

Nonverbal codes are also learned during the process of one's socialization. Speakers often use their hands to emphasize a point. Yet many children are taught that it is impolite to "speak with their hands." Certain gestures (a wave) are understood by all members of the culture. Others (a clenched raised fist) may have meaning only for some.

Just as one learns nonverbal codes as part of his field of experience, so too does he learn that the communication environment is a determinant in the ways in which he encodes his message nonverbally. A smile and nod of the head is sufficient for greeting a friend at an exam where talking is prohibited, but at a beer party it might seem standoffish. In an open field one can run, jump, and romp around much more than at a lawn party given by the dean and his wife.

The sender must be aware that his verbal and nonverbal codes have been learned as part of his own personal experiences. This will help him avoid the trap of assuming that just because he and another person "speak the same language" that the words will be understood by both. It puts him in the position of testing out that assumption whenever he feels the need.

Knowing this can also increase the sender's understanding that the potential meaning in his nonverbal as well as verbal behavior is open to interpretation. If being understood as he had intended matters to him, some attention needs to be paid to the response of his receiver. If one winks at another and says, "You look real bad," meaning, "You really look great," the response of bewilderment, anger, or withdrawal on the part of the receiver can give a clue that he has not received the message as was intended.

The choices the sender makes are also influenced by the communication environment in which he finds himself. His past experiences have taught him how to communicate in this kind of situation. The kind of language he chooses, for example, may be the product of the context (e.g., a classroom) and his relationship to his intended receiver (e.g., the professor). Even if the thought he wanted to express was on the same subject he and his fraternity brothers had discussed over coffee at 2 A.M. the other night, the way in which the sender now expresses himself to his professor in the lecture hall may differ very much in language and tone, if not in content. His awareness of the communication environment and its demands helps him decide on the way in which to express his thought. The communication environment is one of the important dynamics affecting the sender's choices for encoding his message.

Interference with Intentional Communication

This chapter has focused on the human being who plays the role of sender. Specific emphasis has been on those dynamics that affect that person and his message making. Interference with intended meaning results from any inadequacy or complication related to these dynamics.

A serious interference with intended communication occurs when the sender is unaware of one or more of the dynamics discussed. The sender who is unaware of his own socialization and attitude formation as they affect him as a communicator, may be blind to the fact that others have had different experiences and thereby interpret the messages he conveys through a set of filters very different from his own.

In some segments of our culture, for example, profanity is not acceptable in "polite society." A person who swears in public is frowned upon. In such circumstances people receiving his message would be affected negatively by the encoding choices he makes. Other segments of our society, however, consider any word that accurately expresses the speaker's feeling as appropriate. To these receivers the use of such interjections as "Oh sugar!" "Gosh darn!" or "My word!" would be a distraction rather than an effective way of communicating.

The sender must at all times use his awareness of self and others to try to avoid unintentional message making. Effective intentional communication requires the sender's constant attempts to understand the person with whom he tries to communicate. Without this kind of awareness and attempt to reach the other person, the sender is limited in the communication interaction.

Lack of awareness of the context and role of relationships in which he attempts to communicate can also damage intentional communication. Everyone is affected by the context and relationship in which communication occurs. Persons most effective in getting their messages across as intended are most sensitive to the differences between one communication environment and another. Interference with intentional communication occurs when one forgets that the setting, timing, or relationship calls for different ways of expressing one's message. An intimate conversation is not as appropriate in one setting as another; one friend can be criticized more directly than another who is overly sensitive; a joke must be told at an appropriate time.

The sender cannot not communicate. But, he can fail to communicate as he intended. Since communication is a complex transaction open to interpretation by the sender and his receiver, awareness of the dynamics related to any communication interaction add dimensions to the sender's ability to communicate intentionally.

Summary

In this chapter communication has been discussed from the vantage point of the sender by exploring the dynamics that affect his message making. These are the important points to understand:

1. The communicator's field of experience includes all of the living experiences he has had.
2. These experiences are brought by the communicator to the given communication interaction, coloring her perceptions and interpretations of self, others, and messages.

3. One's culture and the social systems to which she belongs are a significant part of her field of experience, shaping her communicative behavior.

4. One's culture is transmitted to him by his primary and secondary socializers. Their individual interpretations, rather than those of culture itself, are transmitted to the child being socialized into that culture.

5. One's attitude and value formation are significant aspects of his field of experience. Attitudes are his predisposition or approach toward a person, place, idea, or thing. Values are his standards for behavior.

6. One's attitudes and values are the filters through which he perceives any interpersonal interaction.

7. One's attitudes and values may also convey metamessages to her receiver.

8. The communication environment influences the sender's message making. It is composed of the physical and psychological ramifications of the space, setting, and time in which the interpersonal exchange takes place.

9. The sender is the encoder of the message. His encoding choices are affected by his field of experience and the communication environment of the given communication interaction.

10. Interference with intentional message making exists if the communicators lack a common socialization. It also occurs if one violates the bounds set by the physical and/or psychological structure in which the communication occurs.

Questions for Discussion

1. Interview a fellow student regarding his feelings about his math professor. In what ways do his feelings constitute an attitude, and what is the resultant effect of that attitude on the communication between the student and teacher?

2. Discuss a situation in which one's feelings of discomfort or inadequacy would affect his communication. Describe some of the metamessages in which that feeling would manifest itself.

3. In what ways does the communication environment affect the day-to-day communication of a college student?

4. Compare and contrast cultural backgrounds among class members. What, if any, uniqueness in socialization can be pinpointed?

5. Discuss the relationship between perception and interpretation.

6. Describe how the nonverbal cues may undermine or reinforce the verbal.

7. What areas of one's field of experience are irrelevant to her interpersonal communication?

8. What determines the sender's choice of codes for his message?

9. Describe a violation of a given communication environment.

Notes

1. Refer to Peter Berger and Thomas Luckmann, *The Social Construction of Reality* (Garden City, N.Y.: Doubleday, 1967) for a thorough discussion of socialization and reality.

2. Ibid., p. 103

3. Milton Rokeach, *Beliefs, Attitudes, and Values* (San Francisco: Jossey-Bass, Inc., Publishers, 1972), p. 118.

Selected Bibliography

Berger, Peter and Thomas Luckmann. *The Social Construction of Reality.* Garden City, N.Y.: Doubleday & Company, 1967. A challenging exploration of human reality construction. Difficult reading for the beginning student.

Johnson, Wendell. *Living With Change: The Semantics of Coping,* edited by Dorothy Moeller. New York: Harper & Row, 1972. An introduction to language as it affects reality. Especially recommended for those interested in words and meanings.

Rokeach, Milton. *Beliefs, Attitudes and Values.* San Francisco, Calif.: Jossey-Bass, Inc., 1972. A philosophical/scientific exploration of attitude and value formation.

Smith, Alfred G. *Communication and Culture.* New York: Holt, Rinehart and Winston, 1966. An anthology of writings on many aspects of communication. In-depth treatment of important areas such as information theory, nonverbal communication, and language/meaning.

The Sender: As Receiver

5

Introduction

While distinctions are made between the acts of sending and receiving messages, it is crucial to understand that all people in the interpersonal communication process do both.

This chapter approaches the analysis of the role of the sender in the communication process by addressing itself to this dual role. The sender is viewed as a communicator involved in a range of behaviors that includes receiving messages.

Communication Goals

This chapter uses the theoretical and experiential approach to explore the multifaceted role of the sender in the communication process. It is written to enable you to understand that:

1. The difference between the initiator (or sender) and receiver in interpersonal communication is a matter of timing rather than behavior.
2. Distinctions made between sender and receiver are necessary for purposes of analysis, yet they are somewhat arbitrary.
3. The role of the communicator designated as sender is a complex multifaceted one.
4. The function of feedback is a response from the sender's perspective; message making from the receiver's perspective.
5. Communicators exert mutual control over one another.
6. The sender who is a complex world unto herself uses communication behaviors to touch the complex worlds of other human beings.
7. The sender must be understood as a receiver as well as an initiator.

Defining the Sender: A Question of Timing

The sender of the message in the communication process has a complex role. He perceives in himself or in the external world stimuli to which he responds with some internal thought, feeling, or idea. He then initiates a communication exchange if he has some need or desire to encode and share that thought, or feeling with another person. Because he is the one who began the interaction, he is referred to thereafter as the sender.

The difference between the sender and the receiver is contingent upon timing rather than behavior. The labels *sender/receiver* and *receiver/sender* are ways of saying that it is the sequence in which one acts rather than the action itself that distinguishes the sender (sender/receiver) from the receiver (receiver/sender). In the course of daily affairs, who starts the exchange may be difficult to decide. In a street fight, the person who threw the first punch might be called the initiator. But from a different place in the timing of the actions, the initiator might be the person who said something to provoke the other to respond with the first punch. The same is true in the verbal communication interaction. Who starts it is another way of saying who the sender is. Deciding who the sender is depends on what we choose as the beginning point. The first person to speak is not necessarily the initiator any more than the first person to throw a punch.

In settling a fight, one is interested in establishing blame. It then becomes important to decide who started what. If we study the fight as an instance of nonverbal communication, we are interested in understanding the processes involved. Blame or responsibility is not our prime concern in the transaction. It is arbitrary in that we are concerned with picking some point at which to begin an analysis. It does not matter so much who started it. What does matter is what happens from the point at which we agree to observe and analyze the exchange.

Once we pick a point in time from which to analyze a communication exchange, we designate the sender as the initiator of the interaction. He has some reason for wanting to interact with another person and his message-making behavior is his way of making that contact. At a cocktail party, the sender may initiate the conversation just to have someone with whom to talk. A person who wins a contest tells the good news to a friend to share the news itself. In either case, the message is what supplies the link between the people. Its reasons for being framed reflect the different needs of the senders.

When the sender constructs the initial message, he begins to take note of himself, his message, and the person to whom that message is being addressed if he is concerned with communicating intentionally. Part of the role of the sender is awareness of himself and the person with whom he is interacting. The other person is also a communicator. He is distinguished from the sender in that he is not the initiator.

Interpersonal communication runs its course as the communicators shift back and forth as sender/receiver and receiver/sender of messages. Each person in the interaction performs each of these roles simultaneously. At times the roles of sending and receiving in a communication interaction are as indistinguishable as deciding which person in a game of catch is throwing the ball and which is catching. There are differences between throwing and catching behaviors just as there are differences between sending and receiving behaviors. Each participant, however, performs both sets of operations if the interaction is to occur.

There are four aspects into which the complex role of the sender in the interpersonal process can be divided. First, he is the one who initiates the communication exchange. Within this facet fall all his reasons for communicating and all the encoding behaviors and skills he has at his command. In initiating the message, he steps into the role of sender. The second aspect of that role is his ability to monitor himself. In the process of expressing himself to another human being, the sender who cares about intentional communication is continually evaluating the ways in which he is expressing those thoughts and feelings he is attempting to share. Third and closely related to the second aspect is his attention to the person with whom he attempts to communicate. His awareness of that other person is his way of looking for any messages that may give him information regarding one of two things: his effectiveness in expressing himself, and/or the wishes of the other person regarding the course of the interaction. Finally, the sender is responsive to his receiver, or more accurately, his receiver as he perceives him. What the sender says or does next is affected in some way by what the other person has said or done in reaction to the sender's previous message.

These aspects are a part of every step in the process of message exchange between people. John says hello to Jim. He is aware of Jim, of his desire to make some contact with Jim, and of the way in which he tries to do so. He is aware of Jim before, during, and after the brief moment when he says hello to him. He is also aware of Jim's response. What John does or says next evolves from this. The degree to which a person is consciously aware of all these facets of the process depends on several things: (1) how analytical of himself and others he is as a result of his nature or training; (2) how important the given transaction or other individual is to him; and (3) the other things with which he is concerned at any given time. Undoubtedly many of the interactions in which we engage go consciously unnoticed by us due to other preoccupations.

"That's my side of it—Now I'll tell you his!"

JOHNS

This understanding of communication interactions leads to some important considerations for understanding the nature of the communicator as sender in the process of human communication: (1) it explains the multifaceted nature of the role of the sender; (2) it explains the mutuality in a communication transaction—it leads to an understanding of communication as an interaction in which all participants have some control; and (3) it leads to the conclusion of individuals as worlds unto themselves, communicating as a means of contact between those worlds. Investigating each of these conclusions is the way to have a complete understanding of the communicator as sender.

Multifaceted Role of the Sender

While it is conceptually true that all communicators are senders and receivers, not all people understand this or behave accordingly. The mother who talks "at" her child and ignores anything but her own words is an example. This is also true of the person so engaged in his own thoughts that after he says something he is too busy thinking of what he will say next, rather than attending to the effects of his initial remark. Another example is the teacher who states an assignment and takes the silence of the class as an indication of agreement or a sign of comprehension. One reason for considering the roles of sender and receiver separately is to emphasize that each role ideally includes sending and receiving behaviors. Even though a person may see himself as filling one role or the other, looking at each role separately is a way of showing how each incorporates the other.

The primary role of the communicator as sender, then, is his message-making behavior. He feels a need to communicate, so he decides on the ways in which to express his thought or feeling, and then encodes and directs his message toward his intended receiver. This in itself is a complex process: encoding is verbal and nonverbal at the same time; and message making is intentional and nonintentional, as well as explicit and implied. In the simplest greeting between two human beings, there are verbal and nonverbal aspects (words and greeting gestures); purposeful and unintentional messages (the communicators' intended meanings and those that can also be interpreted from their words and actions); and explicit and implicit meanings (what is said overtly; what is implied by what is said or not said).

In this process the sender is the encoder. She is also in the process of decoding the responses to her and her message that she sees as coming from her receiver. The sender is in a continuous state of evaluating her own success or failure in her message-making attempts, as reflected by the response or lack of response from her intended receiver. Before initiating a message, the sender has some sense of the appropriateness of what she wants to say and the ways in which she is going to express herself. Words mean different things to different people. Nonverbal behaviors can also be interpreted in different ways. The response received by the sender reflects some information about the accuracy of her perceptions of the situation prior to attempting to communicate. They provide her with some sense of what needs to be done to reassess the situation. A play on words that makes the receiver groan rather than laugh or an intended compliment that gains the response of silence or a strange look are sources of information that the sender uses in monitoring his communication behavior. The communicator is the sender of his original message. He is the recipient of the other person's responses (feedback). Feedback is the receiver's message. In attending to the receiver's feedback, the sender shifts roles with the receiver. He becomes the decoder of a message. The message is in response to his original message and from the sender's perspective is feedback.

Feedback, the receiver's message, is one source for the sender of cues to the effectiveness of his message making. Communication experience 5.1 is designed to illustrate the sender as the processor of feedback from his receiver.

Communication Experience 5.1

Principle

The receiver presents the sender with an ongoing series of clues regarding his understanding of and reaction to the speaker's message.

Procedure

1. Work with a partner.
2. Either you or your partner is to think of an object, writing it down on a piece of paper.
3. The other person tries to guess the object. The person knowing the object acts as receiver and helps his partner by giving him as much verbal and nonverbal feedback (response) as possible. However, verbally he can use only the words *hot,* if the speaker is getting close, or *cold* if he is way off the track, and degrees (*warm, warmer, cool,* etc.) to indicate how close he is to guessing the object.
4. Switch roles.

Discussion

What kinds of things guided the person trying to guess the object? What effect did limiting the verbal code have? Did feedback guide the course of the interchange? In what ways? What are the implications?

As illustrated in communication experience 5.1, the process of interpersonal communication is an ongoing evaluative process in which the sender is processing cues as to the effectiveness with which he has expressed himself. How a sender presents himself and his message, and how accurate his perception of others is, is subject to ongoing scrutiny.

Word choice, nonverbal behaviors, and credibility-establishment, as examples, can only be evaluated after receiving clues from the receiver as to the impact these things have on the thought, feeling, or idea the sender is attempting to convey. The question becomes one of precision: how important is it to be understood as exactly as possible? And, this question can only be answered in the context of the given interaction and by the people involved in the interaction. The importance of the topic and the degree of need the sender has for being understood are defined by his own needs in that given interaction. The patron in a restaurant who requests that his food be cooked in a special way may do so out of habit, or because he feels irritable and wants to assert himself, or because he is trying to impress the waiter or the others with whom he dines as to how much he knows about food preparation. In any of these instances, he may not need to be understood as much as he needs to say what he is saying, for whatever the effect he wishes to achieve. On the other hand, a patron with a health problem (diabetes, overweight, allergy) might need very much to be sure that he is understood and that his directions are followed explicitly. It may be a serious matter if he is not. He then has a high need to be understood as intended, and need pay attention to any feedback that helps him evaluate the waiter's understanding of his instructions. Communication exercise 5.2 presents a situation in which you can evaluate your own behaviors as the receiver of your intended receiver's feedback.

Communication Experience 5.2

Principle

The receiver's feedback provides the sender with clues as to how effective and believable he is in his attempts to communicate.

Procedure

1. Work in groups of five.
2. One person is designated as speaker and has the task of trying to sell something to the others.
3. The rest of the group provides him with feedback to indicate whether or not he is believable to them.
4. Each member of the group takes a turn as salesperson. Compare and contrast styles and effectiveness.
5. After each speaker finishes his turn he rates himself on a scale of 1–10 (10 being the highest), as to how credible he thinks the group found him. The group members also rate how credible they found him. Compare ratings. Discuss how those ratings were arrived at.

Discussion

In what ways did people show their belief or disbelief? Did these responses change with different speakers? Why or why not? Did group members know each other before? How well? What, if any, effects did this have? Why? Were the speakers accurate in estimating their credibility? Why or why not? What were the bases for their estimates?

As illustrated in communication experience 5.2 the receiver may present the initial sender with a good deal of evidence as to how he feels about the sender and his message. In this communication experience as well as in the example of the patron giving cooking instructions to the waiter, we see instances in which the receiver gives the sender some sign of his reaction to the sender and his message. It is then possible for the sender to add to or correct that perception as he chooses, or is able.

Feedback as Information About Code and Channel Selections
The sender can also use feedback as information regarding his code and channel selection. It is all too easy for a speaker to make the false assumption that the language he speaks is clear to others. The ways in which such an assumption can be tested has to do with the sender's attention to and use of his receiver's responses. Whether or not a message is clear either in its intended meaning or in terms appropriate to the channel through which it has been transmitted is a product of the interaction between the communicators. The sender is provided with clues from his receiver as to the appropriateness of the choices he makes in the given circumstances. A person may wish to express affection to another and may thus choose to do so by a physical overture. Whether or not the message is received as intended may become apparent by the receiver's response. While talking to an acquaintance at a meeting, a young woman noticed a hair on a young man's shirt sleeve. She unconsciously reached over to remove it. But his loud, pained response made her aware of what she had done; the hair was not really a loose one, but was attached to his arm and somehow protruded through the fabric of his shirt sleeve.

The appropriateness of the sender's choice of codes and channels is a product of the people participating in the communication. Factors such as the sender's field of experience, socialization, culture, the communication environment, and role relationships of the communicators, all have some effect on the choices he makes for encoding his message. They also have effects on how that message is decoded or interpreted by his receiver. The effects may be very different. Attention to the reactions and response of the receiver give the sender some way of judging whether or not their perceptions are similar. Once again, then, the sender is a communicator receiving clues from which to gather information about the interaction in which he is participating. Communication experience 5.3 is designed to illustrate the difficulties you can encounter as sender of a message if you fail to attend to your intended receiver's feedback.

Communication Experience 5.3

Principle

The receiver's feedback provides the sender with clues as to whether or not he has been understood and in what ways.

Procedure

1. Work with a partner.
2. Role play a relationship with your partner, designating yourselves as student-teacher; mother-child; friend-friend; man-woman; doctor-patient, etc.
3. One member of the pair is designated as sender; the other, receiver.
4. The sender's task is to describe an event that occurred during that day in a manner appropriate to the relationship the two have decided upon. He relates the event, irrespective of his partner's feedback, until he has finished. The incident must take him at least four minutes to relate.
5. The person designated as receiver attempts to interject verbal feedback in the form of question-asking wherever he can; and whatever nonverbal feedback he feels would be appropriate to his designated role in relation to the speaker.
6. The speaker's task is to tell his story while ignoring the feedback from his partner. The receiver's task is to interrupt in whatever ways he can in the given relationship to get the speaker to hurry up.
7. Switch roles.

Discussion

In what ways did role playing affect the exchange? Would the behavior be different if the two people just played themselves? How did it feel to be the speaker; the listener? Do people communicate without paying attention to their receivers' feedback? What are the implications of the experience for interpersonal communication?

Communication experience 5.3 illustrates the sender's use of feedback in a communication interaction. At the same time a person is creating messages to direct toward another communicator, he is attending to clues from that other person, regarding how he should communicate. The sender is in the process of encoding the messages he wishes to express and decoding those he perceives to come from his receiver. Doing both these things explains two things: (1) the complexity of the process in which the sender is involved, and (2) why he must be remembered as a communicator sending and receiving messages in his exchange with another person.

Sender and Receiver: Mutually Controlling Interactants

From the perspective of the sender, the receiver's response or feedback is data he can use to correct his message making. The sender uses the receiver's feedback as a message about his effectiveness in communicating. From the perspective of the receiver, his reaction is not feedback; it is his message. His reaction is his message-making behavior. It is in reacting to the sender that the receiver shifts and becomes the encoder.

The original sender is not the controller of the communication exchange. He is only one of two or more participants. He is designated sender because he initiates the exchange. How that exchange proceeds is determined by all interacting parties. For this reason communication is viewed as mutually causal; each participant affects the other. Communication experience 5.4 is designed to help you evaluate the role of feedback in the mutually causal relationship between sender and receiver.

Communication Experience 5.4

Principle

Communication is a mutually causal activity. Feedback plays a vital role in permitting communicators mutual control over the course of their communication.

Procedure

1. Draw a pictogram such as that illustrated below.

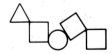

2. One person sits in the front of the room with a pictogram, describing it to the class members who have not seen it previously and who are not permitted to see it at this time. Each class member draws a pictogram based on the verbal description given by the person at the front of the room.
3. The class members may not ask any questions.
4. When the person describing the pictogram has finished he stops and estimates how many people have an accurate representation of the pictogram he has described.
5. He then shows the pictogram to the class members and they compare theirs to his.

Discussion

How correct was the describer's estimate of accuracy? What were the errors made? Would question-asking have helped in accuracy? In efficiency? Repeat the experience with a new pictogram. This time allow questions. What are the implications?

As illustrated in communication experience 5.4, feedback in itself is message-making behavior. It is the receiver's exertion of control in the communication interaction. It is not merely a response to let the sender know if he has been effective. It is an expression of the direction in which the receiver wants the communication to go. Feedback, the receiver's message making, is the way in which he exchanges roles with the sender. It is this interchangeability of role relations that underlies our model for communication. It is why the communicators are designated as sender/receiver and receiver/sender.

In the context of human communication, feedback is used to refer to information about the outcome of attempting to communicate that is rechanneled back to the originating communicator for his use in continuing his message-making attempts.[1] In our model of communication as a mutually causal activity, feedback becomes the mechanism for facilitating at least a two-directional, mutually causal relationship. That is, feedback is the response to the sender's original message making; but it can also be discussed as the receiver's message (about the message he has received) to which the initiating communicator need attend. It is thereby the part of the interaction that explains why we consider interpersonal communication mutually causal and the reason that the participants in interpersonal communication are viewed as senders/receivers of messages rather than one or the other.

While the more traditional feedback-oriented models of communication view the process of human communication as a one-way,

cause-effect relationship in which the sender creates a message that he transmits over one of the various channels to an intended receiver, causing an intended effect on him, Ruben raises the question as to whether the mutually causal model doesn't imply that it is the receiver who causes messages to have their meaning and significance, and thereby influences how the communication affects him.[2] Feedback can be viewed in two different ways: (1) as information about, or a response to, the sender's message, which the sender can use to evaluate his effectiveness, as heretofore discussed, and, (2) as the receiver's indication of what he thinks the message means, thereby allowing him a control he can exercise

over the initial sender as to the direction in which the sender must go to deal with his receiver.

There is a mutually controlling relationship between sender and receiver. It is their message-making behaviors that link them to one another. They therefore not only exchange roles but are mutually fulfilling the sending/receiving aspects of communication throughout their exchange. An understanding of the sender in communication means understanding him as a sending/receiving participant in the process. His message making is an attempt at bridging the gap that separates human beings from each other.

"When You Are Old and Gray"

Since I still appreciate you,
Let's find love while we may,
Because I know I'll hate you
When you are old and gray.
So say you love me here and now.
I'll make the most of that.
Say you love and trust me,
For I know you'll disgust me
When you're old and getting fat.
An awful debility, a lessened utility,
A loss of mobility is a strong possibility.
In all probability I'll lose my virility
And you your fertility and desirability.
And this liability of total sterility

Will lead to hostility and a sense of futility.
So let's act with agility while we still have facility
For we'll soon reach senility
And lose the ability.
Your teeth will start to go dear.
Your waist will start to spread.
In twenty years or so dear,
I'll wish that you were dead.
I'll never love you then at all
The way I do today.
So please remember, when I leave in December,
I told you so in May.

Tom Lehrer

Sender: World unto Herself

We have spent a good deal of time distinguishing between the sending and receiving functions of the original sender in the communication process to highlight the complexity of attempting to communicate intentionally with another human being. The sender is a communicator who must be analyzed in terms of her encoding and decoding skills; her message-initiating and response-receiving behaviors; her attention to her own needs and the needs of the person designated as her receiver. Looking at the sender in this way underscores the interactional nature of the process of communication. The sender is a human being. She has her own sets of needs, desires, skills, and goals. Her attempts at communicating with another human being are her efforts to make human contact. The sender is a world unto herself. She moves in and out of relationships with other humans. Those relations are engineered by her communication attempts. It is during the process of interactions with others that she learns about herself, her world, and that other person, who is also a world unto herself. One facet of her communication behavior is her desire and ability to express herself to others. In the same frame of time during which she is engaging in those behaviors, she is also receiving those things that the other person is willing to share. All communicators are interactants. All send and receive messages that they process through their own set of perceptions, interpretations.[3]

Sender as Receiver

The process of interpersonal communication involves people and their messages. Meanings are within people. Their messages are the symbol systems that they invent in order to translate their experience in hopes of sharing them with others. The words printed on this page for example are the arrangement of symbols used to convey the author's understanding of the phenomenon of communication.

In order to analyze so complex a process as communication, we divide it still further than into people and their messages. We look at messages in a variety of ways. Messages are analyzed as intentional and unintentional, verbal and nonverbal, implied and explicit. Each of these is a way of dividing up the message aspect so as to make analysis of it more manageable.

The people in the interpersonal process are also looked at in a variety of ways. They are called communicators, and are distinguished from one another as sender and receiver. The most important thing for the student of communication to understand is that in the everyday interaction each participant must be able to engage in all of the behaviors described and analyzed theoretically as sending or receiving functions. It is the shifting of roles between people that makes communication a mutually controlled interaction. It is the duality in nature of the role of any communicator that makes his task so demanding. For while he speaks, he must also watch and listen. He needs to be aware of the other person and to view his needs and desires as his own. The most effective communicator understands and perfects his ability to be a receiver even as he is the encoder and sender of his own message.

Interference with Intentional Communication

Encoding one's messages is only one of the functions of the sender in the interpersonal interaction. Anything the sender does that fails to fulfill his function as the decoder of his receiver's responses interferes with intentional communication. If the sender is oblivious to the feedback from his receiver, he has no way of evaluating whether or not he has been understood. He also misses the information that the receiver is sending out concerning the direction that he wishes the communication to take. In both instances, the sender blunders along unaware of the ways in which he is being received or understood. If his purpose in communicating is to be understood as intended, then he has no way of evaluating his effectiveness.

Interference with intentional communication also exists when the sender misinterprets the feedback of the receiver. The sender must be able to decode his receiver's feedback. When he does so incorrectly, he cannot understand the receiver as the receiver means to be understood. Instances of this include misunderstanding the receiver's verbal responses and/or misreading the receiver's nonverbal behaviors. If, for example, the sender is telling a story and notices that the receiver's eyes are scanning the room, the sender can read this as inattention. If he does not test out this assumption, he has no real way of knowing whether or not it is true.

Interference with intended meaning can also exist when the sender is unaware of the person with whom he tries to communicate at the time. The sender wants his receiver to do something for him and gives the receiver complicated instructions. At the same time, the receiver is involved with his own thoughts and is not receptive to the sender. If the sender is unaware of this, he does not realize that he is not accomplishing his ends. One cannot communicate as he intends if he fails to remember that the other person with whom he is intending to communicate is himself

RICHARD CORY

Whenever Richard Cory went down town,
   We people on the pavement looked at him.
He was a gentleman from sole to crown,
   Clean favored, and imperically slim.

And he was always quietly arrayed,
   And he was always human when he talked;
But still he fluttered pulses when he said,
   "Good-morning," and he glittered when he walked.

And he was rich — yes — richer than a king —
   And admirably schooled in every grace:
In fine, we thought that he was everything
   To make us wish that we were in his place.

So on we worked, and waited for the light,
   And went without the meat, and cursed the bread;
And Richard Cory, one calm summer night,
   Went home and put a bullet through his head.

Edwin Arlington Robinson

a complex human being, a world unto himself, who has his own needs and desires.

Related to this problem is that of code and channel selection. It is not only what the speaker says but how and when he says it that maximizes or minimizes his chances of being understood as intended. Everyone, for example, needs to feel appreciated. There are different ways in which different people show their appreciation. The sender who wants to show his gratitude toward another and puts it into words may be insensitive to the other person's needs for a more concrete expression. The secretary who would rather have a raise than a statement of appreciation, the wife who would prefer flowers, and the child who wants a reward for his good grades at school are examples of people whose needs have not been understood.

Finally, the sender needs to act as responder to his intended receiver. If he is unresponsive to his receiver's feedback, he discourages interest on the part of the receiver. A person telling a long tale of woe and asking for suggestions while ignoring anything that his receiver says is a case in point. After a while the receiver takes this lack of attention as a message in itself. If that is not the case, then the sender has not communicated as intended.

Anything that the sender does to discourage or misread the active participation of his receiver in the communication process is a source of interference with intended communication. The process is a complex one demanding that the participants do many things at once. Anything that interferes with one's abilities to do many things at once interferes with communicating as one intends.

Summary

In this chapter we have viewed the sender as a communicator with the complex task of sending and receiving messages. The important points are:

1. The difference between the initiator as sender and the receiver in interpersonal communication is one of timing rather than behavior.
2. Such distinctions are necessary for purposes of analysis, yet they are arbitrary in nature.
3. The complex role of sending can be divided into four aspects:
   a. *Encoding/initiating the exchange.*
   b. *Monitoring self and others as the exchange runs its course.*
   c. *Attention to the other in the interaction.*
   d. *Responsiveness to the other; receiving the other.*
4. The role of the sender is multifaceted; she does many things at the same time.

5. Feedback is that response the sender uses to monitor his effects.
6. Feedback is the receiver's message. It can be discussed and defined differently from the perspective of the sender than from that of the receiver.
7. The sender and receiver exert control over one another; there is not cause-effect or one-way relationship necessarily.
8. Each communicator is a world unto herself, sending and receiving messages.
9. Interference with intentional meaning has to do with the sender's failure to perform all the functions of the role of sender.

Questions for Discussion

1. What is feedback?
2. Compare and contrast the different functions of feedback.
3. Who determines the meaning of the message in the interpersonal interaction?
4. Describe an unresponsive sender.
5. What is self-awareness, and its relationship in one's ability to communicate with others?
6. Are words or actions a more effective means for demonstrating that one cares for another person?
7. In a classroom situation, how must an instructor function as a receiver of messages?
8. What is the most important attribute for one to possess to be an effective message maker?
9. Discuss one's sensitivity to self and others as an asset in interpersonal communication.
10. What are the benefits of defining communication as mutually causal? Would a different model be more reflective of the ways in which people communicate?

Notes

1. Brent Ruben, "General Systems: An Approach to Human Communication" in *Approaches to Human Communication,* ed. Richard Budd and Brent Ruben (New York: Spartan Press, 1972) p. 133.

2. Ibid.

3. Refer to the writings of Peter Berger (*Social Construction of Reality*), Lee Thayer (*Communication and Communication Systems*) and Herbert Blumer (*Symbolic Interactionism*) for in-depth analysis of this point of view.

Blumer, Herbert. "Symbolic Interaction: An Approach to Human Communication." In *Approaches to Human Communication,* edited by Richard Budd and Brent Ruben. New York: Spartan Press, 1972. A brief synthesis of the symbolic nature of our reality recommended to the student with some background.

Frank, Lawrence. "Cultural Organization." In *General Systems Theory and Human Communication,* edited by Brent Ruben and John Kim. Rochelle Park, N.J.: Hayden Book Company, Inc., 1975. A good introduction to the ways in which we interact with one another, within the systems we create.

Ruben Brent. "General Systems: An Approach to Human Communication." In *Approaches to Human Communication,* edited by Richard Budd and Brent Ruben. New York: Spartan Press, 1972. Recommended as a fine introduction to systems theory and its impact on human communication.

Watzlawick, Paul; Janet Beavin; and Don Jackson. *Pragmatics of Human Communication.* New York: W. W. Norton & Company, 1967. A complex book. Important book for the student who wants to add to his knowledge of communication interactions.

Selected Bibliography

The Message: Words and Things

6

Introduction

An artist takes a lump of clay and creates a sculpture. A musician uses a series of lines, dots, and slashes to compose a piece of music. A person takes paper and scissors and creates a series of shapes that look like people. Another person uses matchsticks to build something that looks like a boat. Each object created has some meaning for its creator. And each means something to others who view it. Humans can express themselves and their visions of things in many ways. A code is any set of symbols that can be used to carry meaning. It can be a series of visual symbols such as dots and dashes of the Morse Code. It can be numerical symbols with which to describe the quantity of things.

In order for one human being to communicate with another, he needs a language or code into which to translate that inner experience, referred to as a thought, feeling, or idea. The *verbal code* into which the message can be translated is composed of *words.* An investigation of the interpersonal process from the vantage point of the message can begin by an analysis of words, the vehicles through which the communicator can transmit his experiences verbally.

Communication Goals

This chapter uses the theoretical and experiential approach to explore the function of language in the communication process. It focuses on the verbal message and is written to enable you to understand the role of message maker by:

1. Understanding the symbolic nature of verbal language.
2. Differentiating between the vocal languages of other animals and human verbal language.
3. Exploring the question of meaning and wherein it lies.
4. Familiarizing yourself with the chronology of language acquisition to understand the effect of context and environment on words and meanings.
5. Distinguishing between denotative and connotative meanings of words and their relative significance.
6. Appreciating words as a crude but workable symbolic system into which knowledge is encoded, transmitted, and stored, from person to person, and from generation to generation.

There are many kinds of language. Examples of the kinds of language available to the communicator range from sign and body language to language composed of words, music, or pictures, and includes the ways in which we communicate, referred to as the language of love. Any coding system can qualify as a language so long as it is a medium by which to express oneself. Using this broad definition of *language,* systems of expression as different from one another as the Morse Code and kinesics (body language) can be included within this scope. The specific language with which we will concern ourselves in this section of the text is verbal language, the language of words. While verbal language may be written or spoken, in the interpersonal communication process the verbal message is generally spoken language, especially when the communicators are in a face-to-face situation.

The Symbolic Nature of Words

Verbal language is a symbolic, conceptual language process. Its symbolic nature is of importance to the student of language and/or interpersonal communication. Just as flags, crosses, plus and minus signs are symbols because they stand for or represent something, so, too, are word symbols. They stand for whatever it is that they are used to represent. A useful way to make the distinction between the word and the thing it stands for, or its **referent,** is to draw an analogy to the relationship between a map and a territory.[1] A word is to a thing (referent) as a map is to a territory. It gives a picture of what is being referred to but is not one-and-the-same as that which it represents. A map of New Jersey provides information about that area of the country known as New Jersey, but it is not one-and-the-same as the area. So, too, the word *rifle* stands for the object that one can use to shoot. Having the symbol *rifle* allows the communicator to indicate to another person that he has a rifle by saying, "I have a rifle." If a word was not available to stand for the object, the person would have to carry the rifle around and show it to other people every time he wanted to declare his ownership of it.

It may be that one of the reasons why it is difficult to accept that words are not things but merely symbols of things is that language is taught as if the word were the thing. An infant pointing to a four-legged creature wagging its tail indicates the child's curiosity about the strange animal. In responding to the child's curiosity, someone says, "That's a doggie," as opposed to "We *call* that a doggie." Confusion between the symbol and the object for which it stands could be avoided if one were to say, "You call this a cat, but this you call a kitten," rather than saying,

"This *is* a cat." But since this is not often done the result is that when children were asked to define various terms, Johnson says they replied:

The *sun* is so called because it behaves as if it were the sun.

Pigs are so called because they are such dirty animals.[2]

Obviously, if words were defined in such a manner, then there could be only one verbal language. If the thing to which we refer were called a chair because of its innate "chair-ness," then it would have to be referred to as chair in all verbal languages. If a day were so called because of its "day-ness," then how could the French refer to it as "jour"? If a dog were called dog because of its "dogness," then why would the Germans call it "hund"?

MORSE CODE

HOBO SIGNS

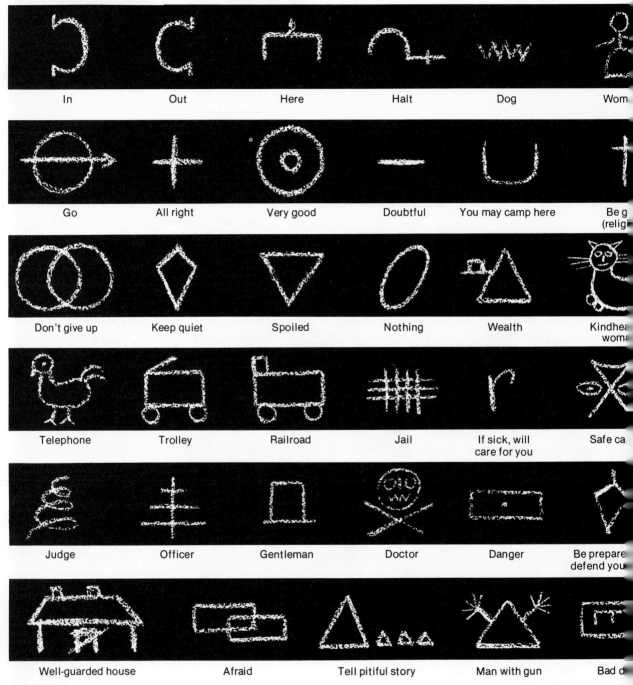

In	Out	Here	Halt	Dog	Wom
Go	All right	Very good	Doubtful	You may camp here	Be g (religi
Don't give up	Keep quiet	Spoiled	Nothing	Wealth	Kindhea woma
Telephone	Trolley	Railroad	Jail	If sick, will care for you	Safe ca
Judge	Officer	Gentleman	Doctor	Danger	Be prepare defend you
Well-guarded house	Afraid	Tell pitiful story	Man with gun	Bad d

Any word, then, is a symbol—a representation of something else. These symbols are arbitrary combinations of noises (or letters) meaningful within the particular language system within which they were invented, just as the dots and dashes of the Morse Code or hand and face gestures of sign language are meaningful within their given structures to those who have learned the coding system of one of those structures. Communication experience 6.1 is designed to illustrate the symbolic and arbitrary nature of language coding.

Communication Experience 6.1

Principle

Words are arbitrary symbols that stand for the things they represent. Meaning lies in the referents, not in the symbols themselves.

Procedure

1. Work in groups of five-to-seven people.
2. Select three words, such as *food, clothing, house, face, help,* and *dog.*
3. Compose a list of as many different symbols for each of the three words that the group members can think of (English words, words in other languages known to any group member, sign language, braille, etc.).
4. Compare and contrast lists prepared by other groups.
5. Compose a final list to incorporate all the symbols found by each group.
6. Decide which symbol most accurately corresponds to its referent.

Discussion

What were the similarities and differences between the different symbols used to refer to the same thing? Did any particular symbol contain any innate quality of the referent for which it stood? If group members were to invent their own symbols for the referent, would they correspond more to it? What are the implications about language?

As illustrated by communication experience 6.1, words are arbitrary combinations of sounds, meaningful within a given language system to those communicators familiar with that system. Any sound can be used for any meaning, as long as it fits the basic structure of a given language system.

CB slang

There's nothing worse than finding yourself in a strange country and not knowing the language. Much the same situation prevails for newcomers to CB Land, that invisible "nation of the airwaves" that now numbers more than fifteen million inhabitants and whose borders stretch from coast to coast across the North American continent. In CB Land, even the simplest questions — What time is it? How do I get there? Does anybody hear me? — can go unanswered if you don't know the language . . .

. . . CB Talk, you see, is not only a new language — it's also a whole new way of talking, and that includes accent, tone of voice, speed of delivery, and a reasonable knowledge of radio etiquette.

Springing from the tough, terse terminology of the long-haul trucker, CB Talk grew up over the years as an unlikely mixture of highway, police, and military slang . . . Since truckers drive for a living and haven't got either the interest or the time to develop much refinement in their language, CB Talk quickly emerged as a mirror reflection of the terse, blunt exchanges truck drivers had formerly reserved for their brief verbal confrontations with each other at truck stop counters. Not without humor, this trucker talk provided the foundation for the language of CB and as the trucker mythology took on all the trappings of folk heroics, CB Talk became inseparable from the language of the professional driver.

. . . When the Citizen's Radio Service was first established in 1958, the few thousand early CBers felt like second cousins to the more sophisticated shortwave or amateur (ham) operators. So, early on, CBers tried to develop a language that could best be called "sham." Full of Ten Codes and Q Signals, early CB Talk was almost incomprehensible to over-the-road drivers.

Suddenly, in the early 1970's, truckers found themselves in need of cheap, convenient two-way communications to locate difficult-to-find sources for fuel, and then (after the imposition of the nationwide 55 miles per hour speed limit), to stay one jump ahead of smokey bear and his new picture-taking machinery. So, once they had their hands on CB, the truckers quickly made it their own and soon had integrated their own colorful language into the modulations of those early CBers.

The truckers' own rising popularity then helped spread the word about CB and, in turn, convinced millions of new CBers that they could best share the "romance of the road" by learning to sound like honest-to-good truck drivers . . . Soon the mass media discovered CB. Films like "White Line Fever" and "Truck Stop Women" began to catch the public fancy; the television series, "Movin' On," picked up where Broderick Crawford and his old "Highway Patrol" show had left off and brought CB and trucker talk into the nation's living rooms. Then, all of a sudden, Walter Cronkite and Harry Reasoner were reporting the 1974 Truckers' Strike on network news and pointing out that the whole thing had been coordinated by Citizens Band radio. In no time, C. W. McCall, Dave Dudley, Cledus Maggard, and a score of others, had chart-busting hits just filling the general Public's ears with this new language of CB.

Now, of course, the development cycle is almost complete, since the once "secret" language of CB has now gone "public" and begun to work its way into everyday conversation . . .

Addict A non-stop CB broadcaster.

Advertising Markings identifying a police car. Also a police car's flashing lights.

Ancient Mary AM radio.

Aunt Fanny The Federal Communications Commission.

B-man Businessman, particularly a travelling salesman.

Back Door 1. Last vehicle in a line of two or more. 2. The road behind.

BCB Before Citizens Band, (prior to September, 1958).

Bear Any kind of law enforcement officer.

Bear Meat (Or Bear Food) Motorist not equipped with CB.

Big Bird Any airplane, but usually a jetliner.

Bird Bath Car wash.

Bite in the Britches A speeding ticket.

. . . part your hair . . smokey's on the front porch . . . .

. . . gonna eat up the white line . . . .

ggy bank took it all . . . .

. . . lights green . . . . mule's l

Black List Published list of convicted CBers who have violated FCC Rules and Regulations.

Blowing Off (Your doors) Passing at high speed.

Blue Slip Driver's license.

Brown Bottle Beer.

Brown Paper Bag Unmarked police car.

Brush Your Teeth and Comb Your Hair Slow down to 55 mph, speed trap ahead.

Bumblebee An annoying CBer who "buzzes" from channel to channel, but never has anything to say.

Camera (also Kodak, Polaroid) Radar speed trap.

Carbon Copy Repeat message.

Check Your Eyelids for Pinholes Try to keep awake.

Chicken Coop ICC weigh station.

Coke Stop Stop for Mother Nature.

Comic Book Trucker's Log.

Cut Some Z's Get some rest and/or sleep.

Ears 1. CB radio. 2. Antenna. 3. CB operator.

Eat Gravel Leave the road continuously, especially in bad weather.

Eat Up Them White Lines Make excellent time, travel at top speed.

Eyeball to Eyeball CBers meeting each other in person.

Feed the Ponies Bet on horses.

Fifth Wheel 1. Device used to connect a truck tractor to a semi-trailer. 2. A CBer who is listening in on a conversation but saying nothing.

Four Lane Parking Lot Crowded highway or expressway.

Fox Charlie Charlie The Federal Communications Commission.

Front Porch Bridge or overpass over a highway.

Goldfish Drivers of tiny, compact cars.

Haircut Palace Low bridge or overpass.

Hammer Accelerator (also volume control on CB Transceiver).

Handle CBer's nickname.

Happy Hooker Any fourwheeler pulling a trailer.

High Ball Proceed at top speed.

Jimmy GMC truck ("general mess of crap").

King Kong Driver who won't let anyone pass him.

Kitty Litter Mixture of sand and salt spread by highway department sander on slick or icy road surface.

Light's Green, Bring on Your Machine The coast is clear, let's make some time.

Lying Fool Weatherman.

Mama Bear Policewoman, especially one who occupies a desk at a police station.

Mercy Wow! One of the most overused expletives in CB talk.

Mule Engine.

Open Season Police everywhere, picking speeders off like flies.

Part Your Hair Slow down, smokey's operating a speed trap up ahead.

PF Flyers Truck wheels.

Piggy Bank Toll booth.

Pimple Flashing red (or yellow) light which an unmarked police car suddenly sprouts when in hot pursuit.

Play Ball Begin modulating, start a conversation.

Poacher An intruder who breaks into a CB conversation without an invitation.

Also a CBer who continually blocks channel by "keying mike."

Preacher Noxious CBer who feels compeled to quote FCC regulations over air everytime he hears a possible infraction.

Pregnant Roller Skate Volkswagen, especially a VW Beetle.

Red Eye Flashing red light on police patrol car.

Red Run Travelling on little or no fuel, empty.

Reefer Refrigerated semi-trailer.

Road Tar Black coffee.

Rubber Duck Flexible, rubber-covered antenna used on walkie-talkies.

Situation Smokey report. What's the situation at marker forty-five, northbound.

Smokey (Smokey Bear) Policeman, any law enforcement officer.

Smow Combination of smog and snow, a frequent driving condition throughout the midwest in winter.

Snog Combination of snow and fog.

Spaghetti Paper Road map.

Starve the Bears Keep your speed below the legal 55 mph limit.

Stuff Your Sinuses Move into a very congested area, become part of a traffic jam.

Sweetheart Truckstop waitress.

Ulcer Congested traffic.

Uncle Charlie's Uncle President of the United States.

Wakie, Wakie Hello, is anybody out there?

Walker-Talker Hitchhiker with "ears."

Welfare Station CB unit purchased with unemployment or welfare check.

Zoo Police headquarters, particularly if in city center.

"...C.B.? I think it means "construction battalion"..."

"...mercy sakes alive good buddy...."

Every Symbol Has a Referent

Often children make up words when the real word is too hard for them to say or is somewhat confusing. *Spaghetti* may come out "pssgetti," *dog* may be "bow wow," or a big sister named *Dorothy* may be called "Dossie." Eventually the child is corrected and taught the "real" word. This may be necessary in order for the child to be able to communicate with people who would otherwise not understand the symbol he uses. But the inherent danger is treating words as things—treating the symbol and its referent as one-and-the-same. In teaching a child the "real" word, our metamessage is that meaning lies in the word rather than the person using the word.

All words, then, are symbols, and every symbol has a referent. The *referent* is that to which the symbol refers, or points. A symbol stands for, replaces, or represents its referent. It is easy to grasp that the symbol *dog* represents a certain animal, *table* stands for a piece of furniture, and *book* represents printed pages that are bound together.

Understanding the symbolic nature of language becomes more difficult when the symbols are such words as *democracy, love, is,* and *beautiful.* Each of these words, too, is a symbol and stands for something— *democracy* for a philosophy of government, *love* for an emotion or feeling of a particular sort, *is* for the process or state of being of the other symbols with which it is used at a given time, *beautiful* for a quality perceived in something. But in these cases the referents are not concrete objects. They cannot be pointed out physically as can a *chair, table,* or *dog.* When the thing represented by the word is less tangible, the tendency is to fall into error by confusing the symbol with what it actually stands for; the difficulty rests in understanding that the word is only a symbol, and not the thing. Communication experience 6.2 is designed to illustrate that *all* words are symbols, but some are more easily understood as such symbols.

As illustrated in communication experience 6.2, all words are symbols and all words as such have referents. Every word has a referent despite how concrete or vague that referent might be. Referents can be divided into three categories. Referents may be **object, concept,** or **process** referents. Object referents are the most concrete. The earlier examples of *table, dog,* and *chair* are object referents. Concept referents are more abstract since they are ideas for which we have symbols. "Democracy" is an obvious example of a concept referent. Other words like *beauty, religion,* and *sexual values* are concept referents, and less concrete than object referents. The third category includes process referents; any words that stand for how something is being done or happening or the state in which it is, is a process referent; examples include all forms of the word *to be,* running, jumping, etc.

Communication Experience 6.2

Principle

While all words are symbols, it is easier to understand the symbolic nature of words with more concrete referents.

Procedure

1. Work with a partner.
2. One person composes three sentences. These must be written down on paper, but are not to be shown to the partner.
3. On a separate piece of paper, he writes down those symbols from the sentences that have object referents. These are to be put in sequence according to how they appear in the sentences that have been written down. (Example: In the sentence, "The boy ate the ice cream," *boy* and *ice cream* are the object referents.)
4. The list of symbols are shown to the second person until he feels he can guess the exact wording of the sentences from which they had come.
5. These sentences are then written down and shown to the person who created the original sentences. The two versions are compared.

Discussion

Compare and contrast the two versions. In what ways are they the same? In what ways are they different? What were the hardest parts of this assignment to fulfill? What are the implications about words and referents? Is there any clear implication about the symbolic nature of process referents?

The Significance of Words as Symbols

The symbolic nature of verbal language allows communicators to translate their inner experiences into a code capable of being transmitted to others. At the same time, it creates ambiguity and imprecision in communication. That is to say, verbal language is symbolic and thereby permits us to use words to stand for things (objects, concepts, processes). Many of these things could not be shared if humans were not capable of being symbol makers. There may very well have been geniuses among the apes, but without a symbolic and conceptual language to record their deeds, their achievements have been lost to future generations.[3] Today, much research is devoted to trying to understand the nature of the language of some animal forms of life other than human life, but evidence to support the theory that other animals are capable of creating symbols has, as of this time, not been found. Animal language, other than human language, is presently understood as vocal language, capable of communicating but nonsymbolic in nature.[4]

Human language is symbolic. Humans are therefore referred to as **symbol makers.** The significance of this ability to make symbols is referred to by Korzybski as *time-binding;* it is one of the distinctions made between humans and other animal forms.[5] According to Korzybski, humans have the unique capacity to pass along accumulated knowledge from one generation to the next. Each new generation builds on the knowledge received from previous generations and passes its knowledge on to future generations. The ability to time-bind is the result of the symbolic nature of our language system, which permits us to verbalize and/or write down our knowledge. We know what the ancient Greeks knew about human nature because they had a symbolic language to record their knowledge.

Paradoxically, however, the symbolic nature of language also allows for imprecision in communication. Because a word is only a symbol and not the referent itself, it only stands for that referent. People are different from one another and therefore they use words in different ways. Since the word is not the referent itself, one has a choice of using whatever word seems most suitable to stand for the referent. One person may refer to a piece of furniture in a classroom as a *chair,* while another may call it a *desk.* If we do not see the object itself, we may not know that both have the same subject in mind. Communication experience 6.3 is designed to illustrate this point.

As illustrated by communication experience 6.3, words mean different things to different people. The implications of this exercise are very important: *Meaning* lies in people, not in words. Words are the medium by which people transfer the ideas they wish to convey. What those words mean depends on the people using (saying or hearing) them. This relationship between words and thoughts is illustrated in the triangle of meaning shown in figure 6.1.[6]

Figure 6.1
The Triangle of Meaning.

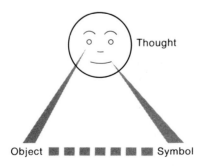

Thought

Object ■ ■ ■ ■ ■ ■ Symbol

Communication Experience 6.3

Principle

A word is a symbol. Its meaning may differ depending on the interpretation derived by its user.

Procedure

1. Make ten copies of the following form and distribute them to ten people.

Interview form

> As part of a project in human communication, you are asked to *define* the following words:
>
> 1. Freak:
> 2. Sexual:
> 3. Door:
> 4. Leader:
> 5. Happiness:
>
> Name:_____
>
> Time and Place of Interview:

2. Compare and contrast the forms after they have been completed.

3. Compare the results with those collected by other class members.

Discussion

What similarities and differences occurred in the responses? Did the participants "define" the words? What is a "definition"? What were the effects of asking for a person's name? What kinds of things influenced the "definitions" a person gave?

The triangle of meaning illustrates that meaning starts with a thought and that the symbol (used to refer to the object), and the actual object are never exactly the same. This same point was raised earlier by drawing an analogy to the relationship between a map and its territory, and is now being reiterated to underscore the ambiguous nature of language and the consequent lack of precision in communicating the human language. Communication experience 6.4 is designed to illustrate the difference between human and artificial language in terms of precision.[7]

Communication Experience 6.4

Principle

The symbolic nature of human language is ambiguous. This ambiguity not only allows for greater error in interpretation; it also permits more flexibility than could be afforded by an artificial language.

Procedure

1. Work in groups of five.
2. Each group is to select a paragraph in English and translate it into Morse Code, computer language, or some other artificial language, either already familiar to the group or one that the group is willing to learn.
3. Translate the paragraph. Compare the procedures used by your group with those of the other groups.

Discussion

What were the most common sources of errors in translation? What difficulties did the group have to overcome? What comparisons and contrasts can be made between English and artificial languages? In what ways are group members more aware of their language skills after the completion of this exercise?

As illustrated by communication experience 6.4 and as heretofore discussed, the symbolic nature of language is a source of imprecision in verbal communication. Meanings are in people, not in the words themselves. Meaning is the product of the ways in which people use words and what those words mean to speakers and listeners. The studies of general semantics as formulated by Alfred Korzybski[8] and Charles Morris's level of language study, which he called Pragmatics,[9] are cornerstones in the field of human communication. Each contributes to our understanding of people and how they use word-symbols. **General semantics** is the study of language as it relates to behavior and is concerned with the meanings words have in relation to the behaviors of the people using those words. **Pragmatics** is a similar area of study that focuses on meaning not as residing in the words themselves or literally as defined in a dictionary, but rather the meanings those symbols have to the people using them. In our exploration of the message aspect of the interpersonal communication interaction, we also look at words as those symbols that carry the meanings people attach to them through use. Our concern is with meaning as a product of people rather than as inherent in the words themselves.

WHAT ALL THAT CARNIE TALK MEANS

by Sheila Anne Webb

Behind those carnival rides, concessions, sideshow wonders, tents and trailers is a language all its own. Carnival workers, or carnies, call themselves keyasarnee. They talk in Carnese, a language designed to confuse outsiders.

The scene: the flatie cracks and pops his gum as he leans on the counter of his joint. Three marks wait. He shakes the dice cup and studies them. The one in the straw hat already has lost half a C note. The flatie will jackpot him. He needs the rush. But the mark on the right wears glasses. That means trouble. The other isn't worth a sawbuck, but the flatie will squeeze him.

The stick wanders up to the counter. "Meeizark geeizot meeizore C's a suisant a leeziali?"

The flatie winks, "Call 'em under seven, gentlemen!" He shakes the dice cup and while the bets are being made, casually says to his stick, "Beeizet yeeizour keester."

Here's a list of Carnese terms for translation:

- **a suisant a leeziali** — meaningless phrase used by carnival workers to confuse outsiders and keep them from cracking the Carnese code. Also see "eeiz."

- **add on** — method of gambling encouraged by concession spieler. He suggests player will win if he increases his stakes by multiples. For instance, first bet is 20c, second 40c, third 80c.

- **agent** — operator of concession for owner.

- **alibi joint** — concession with no front counter. Spieler walks into crowd as he talks.

- **at show** — fake athletic show, such as wrestling.

- **bally** — talker who comes out in front of tent. He may bring girls or some representative attraction from inside.

- **bally cloth** — display banner outside tent.

- **bally stand** — stage outside tent.

- **barker** — talker outside show who encourages crowd to come in. Distinguished from grinder.

- **blank** — a place where an operator didn't make any money. The last spot was a blank.

- **blowed** — when the gimmick on a game breaks down and it accidentally pays off. The gaff blowed. See gaff.
- **blow down** — destruction of a carnival by a bad storm.
- **blowoff** — crowd coming back on the midway from the grandstand or large sideshow. Here comes the blowoff.
- **burned up** — an overswindled town. Sponsors won't allow concessions to come again.

- **Carnese** — special language developed by carnival workers to protect their secrets from outsiders. See "eeiz" and "a suisant a leeziali."
- **carnies** — term applied by public to people who travel with carnival. See keyasarnee.
- **C note** — one hundred dollars.
- **corn game** — Bingo game.
- **cuter** — twenty-five cents.
- **cut in** — to get electricity connected to concession or ride. Also called hook up.
- **cutting jackpot** — carnival people telling carnival stories to each other.

- **deemer** — dime.
- **deuce** — two dollars.
- **donniker** — toilet.
- **doodle e squat** — to be broke.
- **double sawbuck** — twenty dollars.
- **ducats** — money.

- **"ee-iz"** — two syllables forming the base of Carnese. These syllables are inserted after the first consonant or first syllable of a word. The rest of the word follows this addition.
- **ex** — exclusive right to run only one concession of that type on a particular show. For instance, one cotton candy concession per town.

- **fin** — five dollars.
- **First of May** — term applied to show people who don't start their season until May 1.
- **flash** — display of good prizes.
- **flat** — to play a game for money.
- **flat joint** — gambling concession. The prize is money.
- **flatie** — operator of a flat joint.

- **flat ride** — a ride that runs close to the ground.
- **flat store** — concession with a counter.
- **floss** — cotton candy.
- **forty-miler** — inexperienced carnival person who's afraid to go more than forty miles from home.

- **gaff** — device an operator of a concession uses to control the game he's running. The odds are in his control. Not all games have gaffs.
- **gilly** — transfer a show from railroad cars to the lot.
- **grifter** — agent of gambling concession.
- **grind** — to spiel or talk drawing crowd to concession.
- **grinder** — person who grinds.
- **grind show** — show where spieler talks continuously all day to draw people.

- **"Hey Rube!"** — alarm yell for help by carnival people. This signals trouble. Show people will run to aid their cohorts.
- **H.O.ing** — holding out. Ride or joint help who collect money on the sly and don't turn it over to attraction owner.
- **hot wagon** — electricity transformer truck.

- **ink a pot** — to book a ride or concession.

- **jackpot** — means of encouraging a player to continue betting by raising percentage of possible payoff.
- **jenny** — merry go round ride.
- **jit** — five cents.
- **joint** — concession.
- **jump** — move from one town to the next. The show took a short jump between Clinton and DeWitt.

- **keester** — a person's backside.
- **keyasarnee** — term carnival people apply to themselves.
- **kick** — purse or wallet.

- **make a score** — make money from a mark. See mark.
- **mark** — any player the carnival operator can convince to spend his money.
- **midway** — main street of carnival.

- **mud** — plaster figurines given away as prizes or sold at novelty stands.

- **next spot** — next town where show is moving.
- **no grift** — no gambling.
- **nut** — charges for booking.

- **pasteboards** — tickets.
- **patch** — show employe who pays for law enforcement protection and helps take care of squabbles as they arise.

- **re-hashing** — selling tickets a second time that have already been torn off the roll.

- **sawbuck** — ten dollars.
- **score** — amount of money made from a single player.
- **slug** — one dollar.
- **stick** — show employe who plays a concession for the house and wins. His job is to draw a crowd.
- **still spot** — town that has no fair, just the carnival.
- **superstitions** — common superstitions among carnival people are: unlucky to have a bike on midway; anything yellow; an umbrella unless it's a rainy day. Many agents won't play to a man wearing glasses or smoking a pipe.

- **take** — money carnival people make.
- **ten in one** — sideshow with many attractions.
- **tip** — crowd of people.

- **walkaway** — customer who leaves his change on the counter and walks away.

How Meaning Is Learned

Words, then, are the verbal symbols the communicator uses to try to express his inner thoughts. He chooses symbols that *to him* represent what he has in his mind. Ideally, the sender and receiver have similar referents for the words the sender uses; however, this is not often the case. A student speaks of his dorm and his listener pictures whatever it is that dorm means to him. This may be her own dorm or, if she never lived in a dorm, whatever it is that the word *dorm* brings to her mind. By exploring the ways in which words and their meanings are learned, it will be more clearly understood why this is the case.

Although we have dictionaries that record words and their "meanings," the dictionary presents us with only one level of meaning: the *denotative* or literal meaning. The dictionary meaning of a word is its standard meaning as determined by the standard setters of that language. But the dictionary does not give the connotative or associative meanings of a word, primarily because words are as varied as the people using them. Communication experience 6.5 is designed to illustrate this point.

Communication Experience 6.5

Principle

All words have denotative and connotative meanings. The connotations of a word relate to the meaning that word has for the person using it.

Procedure

1. The class works as a group.
2. One person reads the following words and asks the members of the group to each write down the meaning for each of the words.

   a. Love   c. Building   e. Flower
   b. Learning   d. Shoe   f. Friend

3. Compare the meanings given for each word.

Discussion

What were the similarities and differences in the definitions given? Were some words more universal than others in terms of how people defined them? Why, or why not? Were any of the words unfamiliar to class members? What are the implications of this experience for classmates communicating with one another about any of the referents for which these words stand?

As illustrated by communication experience 6.5, what words mean and the connotations about words vary from person to person. Dictionaries provide only literal and/or standard meanings for words. But there are other ways in which the meanings for words are learned. Words are learned in a context and the context provides part of the meaning of the word for the person learning it.

Contexts color the meanings of those words for the person learning them. It is of great significance to note the relative importance of the denotative and connotative meanings of the same word. The connotative meanings of words can have enough impact to actually mask the literal meaning of those words. Such connotations may be strongly positive as, for example, the esteem in which many people hold the concept "patriotism." The connotations may also be strongly negative as, for example, the effect of referring to one's political views as "conservative" has when speaking to a "liberal" friend, or vice versa. A word's literal meaning may be essentially neutral, yet the connotations of that word may evoke an entirely different flavor. By this explanation we can see one reason how confusion between a word and its referent evolves. When a referent has strongly positive associations, use of the word is enough to inspire respect in the listeners. However, if the associations are very negative, saying the word is interpreted by some listeners to mean that the encoder favors that which the word represents. For example, the word *abortion* was not used in "polite" society until very recently, as if to suggest that to know the word meant the person using it was in support of abortion.

Words are learned in contexts. Just as we have talked about the communicators and the ways in which they have learned to communicate as part of their socialization, so too the language code that one learns and the values placed on words within that code are part of one's socialization.

Chronology of Learning Words

One begins to learn words in the first years of his life. For this reason, many people assume that talking is "natural" rather than learned, and take for granted that all people use words to mean the same things. The early cries of a baby are not symbolic language but rather a vocal language shared with some other forms of animal life. It is during the interaction with the people in the infant's environment that the cries are decoded as having definite meanings. The infant learns ways to have his needs fulfilled, whether by crying or behaving in other ways to which the adults will respond. By the time a child reaches his second year he begins to use words; at first, one at a time, then in combinations, and eventually

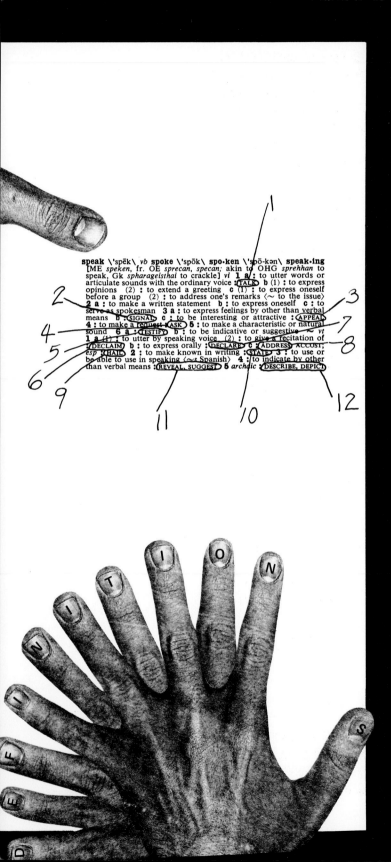

talk \'tók\ *vb* [ME *talken;* akin to OE *talu* tale] *vt* **1 :** to deliver or express in speech **:** UTTER **2 :** to make the subject of conversation or discourse **:** DISCUSS ⟨∼ business⟩ **3 :** to influence, affect, or cause by talking ⟨∼ed them into agreeing⟩ **4 :** to use (a language) for conversing or communicating **:** SPEAK ∼ *vi* **1 a :** to express or exchange ideas by means of spoken words **:** CONVERSE **b :** to convey information or communicate in any way (as with signs or sounds) **2 a :** to use speech **:** SPEAK **b :** to speak idly **:** PRATE **3 a :** GOSSIP **b :** to reveal secret or confidential information **4 :** to give a talk **:** LECTURE **syn** see SPEAK — **talk·er** *n* — **talk back :** to answer impertinently — **talk turkey :** to speak frankly or bluntly

sig·nal \'sig-n²l\ *n* [ME, fr. MF, fr. ML *signale,* fr. LL, neut. of *signalis* of a sign, fr. L *signum*] **1** *archaic* **:** TOKEN, INDICATION **2 a :** an act, event, or watchword that has been agreed upon as the occasion of concerted action **b :** something that incites to action **3 a :** a sound or gesture made to give warning or command **b :** an object placed to convey notice or warning **4 :** an object (as a flag on a pole) centered over a point so as to be observed from other positions in surveying **5 a :** an object used to transmit or convey information beyond the range of human voice **b :** the sound or image conveyed in telegraphy, telephony, radio, radar, or television **c :** a detectable physical quantity or impulse (as a voltage, current, or magnetic field strength) by which messages or information can be transmitted

ap·peal \ə-'pē(ə)l\ *n* **1 :** a legal proceeding by which a case is brought from a lower to a higher court for rehearing **2 :** a criminal accusation **3 a :** an application for corroboration or decision **b :** an earnest plea **:** ENTREATY **4 :** the power of arousing a sympathetic response **:** ATTRACTION

ask \'ask\ *vb* asked \'as(k)t\ **ask·ing** [ME *asken,* fr. OE *āscian,* akin to OHG *eiscōn* to ask, L *aeruscare* to beg] *vt* **1 a :** to call on for an answer **b :** to put a question about **c :** SPEAK, UTTER ⟨∼ a question⟩ **2 a :** to make a request of **:** BEG **b :** to make request for ⟨she ∼ed help from her teacher⟩ **3 :** to call for **:** RE·QUIRE **4 :** to set as a price **5 :** INVITE ∼ *vi* **1 :** to seek information **2 :** to make a request ⟨∼ed for food⟩ **3 :** LOOK — often used in the phrase *ask for trouble* — **ask·er** *n*

tes·ti·fy \'tes-tə-,fī\ *vb* [ME *testifien,* fr. L *testificari,* fr. *testi-* witness] *vi* **1 a :** to make a statement based on personal knowledge or belief **:** bear witness **b :** to serve as evidence or proof **2 :** to express a personal conviction **3 :** to make a solemn declaration under oath for the purpose of establishing a fact (as in a court) ∼ *vt* **1 a :** to bear witness to **:** ATTEST **b :** to serve as evidence of **:** PROVE **2** *archaic* **a :** to make known (a personal conviction) **:** PROFESS **b :** to give evidence of **:** SHOW **3 :** to declare under oath before a tribunal or officially constituted public body

de·claim \di-'klām\ *vb* [ME *declamen,* fr. L *declamare,* fr. *de-* + *clamare* to cry out; akin to L *calare* to call] *vi* **1 :** to speak rhetorically; *specif* **:** to recite something as an exercise in elocution **2 :** HARANGUE ∼ *vt* **1 :** to deliver rhetorically; *specif* **:** to recite in elocution — **de·claim·er** *n* — **dec·la·ma·tion** \,dek-lə-'mā-shən\

de·clare \di-'kla(ə)r, -'kle(ə)r\ *vb* [ME *declaren,* fr. MF *declarer,* fr. L *declarare,* fr. *de-* + *clarare* to make clear, fr. *clarus* clear] **1** *obs* **:** to make clear **2 :** to make known formally or explicitly **3 :** to make evident **:** SHOW **4 :** to state emphatically **:** AFFIRM ⟨∼s his innocence⟩ **5 :** to make a full statement of (one's taxable or dutiable property) **6 a :** to announce (as a trump suit) in a card game **b :** MELD **7 :** to make payable ∼ *vi* **1 :** to make a declaration **2 :** to avow one's support — **de·clar·er** *n*

ad·dress \ə-'dres\ *vb* [ME *adressen,* fr. MF *adresser,* fr. *a-* (fr. L *ad-*) + *dresser* to arrange — more at DRESS] *vt* **1 a :** DIRECT, AIM **b :** to direct to go **:** SEND **2** *archaic* **:** to make ready; *esp* **:** DRESS **3 :** to direct the efforts or attention of (oneself) **4 a :** to communicate directly **b :** to communicate directly to; *esp* **:** to deliver a formal speech to **5 a :** to mark directions for delivery on ⟨∼ a letter⟩ **b :** to consign to the care of another **6 :** to greet by a prescribed form **7 :** to adjust the club preparatory to hitting (a golf ball) ∼ *vi, obs* **:** to direct one's speech or attentions — **ad·dress·er** *n*

hail \'hā(ə)l\ *n* [ME, fr. OE *hægl;* akin to OHG *hagal* hail, Gk *kachlēx* pebble] **1 a :** precipitation in the form of small balls or lumps usu. consisting of concentric layers of clear ice and compact snow **b** *archaic* **:** HAILSTORM **2 :** something that gives the effect of falling hail

state \'stāt\ *n, often attrib* [ME *stat,* fr. OF & L; OF *estat,* fr. L *status,* fr. *status,* pp. of *stare* to stand — more at STAND] **1 a :** mode or condition of being ⟨water in the gaseous ∼⟩ ⟨∼ of readiness⟩ **b** (1) **:** condition of mind or temperament ⟨in a highly nervous ∼⟩ (2) **:** a condition of abnormal tension or excitement **2 a :** social position; *esp* **:** high rank **b** (1) **:** elaborate or luxurious style of living (2) **:** formal dignity **:** POMP — usu. used with *in* **3 a :** body of persons constituting a special class in a society **:** ESTATE **b** *pl* **:** the members or representatives of the governing classes assembled in a legislative body **c** *obs* **:** a person of high rank (as a noble) **4 a :** a politically organized body of people usu. occupying a definite territory; *esp* **:** one that is sovereign **b :** the political organization of such a body of people **5 :** the operations or concerns of the government of a country **6 :** one of the constituent units of a nation having a federal government ⟨the United *States* of America⟩ **7 :** the territory of a state

re·veal \ri-'vē(ə)l\ *vt* [ME *revelen,* fr. MF *reveler,* fr. L *revelare* to uncover, reveal, fr. *re-* + *velare* to cover, veil, fr. *velum* veil] **1 :** to make known through divine inspiration **2 :** to make publicly known **:** DIVULGE ⟨∼ a secret⟩ **3 :** to show plainly **:** DISPLAY — **re·veal·able** \-'vē-lə-bəl\ *adj* — **re·veal·er** *n*

sug·gest \sə(g)-'jest\ *vt* [L *suggestus,* pp. of *suggerere* to put under, furnish, suggest, fr. *sub-* + *gerere* to carry — more at CAST] **1 a :** to seek to influence **:** SEDUCE **b :** to call forth **:** EVOKE **c :** imply as a possibility **:** INTIMATE **d :** to propose as desirable or fitting ⟨∼ a stroll⟩ **e :** to offer for consideration or as a hypothesis **2 a :** to call to mind by thought or association **b :** to serve as a motive or inspiration for — **sug·gest·er** *n*

de·scribe \di-'skrīb\ *vt* [L *describere,* fr. *de-* + *scribere* to write — more at SCRIBE] **1 :** to represent or give an account of in words **2 :** to represent by a figure, model, or picture **:** DELINEATE **3 :** trace or traverse the outline of ⟨∼ a circle⟩ **4** *obs* **:** DISTRIBUTE **5** *archaic* **:** OBSERVE, PERCEIVE — **de·scrib·er** *n*

de·pict \di-'pikt\ *vt* [L *depictus,* pp. of *depingere,* fr. *de-* + *ping-*

in sentence form. "Go store" is a two-year-old or younger child's version of a more complex sentence. Adults, unaware that a two-to-three-year-old child is hearing what they are saying in his presence and is able to repeat it, may be in for a painful experience when the child repeats certain words he has heard. ("Where did he ever learn language like that?")

It has been reported that by the age of four a child may be uttering 10,000 to 12,000 words a day; and that by six, a child has a vocabulary of 2,500 different words.[10] This supports the point that most words are learned in a context, rather than from a dictionary. The meanings of much of one's most basic vocabulary are shaped by the context in which those words are learned. Certain words are associated with certain people. Such associations become part of the word's meanings for the individual. The most universal example involves people's names. We often associate the names of people we have known with certain personal attributes possessed by those people; all Barbaras must be like the Barbara one has known. This is especially true if only one person by that name has been known, or if the person with that name had a strong impact on the person. If Allan was the name of one's most popular classmate, the name Allan may carry that positive connotation.

By the time a child enters elementary school he has absorbed much of the language he will know. This underscores the significance the context in which one learns words and the impact those teaching us the words have on what words mean to us. A person's field of experience and early socialization have a great deal to do with his message-making skills. His verbal language and the attitudes toward words are learned in that language as part of this socialization long before the child learns formal ways of learning to read and write.

Human language is a symbolic process enabling people to share their experiences with one another. It not only allows us to profit from the experiences and knowledge of our ancestors but it enables us to pass along the knowledge we have gained to future generations. We have described words as the symbols within the verbal code, how they are learned, and the chronology of learning them. In the next chapter we will continue our analysis of the message aspect of interpersonal communication by defining and distinguishing between different kinds of language.

Interference with Intentional Communication

It is the symbolic nature of verbal language that enables the communicator to express those experiences she wishes to share. But it is also the symbolic quality that leads to complexity in communication. Words are symbols for the things they represent. People choose words that seem to

Elements in the Interpersonal Cycle

them to stand for the referents they have in mind. Communication complications arise by the very nature of this process, for no two people share the same exact meaning for any given word. This provides the source for two possible interferences with intentional communication: (1) the same word may be used by two communicators to mean different things, to stand for different referents, and (2) two communicators may use two different words to refer to the same object. In each case the communicators cannot share meaning.

Interpersonal communication relies on a shared-language system. In order for the message maker to communicate as intended, he must use language that is comprehensible to his intended receiver. Another interference with intentional communication occurs when the message maker uses symbols for which his intended receiver has no referent. The use of jargon is a case-in-point. Professors share a vocabulary related to their work, which they use freely amongst themselves when referring to certain referents. The same is true for doctors, lawyers, engineers, housewives, truckers, and butchers. Problems can arise, however, when that jargon becomes so familiar and comfortable for them that they use it with people who do not share its usage; therefore they have no referents for the symbols. This creates an interference with communication, which can only be overcome when the message maker is aware of the problem and can translate those ideas into symbols comprehendible to the receiver. In effect, the words common to jargon, even though they are part of the English language, are "foreign" to people unfamiliar with them.

In discussing the referents of words we distinguished between object, concept, and process referents. Object referents are the most concrete and therefore the most easily pinpointed in terms of their referents. The more abstract the referent, the more misleading the symbol may be since its meaning may not be shared by the communicators.

Another factor that explains the possible complications in communicating verbally is the chronology and context in which language is learned. If languages were really learned by reading dictionaries, more people would share the same meanings for words. But much of one's vocabulary is learned in some context and that context becomes part of the meaning of the word for the person learning the word. These connotations are highly personal. One cannot communicate as he intends without some attention to his choice of language and feedback from his intended receiver as to how well he is being understood. When a word is used in such a way that it makes no sense to the receiver, the receiver verbally or nonverbally indicates this. Often the word makes perfect sense to the receiver, just as it makes perfect sense to the sender, but each perceives a somewhat different sense of the meaning.

These, then, are the most basic problems arising from the symbolic nature of language. The human being's ability to symbolize permits him a vast range of verbal and nonverbal expression. It also places on him the burden of evaluating himself as a symbol maker.

Summary   In this chapter we have begun analysis of the verbal message element in interpersonal communication. The important points are:

1. Verbal language is a code of agreed upon symbols; a system of phonetic symbols used to express a thought or feeling.
2. Animals other than human beings have languages, but their languages are not composed of symbols. The symbolic quality of language allows humans to be "time-binders," to pass knowledge from generation to generation.
3. Words are the arbitrary symbols of which language is composed.
4. A word is a symbol because it stands for or represents something else.
5. Every word has a referent, or that which the word represents. Referents are classified as object, concept, and process referents.
6. Meaning lies in people, not in words. People choose words—symbols—to try to convey meaning.
7. The triangle of meaning illustrates that meaning starts with a thought, and the object referent and its symbol are never quite the same.
8. Words and meaning are learned from infancy on in an environment and context.
9. Attached to every word are two kinds of meaning: denotative and connotative. Dictionaries provide denotative meaning.
10. Interference with meaning as intended by the message maker arises from the symbolic nature of language.

Questions for Discussion

1. What is the significance of knowing that the word is not the thing?
2. Compare human language and the languages of other forms of animal life.
3. Discuss any personal experiences in which there was interference with intentional communication because of confusion over referents for a given word.
4. How is it possible for a man and woman who do not speak the same language to meet and communicate enough to fall in love?
5. What is the purpose of a dictionary if meanings lie in people rather than in words?
6. Why is the symbolic nature of man's language significant?
7. Discuss the three different categories of referents.
8. Diagram the triangle of meaning using a specific word, thought and referent. What, if anything, does this diagram help clarify?

9. Explain how the context in which one learns a word becomes part of that word.

10. Discuss and distinguish between the denotative and connotative meanings of a given word. How does the connotative affect the denotative?

Notes

1. This analogy comes from the work of Alfred Korzybski, father of general semantics. Used in literature by Hayakawa, Johnson, Budd, et al.

2. Stuart Chase, *The Power of Words* (New York: Harcourt, Brace and Co., 1953), p. 71.

3. Irving J. Lee, *Language of Wisdom and Folly* (New York: Harper and Bros., 1949), p. 39.

4. Cf. studies at Yerkes Institute, Stanford, California. Research on Lana and other chimps.

5. Alfred Korzybski, *Science and Sanity,* 3d ed. (Lakeville, Conn.: The International Non-Aristotelian Library Publishing Company, 1948), p. 89.

6. Charles K. Ogden and I. A. Richards, *The Meaning of Meaning* (New York: Harcourt Brace and Co., 1946), p. 11.

7. "Theories of Information" in *Essays for Ralph Shaw,* ed. Norman Stevens (Metuchen, N.J.: Scarecrow Press, 1975), p. 160. Artandi and others use "artificial" language to refer to language that is invented by humans with strictly de jure rules: prescriptive language, such as the language of computers, indexing, etc.

8. Korzybski, *Science and Sanity,* p. 89.

9. Charles Morris, *Signs, Language, and Behavior* (New York: George Braziller, Inc., 1946).

10. Chase, *Words,* p. 68.

Selected Bibliography

Brown, Roger. *Words and Things.* Glencoe, Ill.: The Free Press, 1958. A good introduction to the symbolic nature of language.

Chase, Stuart. *The Power of Words.* New York: Harcourt, Brace and Company, 1953. Recommended as enjoyable reading to the beginning student of language.

Lee, Irving J. *Language of Wisdom and Folly.* New York: Harper and Brothers, 1949. Recommended to the beginning student of language. A good introduction to semantics.

Ogden, Charles K. and I. A. Richards. *The Meaning of Meaning.* New York: Harcourt, Brace and Company, 1946. An important analysis of the nature of meaning. Recommended to the student with some background in semantics.

Sapir, Edward. *Culture, Language and Personality.* Berkeley, Calif.: University of California Press, 1966. Language and culture are related. The student interested in the relationships between language structure and one's perception of self and others will find this book useful.

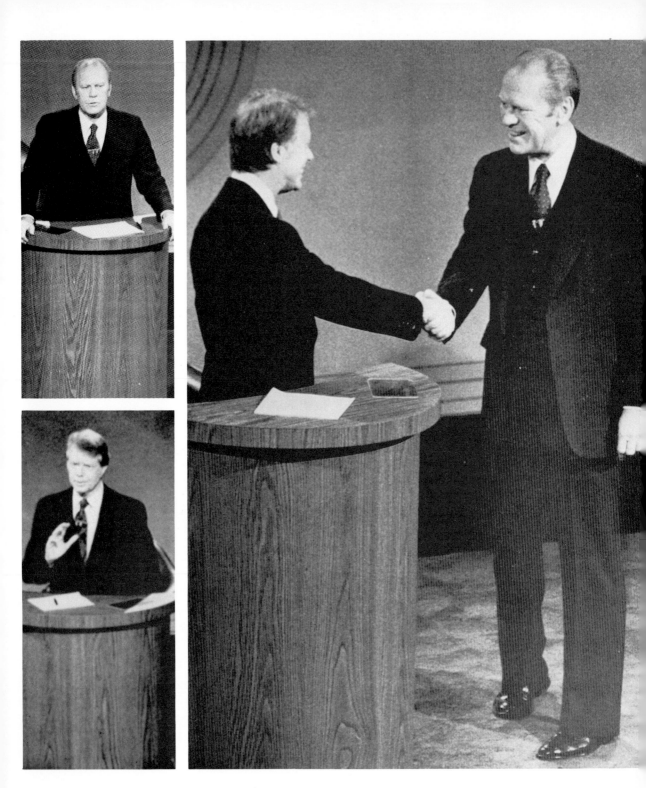

Encoding the Verbal Message: Types of Words

7

Introduction

In our daily living, we are all virtually swimming in words, both oral and written. Words are used to chat, to sell, to instruct, to amuse, and to teach. From the time we rise in the morning until the time we retire at night, each of us is bombarded by messages, most of which are composed of words.

In this chapter we will continue to study the message aspect of the interpersonal communication interaction by looking at the different kinds of verbal language into which the message can be translated. Within any verbal language, there are different kinds of words into which the message can be encoded and which have an impact on the meaning or apparent meaning of that message. This chapter will explore the differences and distinctions between **judgmental language** and **reporting language,** and the impact language choice has on messages and meanings.

Communication Goals

This chapter uses the theoretical and experiential approach to explore the impact the kind of verbal language used by the message maker has on the intended message. It is written to enable you to evaluate the language of the message by:

1. Being aware of the *kinds* of language composing the message.
2. Detecting euphemisms used to make things sound better than they are.
3. Distinguishing between statements of fact (reports) and opinion (judgments) by analyzing the kind of language used to express the ideas.
4. Detecting judgmental language.
5. Being more sensitive to implied meanings.
6. Understanding that even reports may be judgmental.

Communication Concepts and Theories

The relationship between a word and its referent is analogous to the relationship between a map and its territory. A map is only good if it presents an accurate description of the terrain it represents. The same is true for a word. Its worth can be measured in terms of how accurately it maps its referent. Words are the arbitrary combinations of sounds (letters) that we invent and to which we attach meanings. Once this has been done, some standard denotative meaning is attached to that word. The word is then used to stand for a certain referent. But this does not imply that any one word has the same meaning for all the people who use it. However, at its core, there is a common, basic literal meaning attached to that symbol. Communication experience 7.1 is designed to illustrate the kinds of language available to the message maker.

Communication Experience 7.1

Principle

The kind of language a person uses to frame his message affects the receiver's image of the referent being described.

Procedure

1. Work individually.
2. Write a brief ad (50 words or less) for a newspaper describing an item for sale: car, house, coat, boat, etc.
3. Analyze the use of language in the ad.
4. Compare and contrast your use of language with what other students have done, and with ads in the local newspaper.

Discussion

How do the "maps" correspond to the "territories"? What else do they reflect? Did your language bear a resemblance to the language found in newspaper ads? What implications can be drawn from this exercise?

As illustrated in communication experience 7.1, even words with neutral denotative meanings may have connotations that overshadow the literal meaning, evoking strong reactions in the receiver. Sometimes a word can come to have unpleasant connotative meanings. To overcome the effects of these negative associations, a sender might choose to substitute another word for the one with unpleasant associations. The substitute, having a similar literal meaning—if a literal meaning is definable in relation to that word—will have more pleasant connotations. Such a substitute is known as a **euphemism.** Communication experience 7.2 is designed to illustrate the usage of euphemisms.

Communication Experience 7.2

Principle

Euphemisms are words having pleasant connotations and are used to substitute for words having unappealing connotations.

Procedure

1. Work in groups of five.
2. Role play. The group acts as part of a public relations team for a political candidate, corporation, or resort area.
3. The person or place represented by the group has received a great deal of bad publicity due to a recent scandal.
4. Invent the scandal.
5. Invent a news release designed to turn the scandal into some good publicity for the group's person, or place.

Discussion

What did the group have to do to change the image of the person or place? Did the actual referents change? What are the implications for communication?

"I understand you perfectly, Harold. When you say you want to extend your parameters, it means you want floozies."

Euphemisms: The Effects of Language Choice on the Image of the Referent

The dictionary defines *euphemism* as the exchange of an agreeable or inoffensive word for one that is unpleasant, undiplomatic, unmentionable, or taboo. In other words, rather than using one symbol to refer to a given referent, the sender selects another. Instead of telling the instructor that the test was "unfair," or "too difficult," the student says, "It was challenging." The use of euphemistic language is another way in which we behave as if the word were the thing. In using a euphemism one changes the symbol, not the referent. And yet in the process of changing the symbol (word) to a more pleasant one, it appears as if the referent has been changed.

A man at a cocktail party was introduced to another man. As they made small talk, he asked his new acquaintance, "Where are you from?" The second man replied that he lived, "Near Princeton (New Jersey)." The first man being familiar with the area pursued the matter further by asking, "Whereabouts?" The second man replied, "Kendall Park." The first man responded, "So am I," chuckling to himself at the different ways in which he and the other man refer to their hometown. Kendall Park does not have the significance that Princeton does. To say "Near Princeton" while not untrue, nevertheless gives an impression of more status than saying "Kendall Park." This is an example of euphemistic language: putting something in words to color it positively.

Euphemisms, however, are used most often when the connotations of a word are either unpleasant or unmentionable. Whether or not a subject is taboo is determined by cultural norms. Subjects such as death, health, sex, or urination have been taboo in our culture in the past, and even today remain taboo in some subcultures of our society. If a person has to urinate and is in a restaurant, at someone's home, or stopping at a gas station, asking for the "lounge," "powder room," "rest room," "bathroom," "john," or "head," etc. is very common. All of these are euphemisms. None of them really indicate what the room is really for. These substitutes do not refer to the "toilet," which is what the person is looking for and the real reason why he is asking where the room is: the person needs to urinate, not to rest or take a bath.

While eating in a restaurant in the Greek Islands, a visiting American asked for the "bathroom." After repeating herself several times, the bewildered looking waitress led her to the back of the restaurant, out a door, up some back steps, and into a room with a bathtub. "No," said the American, "I want a toilet." "Oh," said the waitress as she led her back to the restaurant to the room with the toilet. Imagine what was going through the waitress' mind as the tourist got up in the middle of dinner and asked to take a bath (bathroom). Hayakawa says, "Indeed, it is impossible in polite society to state, without resorting to baby talk or medical vocabulary, what a "rest room" is for. (It is where you 'wash your hands'!)"[1]

There are many examples of how euphemisms are used in our culture; for instance, take the subjects of age and death. Rather than saying that someone "died," we often hear people say he "passed on," or "is no longer with us." Rather than describe one's seventy-three-year-old grandmother as "old," one might describe her as "aged," in her "golden age," or a "senior citizen."

Euphemisms are often used during instances in which people describe themselves, their work, or state in life. A person who considers herself too heavy might prefer to be called "plump," "chubby," "husky," or "zophtic," rather than "fat." A person who feels she is too thin might prefer "slender," "lean," or "lanky." Euphemisms may also be used by a person to give his work more status: "sanitation engineer" (garbage man), "restauranteer" (candy store owner), "administrative assistant" (secretary), "financial adviser" (bookkeeper).

Euphemisms are used at times to refer to one's physical or mental health. In recent years, children who were once referred to as "emotionally disturbed" are now called "exceptional children." Literally, the word *exceptional* refers to anything that deviates from the norm. Therefore something can be exceptionally good or exceptionally bad. The connotations of the word, however, are very positive. When one says thank you to someone for an "exceptionable" meal, he usually means it was exceptionally good. In this context, we see the possible confusion in terms of the referent when Mrs. Smith says that her Johnny is in the class for "exceptional" children. A person unfamiliar with this euphemistic usage of the word *exceptional* may have an image of Johnny that is almost diametrically opposed to the reality. As semanticists, we consider this confusing and questionable. Educators who work with these children have rationale for this practice; as do any of us who use euphemisms in dealing with a difficult subject.

In these examples, we see euphemisms as a method by which the message maker attempts to give a more favorable impression of the referent than other words would evoke. Another purpose of euphemisms is to describe and/or disguise behavior about which the speaker would rather be vague or misleading. A camp counselor who is having difficulty with a child but who cannot risk offending the child's parents might describe the child as "active" rather than "difficult to control"; as "inquisitive" rather than "nosey"; as "very verbal" rather than "loud-

I got fired last year, in Las Vegas, from the Frontier Hotel, for saying "Shit," in a town where the big game is called Crap. That's some kind of a double standard, you know? I'm sure that there was some out in the Casino there was some Texan, yelling, "Oh, shit, I crapped!" And they fly those guys in free, you know? Fired me. Shit! You can get in as much trouble saying "Shit" as you can smoking it down there, man.

Shit's a nice word. It's a friendly, happy kind of word. Handy word. Middle class has never really been into shit, as a word. Not really comfortable with it, not really relaxed with it. It's it, not really — you'll hear it around the kitchen. if someone drops a casserole. "Oh, shit, ooh! Oh, look at the noodles. Oh, shit! Don't say that. Johnny, just hear it! Oh shit!" Sometimes they say "Shoot." But they can't kid me, man. "Shoot is "Shit" with two Os.

mouthed." A teacher on strike who by law is prohibited from striking calls his actions "work stoppages"; a war correspondent refers to our attacks on enemy bases as "surprise raids," and the same kind of action committed by the enemy against us as "sneak attacks."

Obviously, euphemisms serve an important function, otherwise they would not be used. They give a desirable appearance to something that if called by another name would seem far less appealing. But if we refer back to our map analogy, we can see what is wrong with euphemisms. They mislead; they do not accurately represent the territory about which they supposedly refer. They are a language device that allows the sender to feel more comfortable about what he is saying, at the expense of misleading his receiver by making it impossible for him to have an accurate understanding of the referent.

Communication experience 7.3 is designed to illustrate some things about the use of euphemisms.

Communication Experience 7.3

Principle

While euphemisms enable us to discuss things in terms that are pleasant or comfortable to use, the drawback is that they provide poor maps, giving little information about their territories.

Procedure

1. Work individually.
2. Compose a list of twenty or more words that are self-descriptive.
3. Evaluate each term. Is it a euphemism, and why or why not?
4. Select those descriptors that are not uncomfortable to tell other people.
5. Compare this new list with lists prepared by other classmates.
6. What degree of agreement can be arrived at regarding the use of euphemism in these descriptions?

Discussion

How many self-descriptors were euphemistic? Was this easier to detect in one's own choices or those made by another? What was the basis for disclosing particular self-descriptors to classmates? In what ways does this experience affect future self-description? Why?

As illustrated by communication experience 7.3, euphemisms can make us feel better by allowing us to talk about things in more pleasant terms. We use them at the risk of misleading our intended receivers, and ourselves, as to the referents of which we speak. We do nothing to make a person's living conditions better, or his looks or behavior more presentable by changing the words we use to describe the situation. In fact, our manipulation of words allows us to avoid the issue altogether. The more uncomfortable we are with the given reality, the more likely we are to indulge in euphemisms, defend our use of them, and be blind to or defensive about questions raised as to their value in intentional communication.

Judgmental Language Versus Reporting Language

Judgmental language is language containing a conclusion. In this sense it presents a shortcut. The language itself contains a decision without forcing (or allowing) one to go through the steps necessary to arrive at the conclusion. Moreover, judgmental language includes not only a conclusion but an attitude toward the referent of the word without directly acknowledging that it does so. Judgmental language not only gives information about the referent, it also includes the judgment of the speaker. Communication experience 7.4 is designed to illustrate the comparisons and contrasts between judgmental language and the language of reports.

I don't know who you are, but I hate you!

Communication Experience 7.4

Principle

The difference between judgmental language and reporting language is that judgmental language presents opinion, which is neither true nor false; and reporting language presents statements capable of some degree of verification.

Procedure

1. Work in groups of three.
2. Select a subject about which each of the three people will write a short paragraph.
3. Agree on any basics of the topic on which all three paragraphs are to touch.
4. Each person writes one paragraph. The first paragraph is to be an objective description of the topic; the second, a positive description; and the third, a negative description.
5. Compare paragraphs.
6. Each triad reads its three paragraphs to the class.

Discussion

In what ways do the descriptions differ? Can any of them be verified? If so, how? Do the referents change or appear to change? Which version is the most desirable? Why? What are the implications for communication?

As illustrated by communication experience 7.4, there are differences between judgmental language and reporting language. The most important distinction is that judgmental language provides more information about the encoder than about that to which the words supposedly refer. It tells more about the sender and his attitude toward the referent than about the referent. Judgmental language appears to give information about the referent while in fact being far more informative about the encoder and his perception of that referent. When, for example, someone recommends a certain movie as a "great film," she tells more about her attitude toward the film than about the film itself. Only when we know her well enough to know what kinds of movies she considers "great," do we know whether or not to see the film. Many kinds of language used by communicators incorporate as much about the speaker's perception of the referent as information about the referent itself. We will discuss *slanting language, inferences,* and *assumptions* as some other forms of judgmental language.

The counterpart of this colored language is the *language of reports*. Reporting language is verifiable and excludes judgments, inferences, and assumptions. Reporting language refers more strictly to that which is being referred to without the coloring of the speaker, thereby permitting the receiver to draw his own conclusions. Having briefly described and distinguished between the language of reports and judgmental language, let us develop each separately and more fully.

Judgments: Words with Conclusions

We have already described judgmental language as including the speaker's attitude toward his referent as well as a conclusion. When someone wants to fix up a blind date for a friend, what kind of language does he use to describe her? If he says, "She's a doll, gorgeous, curvy, outrageous, and a swinger from the word go," he has told his friend nothing about the woman at all. He may sound as if he has, and if his friend either hastily accepts the date or tactfully refuses it, he would be behaving as if he had learned something about the woman. But unless one knows the speaker well enough to know what *he* likes in a woman, what *he* thinks is gorgeous, what *to him* is a swinger, the speaker has given his friend no information at all about her. If one is not aware of this and does not act accordingly, he finds himself in the same position as reported by a student. A friend of his offered to fix him up with a woman he claimed looked just like a movie star. The student readily accepted without asking, "Which one?"; and to his dismay, he found out.

When someone says she lives in a "big" house or just bought a "wonderful" car, the receiver must be aware that this is her opinion. One must know what these words mean to the speaker to understand their meaning. If one student says an exam he took was a "snap," this is relative. Another student might find it exceedingly difficult. In all of these instances the descriptive words used contain the speaker's attitude toward the thing. Without knowing anything about the sender, one may be misled into thinking he's given information about the referent. A woman asked a male companion, "Do you have *thin* legs?" Most people would have answered "yes," "no," or "it's none of your business," thereby missing the fact that "thin" is a relative judgment. In this case, the man replied, "Compared to what? An elephant, Yes! A piano, No!"

Judgmental language includes a conclusion. It is a shortcut that eliminates the steps used to arrive at that conclusion. Sometimes this is necessary and useful. When asking a friend "How does this new outfit look on me?" all one wants to hear is the other's judgment, the conclusion. On the other hand judgmental language is often uninformative. When one asks someone about a restaurant and receives the reply, "Terrific," one hasn't really received any information. He would be in the position to draw his own conclusions if instead, he receives the answer, "Well, it serves French food, dinner prices range between $5.95 and $10.00, and dinner is served by candlelight." Judgmental language includes a conclusion in that it makes a statement about the speaker's attitude toward the referent without giving the basis on which the attitude is founded. Communication experience 7.5 is designed to illustrate this point.

"I have a pet at home"

"Oh, what kind of a pet?"

"It is a dog."

"What kind of a dog?"

"It is a St. Bernard."

"Grown up or a puppy?"

"It is full grown."

"What color is it?"

"It is brown and white."

"Why didn't you say you had a full-grown, brown and white St. Bernard as a pet in the first place?"

Communication Experience 7.5

Principle

Judgmental language tells more about the person making the observations than about that which he observes.

Procedure

1. Work in groups of five-to-seven people.
2. The group members must decide whether or not they would select the person described in the following paragraph to teach a course next semester:

   I liked having Professor Harper as a teacher. She is warm, friendly, and really cares about her students. She tries to help everyone learn as much as they can and only criticizes when absolutely necessary.

   Almost everyone in the course got an A or B and anyone who was unhappy with the course felt it was not her fault. She creates an open atmosphere in class. Her tests are fair.

3. Read and discuss the description of Professor Harper. Discuss the basis for the group's decision.
4. Compare the results with other groups.

Discussion

What were the bases for the group's decision? Did they like the sound of Professor Harper? Why or why not? Did the group have enough information from the paragraph to come to a decision? If this were a real life situation, how would the group operate?

As illustrated in communication experience 7.5, judgmental language tells more about the speaker and his attitudes than about that to which his language *appears* to refer. Based on the given criteria, most of what is said or written is framed in judgmental language. Both the sender and receiver must be aware of this. Where detailed information that is free of the speaker's attitudes is needed, the receiver must be aware of whether or not she's getting it. If, for example, a teenager is describing a rock concert that she attended, she may not care that her entire description is highly judgmental. ("Man, I mean like I dig them. They were so cool.") On the other hand, a crew on a lunar flight receiving orders from the space center like: "Okay you guys, you're a *little off* (10 inches? - - - - 6,000 miles?) your planned path. Take your ship up a *bit* (how far is a bit?) to the *left* (of what?) and then *ease* (how?) her into a *better* position (relative to what?)

Inferences and Assumptions: Implied Meanings

Just as some language is colored by the attitudes of the speaker incorporated in the words he selects, so too some language makes statements about its referent beyond what is explicitly stated. This is called an **inference.**[2] An inference draws from the known some conclusion about the unknown. It is meaning the receiver gathers from what is said. Suposedly, an inference is the counterpart of that which is implied. That is, the speaker "implies" something from which the receiver draws an inference. We say "supposedly" because the speaker may unconsciously lead the receiver to draw an inference, or the receiver may get an inference without the speaker implying anything. In the latter case the receiver himself would be supplying the inferential meaning.

Closely akin to the process of inference making is the process of assumption making. In effect, one (inference) may precede the other (assumption). The inference received from what someone has said may lead to an assumption. A friend says "It's cold in here." From this, one gets an inference that may lead her to assume her friend would like her to put another log on the fire.

When making an assumption, something is taken for granted. If it has never rained where one lives, one may assume it never will. When one goes to bed at night, he assumes he will wake up in the morning. When one's gas tank registers "empty," he assumes he needs gas. In assumption making one uses past experience and takes for granted that the future will be like what one has already known. In both inference and assumption making, one tries to interpret the unknown based on the known. These are vital and necessary processes. In many instances, one could not function were one to act solely on the known. In such cases, one's ability to interpret the known and infer or assume things from that which is known determines how effective one is in functioning. If a person hears footsteps behind him while walking home down a dark alley, he has to make some assumptions about his safety. Or, if someone starts to say something and as he continues to talk his voice gets louder as he pounds his fist on the table, one might draw the inference, "He is angry."

The dangers of drawing these kinds of conclusions must not be overlooked. When using the known to evaluate the unknown, there is always the possibility of making an incorrect assumption or drawing a wrong inference. This in no way means that one must not make assumptions or draw inferences. It does mean that the person must know what he is doing. If a person knows he is making an assumption, he can be receptive to any new information that comes his way in order to either verify or discredit the conclusions he has drawn. While driving down a highway behind someone who signals for a right turn, one better know

LEGLESS GRANDMA HITCHHIKES AROUND THE U.S.

EXORCISTS RID GIRL OF 13 DEVILS

MAN WALKS 8,000 MILES BACKWARDS

Communication Experience 7.6

Principle

The difference between what we know and what we think we know is the difference between information and inference making.

Procedure

1. Work in groups of four: two males and two females, if possible.
2. The group goes out to dinner together.
3. Select two tables near your table and take note of the people at those tables.
4. Decide how the people at the tables are "related" to one another.
5. Compare conclusions and the bases for those conclusions.

Discussion

What were the similarities and differences in the conclusions? On what did the group members base their decisions? Was it possible to check for accuracy? What would others in the restaurant have thought the relationship to be among the four people in your group?

BLONDE BOMBSHELL DOUBLES FOR KOJAK

ARCHIE BUNKER MEETS THE POPE

I FOUGHT A KILLER SHARK

WAS JACKIE A CIA SPY?

as one passes on the left that he is making an assumption. Communication experience 7.6 is designed to illustrate the use of assumptions and inferences.

Assumption making is a necessary part of interpersonal communication as illustrated by communication experience 7.6. A person cannot function without making assumptions or drawing inferences. Much of what we do and much of what we know is based on our abilities to draw inferences and make assumptions. A guest ought not wait until his hostess directly asks him to go home. He should be able to infer from how late it is getting, the time he arrived, the kind of occasion, and the kind of people his hosts are, what is an appropriate time to leave. A student learns things in class that he assumes he can then apply to similar problems outside of class.

Sometimes we act on assumptions without realizing that we are doing so, but with no serious consequences. We drive down the highway at a comfortable speed, only five miles over the speed limit, assuming that we won't be stopped. If we are wrong, we find out and must attempt to talk our way out of a ticket. In other instances, by the time we find out, it may be too late to remedy the situation. If, on a hot summer day, one reaches for a glass of soda assuming it's dietetic, it may not matter whether or not

one is aware of his assumption unless he's a diabetic or on a very strict diet. But if one goes around drawing inferences about people by the way they're dressed and doesn't even know that what he thinks is merely a guess, he is in no position to reevaluate his assumption.

We have discussed these processes because they come into play during the sending and receiving of messages. Both processes are part of how the receiver gets messages from the verbal messages that are sent by the speaker, but are beyond what is specifically said. If the receiver is accurate in the inferences he draws or assumptions he makes, he may be a far more receptive and valuable responding communicator. His effectiveness, however, can be measured in part by how aware he is of the inherent risks in whatever he does, and his flexibility in reinterpreting his position.

Slanting: Leading Language

Another way in which the language of the message may be colored is the process of **slanting**.[3] Slanting refers to the inclusion of only those details that are favorable or unfavorable regarding a given subject. Even a listener who is aware of judgments, inferences, and assumptions may be given a very biased description composed of only "the facts." If one person says to another, "I don't want to influence you. Use your own judgment. But, here are the facts: the temperature is 40°; the skies are almost half cumulus clouds; the wind is 60 miles an hour. Now you decide whether or not we should go on that picnic." No real choice is given here. Especially since a few important details were left out: "It's 40° now," but one hour ago it was 30° and it's only 7:00 a.m.; "the skies have cumulus clouds," but 60% of the sky appears to be blue; "the winds are 60 miles an hour" in another part of the state.

ON CHRISTIANITY AND THE HORRORS OF SLAVERY

by Malcolm X

"My brothers and sisters, our white slavemaster's Christian religion has taught us black people here in the wilderness of North America that we will sprout wings when we die and fly up into the sky where God will have for us a special place called heaven. This is white man's Christian religion used to *brainwash* us black people! We have *accepted* it! We have *embraced* it! We have *believed* it! We have *practiced* it! And while we are doing all of that, for himself, this blue-eyed devil has *twisted* his Christianity, to keep his *foot* on our backs . . . to keep our *eyes* fixed on the pie in the sky and heaven in the hereafter . . . while *he* enjoys *his* heaven right *here* . . . on *this earth* . . . in *this life.*" . . .

"We didn't land on Plymouth Rock, my brothers and sisters — Plymouth Rock landed on *us!*" . . . "Give *all* you can to help Messenger Elijah Muhammad's independence program for the black man! . . . This white man always has controlled us black people by keeping us running to him begging, 'Please, lawdy, please, Mr. White Man, boss, would you push me off another crumb down from your table that's sagging with riches . . .'

" . . . my *beautiful*, black brothers and sisters! And when we say 'black,' we mean everything not white, brothers and sisters! Because *look* at your skins! We're all black to the white man, but we're a thousand and one different colors. Turn around, *look* at each other! What shade of black African polluted by devil white man are you? You see me — well, in the streets they used to call me Detroit Red. Yes! Yes, that raping, red-headed devil was my *grandfather!* That close, yes! My *mother's* father. She didn't like to speak of it, can you blame her? She said she never laid eyes on him! She was *glad* for that! I'm *glad* for her! If I could drain away *his* blood that pollutes *my* body, and pollutes *my* complexion, I'd do it! Because I hate *every* drop of the rapist's blood that's in me!

"And it's not just me, it's *all* of us! During slavery, *think* of it, it was a *rare* one of our black grandmothers, our great-grandmothers and our great-great-grandmothers who escaped the white rapist slavemaster. That rapist slavemaster who emasculated the black man . . . with threats, with fear . . . until even today the black man lives with fear of the white man in his heart! Lives even today still under the heel of the white man!

"*Think* of it — think of that black slave man filled with fear and dread, hearing the screams of his wife, his mother, his daughter being *taken* — in the barn, the kitchen, in the bushes! *Think* of it, my dear brothers and sisters! *Think* of hearing wives, mothers, daughters, being *raped!* And you were too filled with *fear* of the rapist to do anything about it! And his vicious, animal attacks offspring, this white man named things like 'mulatto' and 'quadroon' and 'octoroon' and all those other things that he has called us — you and me — when he is not calling us 'nigger'!

"Turn around and look at each other, brothers and sisters, and *think* of this! You and me, polluted all these colors — and this devil has the arrogance and the gall to think we, his victims, should *love* him!"

It is easy to take almost any subject and slant it to make the point one wants to make. Even if the language of the message seems free of judgment, the details selected may give it a definite coloring. Communication experience 7.7 is designed to illustrate this.

Communication Experience 7.7

Principle

A statement of fact (report) can be as slanted as a highly judgmental description.

Procedure

1. Work in groups of three.
2. Role play a murder trial situation. One group member acts as judge, one as attorney for the defense, and one as attorney for the state.
3. Agree on any necessary facts of the case.
4. The two attorneys take turns stating why the defendant should be judged innocent or guilty.
5. If either makes a judgmental statement, the judge calls "out of order" and penalizes him.
6. The judge decides what should happen to the defendant based on the statements.

Discussion

How often did the judge have to say, "out of order"? What did the attorneys do to compensate for judgmental language? Were the statements of the defense and prosecution any the less slanted for being free of judgmental language? What was the basis for the judge's decision? In what ways can facts be manipulated to make one's case? What are the implications for communication?

As illustrated by communication experience 7.7, slanting has to do with what one includes in his description. But not all slanting is free from judgmental language. Just as one can slant something by choosing only those details that make the case he wants, one can also slant something by using highly judgmental descriptive language. Since judgment includes one's attitude or opinion, it is never either right or wrong. It can never be proven or disproven. In describing Mary, one person may slant her image by saying, "She's beautiful." Another might say, "She's an ugly mutt!" Neither statement is true nor false. Both are opinions. Both are subjective reactions, and are therefore relative. To one person she appears beautiful, to another she is ugly. Judgmental language gives a slant to a message especially where the receiver forgets to keep in mind that a judgment is only the opinion of the judge, revealing more about the observer, than what he observes.

The language in which the message is framed colors the meaning of the message. In developing this point we have discussed judgment, inference, assumption making and slanting. "Reporting" language is language that attempts to be free of judgment or coloration.

Reporting Language: Referent-Oriented Words

A message as a report is testable if it is verifiable and if it excludes judgmental language.[4] By knowing what constitutes judgment, inference, assumption making, and slanting, a message can be evaluated as to whether or not it is free from such language. However, knowing what is meant by a message or statement being "verifiable" is another matter. A report need not be true to be verifiable; it must be subject to proof. A judgment cannot be proven or disproven. We cannot prove whether something is "tall," "hot," "fat," or "beautiful," because these words are relative and matters of opinion. If a person is taking a hot shower and his roommate opens the bathroom door to tell him something, he may say "Wow! is it *hot* in there"; at the same time the person in the shower reacts by saying, "Close the door, it's *freezing."*

A report, on the other hand, is measurable and therefore can be proven to be right or wrong. If one says, "It is 90° in the bathroom," this statement could be measured with a thermometer. Any report must be verifiable. According to Hayakawa, you can't test every report yourself, but somewhere there must be a measure.[5] And so whereas "tall" isn't verifiable, you can test whether or not someone stands seven feet. It can't be proven that someone is "fat," but it can be verified that he weighs 200 pounds. A pair of shoes cannot be proven "beautiful," but can be verified as being made of 100 percent baby calfskin leather.

Something is verifiable if it is capable of being measured. Judgments cannot be subjected to objective measurements and thereby are considered nonverifiable. One person has as much right to call the television star Cher Bono sexy, as another does to call her skinny. These are only opinions. The only important caution is for the statement maker as well as the person he addresses to understand that the statements are opinions. A verifiable statement about Cher would be, "Cher is five feet six inches tall and weighs one hundred and three pounds." This is measurable

STAR GAZER

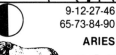

By CLAY R. POLLAN

Your Daily Activity Guide
According to the Stars.

To develop message for Wednesday, read words corresponding to numbers of your Zodiac birth sign.

1. You	31. Into	61. Which
2. Get	32. New	62. Want
3. Push	33. Luck	63. Share
4. Your	34. Anything	64. Appeal
5. Take	35. And	65. Things
6. You	36. You'll	66. Integrity
7. Will	37. Lot	67. Action
8. Going	38. Into	68. Much
9. A	39. For	69. A
10. Your	40. Heed	70. Hunches
11. Advantage	41. Without	71. Will
12. Routine	42. And	72. Good
13. Sweet	43. What	73. As
14. Do	44. Get	74. Profit
15. See	45. Motives	75. Of
16. Put	46. Take	76. Today's
17. Sound	47. Sympathize	77. Rewards
18. Ask	48. Compelling	78. Deed
19. Money	49. Shady	79. For
20. Charm	50. Your	80. Appears
21. Money	51. Quick	81. Of
22. Avoid	52. Do	82. Magnetic
23. Deeper	53. Opening	83. Sympathy
24. A	54. Fair	84. They
25. Of	55. Turn	85. Today
26. Empathize	56. Accomplishing	86. Others
27. Day	57. And	87. Good
28. Early	58. You	88. Work
29. Is	59. Your	89. Today
30. Plans	60. In	90. Come

10/13

 Good   Adverse Neutral

ARIES
9-12-27-46
65-73-84-90
MAR. 21
APR. 19

TAURUS
36-44-54-63
75-76-77
APR. 20
MAY 20

GEMINI
5-11-25-32
53-61-80-85
MAY 21
JUNE 20

CANCER
2-8-28-35
55-60-87-88
JUNE 21
JULY 22

LEO
3-4-19-33
40-59-70
JULY 23
AUG. 22

VIRGO
10-13-20-29
48-57-82-89
AUG. 23
SEPT. 22

LIBRA
16-17-21-30
38-51-67
SEPT. 23
OCT. 22

SCORPIO
1- 7-15-23
31-45-81-86
OCT. 23
NOV. 21

SAGITTARIUS
6-14-24-37
41-56-68
NOV. 22
DEC. 21

CAPRICORN
26-42-47-52
69-72-78
DEC. 22
JAN. 19

AQUARIUS
22-34-49-50
66-71-74
JAN. 20
FEB. 18

PISCES
18-39-43-58
62-64-79-83
FEB. 19
MAR. 20

by an objective measurement, a scale and a yardstick. But questions can be raised even about the accuracy of a scale or a yardstick with which we measure such things as weight and height. Even objective standards are based on the assumption that they measure accurately.

The question, then, becomes one of precision; how accurate does the measure need to be? All yardsticks in a sense are "rubber"; all are open to interpretation and are less accurate than some more perfect yardstick. The question becomes one of degree. At some point we "agree to agree" on certain kinds of measurement as if they were accurate. We use them in the absence of more perfectly objective instruments. Awareness of one's bias and the attempt to eliminate or control it are the essential ingredients. For example, we can agree to agree that a scale is the most accurate measuring device we presently have for weighing something. At the same time, we acknowledge that at some point we may discover that there are distortions or imperfections in the scale that have not allowed us to measure weight accurately. Perhaps, a more perfected device may be found to afford us greater accuracy. For example, a bathroom scale is not as precise as a doctor's scale. While those of us who use the scale are acting on the assumption of its accuracy, being aware that this is an assumption enables us to be receptive to new and better sources of information when they arise. This way of thinking is contrary to that of the person who does not even know he is making an assumption; he can therefore never separate his interpretations from that which he is interpreting.

The Language of the Message

The distinctions previously discussed have implications for the language of the message. The language of the message is often filled with the various types of judgmental language we've discussed. Only occasionally is it a report; it would be virtually impossible, and improbable, for the message to be strictly a report. A report is long, and detailed, and may be meaningless without someone to synthesize it. A report is verifiable; it permits one to come to his own conclusions regarding the referent. But, in addition, it is cumbersome and demands the time and ability to analyze its details. If messages were reports, they might be too complex or demanding for one's intended receivers. This does not mean that reports are never desirable or valuable. It all depends on what one needs to know. If the subject is a friend's new job, a descriptive, judgmental summary is sufficient. To hear every detail of the day stated in language that could be verified would be inappropriate to the receiver's needs. On the other hand, in a scientific report, verifiable language is necessary. The same holds true in cases in which the message relates information regarding health matters or the method by which grades are computed.

The language framing the message is crucial to the kind of communication that can occur thereafter. How effective or desirable the language is for any given communication interaction is dependent upon the nature of the subject, what the listener needs to know, how agile the speaker is in handling the language, and the message maker's intent.

Language can be compared on the basis of how judgmental or reportlike it appears, and in terms of how abstract (ambiguous) or concrete (detailed) it is. Judgmental language is more abstract language, the message maker having left out details about the referent in the process of making his conclusions. We have described the language of reports as more verifiable. It can also be described as more "operational"; that is, it is measurable in terms of how it works, functions, or operates. This chapter has described and distinguished between these two large categories of kinds of language. In the next chapter, we will discuss the semantic devices that the message maker uses in moving from one category of language to another in his message making.

Interference with Intentional Communication

General semanticists point out that a measure of a person's sanity is how well his word symbols depict the external reality they represent. Euphemisms do just the opposite. They distort the image of the referent. They make it appear to be something other than it is. This has serious implications in terms of confusion in communication, and is one source of interference with communication in which the communicators share meaning.

Another interference with effective communication results from the use of highly judgmental language. If one is concerned with information about the referent and not the speaker's attitude toward it, then he is not getting what he needs when the message is couched in highly judgmental language. A question regarding the political state of affairs when answered by the response "Much improved" tells the questioner little.

Reporting language can also be misused in communication. If one asks a question that calls for a quick, to-the-point answer but gets a detailed report, there's a lack of desired communication. Either highly judgmental or very factual language can be inappropriate to the given communication interaction if it is not the language called for in that situation. The language of the message must be appropriate to the situation and must satisfy the needs of those who are attempting to communicate.

When the receiver draws an inference or makes an assumption without realizing that he is doing so, there is potential interference with the communication as intended by the receiver. If one takes inference or assumption as fact rather than as speculation one fails to test out the validity of his inference or assumption. If one infers from the way a friend says hello that he is angry, when in fact he feels ill, there is an absence of intentional communication.

Our ability to communicate symbolically distinguishes us from other animal life and frees us to learn from the experiences of others. All the kinds of language discussed in this chapter are necessary, vital components of a rich creative language. If we misuse our language we contaminate it so that it is no longer capable of conveying our inner experiences to another.

Summary   This chapter has explored the different kinds of language used in the message. These are the important points:

1. A word should correspond to its referent as a map to a territory.
2. A euphemism is a word with pleasant connotations that is substituted for one that is harsh, indelicate, or otherwise unpleasant or taboo.
3. There are distinctions between judgmental language and reporting language.
4. Judgmental language contains a conclusion and thereby expresses an attitude toward the referent.
5. Judgmental language is colored by the attitudes of the speaker; inferences are meanings implied by the sender or imputed by the receiver.
6. An inference draws from the known (that which is stated) some conclusion about the unknown (that which is not stated).
7. Assumptions rely on past experiences to predict a present or future event.
8. Slanting is another form of incorporating attitudes in language.
9. Slanting is the process in which one selects to include only those details that support his point of view.
10. Slanting may be accomplished by incorporating judgments, inferences and assumptions, or by using only those "facts" that make one's case.
11. Language that does not color the meaning, and is free of the kinds of language heretofore described, is called reporting language.
12. Reporting language is verifiable; it can be proven true or untrue. Judgmental language is never true or untrue, since it presents opinion.
13. Interference with intended meaning in communication can occur due to language choice.

1. List euphemisms common in everyday conversation.
2. How does one go about verifying a statement?
3. Can the following weather report be verified?

   "Foggy tonight. More humid weather expected tomorrow. The weekend will be sunny and warm. Some showers."

4. What are the similarities and differences between an inference and an assumption?
5. How does one determine whether the message should be a report or made up of judgmental language?
6. When a doctor tells a patient about his health, is his statement a report or a judgment?
7. Why do general semanticists say that judgmental language tells nothing about the referent?
8. Why should a word conform to its referent as a map to its territory?

1. S. I. Hayakawa, *Language in Thought and Action,* 2d. ed. (New York: Harcourt, Brace and World, 1964), p. 86.
2. For a thorough discussion of inferences as high level abstractions, see Wendell Johnson, *People in Quandaries* (New York: Harper and Brothers, 1946).
3. For a detailed discussion of slanting, read Hayakawa's section on "snarl" and "purr" words in *Language in Thought and Action.*
4. Gordon Wiseman and Larry Barker, *Speech: Interpersonal Communication* (San Francisco, Calif.: Chandler Publishing Company, 1967), p. 132–33.
5. Hayakawa, *Language in Thought and Action,* p. 39.

Budd, Richard. "General Semantics." In *Approaches to Human Communication,* edited by Richard Budd and Brent Ruben. New York: Spartan Books, 1972. An anthology of articles on different approaches to the study of communication. Recommended as a survey for the student interested in more complex explanations of the phenomenon.

Chase, Stuart. *Power of Words.* New York: Harcourt, Brace and Company, 1953. A good introduction to general semantics for the beginning student.

Hayakawa, S. I. *Language in Thought and Action.* 2d ed. New York: Harcourt, Brace and World, 1964. A good introduction to general semantics for the beginning student.

Hertzler, Joyce O. *A Sociology of Language.* New York: Random House, 1965. Recommended for the student interested in knowledge and reality construction.

Rapoport, Anatol. *Operational Philosophy.* New York: Harper & Row, 1953. Recommended for the student with some background in communication and general semantics.

Johnson, Wendell. *Living With Change: The Semantics of Coping,* edited by Dorothy Moeller. New York: Harper & Row, 1972. Recommended for the student interested in general semantics. A clear explanation of the relationship between language and mental hygiene.

Language and Reality: Abstracting and Extensional Devices

8

Introduction

A story is told of a movie director who hired his best friend's sixteen-year-old son to run errands on the set of a movie he was filming. Unfortunately, the boy was so star struck that he was more of a hindrance than a help to the director. The boy arrived on the set at 6:00 A.M. (the cast had all been there since 5:00 A.M.). He was sent out to get coffee but forgot the sugar, and confused the tops of the black coffee containers with those marked regular. When he was given a mop to clean the floor, no one told him to put water in the bucket, so he tried to dry-mop it clean. Since the boy wás so young and the son of the director's best friend, the director did not want to fire him (at least on the first day). He therefore "promoted" him and gave him the title "assistant to the director's assistant," a position in which his chores could be carefully supervised. When the boy arrived home at 7:00 P.M., he proudly told his parents about the day's events. "I arrived at 6:00 A.M.; got everyone coffee; swept the set; bought the lunches, and by afternoon, received a promotion."

The events that occurred in this story, the boy's interpretation of them, and the way in which he framed the message about them, all have to do with the aspect of message making to which we address ourselves in this chapter.

This chapter focuses on the aspect of message making involving perception and selection. The message maker is viewed as a selective responder to certain stimuli and as the encoder of a message that reflects his perception and selection. The process to which we refer is known as **abstraction.** One's choice of language is reflective of the degree to which he has perceived stimuli to which he responds by verbal message making. Some semantic devices enabling him to avoid unwanted loss of the specific will also be discussed.

Communication Goals

This chapter uses the theoretical and experiential approaches to continue the exploration of verbal language processes. It is written to enable you to:

1. Understand the process of abstracting.
2. Learn about the relationship between perception and abstraction.
3. Develop an awareness of the factors affecting the way in which one perceives and abstracts.
4. Learn the semantic devices available to make the "map" correspond more accurately to the "territory."
5. Be more sensitive to the use of language in message making.

Communication Concepts and Experiences

In the story at the outset of this chapter, the teenager did not lie to his parents when he got home. He told them the truth as he saw it. He described to them how he saw his day. He would probably have been startled had he heard the very different versions others would have had of his performance. This is because the object of one's experience is not the thing itself but rather an interaction between the thing and one's own nervous system.[1] The process whereby one perceives stimuli, responds to them, and labels, or names them is known as **abstracting.** Communication experience 8.1 is designed to illustrate the process.

Communication Experience 8.1

Principle

The process of abstraction involves one's selective perceptions of the stimuli in his environment.

Procedure

1. Work individually.
2. Using the language of "reports," compose a list of those things present in the room in which the class is meeting.
3. After ten minutes stop writing.
4. Compare lists.

Discussion

What are the similarities and differences between lists composed by various class members? Were there differences in terms of sequencing as well as inclusion or omission? What factors affected the things a person included? What does this tell about the list makers? What are the implications for communication?

The Process of Abstracting

As illustrated in communication experience 8.1, the human being responds to some, but not all, of the stimuli present in a given situation. Psychologists refer to this process as **selective perception.** Selective perception is the process by which the individual attends to some of the stimuli in a given situation because he cannot, either physically or

AS PICASSO SAID, WHY ASSUME THAT TO LOOK IS TO SEE?

psychologically, attend to all those stimuli that surround him. The process of abstracting is formulated in the general semanticists' view of human's use of language. It simply states that there are limitations upon our abilities to "see" the world around us, and that our language restricts us even further when we attempt to communicate our observations to others.[2] When we speak of *abstracting,* we refer to the ways in which people separate from, draw out, or extract something from a given whole. The story of the boy on the movie set presents an example of the way in which he extracted certain details about his experience. Because his abstracting was different from that of the other people involved, he presented the events as he saw them. Other people, such as the producer, would have given a very different picture of what occurred. In communication experience 8.1, abstracting was illustrated by what different people "saw" and the different words or symbols that they used to encode those things that they included in their descriptions.

    The process of abstracting is a way of understanding that there are limitations on that which we are able to see, hear, smell, taste, and touch. The words we choose to describe our experiences by necessity include some details while omitting others. Before describing the process of abstracting in further detail, let us explore some of the factors that influence the ways in which we abstract, or select.

Factors Influencing Abstracting

The factors influencing the ways in which one abstracts at any given moment can be divided into four categories: (1) one's ability to discriminate, (2) the structure of the abstracting organism, (3) one's position in time and space in relation to that which he observes, and (4) one's life orientation.[3]

One's ability to discriminate refers to how much one has learned, or how discriminating one has become. In other words, how much a person has learned about a given thing will affect what she notes about it. A professional wine taster will abstract more and different details about a glass of wine she is tasting than a young man at his first wine and cheese party. If one knits, or sculpts, or builds things, he will notice more details when looking at a sweater, a sculpture, or a shelf than a person who does not do these things himself. When an actor goes to see a stage play, he notices the set, design, costuming, and actors' makeup. These things are often unnoticed by the ordinary playgoer. One's training or ability to discriminate is one factor influencing the stimuli he selects to respond to in any given situation.

The second factor, the structure of the abstracting organism, influences the way in which one abstracts.[4] In a broad sense, the total human being is the abstracting organism. How fit a person is physically and emotionally determines how able she will be at noting and responding to stimuli. In a more limited sense, however, the abstracting organism

refers to one's five senses. A person who has a hearing loss will not detect as many auditory stimuli as a person with normal hearing. A person who is color blind will not be able to see as much as a person with normal vision, no matter how earnest her attempt to do so may be. A physical (or emotional) impairment in the structure interferes with and limits one's ability to perceive. The opposite holds true, too. A more highly developed sense of taste permits one to get more out of an avocado than someone with a head cold. Whether or not one uses these abilities relates to the first factor: the ability and desire to discriminate.

The third factor that influences abstracting in a given situation is one's position in time and space. What one sees or hears and where one is in relation to it influences what he selects. If one is rushing home late at night, he pays less attention to the trees lining the streets on his route than he would during an early autumn walking jaunt. A spectator at a football game has a different physical perspective than a viewer watching the same game at home on television. Students in the front row of a lecture may be much more aware of the physical mannerisms of the lecturer than those seated in the back, who are more involved in trying to hear what he says.

The last factor we mentioned, related to abstracting, concerns one's field of experience. If a decorator, janitor, and student walk into a classroom, differences in their training and interests explain why they notice different things. For instance, the student is more aware of the people in the room than the decor or the cigarette butts on the floor. A person whose past experiences have made him aware of racial and ethnic groups notices clues regarding strangers' ethnic and racial background on first meeting them. One who is weight conscious is more aware of physiques.

These, then, are the factors influencing abstracting. Thus far, our examples have illustrated abstracting in terms of physical and sensory kinds of things, but the process of abstracting has to do with language. Communication experience 8.2 is designed to illustrate abstraction as a language process.

Communication Experience 8.2

Principle

In terms of communication, the process of abstracting is a language process.

Procedure

1. Work in groups of six-to-eight people.
2. Select several pictures from magazines and/or newspapers.
3. Each member of the group writes down *one* word to describe what is depicted by each of the pictures.
4. After doing this, compare words chosen by the group members to describe each picture.
5. If the selected words differ, determine the reasons.

Discussion

Did the words used to describe the pictures tell more about the pictures or the persons describing them? In what ways did group members differ in their labeling of pictures? If members were to use the words and not the pictures to communicate, what would happen? What are the implications for communication?

The Ladder of Abstraction

The process of abstracting includes both the world of words and the world of not-words, or nonverbal things; and the steps necessary to bridge the gap between these two worlds. We invent symbols, words, to represent those not-words, or referents. We explore the process of abstracting by tracing our steps from observation to symbolization; from selectively

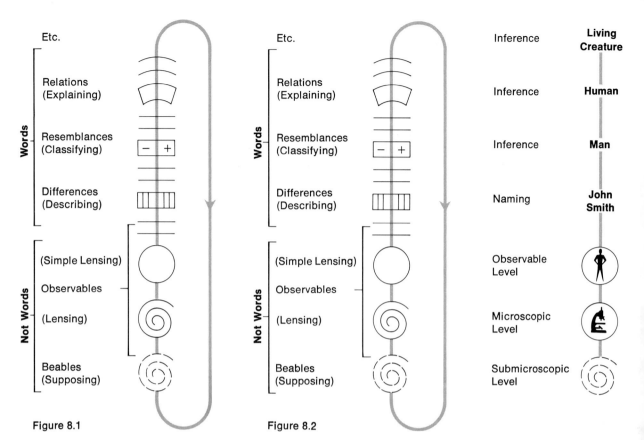

Figure 8.1

Figure 8.2

responding to stimuli to encoding our perceptions verbally. The **ladder of abstraction** shown in figure 8.1[5] is a model by which we can illustrate the workings of this process. Figure 8.2 is an example of it.

The ladder of abstraction is used to show that there are levels of abstraction in language. By levels, we refer to the degrees to which a word selects and includes details about its referent, or limits and omits details about it. In this model, lower level abstractions incorporate numerous detail. The higher the level of abstraction, the less detail is included and thus the more abstract or general the word. For example, the name *John Smith* is a lower level of abstraction than the word *man*, and *man* is a lower level of abstraction than the word *human*. The reason *John Smith* is lower on the ladder of abstraction is because it includes more detail: we know the species, sex, and name. With the word *man* as the level of abstraction, we know less detail; we know only the species and sex. The word *human* is an even higher level abstraction than *man* because it leaves out more detail. The word *human* tells us only the species. We do not know the sex, name, or other details.

Figure 8.1
Ladder of Abstraction.

Figure 8.2
Example of Abstracting.

The metaphor *ladder* for the concept of abstracting is used to show that one can climb up or down in the process of abstraction. We can go from the lower rungs *John Smith* to higher ones, *man, human, living creatures*. We could also start high on that ladder and work our way down: *living creatures, human, man, John Smith*. Of primary significance is the understanding that abstraction is the process of incorporating or omitting details about the thing to which we refer. Communication experience 8.3 is designed to illustrate the ways in which we climb and descend the ladder of abstraction.

Communication Experience 8.3

Principle

Effective communicators need to be able to move up and down the ladder of abstraction verbally as necessitated by the given communication encounter.

Procedure

1. Work in groups of five-to-seven people.
2. Sit in a circle.
3. One person picks a word. The next person selects a word that represents a step up the ladder of abstraction.
4. Each person in the circle takes a turn moving the word up the ladder of abstraction until the group decides it can go no further.
5. The next person names a new word. The same procedure is followed, except this time the group moves down the ladder of abstraction.
6. When this is completed, the group goes around once again. This time each person designates whether the word he offers is a step up or down the ladder of abstraction in relation to the word said by the person directly preceding him.
7. Group members correct any errors as they proceed.

Discussion

Were some words more difficult to deal with than others? Were there any difference between proceeding up and down the ladder? What is the outcome in terms of group members' awareness of the process of abstracting? What are the implications for message making?

As illustrated in communication experience 8.3, the process of abstracting is the verbal method used to symbolize observations of events or referents. It is that process by which details are selected or omitted;

such selection or omission determines the ways in which one refers to the referent. That is, referring to a man as *John Smith* incorporates more detail than referring to him as *a living creature*. It provides the receiver with more detailed information and is therefore to be used when more detailed information is appropriate to the message the sender intends to convey. If a man has just been seen running from a bank with a gun in his hand and a sack of cash under his arm, a policeman questioning an observer at the scene would prefer the description "John Smith" to "a living creature." On the other hand, in response to the question, "What's the population of this town?" the answer "10,000 people" is preferable to a list naming those 10,000 people.

In our discussion of the diagram presented in figure 8.1, we have started at midpoint: the level designated as the *nameable* level. The levels below that on the ladder are grouped together as the levels of *not-words.*

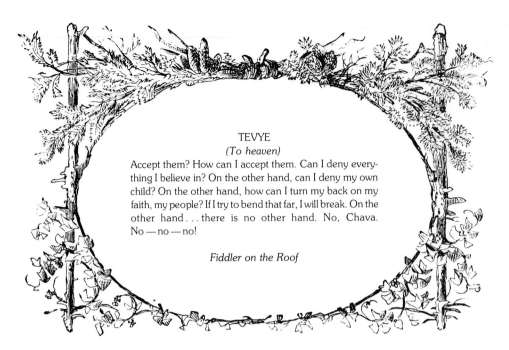

TEVYE

(To heaven)

Accept them? How can I accept them. Can I deny everything I believe in? On the other hand, can I deny my own child? On the other hand, how can I turn my back on my faith, my people? If I try to bend that far, I will break. On the other hand . . . there is no other hand. No, Chava. No — no — no!

Fiddler on the Roof

These are included in the ladder to indicate that even before we reach the level of naming something, more detail exists that we have left out in that naming step. The three levels of the *not-words* part of the ladder are referred to as *simple lensing* (that which we can see; in our example, the man John Smith); *lensing* (that which we can see with the aid of a microscope or some other form of instrumentation, e.g. John's molecular makeup); and *being* (all those details making up matter that we cannot even observe with the instrumentation we have thus far invented). The oval with an arrow to the right in the diagram is there to indicate that as we become aware of our abstracting, we constantly check the word against the thing for which it stands; we move back-and-forth between the verbal world of words and the nonverbal, not-word referents.

Lower level abstractions include more details about the actual referents for which the words stand than higher level abstractions. The map specifies the territory by its inclusion of detail. In moving to higher level abstractions, more detail is left out. The referent becomes more vague and the class of possible referents becomes larger. The word *man* includes a large number of possible referents. *John Smith* limits the possibilities to those men named *John Smith*. Higher level abstractions are more generalized and include more numbers of potential referents while leaving out the details that might enable one to distinguish the exact referent in the mind of the person referring to it. This is indicated in the diagram by making the squares larger and larger on the higher steps. As details about the actual referent are left out, the category to which the word applies is larger. Abstractions then are generalizations. Describing an animal as "domestic" is more of a generalization than saying "dog" or more specifically "my pet poodle." It is this final point about abstracting that has strong implications for the message maker. Communication experience 8.4 is designed to illustrate this point.

Communication Experience 8.4

Principle

High-level abstractions are more generalized statements, more removed from their referent in terms of details than lower level abstractions.

Procedure

1. Work in groups of about ten.
2. Find as many descriptive words as possible that can be used to describe everyone in the group. A word that does not apply to all members is to be eliminated.
3. List the words and discuss their value as sources of information about any given individual in the group.

Discussion

What kinds of words were the group members able to select? At what level of abstraction were the descriptives? How valuable are they as sources of information? What are their drawbacks? What are the implications for communication?

Abstracting and Message Making

As illustrated by communication experience 8.4, the ways in which one abstracts have effects on his message making and the ways in which the message is perceived by the intended receiver. As with the perception of any object, the thing perceived is never the thing itself but an interaction between the thing and one's nervous system. When a person looks at someone and selects his name to refer to him, he is including only certain details and leaving out others. Another person perceiving him might say "blonde," "tall," or "Greek."

Understanding the nature of abstracting is particularly relevant to the judgmental quality of language. Even in a "report," the reporter selects the details she wishes to include and leaves out those she unintentionally misses or purposely decides to omit. The reporter cannot be separated from that which she reports; the reporter is the one who selects what to include in a report. This is true even when one reports about oneself. When asked to describe herself, a woman might say she is a mother, wife, artist, teacher, Catholic, Chicagoan, democrat, etc. In selecting some labels, she excludes others. The higher up the ladder of abstraction one goes, the more details are omitted and the greater the likelihood for two complications to occur in message making. (1) Two different people can have the same referent in mind, but by choosing such different labels it may not be clear that the object is one and the same. One person refers to a woman as Sam's wife. Another describes her as an artist. (2) The same abstraction can be used to refer to two referents that have some quality in common although they differ in most other respects. This is at the basis for such statements as "all Jews are smart," "all politicians lie," or "all women want to be mothers."

The process of abstracting is both unavoidable and necessary. We cannot see, hear, smell, touch or taste everything. In omitting some details, we can pay attention to those that are essential. One must, however, be able to go up and down the ladder of abstraction depending on how much detail is appropriate to the given communication interaction. Abstracting, therefore, is a fundamental process in the message-making aspect of communication. It relates specifically to reports and judgmental language. Higher level abstractions are less inclusive of detail and are thereby more judgmental. Lower level abstractions are closer to reports: they include more detail than do more abstract terms.

Extensional Devices: Language Pollution Controls

Language is a crude tool with which to communicate. So much can interfere with or distort the meaning intended by words that one can question whether or not one person can ever really communicate his exact meaning to another. There are however certain semantic devices to use to ensure a greater degree of accuracy in one's use of language. These are called *extensional devices* and are used to control distortion of language. Since neither people nor the world remains static, one's language and use of it, too, must be dynamic. The purpose of extensional devices is to allow language to be as dynamic and changeable as the reality it depicts.

Despite its detail, no map can show all there is to know about the territory. Neither can words represent everything about an occurrence. As indicated by the process of abstracting, some details are left out in each instance. The purpose of extensional devices is to compensate for those omitted details. Extensional devices are used to fit the language more closely to the physical world it depicts. These semantic devices serve to adjust the map to its territory. The five kinds of extensional devices are: *dates, indexes, etc., quotes,* and *hyphens.*[6]

The first extensional device is the use of **dates.** Dating is used to indicate that objects are in a constant process of change. The person of today is not exactly the same person he was five years ago or even last year. America$_{1978}$ is not the America$_{1888}$. *Dates* help to remind one of the constant evolution of people, places, and things. Where it matters to the message maker to specify when in time and space he is referring to something, then dating is of the utmost significance. The professor who speaks of the college student ought to specify "the college student, 1965" or "the college student, 1975" for his commentary to have and real relation to its referent.

Indexing is the second extensional device mentioned. *Index numbers* are used to show that even when objects belong to the same class, each is unique unto itself. Generalizing can be a misleading factor in terms of communication. By indexing, the awareness that boy$_1$ is not boy$_2$ is not boy$_3$ is indicated. All have one aspect in common; they are male children. But, this does not mean they are all the same. Cat$_1$ is not cat$_2$ is not cat$_3$. Just because Boots is a cat doesn't mean he is as friendly as Tiger. All teachers, all students, all movie stars, all housewives, all CPAs have something in common with the other members of their group; each is a unique person. When one says, "Oh, you know how those Blacks are," we ought to answer, "Yes, Black." The only information the word *black* gives is someone's race. Anything else is inference and assumption.

The third extension device **etc.** indicates that in describing anything some details or characteristics are left out. It is a reminder that the map or word is always an incomplete representative of its referent. Etc. may be verbalized, written, or mental, so long as it is there. It keeps things in a proper perspective. No one knows all or tells all about a subject. When describing a friend, car, or favorite author, only some of the details regarding the referent are told, no matter how many appear to be given.

The fourth extensional device **quotes** are a way of indicating that a statement is neither all-inclusive nor necessarily *true*-to-fact. Quotes call attention to the enclosed word-symbol to indicate that more could be said about the referent. Quotes set the words inside them apart from other words.

In written communication, quotation marks tell the reader to look more carefully at the word in quotes, paying particular attention to the context in which it is used. They remind the reader that words mean

fifty

WAYS

to leave your

LOVER

Paul Simon

The problem is all inside your head
She said to me
The answer is easy if you
Take it logically
I'd like to help you in your struggle
To be free
There must be fifty ways
To leave your lover

She said it's really not my habit
To intrude
Furthermore, I hope my meaning
Won't be lost or misconstrued
But I'll repeat myself
At the risk of being crude
There must be fifty ways
To leave your lover
Fifty ways to leave your lover

You just slip out the back, Jack
Make a new plan, Stan
You don't need to be coy, Roy
Just get yourself free
Hop on the bus, Gus
You don't need to discuss much
Just drop off the key, Lee
And get yourself free

She said it grieves me so
To see you in such pain
I wish there was something I could do
To make you smile again
I said I appreciate that
And would you please explain
About the fifty ways

She said why don't we both
Just sleep on it tonight
And I believe in the morning
You'll begin to see the light
And then she kissed me
And I realized she probably was right
There must be fifty ways
To leave your lover
Fifty ways to leave your lover

You just slip out the back, Jack
Make a new plan, Stan
You don't need to be coy, Roy
Just get yourself free
Hop on the bus, Gus
You don't need to discuss much
Just drop off the key, Lee
And get yourself free

different things to different people. Quotes may also be used in oral communication. They can be either verbal (and I said he's *quote* liberal *unquote*) and/or visual (use of the hands to make quote marks in the air while verbalizing the word *quote*). Since higher level abstractions may often be far removed from the concrete referent, the use of quotes may be essential to indicate that the word can mean many different things to many different people. Even such an ordinary word as *wealthy* is vague enough to merit the use of quotes in particular circumstances.

The last extensional device are **hyphens** a way of indicating the connections between things that ordinarily seem unconnected. They are a way of saying that not all things must be either one thing or the other. Sometimes something is both good-bad, love-hate, right-wrong. The use of a hyphen is a shortcut to say something is both of these things, not one or the other. Our language tends to divide natural phenomena and categorize them. Hyphens are a semantic device indicating the "oneness" of things. The hyphen helps to explain the relationship between things that might otherwise be referred to as if they were two totally separate entities.

Language and Reality

The five devices discussed are methods of extending meaning. By relating words more closely to the world they depict, the gap between the word and its referent created in the process of abstraction is lessened. Language is a human tool for communicating. But, using language to deceive or mislead pollutes language. Promoting a blind date for a woman one considers undesirable physically by saying she "has a lovely personality"; selling a product by calling it "new and improved"; or advocating a politician's candidacy by referring to him as "a man of the people" pollute language by taking advantage of the gap between the word and the thing. These phrases mislead not because they have no meaning, but rather because they each have too many possible meanings. Such statements can mean anything to anyone because there is no recognizable connection between the word and the reality. All words mean different things to different people. This is a problem of language and the whole symbolic process. As message makers people who know this make choices: they use their words as ways of portraying reality as they see it or they use words to distort that reality so as to deceive their receivers. Extensional devices are the semantic tools available to the message maker desirous of presenting as clear a representation of reality as he sees it to the person to whom he addresses his message. They are available to him when and if he sees his role as such. Communication experience 8.5 is designed to illustrate these kinds of choices.

Communication Experience 8.5

Principle

Sometimes the relationship between the map and territory needs clarification. Extensional devices are those semantic tools used to make the symbol more reflective of the referent.

Procedure

1. Work in groups of five-to-seven people.
2. Examine the following hypothetical situations.
   a. John asks Bill, "Who's your speech professor?" Bill replies, "Professor Cook; here's his picture." (Bill shows John a picture of a six-month-old baby on a bearskin rug. It is a picture of Professor Cook.)
   b. Jack tells his friends that his fiancee was president of S.D.S. He does not say that she resigned in 1967 when S.D.S. policy became violent.
   c. Politician X has taken a stand against German nationalism. He is considered to be foresighted by a constituent who reads this in Politician X's biography.
3. Discuss the problems inherent in the statements in these situations.

Discussion

Are these statements very different from the kinds of statements one often hears in everyday communication? What are the problems with them? What can be done to correct the problems? What are the implications about language and message making?

Interference with Intentional Communication

Interference with intended meaning in communication exists wherever high-level abstractions are used without checking for feedback as to the receiver's understanding. Problems in communication always occur unless the speaker relates at the level of abstraction appropriate to the subject and intended receiver. When a patient goes to see his dentist, he doesn't want to hear vague generalities or high level abstractions about health, in general, or dental hygienics. He wants specific information about his teeth and their present condition. On the other hand, if the dentist were to give the patient every technical detail regarding his mouth, he would be as unenlightened as if the dentist were too vague. So, too, when a tennis coach is correcting a beginner's stroke, he must coach using language on the level of abstraction most helpful to the novice.

Interference with intended meaning also occurs when there is a lack of clarity as to what one person means by the words he chooses to use when talking to another. The danger is that communicators are often unaware that anything has gone wrong. If both communicators know the language used, it is very easy for them to assume that they understand it to mean the same thing. This constitutes another possible interference in communication.

Still another interference occurs when one fails to use extensional devices that are mandated by the given communication situation. As explained earlier in this chapter, each device is a way of avoiding ambiguity and of bringing the word into more accurate correspondence with reality. When speaking on a high level of abstracting, failure to indicate *quotes* may leave the receiver unaware of the context in which the sender is using the words. Failure to *index* or *date* creates a statement lacking the essential specifics. Omission of *etc.* may imply that one has "said it all," when, in actuality, this can never be the case. Examples of each of these possible sources of interference with communication abound. Communicating that which one intends means that we have command of the language we use as well as an understanding of the sources of possible confusion when communicating symbolically.

Summary

This chapter has focused on the process of abstracting and the extensional devices one can use to limit ambiguity. The important points are:

1. When observing the same object, different people see and include different details to describe it; this process is called abstracting.
2. The object perceived is an interaction between the thing and the nervous system of the perceiver.
3. Four factors influence the process of abstracting.
    a. *Ability to discriminate.*
    b. *Structure of the abstracting organism.*
    c. *Position in time and space.*
    d. *Life orientation.*
4. The process of abstraction relates to the ways in which one selects language in the process of communication.
5. The ladder of abstraction illustrates that there are levels or degrees of abstraction.
6. Lower level abstractions are those that incorporate numerous detail; the higher the level of abstraction, the less the detail and thus the more vague the referent.
7. Two functions are involved in becoming aware of the process of abstracting.

a. *Understanding that the person reporting affects that which is reported.*

b. *Using language that includes as much detail as is wanted or called for in the given interaction.*

8. Extensional devices can be used to fit the "map" to the "territory"; they include:

a. *Dates*

b. *Indexes*

c. *Etc.*

d. *Quotes*

e. *Hyphens*

9. Interference with intentional communication occurs when the proper degree of abstraction or when extensional devices are not used.

Questions for Discussion

1. Take the word *nation* and make an abstraction ladder that proceeds up and down from the word.

2. Explain a communication situation in which it would be necessary to use *etc.*

3. What value do hyphens serve?

4. Explain the statement: "To perceive everything is to make sense of nothing."

5. Give examples of ways in which one's ability to discriminate and/or one's life orientation affect how one abstracts. In what ways are the two related?

6. What kinds of communication situations call for highly abstract language? Which would mandate low-level abstraction?

7. Why must one be aware of abstracting if it is necessary for everyday living?

8. What are the dangers in abstracting?

9. Why is the object perceived never the actual thing?

10. How is abstracting related to reporting and judgmental language?

11. Explain the semantic value of dating and indexing.

12. Explain the value of extensional devices in communicating intrapersonally.

Notes

1. S. I. Hayakawa, *Language in Thought and Action,* 2d ed. (New York: Harcourt, Brace and World, Inc., 1949), p. 176.

2. Richard Budd, "General Semantics," in *Approaches to Human Communication,* ed. Richard Budd and Brent Ruben (New York: Spartan Press, 1972), p. 103.

3. Gordon Wiseman and Larry Barker, *Speech—Interpersonal Communication* (San Francisco, Calif.: Chandler Publishing Co., 1967), p. 100.

4. This term is used by Hayakawa. Other general semanticists refer to the concept by terms such as "the abstracting process" and "process of abstracting." We use them interchangeably.

5. The model of the ladder of abstraction is a simplification of Johnson's model presented in *Living with Change,* edited by Dorothy Moeller (New York: Harper & Row, 1972).

6. Stuart Chase, *The Power of Words* (New York: Harcourt, Brace and Co., 1953), pp. 139ff.

Selected Bibliography

Budd, Richard. "General Semantics." In *Approaches to Human Communication,* edited by Richard Budd and Brent Ruben. New York: Spartan Books, 1972. Recommended as a synthesis of writings in the area of general semantics. Useful for its evaluation of general semantics as a theory of communication.

Chase, Stuart. *Power of Words.* New York: Harcourt, Brace and Company, 1953. A good introduction to language. Especially recommended for detailed discussion of language acquisition and use.

Hayakawa, S. I. *Language in Thought and Action.* 2d ed. New York: Harcourt, Brace and Company, 1949. A good basic introduction to general semantics.

Johnson, Wendell. *People in Quandaries.* New York: Harper and Brothers, 1946. Recommended for further reading in the relationship between language and mental health.

Thayer, Lee. *Communication and Communication Systems.* Homewood, Ill.: Richard D. Irwin, 1964. An in-depth approach to communication for the student with some background and/or interest in language, behavior, and human organization.

communumicate
CHURCH GAMBLING
STAMP OUT MENTAL HEALTH
COME BACK TRUMAN ALL IS FORGIVEN
INVESTIGATE GOD *
SOME OF MY BEST FRIENDS ARE
EAT FAT
$
MUZZLE MUZAK
TAKE A HIPPY TO LUNCH
UP
WAR IS GOOD BUSINESS $ INVEST YOUR SON
"LEVITATE"
FRODO LIVES
PEANUT BUTTER IS BETTER THAN POT
I'LL NEVER FORGET WHAT'S HER NAME
I AM ANONYMOUS HELP ME
MARY POPPINS IS A JUNKIE
LOVE IS GOD
CHARLES EDWARD WHITE III RULES THE WORLD
DON'T READ THIS BUTTON
CA
TURN ON TUNE IN DROP OUT GET WELL
IF YOU CAN READ THIS YOU'RE TOO CLOSE
come alive!
GREAT SOCIETY
curse you RED BARON
PIGLET LIVES
LEMMINGS ARE SILLY. DINOSAURS ARE EXTINCT. S.P.U.
KISS DON'T KILL
OLD ENOUGH TO FIGHT, OLD ENOUGH TO VOTE
SPU
LOVE IS LOVELY WAR IS UGLY
REPEAL INHIBITION
I HATE EVERYBODY
JESUS SAVES GREEN STAMPS

The Relationship of Language and Culture

9

Introduction

Any set of symbols, or code, is a language. In dissecting the message aspect of interpersonal communication, we are concerned with verbal language, the language of words.

Along with our technological advancements, we have progressed in our contact with and our elementary understanding of cultures other than our own. Most people today are aware that people of different cultures live in ways that differ from our ways of living. Even within our own culture, we become increasingly aware of different life-styles.

Verbal language is one of those things learned in a cultural context. To understand the functions and uses of language, it must be viewed in relation to culture.

Communication Goals

This chapter uses the theoretical and experiential approach to investigate effects of one's culture on his message making. It is written to enable you to:

1. Understand the cultural nature of language acquisition.
2. Become aware of the socializing and uniformizing pressures exerted on communicators by language.
3. Explore the ways in which one's language structure and habits color one's observations and interpretations of the world.
4. Understand "openness" and "self-disclosure" as message-making strategies that have cultural determinants.

Communication Concepts and Experiences

Communicators are affected by the cultures in which they live and the socialization processes of those cultures. In this chapter we will pursue the subject further by exploring the effects of one's culture on language development and usage. At the same time we will investigate the effect of culture on one's perceptions, personality, and message making.

Verbal Language and Culture

It is difficult to talk of language without talking of culture, for the two are hard to separate. There are myths in our culture about abandoned children found and raised by wolves; and sensational stories of children isolated in closets or attics until they are somehow discovered and their abusers punished. What language, if any, such children may have acquired could be no more than vocal grunts, more animallike in nature than human. For language is acquired by a human having been born and raised in a linguistic society. A child in isolation, therefore, would not develop the symbolic human language we have been analyzing.[1]

Speech and a well-ordered language are characteristics of every known group of human beings. In fact, no tribe has ever been found without some form of language.[2] Verbal language, which is a system of phonetic symbols used to express thoughts or feelings, could also be considered gesture. It is gesture that is listened to rather than watched. Speech is gesture made audible.[3] If one wants to communicate to someone to sit down in a chair, he can use gestures or words to convey his message. One distinction between humans and other animals is this ability to have speech replace gesture. The primary function of language is as a means of communication. The more highly developed the language, the more complex the material that can be communicated. Because the symbols in the game of tic-tac-toe are limited to *X* and *O,* there is only two possible players and a finite number of ways of combining those symbols.

Besides serving as a source of communication, language acts as a force in socializing and uniformizing. Through language each society controls the behavior of its members by defining and molding how one is able to express himself. The very forms of our thoughts are affected by the language patterns we learn from infancy on.[4] Communication experience 9.1 is designed to illustrate this point.

Communication Experience 9.1

Principle

Our world and how we perceive it are fashioned by our language structures.

Procedure

1. Work individually. After completing the following tasks, compare answers.
2. Someone reads the following instructions:
   a. *Take a pencil and draw a line on a piece of paper. Place three dots on that line, one to represent the beginning, one the middle, and one the end.*
   b. *With the pencil mark an X on the paper to represent today. Place a Y in relation to the X to indicate Yesterday, and a T in relation to the X to indicate Tomorrow.*

Discussion

How similar were the results? In what ways did they differ? Why? What does this have to do with our language structure? How does one's language affect his perceptions? What cultural concepts affect the answers? What are the implications for communicating with others?

Language, Thought, and Perception

As illustrated in communication experience 9.1, our culture affects our ways of thinking, including our perception of things. Language is a complex system that permits one to communicate with himself and others, and molds his ways of perceiving himself and his world. One's thinking affects his perception of things external to himself and his thinking follows the very specific tracks laid out for him by his language structure. If, for example, a person were given a piece of paper and a pencil and asked to draw a line, he would begin the line at the left and draw it towards the right; our language is constructed left to right—subject to predicate to object. A person whose native language is constructed right to left (Hebrew) or vertically (Chinese) might draw the line quite differently.

Many basic assumptions about the world and how it functions are expressed in terms of the structure of one's language. The grammar used to classify words in our language is also used to organize and classify reality. Rules invented for organizing words into classes and for defining

Viva Yo

In Spain, "viva yo" translates as "hurray for me" with an implication of "to hell with everyone else." A comprehension of the Spaniard's addiction to "viva yo" will help anyone trying to make his way in Spain. But suppose that one tries to make his way not in Spain but in Japan? The self-assertive "viva yo" is quite different from the Japanese concept of "engryo". This concept according to anthropologists is "loosely translatable as hesitance or reserve."

"Viva yo" and "engryo" represent two different ways of making one's way and not necessarily differences between Spaniards and Japanese. Many Japanese urinate in the street, and many Spaniards are reserved. These are not necessarily national or group differences, nor are they differences between people who are self-assertive and those who are submissive. All people are a mixture of both. Different ways of making one's way are simply different responses [to the stimuli or event data of life].

Alfred Smith

the ordering of words into sentences are not necessarily the best rules for organizing reality. Embedded in this kind of language structure is the assumption that things themselves possess qualities, and that those qualities exist irrespective of the observer.[5] Because sentences in our language are structured around a subject, predicate, and object, we express our observations in this sequence. We say, "Mary is sweet," as if sweetness resided in Mary. The reality is that "sweetness" is a product of those vibrations that Mary gives off as interpreted by the person making the statement. Another person observing her behavior might label Mary "phony," "dumb," or whatever word-symbol represents his interpretation of her behavior.

Constructs in our languages such as "beginnings" and "endings" that are necessary to language are used in relation to reality to explain and define it. We have times of day that separate one day from another (12:00 AM is "tomorrow"); and times of year that distinguish one season from another (21 March is the first day of spring despite the weather). These divide up the ongoing process of reality as if it were itself separated in these ways. In fact, it is our language structure that permits (forces) us to impose this kind of structuring on reality. Different languages having different structures would therefore affect those using that language in different ways. It is not unusual to hear someone who is bilingual say that when he speaks and thinks in that other language, he "feels" himself to be a different person, expressing himself and his personality differently.

Language and culture are interwoven. The nature of one's language structure affects the ways in which one perceives the structure of the world he describes by the use of that language. One problem for writers and speakers of which we have become aware of only recently is the use of pronouns in our language structure. In the third person singular, the writer has three choices: *he, she,* and *it.* When referring to a person, *it* is eliminated because the rules of our grammar limit its use to nonhuman referents. *He,* often used to refer to any human, male or female, seems to carry gender associations. But such variations as *he/she, (s)he, his/her,* etc., becomes so cumbersome that they interfere with meaning. In writing this text, I have sometimes used *one* as an alternative to *he* or *he/she;* but *one* has a tendency of formalizing the tone of what is being said. As an alternate strategy, I decided to interchange *he* and *she.* This is a way of neutralizing the sexism in the overuse of *he.* Because we are not accustomed to this method, *she* references may have a tendency to stand out more than is desirable.

The connections between language and culture relate to the process of abstracting discussed in the previous chapter. A person cannot see, hear, feel, or sense all the stimuli in her environment. In abstracting, one selects those stimuli to which to respond. Our culture and the language structure, which is part of that culture, are the filters through which we perceive and abstract stimuli from our environment. Because we are a racially conscious culture, we notice one another's race; not many people in our culture notice one another's shoe size.

Culture and the Message

One's culture molds one's language, at the same time as the structure of that language shapes the culture. Let us look now at the direct relationship between culture and message making.

As with other forms of behavior, language grows organically within any culture, changing as the need arises. In no way do we express ourselves in the formal manner used by the Pilgrims who settled this country, who referred to others as *thou* and *thine.* Nor would words like

atom, automobile, or *automation* have been present in the vocabulary of an American in the 1900s, because no referents existed for these symbols New terms are invented as needed and so language and culture grow hand-in-hand. The verbal messages one chooses to send must be framed in the language available to one in the culture of the time.

A given culture exerts as much pressure on how one expresses himself verbally as it does on the ways in which one dresses or eats his meals. A curse in one society, when translated, might be just a harmless phrase in another society. So, too, with a term of endearment. For example, an American family would not name a son Jesus, yet Spanish families do so frequently. In the American culture to do so would be a blasphemy. In the Spanish culture it is a tribute.

One becomes aware of these cultural differences in studying other languages. The romance languages, structurally more similar than dissimilar to English, manifest an imprint of culture on the message when one tries to translate an idiom. Communication experience 9.2 is designed to illustrate the relationship between culture and message making.

Communication Experience 9.2

Principle

One's culture affects the ways in which he frames his messages and determines those subjects about which one can communicate.

Procedure

1. The entire class works as a group.
2. Have a discussion session in which the goal is to frame some working definitions of the words *culture* and *subculture.*
3. Discuss as much information as possible about the different cultural backgrounds of class members.
4. Discuss what, if any, difference knowing these things will make in future attempts at communicating with one another.

Discussion

What effects do the geographical backgrounds and ethnic groups to which class members belong have on the ways in which they communicate? Are the kinds of things discussed in class of value to know about other people with whom one tries to communicate? What are the implications for communication?

Those terms that are taboo and for which we invent euphemisms are determined unacceptable by the given culture. An interesting example is the use of profanity. One's culture determines what is profane and what is not. It determines who can say what under what conditions. In the 1930s film *Gone with the Wind,* the climactic scene is one in which the hero rebuffs Scarlett O'Hara by saying, "Frankly, my dear, I don't give a damn." The inclusion of this line was a milestone in 1939 when the picture was made. Cultural norms were such that this language was considered offensive. The scene was retained in the film only when the censors had been convinced that the drama of the moment would be lost were Rhett Butler, the very angry hero, to say, "Frankly, my dear, I don't give a garsh darn."

Subcultures, Language, and Communication

A **subculture** is any group or subset of the general culture that has its own social and behavioral norms and plays a part in the socialization of the individual.

One way of dividing subcultures is geographically. Another is to divide subcultures along socioeconomic, ethnic, age, and sexual lines.

Geographically speaking, there are attitudinal, behavioral, and linguistical differences. In general, Southerners tend to express themselves in a manner somewhat different from New Englanders. Certainly, as with any high-level abstraction or generalization, there are many exceptions. Nonetheless, one's geographical locale affects his manner of expression. In Providence, Rhode Island, a New Yorker went into a coffee shop and asked for a chocolate milk shake. What she had in mind was a mixture of chocolate ice cream, milk, and chocolate syrup beaten together into a thick mixture. What she got instead was a glass of chocolate milk that had been beaten. She explained what she had in mind. "Oh, you mean you want a 'cabinet'," said the waitress. If one is from Providence, Rhode Island, this would not seem the least bit peculiar. But if one is from another geographical locale where the same referent is referred to as a "milk shake," "malted," or "frappe," it might seem strange indeed to ask for a "cabinet," except in a furniture store.

The geographical area, therefore, determines some kinds of language usage. But even within these geographical boundaries, there are other subgroups that have their own influence on how the members of the group express themselves.

Communication experience 9.3 is designed to explore the effects of one's subculture on his message making.

Little Boxes

Malvina Reynolds

1. Little boxes on the hillside,
   Little boxes made of ticky tacky,
   Little boxes on the hillside,
   Little boxes all the same,
   There's a green one and a pink one,
   And a blue one and a yellow one,
   And they're all made out of ticky tacky,
   And they all look just the same.

2. And the people in the houses
   All went to the university,
   Where they were put in boxes
   And they came out all the same,
   And there's doctors and lawyers,
   And business executives,
   And they're all made out of ticky tacky
   And they all look just the same.

3. And they all play on the golf course
   And drink their martinis dry,
   And they all have pretty children
   And the children go to school,
   And the children go to summer camp
   And then to the university,
   Where they are put in boxes
   And they come out all the same.

4. And the boys go into business
   And marry and raise a family
   In boxes made of ticky tacky
   And they all look just the same.
   There's a green one and a pink one,
   And a blue one and a yellow one,
   And they're all made out of ticky tacky
   And they all look just the same.

Communication Experience 9.3

Principle

One's membership in subcultures influences the ways in which one communicates.

Procedure

1. Work in groups of three.
2. Draw up individual lists of the subcultures to which members of the group belong.
3. List three things that each subculture values highly; three taboos.
4. Compare and contrast lists.
5. Discuss what conclusions this leads to for interpersonal communication.

Discussion

Did members of the group hold any norms or values in common? Which of these could be attributed to socialization by the subculture? Were there differences in norms and values? Can these be traced? Did members agree with the subgroups' definitions of things? If so, why? If not, why not? What are the implications for communication?

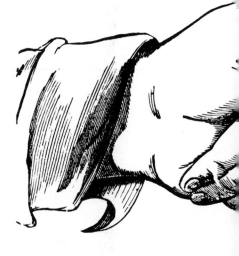

As illustrated in communication experience 9.3, one's subculture membership affects his message making.

Cutting across geographic lines are socioeconomic classes, and ethnic, age, and sexual reference groups all constituting separate subcultures. The subcultures and their influence on the language and behavior of the members of their group are not clear-cut. All communicators have overlapping "membership" in more than one subculture, and conflicting pressures as to what constitutes appropriate behavior (including language usage).

Ethnic subcultures, for example, exert influence on the use of language in several ways. In studies of American Indian and Puerto Rican children living in poor urban areas, it was found that the children had too many languages.[6] In school these children had difficulty learning English, or keeping up with the English of their peers. The problem was in part that their subculture socialized them in Spanish or Indian dialect. Their language learning at home (where most language is learned) was non-English.

Ethnic subcultures have norms and values regarding accepted ways of expressing oneself. This is a second way in which the subculture influences message-making behaviors of its group members. Hall cites an example of a Japanese and an American businessman trying to communicate when the former has been conditioned to avoid direct questions as they are potentially embarrassing to the person with whom he speaks, and the latter continues to ask direct questions.[7]

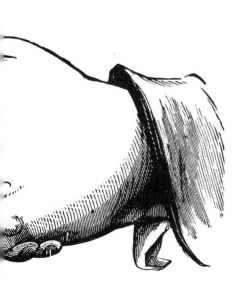

Finally, ethnic groups exert pressure on their members to hold onto group customs and to limit assimilation of the greater culture of which they are a part. Labels such as "Afro-American," "Jewish-American," and "Italo-American" are instances of the subculture encouraging pride in one's heritage.

Many other groups within society can be classified as subcultures exerting their own influence on group members and their message making. Most significant among them are racial, sexual, and age groups. These groups influence their members' use of language, and they also exert influence on the culture-at-large by calling attention to the ways in which the culture-at-large refers to the subculture and its members. In the early 1960s, for example, the black subculture asserted its strong preference for the label "black" rather than "negro" or "colored." The point was to make black and white Americans aware that racial prejudice was as evident in our language as in our behavior. Ossie Davis, the black actor, wrote that inspection of Roget's Thesaurus showed that the word *whiteness* had "approximately 134 synonyms, 44 of which were favorable and/or pleasing (*purity, clean, bright, chaste*) whereas the word *blackness* had 120 synonyms, 60 of which were distinctly unfavorable and none of which were even mildly pleasing (*smut, murky, wicked, evil, unclean*)."[8] The rhetoric of black power in the 60s in which a key slogan was "black is beautiful" was

one way in which the subculture tried to change the meaning of a word so as to use it to refer to themselves without incorporating negative attitudes.

A good deal of rhetoric in the late 1960s and early 1970s has been focused on "sexism" in the English language. *Ms.* became a new way to refer to a woman that paralleled *Mr.* for a man. Neither word gives information about marital status. Attempts have been made and are still being made to erase sexist terms from our language: the use of *he/she* instead of *he; person* instead of *man* and elimination of other word forms that make a distinction that the person to whom the word refers must be male (firefighter instead of fireman, etc.).

One's age group, too, affects one's language acquisition. The slang, jargon, or "in" words of one age group differ from another's. The "hep" person of the 1940s was referred to as "hip" in the 1960s. "Hot" jazz became "cool" until the advent of "hot" rock. Words like *freak* which are negative descriptions to one generation, are used as compliments by another.

Communication experience 9.4 is designed to explore further the effects of culture on language.

Communication Experience 9.4

Principle

Language grows and changes as does culture. Words and their meanings change as the times change.

Procedure

1. Work in groups of five-to-seven people.
2. Discuss what "dirty" words are.
3. Make a list of as many as possible.
4. Discuss who can use these words—when, how, and where? Is this different today than ten years ago?
5. Discuss why it is that everyone knows these words but not everyone is permitted to use them.

Discussion

How did group members feel about working on this task? Why? Are their feelings reflective of cultural conditioning? In what ways? (In what ways are they not reflective of cultural conditioning?) Did group members know one another beforehand? In what ways does this matter?

As illustrated by communication experience 9.4, a person's culture and subculture influence the ways in which one expresses oneself. These influences have implications for interpersonal communication.

The Significance of Cultural Influence on Language

The most important consequences of cultural influences on language are its effects on one's perception of the world, and one's attempts to communicate with others.

Since culture influences language and language influences the way we think and perceive, we have a complex problem in terms of understanding one another. We can translate a word from language to language, but we cannot translate the experience connected with that word. We cannot translate how the language and its structure are intertwined with the perception of the world of the speaker when we translate from one language into another. Because Orientals see humility and "saving face" as highly valued behavioral mores, and Westerners want to aggressively fight until the "better man wins," it is difficult if not impossible for them to translate a statement from one language to the other.

As serious as communication problems between people of different cultures with different languages are communication problems between subcultures sharing a common language. When translating from one language to another, one is aware that problems exist. But when we speak the "same" language we falsely assume that we speak the same "language."

The kinds of language used in message construction become ways for communicating what can be analyzed at different levels. First, the level of the words themselves and whether or not they are understandable to the receiver as well as to the sender of the message is important. On another level, language gives a great deal of information about a person's attitudes, values, and perceptions, and the very way he organizes and is organized by his experience with the world about which his language is supposedly descriptive. The words used tell more about the person using them than about that to which the words refer. The speaker cannot be separated from that about which he speaks. What one selectively notices and responds to and the words one uses to describe those observations are a product of the interplay between the event to which he refers and his own perceptions of that event. His culture is the environment in which he learns his verbal language and the rules of that language. It is also where he acquires the attitudes that govern his perceptions of acceptable and unacceptable verbal behavior.

COLOR

The way people talk about the color spectrum, and even perceive it, varies from one speech community to another, even though all human eyes see the same colors because colors have their own reality in the physical world. Color consists of visible wavelengths that blend imperceptibly into one another. No sharp breaks in the spectrum separate one color from another, such as orange from red. But when speakers in most European communities look at a rainbow, they *think* they see six bands of color: red, orange, yellow, green, blue, and purple. Chopping the continuous spectrum of the rainbow into color categories in this way is an arbitrary division made by European speech communities. People elsewhere in the world, who speak languages unrelated to European ones, have their own ways of partitioning the color spectrum. The Shona of Rhodesia and the Bassa of Liberia, for example, have fewer color categories than speakers of European languages, and they also break up the spectrum at different points, as this diagram shows:

ENGLISH:

red	orange	yellow	green	blue	purple

SHONA:

cipsuka	cicena	citema	cipsuka

BASSA:

ziza	hui

The Shona speaker divides the spectrum into three portions, which he pronounces approximately as *cipsuka, cicena,* and *citema* (*cipsuka* appears twice because it refers to colors at both the red and purple ends of the spectrum). Of course the Shona speaker is able to perceive and to describe other colors—in the same way that a speaker of English knows that *light orangish-yellow* is a variant of yellow—but the Shona's basic divisions represent the portions of the spectrum that his language has convenient labels for.

Peter Farb

Culture affects language and personality. It affects one's perceptions of what is personable as opposed to crass; polite as opposed to gauche; tactful as opposed to blunt or devious. In completing the exploration of culture and other factors affecting the verbal message in interpersonal communication, let us talk of openness and self-disclosure as strategies of message making affected by socialization into a culture.

Culture, Personality, and Self-Disclosure

Communication experience 9.5 is designed to explore how openness and self-disclosure are strategies for message construction and communication.

Communication Experience 9.5

Principle

Self-disclosure and openness can be viewed as culturally determined strategies for message making.

Procedure

1. Work in groups of three.
2. One member of the group is given three-to-four minutes to speak on the question, "What is it that others need to know about me in order for us to communicate?"
3. While the first person speaks, the second member of the group listens and then repeats back a summary. The original speaker may correct him whenever necessary.
4. The third member of the group serves as an objective listener giving assistance to the other two when necessary.
5. Each person in the group must play each of the roles.

Discussion

Did group members "know" one another beforehand? Does this matter? Did they "know" one another after the experience? Why? How did group members feel about the roles they had to take? Which role was most/least comfortable to each group member? Why? Did each learn things about the others? What effects did the kinds of things the others chose to say have on the two group members listening to the speaker? What are the implications for self-disclosure in everyday interactions? In what ways do the communicators' cultures and subcultures affect what they disclose about themselves and how they go about it?

One way of analyzing the verbal message is to evaluate the degree to which the message maker is open and/or self-disclosing. **Self-disclosure** relates to how much a person reveals information about who he is and what he thinks and feels at any given time on any given subject. The apparent openness of the sender is a product of the clues he gives off as translated by his receiver. To say someone is "open" is to attribute to him a characteristic that really resides in the perception and interpretation of the receiver. There are, however, behaviors that a message maker exhibits that lend themselves to the interpretation that he is more "open," self-disclosing, than others. At this juncture we will analyze these verbal behaviors. In the next section of the text, we explore the role of the receiver and will talk of the effect these behaviors have on the intended receiver.

All messages reveal something about the message maker even when they seem to be about something to which the sender refers. When one says something about another person, he is really saying something about himself. "Jackie is smart" seems to say something about Jackie. What the statement actually reveals is something about the statement maker. If we know Jackie, we know what the speaker thinks a smart person is like. Self-disclosing messages are distinguished from other messages in that they are more direct statements about the message maker—statements in which he acknowledges that he is revealing something about himself, rather than statements in which the information about the speaker is implied. The difference between acknowledging explicitly that one is revealing something about himself in the statements he makes and having that revelation implicit, is the difference between statements such as, "I feel that Thelma is kind because she always says nice things to me," and the statement, "Thelma is kind," which is framed as if it says something only about Thelma.

Both statements are expressions of the same thought. In the former, the message maker gives more information about how he arrives at his conclusion, thereby revealing more about himself. In the latter example, what is revealed about him may be something of which he is unaware.

These examples illustrate self-disclosure of the message maker in the broadest sense. Whatever one says tells as much about him as about that to which he refers. There is a more specific sense in which self-disclosing statements are defined, however. Any statement in which the message maker sets out to share with his receiver some insight into himself is a self-disclosing statement. Such self-disclosure can range from superficial data such as one's hometown, education, field of work or study, or anything else that the sender views as low-risk-taking disclosures, to statements about one's more intimate self. Such statements include one's feelings, fears, hopes, desires.

When I am a man, then I shall be a hunter
When I am a man, then I shall be a harpooner
When I am a man, then I shall be a canoe builder
When I am a man, then I shall be a carpenter
When I am a man, then I shall be an artisan
Oh father! ya ha ha ha

Kwakiutl Indian

In terms of language use, self-disclosing statements are easily discernible. Intentionally open statements are those that refer to the sender and his ideas, thoughts, and feelings in regard to himself and his perceptions. Any time someone says, "I think [feel, wish, etc.]," he is sharing something about himself. The more personal the subject matter, the more self-disclosing the statement. In terms of how and why one chooses to be self-disclosing, and the degree to which he chooses to reveal himself, determines how complex the analysis becomes.

One's tendency toward self-disclosure is a product of her culture and personality. Where the culture or subculture places high value on openness, the message maker is encouraged to be open in the expression of his ideas and feelings. In our culture, the movements toward T-groups, encounter sessions, and other groups valuing honesty and openness are expressions of a cultural value on self-disclosure. But openness and self-disclosure can also be analyzed as the strategy of the individual within the culture for accomplishing his ends in communicating. As message makers, we construct those messages that we believe best suit our ends. Self-disclosing messages, therefore, are chosen by message makers who view them as effective strategies for communicating. A communicator who wants to get to know someone else better is self-disclosing as a means of encouraging the other person to reveal himself. A communicator who needs help from someone else, must be self-disclosing to indicate that need. A communicator who has any kind of need that he uses his communication to fulfill will be as self-disclosing as his culture and personality permit if he views that self-disclosure as a means of achieving his purposes.

Culture, then, is an important determinant in one's message-making strategies. It influences one's perceptions of his world and the attitudes and values he holds regarding that world. Culture and language affect one another. And both determine many of the ways in which one frames his message.

Interference with Intentional Communication

Our verbal language is the coding system available to us for message construction. When communicators do not share a common verbal language, there is difficulty in communicating verbally. But difficulty even exists when the language is ostensibly the same. The cultural factors influencing one's message making contribute to potential interference with intended meaning. Interference exists when the communicators have learned the same language but come from different cultures using that language, or different subcultures that share a language but have differing norms and values regarding its usage.

Differences in cultural background interfere with intended communication in terms of acceptable language usage, subject matter, and openness and self-disclosure of the message maker. Numerous examples exist to support the hypothesis that differences in culture and socialization into that culture affect one's ability to communicate with another as he intends. Culture shapes our language and language structure shapes our culture, personality and perception of the reality in which we find ourselves. Using words that the message maker holds in common with his intended receiver does not necessarily guarantee that his message will be understood as intended. Awareness of the impact of one's culture on his language usage gives him a tool for analyzing and evaluating his effectiveness or potential effectiveness with another in the interpersonal communication situation.

Summary   In this chapter we have completed our exploration of verbal language by analyzing the relationship between language, culture, and personality. The salient points are:

1. Language is acquired by a human born into a linguistic society.
2. Language functions as a way of communicating and as a socializing and uniformizing force.
3. Our language habits condition us to choose certain interpretations of the world around us.
4. Subcultures also exert pressure in defining acceptable verbal behavior.
5. Openness and self-disclosure are strategies for message making affected by culture and personality.
6. Interference with intentional communication arises from cultural differences of the communicators.

Questions for Discussion

1. Trace the influences of American subcultures on language behavior.
2. What pressures can be created by membership in more than one subculture?
3. Why is it impossible to discuss language without discussing culture?
4. What differences are there between our language structures and those of other languages?
5. How is language a socializing or uniformizing force?
6. Explain how language influences perception and interpretation of external realities.
7. What kinds of words (categories) are considered taboo in our culture?
8. What differences are there among any subcultures within our society as to verbal taboos?

Notes

1. Roger Brown, *Words and Things* (Glencoe, Ill.: The Free Press, 1958), p. 153.

2. Edward Sapir, *Culture, Language and Personality* (Berkeley, Calif.: University of California Press, 1966), p. i.

3. W. A. Sinclair, *The Language of Wisdom and Folly* by Irving J. Lee (New York: Harper and Brothers, 1949), p. ii.

4. Stuart Chase, *The Power of Words* (New York: Harcourt, Brace and Company, 1953), p. 4.

5. Richard Budd, "General Semantics" in *Approaches to Human Communication,* ed. Richard Budd and Brent Ruben (New York: Spartan Books, 1972), pp. 107–8.

6. Ronald Williams, "Race and the World," *Today's Speech* 19 (Spring 1971): 27.

7. Edward T. Hall and William Foote Whyte, "Intercultural Communication: A Guide to Men of Action," *Human Organization,* 19 (Spring 1960): 7.

8. Ossie Davis, "The Language of Racism," in *Language in America,* ed. Neil Postman, Charles Weingartner and Terence P. Moran (New York: Pegasus, 1969), p. 74.

Selected Bibliography

Brown, Roger. *Words and Things*. Glencoe, Ill.: The Free Press, 1958. A good introduction to the relationship between language and the world of "not-words."

Chase, Stuart. *Power of Words.* New York: Harcourt Brace and Company, 1953. An interesting introduction to the symbolic nature of language. Recommended for the beginning student.

Sapir, Edward. *Culture, Language and Personality*. Berkeley, Calif.: University of California Press, 1966. An in-depth investigation of the relationship between the structures of language and personality. Recommended for the student with some background in communication, psychology, or anthropology.

Smith, Alfred. *Communication and Culture.* New York: Holt, Rinehart and Winston, 1966. An anthology that is recommended for in-depth investigation of various aspects of communication.

Thayer, Lee. *Communication and Communication Systems.* Homewood, Ill.: Richard D. Irwin, 1968. While this does not deal per se with semantics, it is recommended for its perspective on communication as behavior.

The Receiver: As Listener

Introduction

Most models of communication begin with the sender of the message. In the mind of the lay person, the term *interpersonal communication* may mean "someone saying something." In reality, however, it is the listener who determines whether or not and in what ways intentional communication will occur. In the parent-child, teacher-student, or any other sender-receiver relationship, the former encodes the message, and the latter decodes the message and decides what to do about it. The parent can tell the child not to bite her nails. The teacher can give the student the reading assignment. The friend can offer advice on the receiver's sexual relationships. But it is the receiver of any message who has the choice of whether or not to listen.

In order to communicate intentionally, senders and receivers need to understand one another.

It is therefore necessary to explore the receiver's ability and desire to listen as the necessary condition preceding any attempt at understanding. We begin our analysis of the receiver in the interpersonal communication process by analyzing her role as listener.

Communication Goals

This chapter uses the theoretical and experiential approach to begin to explore the role of the receiver in the communication process. It is written to enable you to:

1. Understand "listening" as the essential receiver skill.
2. Evaluate some of your reasons for listening.
3. Understand what listening is in relation to other decoding processes.
4. Develop methods for improving your own hearing and listening skills.
5. Increase your sensitivity to any interference with your own abilities to be an effective listener.

Communication Concepts and Experiences

Communication is a mutually causal activity. It is an interaction between people who have the power and ability to share meanings with one another. In any given interaction, the receiver is the communicator to whom the message is addressed.

To assume that the more one talks, the more the other listens is a faulty understanding of the communication process. Communication relies on a receiver who is able and willing to listen as much as a sender who wants to make contact with that other person. The essential receiver skill, the prerequisite for intentional communication, is **listening.**

In this society, adults spend about 42 percent of their time listening and children spend 58 percent of their time in the same activity.[1] Listening is a complex facet of the communication process, considered by some communication researchers as a more difficult activity than that of speaking. Communication experience 10.1 is designed to illustrate the listening process and its difficulties.

Communication Experience 10.1

Principle

Listening is a complex process in which all communicators participate, often without much attention to how they do so.

Procedure

1. Work individually.
2. Select four separate hours during a given day in which to monitor listening behavior.
3. During each hour keep track of how many people speak to you, the percentage of time others speak and you listen and vice versa; and the degree to which you give the other your full listening attention.
4. After each hour of observation, write down the number of people talked with, amount of listening time, the degree of attention, and any explanations of the attention or lack thereof to different people.
5. Bring this information to class and compare with others.

Discussion

Did the self-observation affect the listening behavior? How? Why? Were there differences at different times of day? What were they? Why? Were there differences in listening to different people? What? Why? How did the behaviors compare to other class members? What are the implications about you as a listener?

I'm looking through you,
where did you go?
I thought I knew you, what did
I know?
You don't look different, but
you have changed,
I'm looking through you, you're
not the same.
Your lips are moving, I cannot
hear, your voice is soothing
but the words aren't clear.
You don't sound different,
I've learnt the game,
I'm looking through you,
you're not the same.
Why, tell me why did you
not treat me right?
Love has a nasty habit of
disappearing overnight,
you're thinking of me the same
old way, you were above me,
but not today.
The only difference is you're
down there.
I'm looking through you
and you're nowhere.
Why, tell me why did you not
treat me right?
Love has a nasty habit of
disappearing overnight,
I'm looking through you,
where did you go?
I thought I knew you, what
did I know?
You don't look different,
but you have changed,
I'm looking through you,
you're not the same.
Yeh, I tell you you've changed.

John Lennon
Paul McCartney

As illustrated in communication experience 10.1, listening is a complex process. We begin an analysis of that process by discussing why people listen and then compare and contrast listening with related behaviors *perceiving, attending,* and *hearing.*

Why Listen

In many ways communicators act as sounding boards for others when they function as the receivers of messages. People continually address verbal messages to one another. One listens if there is some reason to do so. There are several things one can accomplish by listening to others and therefore several reasons why one will listen to another.

One reason that a person listens to another is because he knows that at times he needs others to listen to him. All of us at one time or another are in need of good listeners. These are the people to whom we can turn when we need to share our inner experiences, our private worlds. Because we know how it feels to have someone listen to us, we feel some responsibility to listen to other people. This is one reason for listening.

A second reason that anyone listens to anyone else is because he cares about that other person or about what that other person has to say. If the subject matter is of interest or of importance to the receiver, he has a motivation for listening to the speaker, whether or not he likes him as a person.

A third reason for listening to others is because one feels he has to. This feeling results from the receiver's response to the sender. Somehow the sender indicates that it is important for him to be listened to; he conveys that he is attempting to reach out and share his inner experiences and thus inspires the receiver to feel that to avoid listening is to reject that other human being in some very profound way. Whether or not the receiver responds depends on the speaker and whether or not he conveys that it is this particular receiver whose attention he needs. If the receiver feels that the sender will talk to anyone who will keep quiet long enough for the sender to speak, he may not feel obligated to listen to the speaker.

There are many other reasons why one listens to a speaker. It may be that the listener hopes to learn something or profit from what he hears. By attending a class, going to a lecture, or receiving any kind of instruction, the receiver listens because he needs some information. If this need is not met, the listener becomes disinterested and his desire and ability to listen are affected. Communication experience 10.2 is designed to test out the relationship between listening and interest levels.

Dr. Arthus Kellner, a New York industrial psychologist explains: "When a person with a problem talks to someone who does not listen, his 'self-concept' is challenged and his problem becomes more acute. However, when such a person can talk to an interested listener, his 'self-concept' is preserved, or even enhanced, and he goes away feeling better."

Communication Experience 10.2

Principle

Listening is a complex process dependent on the receiver's needs and interests at the times during which a sender addresses him.

Procedure

1. Work with a partner.
2. Attend a religious service or political speech.
3. After the event cross-question one another to evaluate whether or not each of you has listened to the speaker.
4. Discuss why each was able to listen or found it difficult to do so.

Discussion

Did the partners know one another beforehand? How does this affect their post-speech candor? How interested is each in the particular event and/or speaker listened to? What difference does this make? What are some of the motivations that each person had for listening? Were they similar or different from the other person's? Was the listening behavior the same or different from the ways each would have listened if this had not been an assignment? Did others who attended the event listen to the speaker? On what basis can this question be answered?

As illustrated in communication experience 10.2, receivers listen when they are interested in something. The degree of interest influences whether or not they are attentive to the speaker. Listening also occurs if it allows a person to exercise imagination, to somehow share in that other person's experience by listening to it. In hearing what the speaker says, the receiver can sometimes get a different view of the world or enjoy an experience that he would otherwise not have had. He may listen because he enjoys listening in general or because a particular speaker is pleasurable to listen to.

There are many reasons why we listen—to pass time, to enjoy a joke, to add to our knowledge, to share another's experience. But whatever the reason, one listens only when something happens to him if he listens, or because he feels he will miss out on something if he does not. These, then, are the reasons why one listens. Defining listening entails comparing and contrasting it with some similar activities.

Listening, Perceiving, Attending, and Hearing

Perception has been defined as a process of extracting information from the world outside oneself as well as from within.[2] When perceiving something, a person is able to note certain stimuli and draw some kind of information from them. Looking at the sky and concluding that rain is in sight is perception. Looking at oneself in the mirror and deciding to start a diet involves self-perception. The process of perception is much like the steps described in the Westley-MacLean model in which the X's become X_i's, and are attended to by the communicator. The "perceptive" individual, then, is the one who is able to draw accurate information based on the stimuli with which he is presented. One type of perception is "listening," the process by which one selectively attends to certain auditory stimuli. Listening is selective perception and attention to auditory stimuli.

In any situation a multitude of sights and sounds are available as potential stimuli or sources of raw data on which to base messages. If a person speaking says something the listener considers important, she blocks out other potential stimuli and pays attention to what is being said. On the other hand, if her own inner thoughts, or some other stimuli, preoccupy her, she does not pay attention to what the other person is saying. In a lecture class, for example, the professor speaks while the students supposedly listen. But a student's thoughts may be elsewhere. Her priorities shift and she listens if something said is important enough to cut through her private thoughts, for example, the date for an exam is given, the class is dismissed, or her name is called.

Listening is related to perception and attention. It is a process involving both of these activities. It is narrower than either of the other two processes in that it is perception and attention to auditory stimuli rather than the whole range of audiovisual stimuli with which one is presented. This is a literal definition of listening. In a broader sense, the receiver attends to the whole range of verbal and nonverbal behaviors as he listens to a speaker. Using the word **listening** in this narrow sense is to analyze the receiver's function in attending to one set of stimuli (auditory) with which he is presented. Communication experience 10.3 is designed to let the student explore his own listening habits.

Communication Experience 10.3

Principle

Listening is a complex process in which one has to select those stimuli to which he will attend.

Procedure

1. Work with a partner.
2. Go together somewhere on campus for lunch, taking a tape recorder with you.
3. Turn on the tape recorder. One person speaks into it, recording everything that he observes during a five minute period.
4. The second person listens, so as to be able to repeat what the first has said.
5. After five minutes, with the tape still going, the second person repeats what the first has said.
6. When the second has finished, use the taped versions to compare what both persons have said.
7. Then, replay the tape a second time, while still in the same location, to see what was missed.

Discussion

What were the differences between what the first person said and the version stated by the second person? Why? How did both compare to what the pair noticed during either replay? Why? Did the tape recorder affect either person? How? Why? What are the implications about listening? If the pair switched roles, what differences would it make?

As illustrated in communication experience 10.3, listening involves attention to certain kinds of stimuli from among the entire range to which one can pay attention. Listening is related to, but distinct from, *hearing*— another concept mentioned earlier as important in defining the listening function of the receiver.

In the selective process that we are calling listening, the receiver notices those stimuli that are most fitted to his needs or purposes. **Hearing** differs from listening in that it is a nonselective process. It is the perception of all vibrations (sounds) through the sensory receptors (auditory mechanism). If one has normal hearing (hearing that is not impaired), then he *hears* every audible sound occurring in his presence. If he is reading in the library, he hears other people walking, sitting, turning pages, and whispering; he can hear pencils writing, doors opening, the clock ticking, and people breathing. But he does not listen to all of these sounds. The distinction between hearing and listening has to do with selectivity and attention. One hears everything but selects and attends to only some things. Selective attention is a necessary human mechanism. To pay attention to all sounds is like staying on the lowest level of abstraction. It prevents one from "extracting" the essential.

In the library example just cited, the student who is there to socialize or to wait for someone attends to most of the sounds present in order not to "miss" something or someone. But if he were trying to read and digest an assignment on which he expected to be tested, he would block out the sounds (auditory stimuli) and concentrate on what he is reading. This does not mean he does not hear the sounds. He does not listen to them. This means he is unaware of the things he is hearing because they are unimportant to him at a given moment.

The words *listening* and *hearing* are often used interchangeably. They stand, however, for two distinct processes. In one (hearing) the activity consists mainly of the reception of sounds. In the other (listening), one not only receives the sounds, but also attends to them and tries to comprehend their meaning. Communication experience 10.4 is designed to test the student's listening skills.

Communication Experience 10.4

Principle

Listening is a complex process in which the receiver must attempt to understand that which the sender tries to say rather than that which the listener would like to believe the sender is saying.

Procedure

1. Work in groups of three.
2. One person acts as speaker, the second as listener, and the third as judge.
3. The speaker talks about something important to him for 2 to 4 minutes.
4. The listener repeats back what the speaker has said until his version is satisfactory to the original speaker.
5. The judge acts as an "objective" observer and assists the other two when necessary.
6. Switch roles so that each of the triad has a turn filling each of the roles.

Discussion

Which role was the most difficult? Why? What factors caused the most inaccuracies in reiteration? What was done to compensate? How did one's listening behavior differ from the ways in which he listens elsewhere? Why? Was a "judge" necessary? Why?

As illustrated in communication experience 10.4, listening is a complex process. It is related to but differs from perceiving, attending, and hearing. Listening is composed of physiological and psychological components.

The Physiology of Listening and Hearing

Physiologically, listening incorporates the act of hearing. Although one can hear without listening, it is difficult to listen unless one can hear. The physiology of listening deals with how one hears. When a speaker talks, he uses his vocal mechanism to create vibrations with differing frequencies, pitches, and durations. The results are sounds that can be shaped into words and paralanguage. A listener uses her hearing organs to receive those acoustic vibrations that she converts into signals suitable to be understood by the brain. It is the brain that gives meaning to those vibrations. The brain decodes the symbolic nature of the vibration patterns, known as words. For example, a boy whistles and his dog comes running. This is analogous to what happens between human senders and receivers in the communication process. The boy puckers his lips, pushes air through them, creating sounds by the tension between his lips (tongue and teeth) blocking or shaping the stream of air so as to create the acoustic vibrations we call a whistle. The dog's ears pick up the vibrations, convert them into signals that are sent to the brain and understood to mean, "Come running." In human interaction, the sender uses his vocal mechanism to create sounds (words and paralanguage). The receiver uses his auditory mechanism to receive and decipher those vibrations we refer to as sounds and/or words.

The condition of the receiver's hearing mechanism is an important consideration in his function as receiver. If a person has any hearing impairment, it is important to have the proper medical and/or therapeutic help. The inability to hear well affects the receiver's ability to listen. If he cannot listen well, the communication cycle becomes more difficult. Naturally, there are degrees of hearing impairment. The communicator himself can usually evaluate whether or not he has a problem hearing. If necessary, he can seek medical/therapeutic aid or develop compensatory devices just as those developed by the sender with speaking problems. The communicator who is not sure whether or not his hearing mechanism functions properly ought to seek a professional diagnosis.

Physiologically, listening occurs in waves. There are natural peaks and fallings off in the receiver's physiological processing of auditory stimuli. This is an important concept to understand. No one can hear and/or listen to everything. For the speaker, this implies that he needs to make sure that he creates his messages in such a way as to maximize his intended receiver's ability to listen to him. Techniques such as repetition, highlighting, contrasts in content, and/or presentation of that content are available to the sender to help his receiver listen. Public speakers are more trained in these techniques than people interacting interpersonally. Many conversationalists mistakenly believe that they can talk until they finish, leaving their receivers to listen until it is their turn. The speaker must adapt his message to the peaks in attention of his receiver. The receiver learns about his own pattern of listening and attempts to adjust it where necessary to comprehend that which is said to him.

As already discussed, one's ability to hear and to listen has physical determinants. But in tracing one's listening patterns it becomes clear that other factors have influential value. These are the psychological facets of the listening process.

The Psychological Aspects of Listening

Hearing is a prerequisite for effective listening. Unfortunately, there is no close relationship between listening ability and hearing skill.[3] One's hearing may be perfectly normal but that does not necessarily mean he listens well. The degree to which a person is able to listen is psychologically as well as physically determined. Central to listening is a person's ability to pay attention—to focus. Perhaps the most basic reason

I think that the greatness of Freud probably will, in the long perspective of history, pretty much sift down to the fact that he was the first really great listener, just as Galileo was the first great experimenter. I think Freud will become known as the first man who deliberately listened. He knew that was what he was doing. He listened. And so the person to whom he listened was left free to be himself.

WENDELL JOHNSON

anyone pays attention to anything is because it is of interest to him. But the receiver can listen faster than the sender can speak; thus the listener's thoughts can wander if the speaker does not hold his interest.

The reasons for a listener becoming bored and/or his thoughts wandering are functions of his personality and are referred to as the psychological aspect of listening. We all have emotional filters and emotional ears that strongly affect how, if, when, and why we listen.[4] Listening is dependent upon both physiological and psychological abilities to receive messages. Often it has been said that a person hears only what he wants to hear. Despite the listener's hearing ability, he pays attention to, and interprets what he hears, to mean what he wants it to mean. Communication experience 10.5 is designed to illustrate the effects of one's emotional filters on what he hears.

Communication Experience 10.5

Principle

The subject matter and/or the words used in discussing a subject can affect the receiver's ability to be receptive to communication.

Procedure

1. Work in groups of four-to-seven people.
2. Discuss what subject matter and word usage the group thinks are potentially emotionally charged and the kinds of receivers about whom this assumption is being made.
3. Prepare a speech, short story, or newspaper article using those emotionally charged items.
4. Prepare another version differing in word usage and/or using less inflammatory topic development.
5. Each group member takes both versions and shows them to at least ten people, asking each, "which version of what I have written should I present to a speech class (or newspaper for publication) and why?"
6. Compare results and discuss implication. Compare with other groups.

Discussion

What kinds of things did the group assume would interfere with listening? Why? How did these items compare with those chosen by other groups? Why? Were any of the assumptions different from one group to another? What would this indicate? Were any of the topics difficult to discuss in the group? Why? What were the results? What were the implications?

he community may scream because one man is born who will not do as it does, who will not conform because conformity to him is death — he is so constituted. They know nothing about his case; they are fools when they presume to advise him. The man of genius knows what he is aiming at; nobody else knows. And he alone knows when something comes between him and his object. In the course of generations, however, men will excuse you for not doing as they do, if you will bring enough to pass in your own way.

As illustrated in communication experience 10.5, a person's listening is affected by both physiological and psychological factors. Just as one can perfect his listening skills by becoming more aware of the physical peaks in his ability to pay attention, so too can one improve his listening skills by understanding his own psychological makeup.

To be an effective listener, one needs to know herself in several ways. The first is knowing one's physical hearing ability. The receiver must also know and evaluate her own personality to have some way of understanding whether or not she is an effective listener. Communication experience 10.5 was designed to give the student some information about the emotional filters through which she sifts out what is said to her. Attitudes, values, preferences, and prejudices shape those emotional filters. Whatever she knows and/or can learn about her attitudes and values will help her in dealing with these filters.

Psychiatrists refer to filtering as one's ability to separate the observer from the observed.[5] To distinguish between what is being said and what is perceived as being said, a great deal must be known about oneself. Meaning always resides in the interplay between what the speaker says and means and what the listener hears and thinks it means. Attempts to improve intentional communication are attempts to share common meanings. The speaker tries to do this by knowing himself, the situation, and the person he talks to. The listener can do the same by learning to distinguish between what the speaker is trying to say and what the receiver wants to hear. Here lies the first step in improving one's basic listening skills.

Basic Listening Skills: Guidelines

All human beings are potential receivers of messages from all the communicators peopling their world. Because one is not always willing to listen to what another needs to say, he learns to close his ears and mind to those messages he views as unimportant, unnecessary, or in some way unpleasant or undesirable. There is a tendency for us to work more at learning to avoid listening than at learning to improve our listening skills.

Improving one's listening skills is similar to improving one's reading comprehension. In reading comprehension exams, students read passages and answer questions about those passages. The answers are then rated to establish some index of the reader's comprehension of the material. Similar testing can be applied to one's listening skills. The communication experiences in this chapter are tools helpful for evaluating one's listening strengths and weaknesses. They are based on self-knowledge and practice. The key points are: What does a person know about how well he listens? and, what can he do to improve his listening skills if he finds they do need improvement? Since listening experiences bombard all of us each day, one need only use some of these experiences to aid him in his self-evaluation.

There are four essentials for a person to improve listening skills. First, she must be aware of whether or not she is paying attention to the sender. No one pays attention all the time. Effective listening means conscious choices about paying attention. For example, a person on a trip gets lost, and stops to ask for directions. Lack of attention is certainly a problem if he drives away before he even realizes he hasn't listened. If instead the driver's companion talks about something that is not interesting to him, his lack of attention is not poor listening; it is a matter of choice.

The second way to improve one's listening skills is to make distinctions between what the speaker is trying to say and what the listener wants him to be saying. This involves knowing one's own needs and desires in the communication interaction. It means separating one's opinion of the speaker from what one thinks he hears the speaker say. A close friend can say something just as stupid as an enemy. But because he is a friend, one may be tempted not to "hear" his error.

The third way to improve one's listening skills is to find some ways to separate the essential (in terms of what the speaker is trying to convey) from the nonessential. This parallels sorting out the main points and supporting statements in written material. "Essential" here refers to the scheme of thought of the speaker rather than to that which is of interest to the listener.

CATCH-22

Joseph Heller

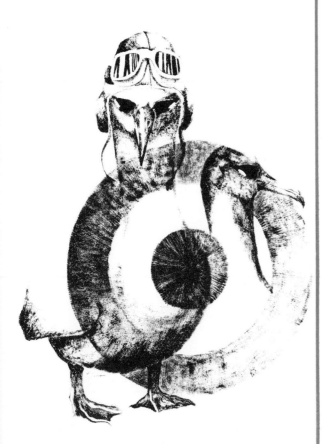

"Can't you ground someone who's crazy?"

"Oh, sure. I have to. There's a rule saying I have to ground anyone who's crazy."

"Then why don't you ground me? I'm crazy. Ask Clevinger."

"Clevinger? Where *is* Clevinger? You find Clevinger and I'll ask him."

"Then ask any of the others. They'll tell you how crazy I am."

"They're crazy."

"Then why don't you ground them?"

"Why don't they ask me to ground them?"

"Because they're crazy, that's why."

"Of course they're crazy," Doc Daneeka replied. "I just told you they're crazy, didn't I? And you can't let crazy people decide whether you're crazy or not, can you?"

Yossarian looked at him soberly and tried another approach. "Is Orr crazy?"

"He sure is," Doc Daneeka said.

"Can you ground him?"

"I sure can. But first he has to ask me to. That's part of the rule."

"Then why doesn't he ask you to?"

"Because he's crazy," Doc Daneeka said. "He has to be crazy to keep flying combat missions after all the close calls he's had. Sure, I can ground Orr. But first he has to ask me to."

"That's all he has to do to be grounded?"

"That's all. Let him ask me."

"And then you can ground him?" Yossarian asked.

"No. Then I can't ground him."

"You mean there's a catch?"

"Sure there's a catch," Doc Daneeka replied. "Catch-22. Anyone who wants to get out of combat duty isn't really crazy."

Finally, listening skills can be improved by exercising control over one's tendency to jump to conclusions. One must not let herself think she knows what the speaker is going to say before he says it. Nor can she let herself be more concerned with what she will say next than with listening to what the speaker is trying to say. Using these guidelines, the communicator can improve her listening skills and work toward whatever improvement she finds she needs as a communicator.

The receiver in the interpersonal process is a listener. Understanding the listening process and evaluating one's own abilities to listen effectively is the first task as an effective receiver.

Interference with Intentional Communication

In this chapter, we have begun to investigate the role of the receiver in the interpersonal interaction. Our focus has been on the receiver as listener. In terms of communication effectiveness, the major interference with intentional communication is an intended receiver who cannot, will not, or does not listen.

There are three common faults in listening, each of which interferes with intentional communication. First, one can "hear" (listen) too little; i.e., listening only to selected parts of a message.

Secondly, one can hear (listen) too much. Hearing too much involves drawing inferences not implied by the sender. If the person speaking criticizes the way Margaret Casey is dressed and the listener "hears" in that statement that the speaker hates the Irish, he is hearing too much, unless he has other evidence on which to base this conclusion. Hearing too much is a pointed instance of failure to separate the observer from that which he observes. The listener thinks he hears something, but it is something he has added to that which was said.

The third common listening weakness is the tendency on the part of many receivers to hear the inessential. What is important in a speaker's message is a matter of interpretation. It differs depending upon the point of view from which it is discussed: the sender's or the receiver's.

It may very well be that the speaker considers the main points he is stating as important, whereas the listener is more concerned with the examples used to measure what the speaker really seems to mean. These are relative judgments and as such both have bases. To evaluate the listener's ability to digest any given message, a relatively accurate measure is whether the listener can reframe that message as originally sent, to the satisfaction of the originating communicator. If he cannot and it is because he has not paid attention to some major points, then he has focused on the inessential from the perspective of a shared understanding of the message.

Weaver cites five specific psychological causes of faulty listening: *habitual inattention, selective perception, selective inattention, inaccurate inference making and the inability to handle concepts.*[6]

Habitual inattention refers to the constant inability of a receiver to pay attention to the messages addressed to him. No one person can listen to everything and no one listens all the time. Habitual inattention is a problem because of the extreme degree to which the receiver fails to listen. When we speak of someone as habitually inattentive, we refer to a general attitude; a continual inability to pay attention. When inattention is this extreme, it is symptomatic of a physical or psychological problem. An unknown hearing loss can make it hard to listen. A person with important problems of his own can't listen to other people's problems. From the point of view of communication, what is important is the resultant inattention that makes communication impossible. Listening requires effort and attention. Inattention gets in the way of good listening.

Selective perception and **selective inattention** are in a sense two sides of the same coin. Both interfere with listening. Listening is selective perception of auditory stimuli. When this selectivity is excessive, the listener filters out many relevant auditory as well as other stimuli and he cannot listen adequately. Selective inattention is a related concept. In *selective perception,* one only listens to some things. In *selective inattention* he blocks out what he does not wish to hear. The difference resides in those kinds of things the listener chooses not to attend to. In selective perception, only those things that are interesting to the listener are listened to. In selective inattention those things that the listener does not want to hear or that bother him are filtered out.

As with habitual inattention, selective perception and selective inattention are signs of a problem. What causes either varies from one individual to another.

The last two causes of inadequate listening listed above are inaccurate inference making and the inability to handle concepts. **Inaccurate inference making** is related to "hearing too much." The listener "reads" meanings into what has been said, but which are not related to anything the sender has encoded. They are his own interpretations. The speaker has not said or implied anything like them.

Interpretation and differences in meaning are part and parcel of the communication process. Inferential meanings are also useful and necessary ways in which people communicate with one another. A communicator does not always want to spell out his feelings or thoughts. Sometimes a look or brief statement is enough to get the idea across. It is not a problem when the listener draws inaccurate inferences if he knows they are inferences. He can test out what he thinks he has heard by asking the speaker questions. But if he has no idea that he has drawn an inference and no way therefore of validating its accuracy, this contaminates his ability to be an effective listener. As with each of the other causes of inadequate listening discussed above, it is the extreme degree more than the mechanism itself that is the problem in terms of effective communication.

Finally, inadequate listening can be a sign of the listener's **inability to frame concepts.** If words cannot be put together in some meaningful way by the listener attempting to decode them, he is left with a series of separate symbols. Any time one tries to acquire new knowledge on an unfamiliar subject, he faces this problem. One takes a course in statistics, communication, or anthropology. He must learn a vocabulary new in that subject. He must also be able to put together the words said in order to understand the concepts for which those words stand. Words are only symbols. If one does not grasp the concepts for which those symbols stand, then they are of little value to him. As a listener, he can be no more than confused.

These, then, are some faults in a listener that can interfere with intentional communication. Anything that prevents the receiver from listening to the sender is an interference with communication whether it be his hearing, his interest, or his reaction to the message maker.

Summary

This chapter is the first of three to explore the part of the receiver in the process of communication. The salient points are:

1. Listening is the essential receiver skill.
2. There are a range of reasons for listening to another person, all of which center on whether or not the listener feels he will benefit as a consequence of his listening.
3. Listening and related concepts are defined as:
   a. *Perceiving: the process of gathering information from internal and external sources.*
   b. *Attending: the selective perception of stimuli from the environment.*
   c. *Listening: the selective perception of* auditory *stimuli from the environment.*
   d. *Hearing: the* nonselective *reception of all auditory stimuli by the auditory mechanism. Receiving the sound without attending to it.*
4. Listening and hearing are not synonyms; they refer to two different concepts.
5. Listening has physiological and psychological aspects.
6. Physiologically, listening incorporates the process of hearing and sound reception.

7. Psychologically, listening ability is largely shaped by the personality of the receiver and the effect of the words on him.
8. Good listening skills can be developed if the receiver follows certain guidelines.
9. Interference with intentional communication can result from poor listening.
10. Three common flaws in listening are:
    a. *Hearing too little.*
    b. *Hearing too much.*
    c. *Hearing only the inessential.*
11. Several causes for the faults or inadequacies in listening are:
    a. *Habitual inattention.*
    b. *Selective perception.*
    c. *Selective inattention.*
    d. *Inaccurate inference making.*
    e. *Inability to handle concepts.*

Questions for Discussion

1. What can one know about oneself as a listener? How does one know whether he is hearing or listening?
2. What is the difference between listening and attending?
3. Why is "hearing too much" a fault in listening? When and why does it occur?
4. What is habitual inattention? What aspect of listening would it relate to?
5. Explain the physiological aspect of listening.
6. Discuss why listening ability and hearing acuity are not necessarily interdependent.
7. When and how is one taught to listen?
8. Take a listening self-inventory. Answer the following questions:
   a. *When do you listen most?*
   b. *When do you listen least?*
   c. *What can a speaker do to keep you listening?*
   d. *What can a speaker do that makes you unable to listen?*
   e. *Are you considered a good listener?*
9. Is listening an art?
10. How does one react to someone who really listens to him?

1. Carl Weaver, *Speaking in Public* (New York: The American Book Company, 1966), p. 58.

2. R. H. Fergus, *Perception* (New York: McGraw-Hill, 1966), p. 1.

3. R. L. Nichols and L. H. Stevens, *Are You Listening* (New York: McGraw-Hill, 1957), p. 2.

4. Ibid., p. 90.

5. Jergen Ruesch, "The Observer and the Observed," in *Toward a Unified Theory of Behavior,* ed. Roy Grinker (New York: Basic Books, Inc., 1957).

6. Weaver, *Speaking in Public,* pp. 68–70.

Notes

Fergus, R. H. *Perception.* New York: McGraw-Hill, 1966. Recommended for the student with some background in communication or psychology. A sound study of perception, its bases and effects.

Johnson, Wendell. *Living with Change.* Edited by Dorothy Moeller. New York: Harper & Row, 1972. A good introduction to the relationship between language and sanity. Recommended for the discussion of the listening process.

Nichols, R. N. and L. A. Stevens. *Are You Listening?* New York: McGraw-Hill, 1957. Recommended for the beginning communication student. A good overview of the entire process of listening.

Ruesch, Jergen. "The Observer and the Observed." In *Toward a Unified Theory of Behavior,* edited by Roy Grinker. New York: Basic Books, 1956. An article suggested for the student with some psychology or communication background. The relationship discussed is important for the discussion of listening and perception.

Smith, Henry. *Sensitivity to Others.* New York: McGraw-Hill, 1969. An interesting presentation of material important to the student aware of the interactional nature of interpersonal communication.

Selected Bibliography

The Receiver: Listener Plus

11

Introduction

While the words *listener* and *receiver* are being used interchangeably in this text, they are not merely synonyms. In order to receive messages, it is clear that one needs to be a listener. But to gather all the messages encoded in the interpersonal situation one needs to do more than listen. In some sense she needs to listen with her eyes as well as her ears. This is one reason we refer to listening as an active process.

The effective listener participates in the communication process with an intent of understanding the other person who is trying to communicate. She is more than a passive receiver of another's word. She is an understander, a person who uses her eyes and mind to try to evaluate what the sender is saying and doing. The listener relates to the range of verbal and nonverbal behaviors presented and attempts to decode and understand them. She does more than listen.

Communication Goals

In this chapter the theoretical and experiential approach is used to enable you to know more about the receiving function by understanding that:

1. Listening is an active process involving the receiver's attempt to understand the sender.
2. Such understanding demands that the listener attend to pertinent nonverbal as well as verbal aspects of the sender's message.
3. Decoding the sender's message involves translating that which the sender has said without distorting it.
4. Distinguishing between the sender and the message enables the receiver to be more accurate in understanding what the message means.
5. The receiver's field of experience and the communication environment in which the message is sent affect his abilities to understand it.
6. An effective listener distinguishes between his observations and interpretations.

Communication Concepts and Experiences

The biggest blockage to human understanding, as mathematician Quine of Harvard once said, is the "uncritical assumption of mutual understanding."[1] Each person as he is talking has the illusion that he is being understood, and that the person to whom he speaks is listening to him. But listening is demanding work, and good listening, the sort that works at understanding the sender, is rare.

Our society as a whole, and the individuals composing it, place more value on the art of using words than on the attempt to listen to how another uses those words. We work more at training ourselves to be "communicators," meaning speakers, than "communicators" in the sense of learning to be effective listeners. This is so despite the fact that a large percentage of our time is devoted to "listening" activities. Listening involves hearing auditory stimuli and paying attention to them. But it is even more. It is receiving and processing all the messages coming from a sender in a given communication interaction.

Receiving Messages: Listening with a Third Ear

In the interaction referred to as communication, good listening is the critical component. It goes further in determining what others say to us and what we say to others than any other single element of that process. Learning about listening and techniques for improving one's listening skills gives him the most effective approach to understanding and improving communication in any interaction.

Listening is defined literally as *attention* to auditory stimuli. In the broadest sense of the word, however, listening is synonymous with receiving messages. It includes the use of one's eyes as well as one's ears to detect meanings in the interpersonal communication encounter. The effective listener knows that the nonverbal behavior of the sender is at least as important as his verbal behavior. He understands that it is sometimes possible to tell how a person feels about what he is saying by observing his facial expressions, gestures, body posture, and combining these with his verbal expression and his paralanguage (the tone, timing, tensing, sequencing and manner of what he says). The effective receiver understands that we do not communicate by words alone. He knows that messages are a complex of verbal and nonverbal behaviors. Communication experience 11.1 is designed to illustrate the role of the listener as receiver of a range of message-coded behaviors.

I know
you believe
you understand
what you think
I said but,
I am not sure you
realize that what
you heard is not
what I meant

Communication Experience 11.1

Principle

Listening is an active process in which one uses his eyes and ears to gather all the components of the speaker's message.

Procedure

1. Work in pairs.
2. One person is the speaker and the other the listener.
3. The speaker talks for five minutes on the topic: the most serious problem facing college students today.
4. The listener must listen with his eyes closed, and respond to the words (not the paralanguage) of the speaker. That is, he responds to the literal verbal message.
5. Switch roles.

Discussion

What effects did the closed eyes have on the listener; the speaker? How did it feel to take each role? Why? What is the difference in responding to the words alone? Did the speaker feel able to get his message across? Did he do anything different in expressing himself from what he would normally do? Why? What are the implications for listening?

As illustrated in communication experience 11.1, listening in the broadest sense of the word involves observing and processing a range of message-coded behaviors. Listening is a demanding activity in that the receiver needs to be an observer, a thinker, and a decoder, using his ability to collect, process, and use the information directed his way.[2] Just as in the sending of the message, one need have certain encoding skills, in acting as receiver, one need be able to decode the messages with which he is presented. He does all of this at the same time that he is selectively tuning out those stimuli he considers irrelevant to the communication interaction at hand.

Decoding Skills: Listening with One's Eyes and Ears

In its most basic sense, decoding is the reversal of the process of encoding messages. The sender has encoded her thoughts or feelings into words and nonverbal behaviors; the receiver observes and decodes those behaviors in order to understand the thoughts and feelings for which they stand. Complications arise, however, because communicators are often far more able and interested in initiating messages than in being responsive to others wishing to do the same. Communication experience 11.2 is designed for the student to evaluate her encoding and decoding skills.

Communication Experience 11.2

Principle

Listening involves one's ability to decode that which the speaker has said and to translate those symbols into that which is comprehendable to him.

Procedure

1. Work alone.
2. Listen to a person speaking a language other than English and attempt to understand as much as possible. The language should be unfamiliar to the listener.
3. Talk with the speaker afterwards and find out how accurate the interpretation has been.

Discussion

How did the listening behavior differ from listening to speakers who speak a familiar language? Why? What was understandable? Why? What things were done by the listener that he ought to do in other listening situations? Why? What are the implications for listening? In what sense is listening to another human being always listening to a foreign language?

As illustrated in communication experience 11.2, encoding and decoding are processes that reverse one another. When discussing them in relation to human interactions, it becomes clear that one communicator is not always as capable or interested in performing one as the other. Decoding involves the ability to receive the message, translate the symbols, and try to understand what it is that the sender attempted to say.

In order to do this with any degree of accuracy, the receiver must be aware of himself and the other person with whom he is trying to communicate. He needs to understand the impact of people, himself included, on their messages. If the receiver is aware of himself in the communication interaction, he knows that decoding a message is translating it. In listening to the message, the receiver is in the process of translating that message, its verbal and nonverbal codes, into his own words. The receiver supplies the code in his own head for the sounds and actions he sees as coming from the sender. In so doing, he translates the language of the speaker into his own language, a necessary and unavoidable function of message reception. Being aware of the ways in which this is done helps the receiver avoid putting the speaker's message into his "own" words, which may alter and distort the sender's original meaning.

The receiver must be aware of himself in order to strive for accuracy in understanding what the other person means rather than what he thinks or wants that other person to mean. The receiver must also be aware of the other person in the communication interaction and his feelings about that other person. In order for the listener to hear what the speaker is saying, and to observe what he is doing, the receiver must be able to distinguish between the sender and that which the sender is encoding. One of the ways in which the meaning of the message can be distorted by the receiver is if he pays more attention to the sender than to what the sender is saying. The relationship between the sender and the message being sent can be analyzed as one of several kinds of factors affecting the receiver and thereby influencing what he "hears" in that which is being addressed to him.

Dynamics Affecting Listening and Meaning

Perception of the Sender

At times, having difficulty separating the message from the message maker can add to the understanding of what is being said, giving some measurement for how much credence to lend to the message. The message in the interpersonal interaction is only the symbolization of the message the sender attempts to convey. The meanings in the interaction are the product of the people involved in that encounter. In decoding the

sender's message, the receiver uses that message as the symbolic vehicle for understanding that other human being and that which he is trying to convey. The danger, however, is that the receiver's feelings about the sender can distort his perception of the sender's message. Liking someone can add "sense" to the nonsense he spouts.

In light of this kind of understanding of the communication process, it becomes clear why communicators need to sort out the interpersonal dynamics that are affecting what is being communicated. These interpersonal dynamics include not only the communicators, but the impact they have on the actual message making and reception; that is, the receiver must be aware of his own needs, feelings, and interpretations as they color his perception of the message maker and thereby influence his understanding of what is being said. He must be aware of the sender's reputation and how that colors the meaning of his message in the given interaction.

One of the most effective tools a receiver can have for understanding and evaluating the sender's message is the ability to separate what the speaker says from whom he is; to attend to the message as separate from the person's reputation, power, influence, or whatever other measure we can use to describe him as a credible or noncredible source. The good sense of what someone has to say is often very separate from his symbols of authority or power. In interpersonal interactions, however, the separation of the message and message maker is often ignored. This explains why it is that the same message can be sent by two different people and received in very different ways. The receiver who is able to separate the speaker's impact from that which is being said exercises some control over her own prejudice or prejudgment. In so doing, he is then in a position to put the two back together.

Communication experience 11.3 is designed to illustrate the difference between separating the message and message maker until one understands what is being said, from making prior decisions about the meaning of the message.

Communication Experience 11.3

Principle

In listening to a speaker, it is easy to confuse what is being said with who is saying it. The effective listener separates the message from the message maker.

Procedure

1. Work in small groups.
2. Select a poem written by a famous poet liked by the group. The poem must be one the group assumes most other people are not familiar with.
3. Write a poem that resembles the style of the selected poet.
4. Copy the two poems, citing the famous author as writer of the group's poem, and the name of a student as author of the selected poem.
5. Show both poems to fifteen people outside of class.
6. Ask each to pick the "better" poem. Have them give their reasons.
7. Compare results with those obtained by other class groups.

Discussion

What were the results? Why? Would group members have made the same choices? Why? What does the activity have to do with listening/receiving messages? What are the implications for receivers?

As illustrated by communication experience 11.3, the meaning of the message does lie, to some extent, in the message maker. But the listener needs to separate the two until after he has a sense of what is being said. The point here is that the reputation of the speaker may be a key factor in the listener's acceptance and/or rejection, as well as comprehension, of what is being said. This does not pose a problem if the listener knows what he is doing and uses it to his benefit by acknowledging it. The most effective way of doing so is to begin by listening to the message itself and then to consider it in light of who is sending it, rather than to respond to the two elements as one and the same. This is very similar to what the receiver does when attempting to separate his own needs and feelings from those he perceives in the sender. The more capable he is at doing this, the safer it is for him to then reverse the process and put the two back together, knowing that one impacts the other and must therefore be evaluated.

Other dynamics of the interpersonal encounter affect the ways in which the receiver receives the sender's message. Among them are the receiver's field of experience, the communication environment, and the code and channel selections of the initiator of the communication.

Field of Experience

The field of experience with which the receiver enters the communication interaction determines the ways in which he listens to and understands what is said to him. All the experiences and dynamics comprising one's field of experience affect his expectations of the immediate communication situation and what he believes the other person means.

What he thinks the speaker means, how he feels it is appropriate for him to respond, and all of his listening behaviors are products of his previous socialization and the listening experiences he has had prior to this particular encounter. Experience is a valuable tool in understanding. Its value lies in the receiver's awareness of its effects on the present. Since any two situations are no more identical than any two people, the past experiences of the receiver provide him with the basis for some assumptions as to what is to be expected of him in the situation at hand. Those past experiences can help him in the interaction at hand. Communication experience 11.4 is designed to illustrate the effects of one's field of experience on message reception.

Communication Experience 11.4

Principle

We use our past experiences to make sense of new experiences.

Procedure

1. Work in small groups.
2. Role play a situation in which two people are given familiar labels (for example, feminists, activists, health food freaks, professors, artists, etc.).
3. The two act as senders. They describe the situation in which they will be speaking. The others act as listeners and write down the meanings of the speakers' messages.
4. The two speakers talk to each other for five minutes while the others listen. They discuss a course of action they feel would solve a problem.
5. When they finish, each listener reads his version of what he has heard.

Discussion

How did the versions compare? Why? What did each listener know about real people with these labels? What were his past experiences with them? Did this affect his observations? How? Why? If it were a real life experience, how would it differ? Why?

As illustrated in communication experience 11.4, the listener's previous experiences affect the ways in which he listens in the given communication interaction and the ways in which he interprets what the speaker seems to be saying. A significant part of one's field of experience is the culture and subcultures by which he has been and continues to be socialized. Just as one learns appropriate message-making strategies as part of the process of socialization, one also learns to understand another's message making as part of one's socialization. The receiver uses his own frame of reference and past experiences including his own message-making strategies for decoding those messages sent his way. It does not necessarily follow, however, that one can understand a speaker's meaning by transferring roles mentally. One cannot necessarily understand the speaker by knowing what he himself would have meant by similar statements in similar situations. Nor is it necessarily accurate for the listener to assume that the person to whom he now listens means the same things by his words as would another person.

One's past experiences are the frame of reference with which he enters the communication encounter. He uses them to try to read the verbal and nonverbal communication of the sender. Their value lies in how wisely the listener is able to use them; how effectively he is able to distinguish, which makes this situation different. Where one's past experiences encourage him to behave or respond in stereotypic ways, he is processing the event-data through a screen that filters out rather than adds insight into the communication interaction. Where he uses them as tentative ways of understanding what the sender means, he has a valuable mechanism necessary for the complexity of the communication encounter.

Communication Environment

The physical and social context surrounding the communication interaction is the **communication environment.** It affects the ways in which the sender makes and transmits his message. The communication environment also affects the receiver's perceptions of what the speaker means by his message. It is the context of the communication interchange, including the role relationships of the communicators and the setting, time, and space in which that encounter occurs. Each influences the receiver in the interpersonal interaction.

Information is not something which inheres in the objects and events of man's world. Information is what a man endows those objects and events with. Man literally informs himself. He may be constrained or even destroyed by his environment. But its meaning . . . its significance, its utility for him; these are ultimately properties of him. Information is thus the lifeblood of his awareness, his consciousness, his knowledge of his environment in the same way that the highly refined and translated products of metabolic processes are the lifeblood of the body. An indigestable or undigested herb is either useless or as troublesome to man as is being unaware of or unable to inform himself adequately of some event in his environment which might have vital consequences for him.

Lee Thayer

The role relationships of the communicators affect what the communicator attempts to communicate. One of the ways in which the receiver decodes the meaning of the message is by knowing who it is that creates the message. In this context, however, the who refers not only to the person's ethos or credibility, but also to who he is in relation to that receiver. What one's superior means by a request as opposed to what one's friend or subordinate may be asking by the same request can be interpreted very differently by the receiver. For example, each could request that the other sit down and listen to something. It is the nature of the role relationship that changes the meaning; in the first instance the request is a tactful or indirect command; in the second, a request; in the third, the role relationship is so potentially inappropriate to the normal flow of communication that unless what follows justifies it, the receiver can interpret it as something to hold against the requester.

The words of the sender are processed through the receiver's perception of their role relationship. The sender offers a compliment and the receiver interprets it in terms of the words themselves, the source from which they come and his interpretation of what a person in such a relationship to him means by such a compliment. Once again, the meaning derived by the receiver is a product of the stimuli as perceived and interpreted by him. Here as elsewhere, effective message reception rests on the receiver's ability to separate that which is said and who is saying it from his own interpretations of it. He does not eliminate his interpretation. He is aware of it and continuously evaluates the bases on which it is made.

Besides role relationships, the communication environment includes the setting, time, and space in which the message making occurs. The setting refers to the physical environment. Just as it affects the sender and his message making, the setting affects what the receiver thinks the message means. The request to sit down and listen, cited by way of the previous example can be used to illustrate this point. These words uttered by the same speaker in the same tone to the same listener can be interpreted by that receiver very differently in different settings. Uttered in the sender's living room, they can be interpreted as an invitation; uttered at a football stadium, they can be interpreted as a criticism of the receiver's behavior or a signal indicating that what is about to be said is earthshaking; uttered in a different context, the meaning changes in as many ways as there are different settings. Of significance here is that often it is not the message, message maker, or receiver alone that is the key determinant to meaning, but the setting in which those people interact with one another and the perceived effects of that setting on what is meant by the message.

The time and space in which the receiver receives the message also affects the meaning of a message. **Time** refers to the time of day or year, both of which have some influence on the kinds of things that are said to receivers. It is also that sense of timing in the relationship between the message makers or the timing of one message in relation to other messages between these two communicators. One of the measures that a receiver uses to test out the sender's meaning in telling him something is the timing of the message. A compliment given just before one has to perform a difficult task may be read very differently from a compliment on first meeting or a compliment from a husband of twenty-seven years who still takes time to notice and verbalize something to his wife. Questions that necessitate lengthy answers can be taken to mean different things. Those asked by someone who will use up his own valuable time to listen to the answer, such as a doctor interviewing an ailing patient, are viewed differently than questions that can be interpreted as time-wasters, such as those designed by a student to take up enough time so that time is not available for the scheduled hour exam.

In each of these instances it is the timing of the message that in some ways is used by the receiver to decode the sender's meaning. His conclusions or interpretations are not necessarily correct nor the same as the intent of the sender; awareness that it is the timing of the message that has led him to the meaning he sees therein gives him some mechanism for validating or invalidating his conclusion.

The **space** in which the communication occurs is a factor in determining how the receiver decodes the message. The space in which communicators find themselves affects communication, because there are cultural norms and standards affecting each of us in our interpretation and feeling of personal and social space. Just as the sender can make use of these, consciously or unconsciously by "saying" something (nonverbally), so too does the receiver decode consciously or unconsciously the sender's use of space as part of the message. The freedom one person has to refuse a request made by another may be as much a product of the physical distance separating these two people as any other facet of their relationship. Furthermore, the receiver can decode the sender's use of space as a means of communicating nonverbally the sender's feelings of power.

Once again, these factors potentially are translatable by the receiver, whether or not intended by the sender or decoded in the same way as they were encoded.

Active Listening: Observation and Interpretation

Underlying almost every dynamic in the process of decoding the sender's message is the distinction between the receiver's observation and interpretation. Communication experience 11.5 is designed to give the student some experiential practice in distinguishing between the two.

Communication Experience 11.5

Principle

In observing another human being, one is continually in the process of interpreting his behavior. There are differences, however, between that which is observed and the ways in which it can be interpreted.

Procedure

1. Work in groups of five-to-seven people.
2. Select a photograph of a woman from a newspaper or magazine.
3. Each group member is to write a description of the person in the photograph.
4. Compare descriptions. Compose one as a judgment-free report.
5. How does it differ from the original versions?
6. Discuss what creates the differences.

Discussion

In what ways were the original descriptions different from the ways each person would have described the picture in situations outside of class? Why? How did they differ from one another? Why? Who did the differences give information about? Why? Was the composite a report? Was it free of interpretation? How can this be measured? What would be the differences if the person described was a group member? What are the implications?

As illustrated by communication experience 11.5, it is important to differentiate between that which is observed and the observer's interpretation. In the broadest sense, listening is receiving and processing the whole range of verbal and nonverbal behaviors. The active listener knows that a person's gestures, tone of voice, posture, etc., can mean as much as the words he says. There is no doubt that anything a communicator does has some meaning, intentional or not. But the meaning derived is a matter of observation, plus interpretation. Interpretation is a very individual thing, based on what the receiver has observed and what those observations mean to him. As necessary and important to effective communication as interpretation is, it is also a very separate process from observation. In everyday communication the two are often confused.

The communication models on which the text is based include the notion that communication is the process in which communicators perceive, respond to, and interpret event-data, and that there is a difference between the stimuli and one's interpretation of them. Nowhere in the analysis of the process is this concept more crucial than in evaluating the function of the receiver in the interpersonal exchange. As stressed throughout the text, meanings are in people, not in words. Words are the vehicles by which people transport their meanings. But because meanings are a matter of interpretation, they are quite individual. A sender and a receiver often have different meanings for the words and actions they use in relation to one another in the communication situation. Differentiating between observation and interpretation is one way of clarifying that people can mean different things when using the same words and actions. It provides communicators with some tools for making their meanings more mutual.

An **observation** is a report of that which the observer takes note. The language of reports is judgment free, capable of verification, and contains information about the referent rather than about the message maker's attitude toward the referent. In this sense, they are low-level abstractions. They include as much detail as is observable and are thereby as free as possible from the kind of judgment that ensues as we select those factlike statements to report from amongst all of the other possible statements that can be made about the referent. Observations are reportlike statements because they are relatively free from the observer's interpretations and/or feelings about those observations.

The **interpretation** is what the communicator's observations mean to him—his response to and decision about the meaning of any bit of event-data. Therefore, it is a product of himself and his observation. It is his perception of that internal or external reality. In interpersonal communication, communicators are continually in the process of observing and interpreting verbal and nonverbal phenomena. Both processes have to do with the observer. A person's observations contain more information about that which is observed than about him. His interpretations on the other hand gives as much information about him as about that which he has observed. For example, an observation would be to say that Carol's eyes are dilating as she looks at Henry; an interpretation, Carol is afraid of Henry. Not only does the interpretation leave out the basis for the

conclusion, although this is not necessarily true of all interpretations, but it supplies only one of many meanings a receiver could attribute to the condition of Carol's eyes. It tells something about the observer and the things that he notices and evaluates.

Part of the function of message reception in the interpersonal process is interpretation. The entire process referred to as decoding rests on one's interpretation of the message making of the sender.

The interpreter–receiver needs to separate what the words and actions are interpreted by him as meaning from the event he observes. Making this distinction allows the receiver to consider his interpretation as something he creates rather than something inherent in the object, other person, or message itself. If his role is to try to decipher rather than to create meanings entirely in himself, then he must go step-by-step from noting events (words and actions) to attempting to decide what they mean.

The student new to nonverbal communication who is very conscious of the physical behaviors of others may fall into the trap of assigning only one meaning to any one behavior. More sophisticated knowledge of nonverbal behavior leads one to understand that any gesture has some meaning. Assuming that all people making that gesture mean the same thing tells more about what that gesture means to the interpreter than to the person he observes. Taking the context and human differences into account and attempting to find out just what it does mean when an individual makes a certain gesture demonstrates more profound understanding of nonverbal communication.

The receiver, then, is an active participant in the communication process. He attempts to see, hear, and understand all that is said or done by the speaker attempting to communicate. He is his own tool for such understanding. He must therefore refine and sharpen his senses and interpretative skills if he is to be an effective instrument of communication. One of the ways in which he makes himself most valuable to the sender is by functioning as an empathetic, supportive listener. He works to understand the sender's meanings and at times even "hears" more than does the sender and functions to help the sender hear himself more accurately. It is in these senses that the receiver is more than a listener and more than an active receiver. He is a responder. His responses cover the entire range of verbal and nonverbal behaviors available to the message maker. It is in his role as responder that the receiver reverses roles with the sender thereby becoming a message maker even as he is decoding and interpreting the messages sent his way. In the next chapter we complete the analysis of the elements in the communication cycle by discussing the receiver as responder.

The Dangling Conversation

Paul Simon

It's a still life watercolor
On a now late afternoon
As the sun shines through the curtain lace
and shadows wash the room
And we sit and drink our coffee
cast in our indifference
like shells on the shore
you can hear the ocean roar
In the dangling conversation
and the superficial sighs
the borders of our lives

And you read your Emily Dickinson
and I my Robert Frost
and we note our place with bookmarkers
that measure what we've lost
like a poem poorly written
We are verses out of rhythm
couplets out of rhyme
In syncopated time
And the dangling conversation
and the superficial sighs
are recorders of our lives

Yes we speak of things that matter
with words that must be said
Can analysis be worthwhile?
Is the theater really dead?
and how the room is softly shaded
and our holy kisses shadow

I cannot feel your hand
You're stranger now unto me
lost in the dangling conversation
and the superficial sighs
In the borders of our lives

Interference with Intentional Communication

In order for the receiver to understand the sender as the sender intends to be understood, he needs to work at it. Anything he fails to do in his attempt to decode what is intended by the sender interferes with intentional communication. The first and most obvious interference is the receiver who does not listen or who listens ineffectively. In terms of the kinds of listening discussed in this chapter, not listening effectively means anything from lack of attention to lack of comprehension of the message in its totality of verbal and nonverbal components.

The receiver who listens to the words alone and does not note other nonverbal messages fails to comprehend all of what the sender wishes to convey. The sender makes a statement that seems to say one thing. In terms of paralanguage and kinetics, however, he says something of a very different nature. In responding to the literal verbal message, the receiver has not understood the sender as he has intended to be understood. Messages do not lie in words alone. The receiver who listens only to the words, ignoring the ways in which they are said and the accompanying nonverbal behaviors, is not an effective listener.

A second source of interference with intentional meaning is a lack of selectivity on the part of the receiver. Listening and observing every potential stimulus in the communication environment makes the receiver incapable of sorting them out and making sense of them. A case-in-point is a receiver who is so busy noticing the sender's clothing, jewelry, cosmetics, hairstyle, etc., that he cannot attend to the pertinent message-carrying behaviors in the given interaction. If the sender is a beauty consultant or decorator then the receiver might indeed take note of these things as a means of evaluating the worth of his advice. But if he is an attorney speaking about a constitutional issue, he is attending to stimuli irrelevant to the communication interaction.

In order that the receiver fulfill his function in the communication interaction, he needs to be able to decode that which the sender says. In the process of translating the message into his own words, the receiver can distort what the sender attempts to say. Decoding necessitates an attempt on the part of the receiver to be as true to what the speaker intends as he is able. Instances in which this becomes difficult are those in which the receiver has strong feelings about the sender. Those feelings color what he wants to believe the sender is saying. It is quite human to want those people we value to say smart things and those we do not like to say things with which we can take issue. The danger to intentional communication is that the receiver's need places him in the role of ventriloquist. He puts meanings into the sender's message that were not there explicitly or implicitly. An effective listener does not do this. He knows he does not have to agree with or like that which the sender says. He does have to work to understand it; understand it as said, not as he wishes it had been said.

Many other dynamics present in the interpersonal interaction interfere with effective listening and message decoding. Interference can result from the role relationship of the communicators, the subject matter discussed, and the receiver's feelings about it; the ways in which the sender expresses himself and their effects on the receiver's ability to listen; the receiver's field of experience; and the communication environment within which that communication takes place.

The receiver comes to the interaction a complex human entity with likes and dislikes, needs and feelings. He needs to know about all of these in order to monitor their effects on his abilities to listen to and understand that which the sender attempts to communicate. His past experiences can help him to understand the present. They can also interfere with understanding the sender if the receiver acts as if each new situation were the same as the old one. Students become aware of this trap during the course of learning to relate to and understand different teachers. If all of the teachers one has ever had have not really meant it when they have said there is a penalty attached to late papers, the student may assume that in the present instance the teacher making this statement does not mean it either. A low grade for late work is his first clue that he has misread the instructor's message.

Finally, and most significantly, the inability of the receiver to separate that which he observes from his interpretation of it is a source of interference with intentional communication. Whenever the receiver forgets that it is a two-step process, one in which he observes some phenomena and then makes sense of them, he is in danger of misreading the situation. He has no way of reminding himself that what he thinks something means may be different from what the sender means. Intentional communication becomes difficult because the receiver may be so unaware that he is making assumptions, that it never dawns on him to check them out.

Interpersonal communication is a complex process. Participating effectively is an art that demands effort on the part of all of the communicators. Whenever a receiver fails to make the necessary effort and settles instead for assumptions about what the sender means there is potential for interference with intentional communication.

Summary   In this chapter we have discussed the receiver as a listener privy to the whole range of verbal and nonverbal behaviors presented by the sender. The salient points are:

1. Receiving messages necessitates listening with a third ear.
2. Decoding messages involves reversing the process of encoding: translating the symbols into that for which they stand.
3. The translation involved demands that the receiver do as little as possible to distort that which the sender attempts to say.
4. The ethos of the sender and his role relationship with the receiver affect the sense of what the receiver thinks he says.
5. Receivers ought to separate the sender from the message in order to understand the message.
6. The receiver's field of experience and the communication environment in which the communication occurs affect his abilities to listen and understand that which is said.
7. The receiver must separate his observations from his interpretations in order to understand the sender as he intends to be understood.
8. Interference with intentional communication exists whenever the receiver lets any of the elements or dynamics discussed above affect his ability to work at understanding that which the sender wishes to convey.

Questions for Discussion

1. Discuss the differences between observations and interpretations. In what ways does the language of one differ from the language of the other?
2. Explain the concept of listening with a third ear. Discuss the circumstances under which one does this. When does one not?
3. How does the receiver decide whether the words or nonverbal behaviors are more significant in a given communication interaction?
4. Analyze a statement by a public official in terms of its timing and the effect its timing has on what the public thinks it means.
5. Discuss the differences between decoding and translating a sender's message.
6. Given that the ethos of the speaker is an important variable in determining one's impression of what he says, why atttempt to separate the message from the message maker? Are there dangers in so doing?
7. What are the most important assets of an effective listener?
8. In what ways is an instructor a listener?
9. Why do senders need effective listeners?

1. Wendell Johnson. *Living with Change,* **Notes**
   ed. Dorothy Moeller (New York:
   Harper & Row, 1972), p. 155.

2. Gerald Miller and Mark Steinberg,
   Between People (Chicago: Science
   Research Associates), 1975.

Bakan, Paul, ed. *Attention: An Enduring Problem in Psychology*. Princeton, N.J.: **Selected**
   D. Van Nostrand and Co., 1966. A good discussion of listening and attention. **Bibliography**
   This book is recommended for the student with some background in psychology.

Johnson, Wendell. *Living with Change*. Edited by Dorothy Moeller. New York:
   Harper & Row, 1972. A good introduction to the relationship between language
   and mental health.

Johnson, Wendell. *Your Most Enchanted Listener*. New York: Harper & Row, 1946.
   Recommended as a good introduction to listening techniques.

Nichols, R. N. and L. A. Stevens. *Are You Listening?* New York: McGraw-Hill, 1957.
   A basic book recommended for any person who wants detailed information
   about the listening process.

Smith, Henry C. *Sensitivity to People*. New York: McGraw-Hill, 1966. Recommended
   for the beginning student as an in-depth discussion of perception and human
   awareness.

The Receiver: As Responder

12

Introduction

As a responder, the receiver is a message maker. What distinguishes her from the sender is that her message making is in response to that initial sender's behaviors. This chapter looks at the receiver as responder. It compares and contrasts her responding functions with the other facets of her role as receiver. It also compares the receiver with that other communicator to whom we have referred as the initiator of communication.

Communication Goals

This chapter analyzes the receiver in the communication process as a responder. It is written to enable you to:

1. Define and recognize the range of feedback mechanisms available to you as a receiver.
2. Distinguish between the responding and message-making functions of feedback, understanding that they are not mutually exclusive.
3. Develop some guidelines for effective feedback strategies.
4. Understand the self-disclosing nature of feedback.
5. Use these concepts to complete your understanding of the communication cycle, and the dual nature of the roles of all communicators in that process.

Communication Concepts and Experiences

The essential receiving function is listening. Listening in its broadest sense incorporates the active process of observing and interpreting with one's eyes and ears. In interpersonal communication, however, the receiver who only listens and tries to understand short-circuits the communication cycle. It is for the ways in which the receiver shows his understanding, his feedback, that the sender relies on him. Feedback is what distinguishes interpersonal from other kinds of human communication. In discussing the receiver as a responder, therefore, we are concerned with his feedback to the original message maker. There are three factors to consider in discussing the receiver's feedback: (1) his choices of feedback mechanisms, (2) the functions of his feedback, and (3) effective feedback strategies for the sender and receiver in the communication encounter.

Feedback Mechanisms

In terms of interpersonal communication, **feedback** is any form of response to the sender's message. It is verbal and/or nonverbal and/or silence. Any response or lack of response is the receiver's message to the original message maker. Communication experience 12.1 is designed to illustrate the range of behaviors constituting feedback.

Communication Experience 12.1

Principle

Feedback is a necessary part of the receiving function; it is that which permits the sender to evaluate his speaking effectiveness.

Procedure

1. Work in small groups.
2. Each group prepares an involved story that the group members feel they could relate to a friend or stranger without it seeming improbable.
3. Each member of the group rehearses the story until he is familiar enough to tell it as if he knew it firsthand.
4. Each group member selects five people outside of class to tell the story to.
5. He tells the story to each noting feeedback: that is, when each responds and the ways in which he does so.
6. After each time, he writes down this information.
7. Group members get together and compare experiences.

Discussion

How did people feel about doing this? How well did they know the people to whom they told the story? What difference did this make? What were the differences in results from telling to telling? Why? What differences were there in the ways group members told the story? Why? Was each speaker more or less aware of feedback than usual? Why? What are the implications?

As illustrated by communication experience 12.1, a wide range of verbal and nonverbal behaviors make up the receiver's potential response to the sender. The skillful receiver is continuously listening, evaluating, and making choices as to the best response to make to the person initiating the interaction. Who the speaker is, what he appears to be discussing, what his relationship is to the receiver, what his demonstrated needs are, the communication environment in which the communication occurs, and the receiver's own frame of reference, including his field of experience, are decisive factors in feedback choice.

In many communication encounters, the exchange is conversational in nature and demands that the receiver respond verbally to the sender. At other times the exchange may be more one-sided. In this latter case the speaker continues to make his points at length, demanding only that the receiver signal his responsiveness nonverbally or by means of paralanguage and combinations of brief verbalizations ("Oh"; "I see"; and short questions). In most cases these choices come from some sort of tacit agreement between the speakers. A good deal of current communication research is devoted to analyzing what is referred to as **turn taking,**[1] the communicator's unspoken but agreed upon exchange of sending and receiving functions.

The effectiveness of the receiver is indicated by his skillful turn taking; by his sense of whether or not the situation calls for him to encourage the speaker by allowing him to continue to talk or by contributing his own verbalizations. Interruptions are not only feedback. They may in fact express the receiver's assertion of control in the communication situation. In effect, then, smooth turn taking indicates that there is mutual agreement regarding how the communication is to proceed.

Feedback in this sense is the response to the original message maker which presents him with some signs as to his effectiveness in communicating purposively. But as indicated by the discussion of turn taking, feedback serves another important function. It is the receiver's mechanism for exerting control over the communication encounter.

Feedback Functions

In each situation feedback serves two differing kinds of functions. First, it indicates the receiver's understanding or misunderstanding of the sender's intended message. Second, it shows the receiver's willingness or resistance to proceed as directed by the sender. In the faculty coffee room, one instructor says, "What do you think of the equal rights amendment?" Another responds, "Pass the sugar, please." The second message is feedback. Each communicator has his own private world. Each has his needs and desires. Each is in a continual process of determining whether or not to enter or continue to participate in the encounter initiated by the other communicator. Feedback can be viewed either as a response and/or an exertion of control in the situation.

Viewed as a response, feedback can be analyzed as providing the sender with information about how effectively she has expressed herself.

Feedback that is other than desired, either in form or content, would be analyzed from this perspective as a measure of her lack of effectiveness. Feedback that is other than desired indicates some error in her message-making strategies or choices. From this perspective, the response "pass the sugar" is viewed as a sign that the question (What do you think of the equal rights amendment?) has not been heard or understood.

But viewing feedback from the other perspective, that of the control over the communication that the receiver can exert, leads to some different conclusions. Feedback that is other than that desired by the speaker is not analyzed in this perspective as a measure of error on the part of the speaker or the receiver's inability to understand him. The answer "Pass the sugar" can mean that the receiver has understood the sender's message perfectly. His feedback indicates that he does not like it. In this perspective, his feedback is his way of saying how the encounter has to proceed if the receiver is going to continue to participate. In our example, the sender has to drop the subject of the ERA or look for a new receiver. Both these functions of feeedback are continuously, and often simultaneously served in the interpersonal encounter.

Viewing feedback only as the response to the sender violates the activeness principle of receiving. It makes the receiver a less than equal partner—one who passively functions only to assist the speaker in accomplishing his ends. In any interpersonal exchange, however, all participants must be accomplishing some sort of personal ends or they would have no reason to participate, actively or passively. Those needs may be by default, that is, it is easier in some situations for a designated receiver to let the sender talk on than to actively silence him. Nonetheless, some sort of needs to communicate exist or one does not enter the communication encounter. Communication experience 12.2 is designed to allow you to evaluate which of the functions, response or control, the feedback serves in a given instance.

Communication Experience 12.2

Principle

Feedback serves two functions: response to the sender and exertion of control in the speaking situation.

Procedure

1. Work with a partner.
2. Together, visit at least three places where the pair can observe, without being noticeable, two or more people in conversation with one another.
3. Bring a tape recorder or notebook. Use this to keep a record of messages and responses.
4. Evaluate the function of each message evaluated as feedback: was it responsive or an exertion of control?
5. Each person does this separately. Afterwards, compare notes and discuss findings.

Discussion

Did the pair know the persons observed beforehand? Would this matter? What differences were there in the pair's evaluation of the feedback functions? Why? Were the functions easy to distinguish? Why? What are the implications?

As illustrated in communication experience 12.2, in any given communication interaction, feedback can serve to assist the sender in accomplishing his communication goals or be the receiver's method for exerting his own influence on the direction he wishes the encounter to take. These two functions are not mutually exclusive. They are negotiable. Each individual in the encounter has his own needs to talk and be understood and/or to listen and/or be listened to. In order for one to satisfy his own needs, which involve the help of the other party, he needs to satisfy the other person's needs in some way.

In evaluating the effectiveness of one's feedback, then, it is necessary to view feedback as a strategy on the part of the receiver for responding to and/or exerting control on the other person with whom he attempts to communicate. In light of these considerations, a communication exchange cannot be considered effective from the perspective of one party alone. What the sender needs to accomplish and his feelings of success or failure are separate from the perception and experience of the receiver. There can be a mutually agreed upon perception and satisfaction but it does not necessarily happen. One can view his accomplishment from a very different perspective than the other.

From the perspective of the receiver, his feedback is effective if it expresses his response and/or control needs in some decipherable way. To make conscious choices about the most effective kinds of feedback strategies, the receiver needs to first evaluate what it is that he wants in the given communication encounter. Based on his defined purposes and whether or not he feels he accomplishes them, he can feel he has communicated as intended. An employer asked a new member of his staff how he liked his office. The employee hated it but felt he could not say that. He knew he had to say something. "It's just as I pictured it, Sir," he replied. He felt satisfied that his answer was vague enough to sound like he meant something quite different from what he felt he couldn't say.

The kinds of feedback strategies chosen by the receiver depend in part on the relationship between him and the sender and the nature of the given interaction in which they are engaging. Some of the most useful techniques that have emerged from sensitivity training, therapeutic communication, and active listening workshops are listening techniques and strategies for response. Despite the fact that a conversation differs from an encounter group session and that both are different from a therapeutic session, all have in common the interpersonal communication that occurs. What has emerged from these areas of study is some understanding of what it is that a sender looks for in a receiver and therefore some strategies for the receiver in fulfilling that role.

Essentially, a sender needs an empathetic receiver, one who understands or attempts to understand her. Understanding and agreeing are not one and the same. In many ways an understanding receiver is of more value than one who agrees. A receiver can seem to agree, thereby making the sender feel good. But if that agreement is not a product of understanding what the sender has been attempting to convey is mere flattery. Unless all the sender needs is some kind of flattery, her need will be better met by a receiver who tries to understand than by one who merely pretends to agree with her. An example is the person who wants so much to be liked by the sender that he will "yes" him. If what the sender wants is someone to understand him, eventually he finds little value in the receiver's inability to give his true response.

One of the reasons for talking to someone else is to clarify one's own thoughts. Sometimes the overt expression of a thought or feeling helps the sender become more sure of what it is that he means. It is in

FUNKY WINKERBEAN   Tom Batiuk

this sense that the responsiveness of the receiver is vital. For it is based on the reaction of the receiver that the sender has some more clear understanding of his thoughts than were he to talk to himself. An effective receiver is one who is responsive. Johnson calls the kind of responsiveness that we refer to here as *self-reflexive*.[2] It is responsiveness built on good listening in which the receiver assists the sender in crystallizing his thoughts.

The central focus of this method of responsiveness is question asking. The receiver responds to the sender by asking the questions: "What do you mean?" "How do you know?" "What then?"[3] The questions are used to help the sender think about what he is saying. He comes to a friend with a problem. The friend uses these questions to help the person help solve the problem himself.

The exact wording of each question changes in the given communication interaction. There are many ways in which one can question the sender regarding what he means. Examples include "Are you trying to say x?" "Are you saying x?" "Is x what you are indicating?" etc. The key is that the question allows the sender to clarify further for himself and the receiver exactly what he is saying, without doing it so artificially that it interferes with the flow of the sender's message making or makes him feel he is being placed under a microscope.

The same holds true for the second question: How do you know? The nature of the exchange and the relationship of the communicators determine how the question is framed. The question is important in helping the sender to clarify his own thoughts and in helping the receiver to know that he has understood the sender. Depending on what has preceded the question, one might ask the sender, "What leads you to that conclusion?" "Why do you say that?" "What basis is there for believing that?" "What do you mean?"

The third question, "What then?" can also be phrased in many ways: "What does it lead to?" "Where do you go from here?" "Why does it matter?" "How does all this affect you?" etc. Once again the thrust of the question is clarification. If the receiver can use them in that sense and not impose them artificially or rigidly, then he is responsive, empathetic, and can be seen as helping the sender in attempting to understand himself and make himself understood to others. Communication experience 12.3 is designed for you to see the effects on the communication interaction when such a response strategy is employed.

Communication Experience 12.3

Principle

One of the strategies for effective responsiveness on the part of the receiver is to be helpful to the sender in being self-reflexive.

Procedure

1. Work alone outside of class.
2. Select a conversation in which you take the role of receiver.
3. Participate by giving the sender verbal and nonverbal cues to indicate that he is being listened to and that you are attempting to understand him.
4. As the conversation progresses, ask the appropriate versions of the questions: How do you know? What do you mean? What then?
5. When the conversation ends, discuss with the sender what effect asking the questions had on him. Record the sender's reactions. During this exchange also use the same three questions.

Discussion

What was the relationship between the communicators? The nature of the conversation? How did the questions affect the conversation? How did the receiver feel about interjecting them? How different was this response strategy than his usual pattern of response? How effective was it? What was the other person's response when told what the receiver was doing? Did the questions facilitate understanding?

As illustrated by communication experience 12.3, a question-asking technique is a strategy for response. It is appropriate in an interpersonal communication interaction if the relationship of the communicators and the nature of the subject being discussed necessitates clarification.

Not all circumstances lend themselves to this technique—for example, a situation in which the sender is more interested in the receiver's own opinions than in being helped to clarify his own position. Practically all of our learning is based on getting information about our performances, and using it to measure whether or not we have accomplished our desired goals. It is the receiver's feedback that the sender uses to judge his success or failure. The guest says to the hostess, "I guess I'd better be getting home." In response she answers, "It's so early, have another cup of coffee." The verbal exchange is their way of deciding whether or not to end the evening at that point. Effective feedback in these circumstances is a responsiveness that gives the sender verbal and nonverbal reaction to what he has said.

There are several criteria that the receiver can use in evaluating the usefulness of this kind of feedback to the sender. The feedback must be *descriptive, specific, timely,* and about *behaviors (or ideas) that can be altered.*[4] In offering feedback in these circumstances, the receiver is attempting to let the sender know how he responds to the sender and the sender's message. Effective feedback is a response that is useful to the sender. For example, feedback that is **descriptive** is reportlike rather than judgmental. It is reportlike in that it is **specific,** including the details necessary to explain what the receiver is reacting to. Its **timeliness** is significant. If it is offered as an interruption or before the sender has completed his thought, it is either not of value to him or it is perceived as an attempt to redirect the communication.

Finally, feedback *is reflective of something about which the receiver believes the sender can take some action.* For example, the sender asks, "Do you like the shirt I am wearing?" For the receiver to ask any version of the three questions discussed above would be inappropriate to the message at hand, unless it was the receiver's feeling that the sender was not really asking the question he had in mind nor the one that he needed answered. Assuming, however, that the evidence at hand is that the question can be taken at face value, it calls for verbal feedback (unless a nod would do). The feedback is most valuable if it is immediate, specific, descriptive, in that it gives the basis for the judgment called for by the sender, and based on something that the sender can do something about. With these as guidelines the receiver responds by saying whether he likes the shirt or not, and why or why not. (In the case in which they are about to enter a job interview, the receiver has to fit his answer to the limitation of the sender's ability to do something about it and what he knows of how his answer will affect the sender's feelings about his shirt and perhaps himself.) Communication experience 12.4 is designed to illustrate the impact of useful feedback on an interpersonal interaction.

Communication Experience 12.4

Principle

For feedback to be useful to the original sender, it must be specific, descriptive, timely, and regarding something about which the sender can do something.

Procedure

1. Work in small groups.
2. Find a tape recorder to use while the group members work in triads and role play.
3. One person acts as sender, making some offensive statement.
4. The second person role plays a receiver who reacts by berating the sender and telling him what he thinks of her.
5. The third person role plays a receiver who interjects feedback fulfilling the criteria discussed in the chapter.
6. Switch roles so that each person plays each part.
7. Listen to the tapes afterwards. What are the differences in the feedback offered?

Discussion

Did the taping affect the conversation? How? What were the differences in the two kinds of feedback offered? How did each make the sender feel? Did the people know each other beforehand? What difference did this make? What are the implications?

As illustrated by communication experience 12.4, useful feedback has an effective impact on the communication interaction. In discussing feedback strategies, the focus has been on feedback as responsiveness to the sender's message-making. As discussed earlier, feedback is also the receiver's means of exerting control over the communication interaction.[5] As such, feedback needs to be analyzed as the receiver's message.

Feedback as Message Making

Another way of analyzing feedback is as message making. The strategies discussed in the last section are messages. They are messages made in response to the sender. The receiver, like the sender, is an equal participant and message maker in the interpersonal process. His feedback

Cues of the Primary Affects.
Can you match the sketches with the correct affects?
(1) Happy (2) Sad (3) Surprise (4) Fear (5) Anger (6) Disgust

Answers: A-5, B-2, C-1, D-3, E-5, F-2, G-6, H-4, I-3.

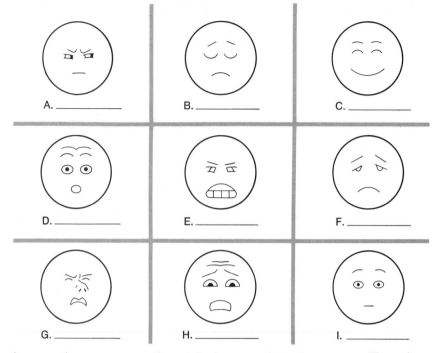

A. _____   B. _____   C. _____

D. _____   E. _____   F. _____

G. _____   H. _____   I. _____

is as much a message as the original communicator's message. **The only distinction between the sender and receiver's message making is one of timing.** Feedback occurs in response to the original message maker rather than as the initial message in the given interaction. Feedback is therefore two things: (1) it is a response, and (2) it is the receiver's message; his exertion of control on the interaction. Most important, feedback is the label given to the message that is a response from the perspective of the sender.

As a message maker, the receiver has the same choices to make about channel and code selection as does any other message maker. His choices are to some extent determined by the fact that he makes his message in response to that other person. If the sender asks the question, "What time is it?" the question calls for a verbal answer. If the sender pauses in a long explanation of something, saying, "okay," all he may be asking the receiver to do is indicate briefly his response, verbally or nonverbally.

Often, however, the receiver has as much to say on the subject as the original message maker. The interaction starts with a statement or question from the sender to which the receiver responds by making his own statement or asking his own question. The sender responds with further statements, or questions, or silence. The receiver continues with another message. The two are interchanging roles acting as sender and receiver simultaneously with one another. This is the most common pattern of interpersonal communication. Two people talk with one another. Who the sender is and who the receiver is depend on the point in time during the conversation. Which behaviors are messages and which are feedback also depend on timing. The statement, "I am thirsty" is a message if the person saying it is labeled sender. If said in response to a sender, it is considered feedback. Feedback, therefore, is the word used to describe the receiver's message.

Remembering this dual nature and function of people in the interpersonal interaction, one can discuss the receiver as a message maker, noting that he must make as careful and articulate choices in expressing himself as that person labeled sender. The feedback strategies viewed from this perspective have to do with the receiver's attempts to be as clear and understandable as any message maker. They also have to do with the receiver's awareness of the sender's understanding of his feedback. His feedback is in response to the sender's message. But it is also a message. Therefore, the sender may or may not understand it as intended by the receiver. The receiver uses whatever he finds in the original sender's response to assist him in clarifying his intentions in the message he has made in response to that original sender. In his message making, the receiver exercises his control over the course of the interaction. Like children playing the game "hot potato," messages travel between people. All communicators use their messages to influence each other. All messages are sources of information about the message makers, analyzed as the receiver's mechanism for self-disclosure.

Feedback as Self-Disclosure

Like any other message, feedback tells as much about the person offering it as it does about that to which his feedback supposedly refers. This is because feedback is judgmental and evaluative no matter how reportlike the receiver attempts to make it. In this sense, feedback is **self-disclosing.** It gives the other communicator information about the receiver's reactions to the original sender's message and/or behavior. Its usefulness to the sender has been discussed in terms of how constructive it is. But it can be looked at as evidence of the receiver's being open and self-disclosing. Communication experience 12.5 is designed to illustrate the self-disclosing nature of feedback.

Communication Experience 12.5

Principle

Although feedback overtly appears to be about the sender and/or the sender's message, it reveals as much about the person offering it as about the one to whom he refers.

Procedure

1. Work individually or in small groups.
2. Attend a campus meeting at which some issue is to be addressed and during which the audience is permitted to address the speakers.
3. Listen to and evaluate anyone giving any feedback regarding another person's statement.
4. Write down the content of his comment and analyze the language to decipher whether it says something about him or the subject he is addressing.
5. If possible, check out the conclusions arrived at by speaking to the person after the meeting and find out if his feelings are in line with what his statements seemed to say about him.
6. Compare conclusions with other group members. Discuss differences.

Discussion

What differences were there in group members' interpretations? Why? What was learned by analyzing the language? Why? Is this analysis different from what one usually does? What are the implications about feedback?

As illustrated by communication experience 12.5, feedback is as self-disclosing as any other kind of message making. The reasons that the receiver is motivated to self-disclose differ only in that his feedback is in response to the sender and something that the sender has said or done. These prior conditions determine the extent to which a receiver will disclose his feelings about the sender, the sender's message, and/or himself. Contemporary communication research finds that the degree to which one human being is apt to manifest his trust of another in terms of verbal openness has to do with how open he perceives the other person to have been with him. The implications for self-disclosing feedback are numerous.

The sender's expression of his own self-awareness and openness to himself and others inspires in his receiver a like degree of openness and self-disclosure. Obviously, the same personality considerations that determine whether or not the sender will be open apply to the receiver. All communicators are first and foremost complex human beings, with differing capacities for openness with others. But given that the receiver has the capacity for openness and self-disclosure, the degree to which he trusts himself and the other and thereby self-discloses, has to do with the ways in which the sender has been open with him.

This raises some interesting implications for the kinds of feedback strategies used by the receiver. Just as with any other communicator, the

"But it's only a word!"

most basic determinant of whether or not one is open and self-disclosing has to do with one's own self-knowledge and self-perception. It also has to do with one's perception of the other with whom one is communicating. The receiver is in the position somewhat different from the sender. He has more than an initial instinct to go on; his decisions about openness and self-disclosure have to do with the ways in which the sender has presented himself and his message.

Earlier in this discussion, we used the example of the sender questioning the receiver as to whether or not he liked his shirt. Such a question can be analyzed as open or not depending on one's interpretation of what it is that the sender really wants to know. If his question is really in regard to the other person's opinion of his shirt, his message making has been a direct expression of his inner question. It is the directness with which he asks and the openness of the accompanying nonverbal behavior that may inspire directness in the response from the receiver. If, however, the question is read by the receiver as different in its implication or if he reads it as a hint or indirect request for a compliment, this too affects what he says in response. It places the receiver in the position of making some assumptions about why the sender has chosen to be indirect, and of himself making some choices about whether he is going to respond to the verbalized question or to the unspoken but implied question. It affects the way in which he will frame his feedback.

Although any kind of feedback is self-disclosing in that it gives information about the thoughts and feelings of the receiver, statements that specifically disclose information about oneself and one's feelings and statements that increase the areas of one's personality designated in the Johari window as the *hidden area* are the most overtly self-disclosing. These kinds of disclosures are most directly responsive to the self-disclosing nature of the original sender's message making. That is, the more directly expressive and self-revealing the original sender is, the more likely is the receiver to participate in the interaction in a similar fashion. The sender who shares his hopes and fears with a receiver and expresses what he really feels about someone or something is most likely to receive feedback that is a true expression of the receiver's feelings about what the sender has said.

Interference with Intentional Communication

In engaging in interpersonal communication, the sender needs someone to listen to him, attempt to understand him, and as stressed in this chapter, to respond to him. Interference with intentional communication exists when the receiver does not fulfill the responding function; when he listens but in no way indicates what his response is to the sender of the message.

The mechanisms available to the receiver as responder are the range of verbal and nonverbal behaviors used by any communicator. Interference with intentional meaning, in this case the meaning of the receiver's response, has to do with the choice of feedback mechanism the receiver makes. A person asks another a conversation-starting question and receives a yes or no answer. The receiver has responded, but the response is so different from that asked for by the sender that it is read by the sender as a lack of interest on the part of the receiver. If this is what he intends, then he has responded appropriately. If it is not, then the ways in which he has framed his response have not communicated that which he intended to communicate. A sender makes a statement and gets no verbal feedback. If he wants a verbal answer he can read the lack of it as an indication of a negative response on the part of the receiver. A sender tells a joke and is met with silence. If the receiver means to indicate that the joke is not funny or that he is in no mood for jokes or anything of the sort, he has responded intentionally. If he enjoyed the joke but does not laugh, he needs to add some verbal feedback to explain his silence.

Feedback serves several functions. It communicates as intended if it accomplishes those functions. It is an interference with intentional communication if it is framed in such a way that the sender reads it very differently. If the receiver is tired of hearing the sender talk but remains silent, the sender may not be able to understand the meaning of that silence. If, on the other hand, the sender asks a question to which the receiver responds by silence, it may mean that he does not wish to talk. Since silence can be highly ambiguous, it is often necessary for the receiver to give some other cues, verbal or nonverbal, as to his response.

Interference with intentional meaning can come about if the receiver chooses a feedback strategy that is inappropriate to the interaction or does a poor job in using the strategy that he selects. If, for example, the receiver feels that the sender needs to clarify some things for himself and chooses to use self-reflexive question asking, he needs to be sure that his assumption is correct. He must use the questions in productive, nonintrusive ways. A wife used this method in talking with her husband, but she did it so artificially and clumsily that it made him very angry. Instead of feeling that she was listening to him, he felt she was talking to him like a child every time she said "How do you know?" "What do you mean?"

Feedback is the receiver's message. It is effective and works as intended if it is responsive to the sender and the sender's message. The receiver who is a poor message maker cannot communicate as intended any more than can a sender with the same problems. Interference with intentional communication results from an inappropriate understanding of what the situation calls for, or lack of recognition of the most appropriate message-making strategies. A message inadequately stated or nonverbal when the sender is calling for a verbal response fails to communicate as intended.

Finally, the receiver's feedback is her mechanism for disclosing her feelings and attitudes about herself, the sender, and the sender's message. Interference with intentional communication arises whenever the degree to which she opens up or remains closed is inappropriate to that which the situation calls for. Interference exists in any instance in which the receiver's choices for expressing herself do not accurately convey what she is trying to convey.

Summary   In this chapter, we have completed our analysis of the elements of the process of interpersonal communication by discussing the receiver as responder. The important points to remember are:

1. Senders rely on receivers to be responders as well as listeners.
2. Responding incorporates the whole range of verbal and nonverbal behaviors available to any communicator.
3. The receiver's feedback serves two functions: first, as indication to the sender of the receiver's responses; second, as the receiver's mechanism for controlling the communication, the receiver's message.
4. Strategies for effective feedback depend on the communication situation and the receiver's perception of what that situation calls for.
5. Self-reflexive question asking is a feedback strategy used by the receiver to assist the sender in clarifying something for himself.
6. Situations that call for more of the receiver's opinions are not handled best by question-asking techniques.
7. In these situations, guidelines for feedback are that it be descriptive, specific, timely, and about behavior that the sender can do something.
8. Feedback is the receiver's message. As such, the same guidelines for message making apply to him as to any other message maker.
9. Feedback is as revealing about the person offering it as about that to which the feedback refers. It is therefore self-disclosing.
10. Reasons for self-disclosure are a product of the person's personality and his perceptions of the other person's openness in message sending.
11. Interference with intentional meaning exists whenever the receiver gives feedback or refrains from so doing in ways that are not construed as he meant.

1. Define feedback and cite examples of it. How do these differ from other messages?
2. What is the purpose of feedback that is comprised of question asking?
3. In what ways can using the self-reflexive method of question asking interfere with effective communication?
4. How can silence be considered a response? Does it provide effective feedback?
5. Is feedback that is other than that desired by the sender indicative of a failure on the receiver's part to communicate? Why?
6. Why should feedback be specific?
7. Must feedback as message making be specific, timely, and about something the sender can do something about? Why?
8. What are the differences between feedback as a response and feedback as message making? Are they mutually exclusive?
9. What impact would a lack of feedback have on communication? What is a lack of feedback?

Notes

1. This term is used in the works of Knapp, Miller, and others.
2. Wendell Johnson, *Living with Change,* ed. Dorothy Moeller (New York: Harper & Row, 1972), p. 164.
3. These are Johnson's questions.
4. Richard W. Budd, "Encounter Groups: An Approach to Human Communication," in *Approaches to Human Communication,* ed. Richard Budd and Brent Ruben (New York: Spartan Books, 1972), p. 89.
5. Brent Ruben, "General Systems Theory: An Approach to Human Communication," in *Approaches to Human Communication,* ed. Richard Budd and Brent Ruben (New York: Spartan Books, 1972).

Selected Bibliography

Budd, Richard W. "Encounter Groups: An Approach to Human Communication." In *Approaches to Human Communication,* edited by Richard Budd and Brent Ruben. New York: Spartan Books, 1972. Recommended as a survey of the theoretical underpinnings of encounter group theory. Presents a valuable assessment of the theoretical shortcomings.

Johnson, Wendell. *People in Quandaries.* New York: Harper and Brothers, 1946. A good introduction to general semantics and mental health; recommended for the student with some background in semantics.

———. *Living with Change,* edited by Dorothy Moeller, New York: Harper & Row, 1972. Recommended for the treatment of feedback strategies. Johnson stresses the role of the listener in our culture.

Smith, Henry C. *Sensitivity to Others.* New York: McGraw-Hill Book Company, 1969. Recommended for the student interested in the interactional nature of communication. Some background in communication or psychology would make the book more meaningful to the student.

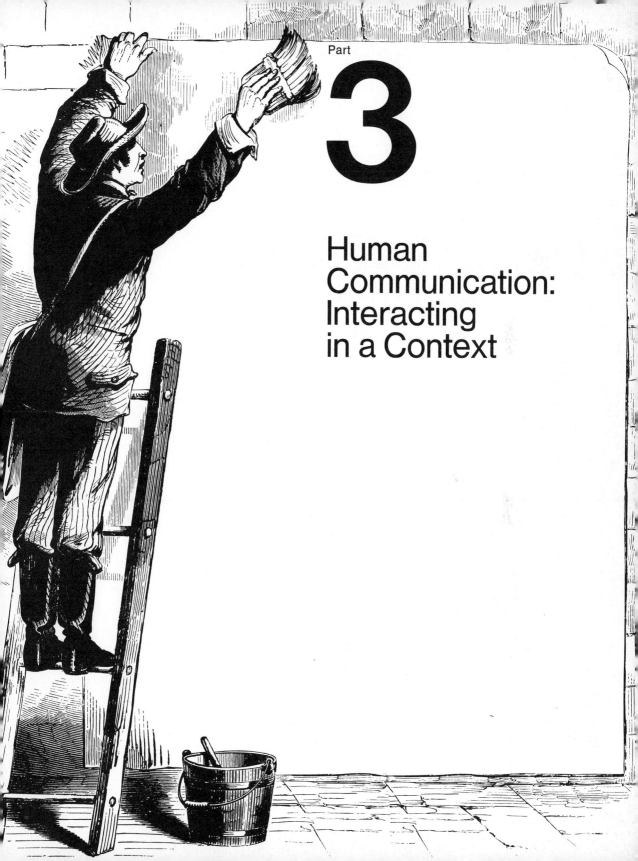

Human Communication: Interacting in a Context

Communication in the Small Group: Interacting with Others

13

Introduction

As humans, we are basically social animals. For this reason we spend a great deal of our time interacting with one another. These interactions occur in dyads (pairs), small groups, and organizations. Groups serve several functions in our society. There are groups that are primarily responsible for the socialization of the individual. Families, religious groups, ethnic groups and educational organizations are among the most influential in an individual's socialization. There are groups that are basically decision-making groups. Governmental agencies, business organizations, and educational systems are managed by groups responsible for decision making. There are groups whose basic function is problem solving. Therapeutic groups, counseling services, and consumer agencies are problem-solving groups.

Small groups can be studied as a social phenomenon, a system of social interaction, and/or as a context in which individuals communicate with one another. Our focus in this chapter is on communication in the group context. Since many of our interactions with one another take place in the context of the small group, the study of interpersonal communication is fostered by examining it in the small group setting. Communication in the small group is interpersonal communication. It is interpersonal communication

in a context. Studying the context, then, involves an exploration of the effects of the context on the communication patterns.

Communication Goals

This chapter focuses on the small group setting and communication within that context. It is written to enable you to:

1. Distinguish the small group from other human assemblages.
2. Understand the characteristics and dynamics of small groups.
3. Understand why an individual joins a group and the effects that group membership has on him.
4. Comprehend communication in the small group in its reality construction functions and in terms of the patterns of verbal and nonverbal interaction.
5. Recognize the several types of small groups, understanding that group types are not necessarily mutually exclusive.
6. Concentrate on participation in decision-making groups.
7. Understand the workings of the dynamics of small groups within the frame of reference of the decision-making group.
8. Develop some guidelines for more effective participation in the decision-making group.

**Communication
Concepts and
Experiences**

There are many different kinds of groups within our society. Each individual is a member of a variety of those kinds of groups. One way of distinguishing between groups is to separate small groups from other kinds of groupings. The term **small group** refers to a number of kinds of groups. It encompasses those groups having certain characteristics, despite the variety of purposes or functions served by any one type of small group.

The Small Group Defined

At certain ages children are notorious question askers. For each answer they have another question. Things that adults have learned and take for granted present food-for-thought for the child during these question-asking stages: "How high is up?" "Why is blue, blue?" "How small is small?" These are the kinds of questions children ask that adults tend to have difficulty in answering and therefore feel annoyed at being asked. But the last question "How small is small?" is one that a student of small group communication ought to ask and have answered. It is the initial question to ask in analyzing small groups, since it is the adjective *small* that distinguishes these groups from other kinds of assemblages of people.

Obviously size is an important element in defining "small" in relation to the word *group.* The lower limit is two people. A group of two is called a **dyad.** In some literature on groups, dyads are treated separate from other groups. Dyads are included within our definition of small group because many of the processes and interactions are common to both. The upper limits of the small group are defined in differing ways in the literature. The extreme is easy to eliminate. One hundred, seventy-five, or fifty people are easily eliminated as too vast a number to be considered a small group. Somewhere from twenty-five people on down to the lower limit of two is where the dividing line becomes cloudy.

There is not a magic number, however, that can be used as the dividing line. Five, seven, and eighteen people are potentially small groups. Obviously, then, number alone is not the determining factor. A small group is that number of people in a face-to-face relationship who can manage direct communication with one another. In this sense the number matters. The larger the group, the less likely the individual to be able to communicate directly with all other group members. **Small** is from two to as many people as can relate verbally to one another. The upper limit for a small group is usually set at somewhere between fifteen and twenty, for reasons of manageability.

The word *group* also needs specific definition. Group is used to mean a variety of things in our everyday language. In small group theory, a **group** is an assemblage of people having certain qualities. First, it is composed of two or more people, as previously discussed. Second, these people are in a face-to-face communication relationship. Many groups are not face-to-face in nature (religious groups, ethnic groups, national organizations). Consequently, these are not the kinds of groups generally analyzed in small group theory. Small group study concerns itself with only those groups in a face-to-face interaction. It is concerned with what happens between those people. It explores the ways in which those events are the products of the nature of the group and the individual's behavior as affected by his group membership.

The third quality of the small group is that there is an interrelationship among group members. This is sometimes referred to as **mutual need** or **interdependence.** Members of the group need one another for some reason. They cannot accomplish their individual purposes without one another. Fourth, there is a mutual purpose for the group's existence. Each individual member has his own set of reasons for belonging to the group. Fulfilling the group's purpose for being is one of the things he agrees to when he enters the group. Finally, the small group exists over a span of time. It comes into being either purposively or spontaneously; thereafter it has a life span. Communication experience 13.1 is designed to illustrate the difference between small groups and other kinds of assemblages of people.

Communication Experience 13.1

Principle

The small group is distinguished from other assemblages of people because it has certain qualities and characteristics not found in other groupings.

Procedure

1. Work individually.
2. Keep a record of all the groupings of people (two or more) with whom you have contact in the course of a forty-eight-hour period. Include friends, family contacts, classes, rides in elevators, buses, trains; attendance at a performance; any situation in which you do something as part of a number of people.
3. Use this chapter to make a checklist of qualities and characteristics associated with small groups.
4. Compare your interactions within the various settings against the items listed on the checklist you have compiled.
5. Then classify your experiences into those that are small group activities and those that are not small group activities.
6. The class as a whole compares activity lists, checklists, and classification lists.

Discussion

What were the similarities and differences of activities included in people's activity lists, checklists, and classification lists? What kinds of things were not included that should have been? What were the bases used for including or excluding activities? What difference does it make in knowing which activities are small group and which are not? What does the individual learn about himself and others from this experience?

As illustrated by communication experience 13.1, a small group has certain qualities that distinguish it from other units in which people participate with other people. George C. Homans sums up these qualities by saying that what distinguishes the human group from other assemblages is the ability of members to communicate with one another over a period of time in a grouping small enough so that "each person is able to communicate with others, not at secondhand, through other people, but face-to-face."[1] A group is a plurality of individuals in face-to-face contact with one another, having some purpose, and some interdependence on one another. Passengers in an elevator are not a group; but, if the elevator breaks down, they might have to become a group in order to survive.

Dynamics of Small Groups

Groups have reasons for existing. These reasons range from the need for the group to maintain itself to a need for accomplishing certain specific tasks. A family circle is a club that exists in some families and meets on a regular basis. Its main purpose is to perpetuate itself; to keep members of the family in touch with one another even though they may live far apart. This is an example of a group that exists to maintain itself. There are many examples of groups with specific purposes. Boating clubs, hunting clubs, bridge groups, therapy groups, and consciousness-raising groups are among the examples. Each of these exists to accomplish a specific purpose.

One dynamic of the small group, then, is that it has a purpose for being. It exists to fill some need. There are six kinds of dynamics associated with all small groups. First, all groups have a **group climate.** The group climate is the atmosphere that the group creates and in which individuals work with one another. *Cohesiveness* is another word for climate. It is a feeling of oneness. It is often called a "we" feeling, "groupiness," or "attraction." The degree to which a group is cohesive or not is a way of measuring its climate.

The second dynamic associated with groups is that they have **pressures and standards** that they exert on group members. Group pressures and standards are the ways in which the group fosters uniformity among group members. These pressures toward uniformity serve several functions. They enable the group to move in the direction it wants to go; they allow it to maintain itself; they create an atmosphere in which the group constructs its vision of reality.

The third characteristic of the small group is the interplay between the individual's motives for joining/participating in the group and the group's goals. **Group goals** are its reasons for being and/or the things it wishes to accomplish. Groups are made up of individuals. Different individuals have different reasons for joining (*attractions*) and different degrees to which they share the group's motives. The group moves along in a balanced state between meeting the needs of individuals and accomplishing its group goals. Without the individual, there is no group. The group must satisfy the individual's needs at the same time it accomplishes its purposes.

Fourth, all groups have **leadership and membership functions.** Participation in the small group is filling a membership or leadership function. The nature of these roles varies in degrees of formality depending on the nature of the group. *Leadership* is another word for influence. Any group has leadership: those who influence the direction a group takes. Some groups give formal titles and responsibilities to their leaders. This kind of leadership is *ascribed* leadership. Leaders in these groups are more recognizable than those in others. But even in what is called the *leaderless* group—the least formal, least structured group—some people exert more influence over others in determining the direction of the group. These people are those who achieve leadership. *Leadership* in a group is ascribed (assigned), achieved, or some cross between the two. *Membership* functions are the ways of behaving in the group. The members carry out the tasks of the group. These behaviors are as formal or informal as defined by the group. Leadership and membership are behaviors; they differ in the functions they serve.

Group membership functions fall into two basic categories: task-related and group-related. First, one can fulfill functions related to the group's task or job. **Task-related functions** are those that help the group accomplish its task. If the group is a problem-solving group, then its task may be a verbal discussion. In such circumstances, task-related functions are those that contribute to the discussion: give or seek opinions; give or seek information; coordinate; elaborate; or record what the group is doing. In other kinds of groups, such as social service groups, there are parallel task-related functions. In a rescue squad, for example, task-related functions would be contributing time, information, and/or equipment; seeking or giving financial or physical assistance for the task of rescuing people; coordinating the efforts of the group; keeping financial or other necessary records. Anything that a group member does to facilitate the group task is a task-related function. The nature of the task determines the kinds of behaviors that are task-related.

The second kind of function in which group members engage are **group building or maintenance functions.** Participation in these ways is oriented toward creating or encouraging a cohesive group climate. Group building roles include acts such as encouraging other group members; harmonizing relationships among them; observing and/or commenting on interactions; leading; following; and setting standards for behavior. All these are ways of interacting in the group; they are behaviors related to the group and its relationships rather than the task per se.

People work in groups as members of those groups. Some also take on the job of leading the group. The leader is one whose behavior affects the direction a group takes. Leadership in a small group is a function just as is membership. Leaders, and leadership, have been defined many ways in the field of communication, as well as in any aspect of life concerned with how people are affected by other people. Among the most popular ways of defining leadership are to look to those people who serve as leaders, and measure their capacities in terms of their traits, styles, or the

Then said a teacher, Speak to us of Teaching. And he said:
No man can reveal to you aught but that which already
lies half asleep in the dawning of your knowledge.

The teacher who walks in the shadow of the temple, among
his followers, gives not of his wisdom but rather of his
faith and his lovingness.

If he is indeed wise he does not bid you enter the house of
his wisdom, but rather leads you to the threshold of your
own mind. The astronomer may speak to you of his understanding of space, but he cannot give you his understanding.

The musician may sing to you of the rhythm which is in all
space, but he cannot give you the ear which arrests the
rhythm nor the voice that echoes it.

And he who is versed in the science of numbers can tell of
the regions of weight and measure, but he cannot conduct you
thither. For the vision of one man lends not its wings to
another man. And even as each one of you stands alone in
God's knowledge, so must each one of you be alone in his
knowledge of God and in His understanding of the earth.

Kahlil Gibran

situations in which they operate. If leadership is defined in terms of traits, we look at the leader as outgoing, verbal, influential, etc. Leadership styles are categorized as democratic, autocratic, and laissez-faire, the distinctions being the degree to which the leader directs the group or allows them to direct themselves. Situations as the criteria of leaders analyzes leadership in terms of what the given occasion calls for and the kind of person most effective to influence a group in such circumstances.

Since our concern is the interaction in the group and the kinds of communicative behaviors that occur, we prefer to define leadership in terms of its function rather than trying to define what kind of person is a leader. Group leadership functions, like membership functions, fall into two basic categories: facilitating the accomplishment of the task of the group and building constructive group climate. The function of leadership is to supply the impetus for the group to work efficiently and effectively along its social and task-oriented dimensions. Defining leadership in this way makes it parallel to membership, rather than related to individual personality.

Fifth, all small groups are characterized by **structural properties.** The structural properties are those qualities of organization within the group. This includes any rules and regulations for membership, leadership, and entry. The structural properties govern individual status, and the ways in which members communicate with one another. The degree to which the structural properties are formalized is a function of the given group.

Finally, all groups have **task and social dimensions.** The task dimension of the group is that which the group has as its job-related purpose. Its task is that which it has grouped together to accomplish. The social dimension of the group is its interpersonal relationships. The strength of the relationships among group members is usually measured by its cohesiveness. Its task orientation is measured by its accomplishment. Since both dimensions are operant in all groups, although some groups focus on one more than another, there is an interface between the dimensions. For example, group climate affects the performance of the group's task; effective task accomplishment influences group climate.

The Individual and the Small Group

There are a variety of reasons for joining a small group. Among them is the belief that some things are accomplished better by a group than by an individual. This is true in terms of tasks: a group has more resources than an individual, it can pool those resources and divide up the labor. It is also true in terms of the social dimension of a group: a group is a source of companionship, affirmation of one's ideas and feelings, and a place to share with others. Some needs (task and social), however, are better suited to individual participation than group work. Groups are slower than individuals, they must achieve consensus among members with varying points of view, and may be costly in terms of demands on one's time, money, and emotional resources.

Motives for Joining a Group

One joins a group because he believes it will fulfill some need and/or is a better way of accomplishing some purpose than individual activity. He chooses the group that he believes will best fulfill his needs. Underlying the specific appeal of any given group are some basic motivations for the individual's entry into and participation in that group. Most basic are the attraction the group holds for the individual, the satisfaction that participation brings, and the identity he achieves with that group.

Attraction

Each of us has certain motives for joining a group. Cartwright and Zander[2] call one's interest in joining a group, the group's **attraction.** Basically, they state that there are one of two things that make entry into a group attractive to the individual. She enters it either because the group itself is the object of some need on her part or because membership in the group satisfies some needs outside the group.

Need Satisfaction

An individual joins a group because he has some need to do so. If this need is satisfied, the group is important to the individual. He therefore sees it as valuable. Group membership can satisfy a variety of needs. They range from the specific purposes of the group to the most intimate individual needs, such as the need to belong. The more valuable one sees the group, the more motivated he is to join and remain in the group. Studies have indicated that the more difficult it is for the person to gain entry to the group, the more valuable he sees membership in that group.[3] This is one way to explain fraternity and sorority initiation rites or the strict rules for membership in such social groups as golf and tennis clubs.

Group Identification

An equally compelling reason for an individual to join a group is the feelings of identification with a given group or the need to have a group with which to identify. The individual's group identification exists to the degree to which he feels himself a part of the group. Identity with a given group can be in terms of its goals, values, life-style, or purpose for being. When an action caucus forms to do something about rising tuition costs, one can identify with its goals and therefore decide to join. A group formed to prevent segregated housing in a town draws members who identify not only with its goals, but also with its values, and the style of life it encourages. In still other groups members identify with the kinds of people joining the group as well as the group's purpose for being.

Effects of Membership on the Individual
Socialization

In the process of interacting with the other members of the group, the individual is socialized into that group's norms, values, and goals. Groups have purposes, goals to achieve, and means for accomplishing them as determined by the norms and values of the group. The individual enters the group for his own reasons. To achieve acceptance, and a feeling of belonging, he must learn the ways in which people in that group interact with one another. His socialization, the learning of the group's ways of operating, is rewarded by his acceptance by the group. To be a member of Alcoholics Anonymous, for example, a person has to agree to say that he is an alcoholic. This is not easy for some people with drinking problems. It is a norm they must accept in order to become part of the group.

Each individual is a mixture of his own personal norms, values, and needs. In interacting in a group he is in a constant state of balancing his individuality with the group's pressures toward conformity. Without conformity the group could not function. If, for example, everyone in a civil rights group were to speak at once, no one would be able to hear or understand another. The group therefore develops its own norms for who is to speak, at what length, and at whose pleasure. In this sense, there is pressure on group members to conform to the norms established by the group for taking turns in speaking one's mind. If these norms differ with the individual's set of standards, he either learns to conform to the group or attempts to influence the group to change. In either case the group exerts some pressure. The individual makes his choices about how to conform to or violate the group's norms. If his needs for acceptance, approval, or continued membership in the group outweigh his individual sense of the appropriate way to act, he goes along with the group. If not, he makes other choices.

Every group has its own structure and organization. The structure includes distribution of power and its agenda setting. The distribution of power can be formal or informal. A group may be highly structured and elect officers who are given prescribed duties and functions and have ascribed leadership status. Or, it may be loosely knit, allowing power to emerge, and leadership to be achieved. A local political party, for example, elects officers who have certain powers. Others who do not hold office may also vie for power. In that sense it is both structured and open to power plays. A therapeutic group, as another example, is generally loosely defined. Power falls where it may.

Agenda setting refers to the tasks the group has to perform and the order in which it does them. Some groups are more formally organized than others about their agenda items. The most formally structured group proceeds by parliamentary procedures. The least formally structured group is open to the items that group members present in the order that suits the group or any individual members.

Reality Construction

The group influences the individual and each individual contributes to and thereby influences the group. **Reality construction** refers to the interactions between group members and the ways in which they affect each other's perception of reality: the way in which people define for themselves and each other what is real, why it matters, and what needs to be done. It is the interpretative process in which we give meaning to the stimuli (event-data) with which we come into contact. Reality construction is part of the process of interpersonal communication. It occurs in the exchanges between group members as well as in any other interpersonal exchange.

In our interactions with others we construct our realities. We learn who we are and what it is that matters in our interactions. In belonging to certain groups, we interact with others in the process of defining reality for ourselves. It is for this reason that part of what is called communication in a group can be considered reality construction. One of the things group membership does is present us with other people who can confirm our ways of seeing things. The reason that a person can identify with one group rather than another is the way in which members of that group define reality. A voters' rights group confirms the interpretation of reality that members of the society share equal voting rights. People joining such a group would have to hold the same interpretation.

Individuals belong to many small groups. Different groups define meanings for different facets of one's life. Some groups overlap one another. The communication, then, of membership within overlapping groups either reinforces or conflicts with certain norms and values. Where they conflict the individual must either choose the values of the group that make the most sense to him or bring the most pressure to bear on him. Communication as reality construction always involves the interplay between the individual and others. None of us is programmed. We all have choices about the degree to which we accept others' definitions of ourselves and the meaning of things. Communication experience 13.2 is designed to illustrate the group's effect on the individual's reality construction.

Communication Experience 13.2

Principle

One of the ways in which communication is defined in the small group is as reality construction. What we know of ourselves, the world, other people, and how to interact is part of communication.

Procedure

1. Work in groups of ten-to-twelve people.
2. Each group creates a verbal (word) and nonverbal (action) symbol to be used for greeting one another and for taking leave (saying good-bye). These symbols must be different from any that are traditionally used.
3. Every time group members see one another in-or-out of class, each must use the greeting and leave-taking symbols of the group. This activity is to continue for as many days as possible.
4. Each group member introduces as many friends and acquaintances as possible to these words and gestures.
5. At the end of the allotted time period (days or weeks), have a group meeting.
6. Discuss feelings about these created symbols, reactions to one another when using them, and reactions of those introduced to these symbols.
7. Compare results with other groups.

Discussion

Did the words and gestures come to feel as if they meant something to participants? To friends? How does this compare with other expressions that we learn? Where do we learn greeting and leave-taking behaviors? What are the implications for how we get meanings? Did the symbol-making experience affect individuals' feelings toward one another? Did they effect a group feeling? Was the group who worked together a "group" within this chapter's definition of a small group?

As illustrated by communication experience 13.2, membership in the small group influences one's perception of one's world. One of the reasons for joining a group is because its members see the world from the same perspective as the newcomer. A chapter of the Daughters of the American Revolution and the National Organization of Women have differing versions of the role of a woman in society. Which group a woman joins depends, among other things, on these differing reality constructions.

Communication in the Small Group

Communication in the small group encompasses all of the message-related interpersonal behaviors of group members. It includes the reality construction behaviors just discussed. It also takes into account the patterns of verbal and nonverbal interpersonal communication patterns of group members. In discussing communication in the small group, we are looking at interpersonal communication in the context of a given social structure. Three important kinds of questions can be addressed regarding the nature of interpersonal communication in the group. First, what are the relationships among members of the group. Second, how do these manifest themselves in exchanges among group members. And third, what are the degrees to which communication is verbal and/or nonverbal.

The relationships among group members refers to their status within the group. This can be measured in terms of assigned status, in which leadership and membership functions carry ascribed titles and responsibilities. Relationships in these circumstances are measured by these titles and interactions based on performing one's duties. Another way of measuring status in groups is by the verbal and nonverbal communication of group members. Verbal communication is the easiest to measure. Who speaks to whom with what degree of frequency is the measure of the verbal communication. Nonverbal communication can also be measured. It has to do with the ways in which people talk to one another; the ways in which they talk to and look at one another; their use of space, and the ways in which they are physically positioned in relation to one another. Communication experience 13.3 is designed to illustrate communication patterns within a group.

Communication Experience 13.3

Principle

Communication within a group refers to reality construction and to the ways in which people interact verbally and nonverbally.

Procedure

1. Work in groups of ten-to-twelve people.
2. Divide each group into two teams.
3. Team A role plays the parts of members of a board of directors of a bank. They sit in a circle. Each person has to introduce herself and the character she is playing. (The name she gives herself, status on the board, and any other pertinent personal information.)
4. After introducing themselves, they have a discussion on the question: "Should the bank give college students interest-free loans based on good grades."
5. Team B sits in a larger circle surrounding Team A to observe the verbal and nonverbal interactions. (Who talks to whom, when, and how often. Who looks at whom, when, and how often, etc.)
6. Allow twenty-five minutes for the discussion.
7. Discuss the observations of the communication patterns observed by Team B.

Discussion

Did the role playing encourage or discourage self-consciousness? What kinds of verbal and nonverbal patterns emerged? Were they because of the roles played or the personalities of the students themselves? How well did students know one another before the activity? How did this affect the discussants? The observers? In what ways did discussants think they behaved differently when being themselves? Was either team a group within the definition of "group" in this chapter?

As illustrated by communication experience 13.3, communication in the small group refers to the patterns of verbal and nonverbal behaviors among group members.

In describing the communication patterns in small groups, some theorists have used geometric figures to represent the patterns of people's verbal and nonverbal interactions. The most common patterns depicted by these kinds of figures are circles, wheels, chains, Ys, and stars. These are represented pictorially in figure 13.1.

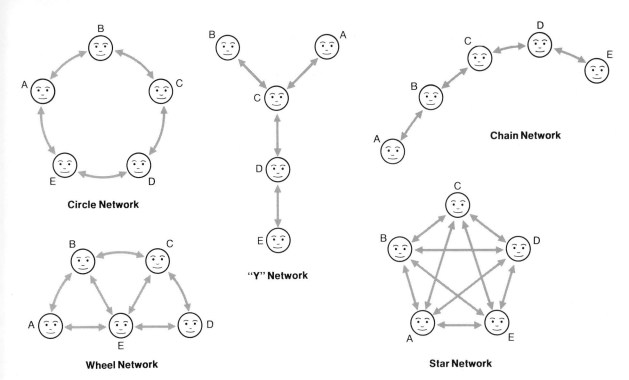

Circle Network

"Y" Network

Chain Network

Wheel Network

Star Network

Figure 13.1
Communication Networks.

Each node (face) in the figure is a member of the group. The lines connecting nodes represent the possibilities for direct communication. In the highly structured, formal small group, direct communication may be encouraged only along the lines defined by the group and represented by one of these figures. Even in the least formal group, however, despite the fact that direct communication with all members is not precluded, some groups function in the more constricted pattern represented by some of the figures (chain, Y, wheel) than in the more open communication figures (circle; star). The communication patterns in the small group indicate two kinds of things. The first thing that the communication pattern evidences is the interpersonal relationships in the group, or who communicates directly with whom and with what degree of frequency. Defining the kind of communication pattern with which a group operates can be the basis for evaluating communication patterns in the group. Questions can be raised as to whether or not this is the most effective way in which direct, face-to-face communication can occur within the given group. One can also evaluate the nature of the group and/or of the group members by their patterns of communication.

A second phenomenon that becomes observable by tracing the communication pattern of a group is the status relationships among group members. Patterns of communication provide evidence for whom it is that dominates group decision making, and who it is that is more passive or submissive. Membership and leadership functions evidence themselves in terms of a communication pattern and the frequency with which members are addressed verbally or are the recipients of nonverbal attentions.

Recognizing the communication patterns that occur within a given group and evaluating them are ways of understanding how a group functions. Effective patterns of communication are those that best facilitate the task and social dimensions on which the given group operates.

Types of Small Groups

Small groups are distinguishable from other interpersonal assemblages because of size, nature, dynamics associated with them, common characteristics, and the effects on their individual members. Within the broad category of small groups, there are several different types of groups. The distinctions among types of groups are made on the basis of three things: the nature of the relationship among group members; purpose of the group's existence; and/or duration of the existence of the group. Tennis teams, families, social clubs, volunteer organizations, and bridge partnerships are all groups within our definition of the small group. What distinguishes them from one another are one or more of the three characteristics mentioned above. By taking these characteristics into consideration, we can distinguish at least five different types of small groups.

First, **primary groups** are mainly responsible for the socialization of the individual. Second, **casual groups** are those in which the individual interacts on a voluntary, usually social or service-oriented basis. Membership is fluid in these groups. While socialization can take place in these groups, it is as ongoing as the primary group. Third, **therapeutic groups** are those in which individuals seek and/or assist one another in dealing with emotional and/or social problems. Fourth, **educational groups** focus on the learning or relearning by group members. Classes, seminars, and caucuses inside and out of formal educational institutions can be classified as educational groups. Fifth, there are **problem-solving** and/or **decision-making groups.** Solving a problem and arriving at a decision are not one and the same thing. They are related. Decision making includes problem solving that requires a high degree of acceptance of a solution.[4] Decision making is choosing between alternatives. Groups whose central concern is the accomplishment of a task are decision-making groups. Decision making is the process in which groups "refine, accept, reject, modify and combine ideas progressively."[5]

These types of groups are not mutually exclusive. In fact, many groups could be classified under two or more categories. A group such as the League of Women Voters is educational and decision making in nature. Its thrust is educating its members and the public. But it is also concerned with issues on which it as a group arrives at a decision and takes a stand.

There are three reasons for classifying groups: (1) to indicate the diverse nature of groups in which individuals participate, (2) to indicate that despite these differences of purpose, function, or relationships, they have enough in common to be called a small group, and (3) to raise as a question the varied nature of the groups to which an individual belongs and the reasons for her membership. Communication experience 13.4 is designed to illustrate the different natures of the groups to which one belongs.

Communication Experience 13.4

Principle

The individual belongs to a variety of groups for a variety of purposes. Membership in different groups is only problematic when the norms, values, or demands of one group conflict with those of another.

Procedure

1. Work in even-numbered groups of people.
2. Brainstorm to compose lists of all the groups to which individuals in the group belong.
3. Separate into dyads.
4. Partners discuss their reasons for membership in each of the groups on the list to which they belong.
5. The dyad reports its findings back to the group.
6. Groups compare their results with other groups.

Discussion

Were group members able to distinguish between small groups and other kinds of groupings? What kinds of motives did they discuss for group membership? What kinds of motives were not discussed? What degree of risk taking did people engage in during motive discussion with one another? Why? Was the group with which the individual worked a small group within the definition of that term in this chapter? Why or why not?

As illustrated by communication experience 13.4, an individual belongs to many small groups. This is known as **multigroup membership.** Multigroup membership explains the nature of the human in his social interactions with one another. We join different groups for different reasons. This becomes a problem only when the goals or requirements of different groups make conflicting demands on the individual.

Participation in Decision-Making Groups: Some Guidelines

While decision-making groups have been defined as one type of group, the process of arriving at decisions is essential in most small group environments. For this reason, the remainder of the chapter focuses on participation in decision-making groups. Participation in a group involves one's interactions with others on the task and social dimensions on which the group operates. Decision making, choosing among alternatives, in terms of the social interaction relates to the ways in which one chooses to communicate interpersonally with those with whom he works. Decision making in terms of task-related matters focuses on the ways in which the individual and group perform the function for which that group exists.

Participating in the decision-making group refers to the individual's fulfillment of the membership and leadership functions necessary to the group's success and survival. A group neither exists without members nor functions without leadership. This does not mean that a group must have assigned or assumed leadership. It does mean that the leadership functions must be fulfilled. In many groups leadership is shared, the group being *leaderless* in terms of a designated or single leader. The leadership functions are fulfilled mutually or by different members at different times.

Effective participation in the decision-making process requires that the individual know and understand what that process is and the ways in which groups arrive at decisions (since these differ from the ways in which individuals arrive at decisions), and be able as well as willing to facilitate the group's effort at achieving its goals. While the process of arriving at a decision differs among groups in terms of the sequence in which a group takes the necessary steps, there are those steps that must be taken. Ideas need to be formulated, shared clearly with others, refined, accepted, rejected, modified, and combined.[6] The group moves ahead on its task as it does these things. While the going can be tedious and slow at times, groups committed to group rather than individual accomplishment of the task must plod ahead. One of the first things to consider in the group, then, is whether or not the task is suitable to group accomplishment. If it is, the group needs to move toward that end. If not, one of the next decisions that a group can make is to designate to individual members those tasks that can most profitably be accomplished by individuals.

A second factor affecting the decision-making process in a group is the fulfillment of membership and leadership functions. The group is composed of individuals who share the rights and responsibilities of evaluating the performance of these functions by themselves and others. Membership and leadership functions should facilitate the task of decision making. If this is not the case, it should be recognizable and acted upon by the group as a whole or the individual who recognizes the problem and guides the group toward doing something about it.

A third dynamic affecting decision making is the interface between the task and social dimensions of the group. Even in the most task-oriented group the individual personalities of participants can affect cooperative decision making. One measure of the effect of the social dimension on group performance is group climate. A group that is cohesive experiences a feeling of "weness" or "oneness" with one another. They experience a sense of kinmanship and accomplishment. Since the absence of such a feeling impedes task performance, even the most task-oriented group might spend its time well to air feelings that are impinging on task accomplishment. Feelings that are under the surface but interfering with task performance are referred to as **hidden agenda.** Exposing hidden agenda often disposes of it.

Another way of measuring the interface between the social and task dimensions is the interpersonal communication patterns. Each of the five patterns or networks defined earlier in the chapter are contributory to decision making, depending on the task and the nature of the people involved. Obviously, some groups and some tasks are performed better with one pattern of communication than another. In a group with factions, the Y pattern is a way of facilitating cooperation, with one person emerging as the bridge between factions. If, however, a person takes on such a role when it is unnecessary, this may prevent people from communicating directly who could and would normally do so and it also interferes with task accomplishment.

Finally, decision making can either be aided or interfered with by the structural properties of the group and its group pressures and standards. The structural properties, like the interface between social and task dimensions, can be measured by communication patterns. The structure of the group must be compatible with the kinds of decisions it has to make and the ways in which it goes about making those decisions. Some kinds of decisions demand formal procedures; others are impaired by such formal structuring. Groups and members need to evaluate the effects of the structure, or organization, on the ability of the group to carry out the decision-making process.

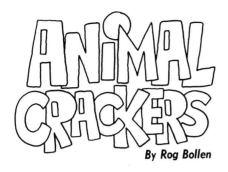

ANIMAL CRACKERS

By Rog Bollen

Closely related are the pressures and standards that the group brings to bear on individuals. Because decision making is an intricate process, groups must have some standards for carrying out the process and exert some pressures on members to do so. Effective participation involves awareness of this aspect of group nature and willingness to evaluate and change where necessary.

All of us have needs to interact with others. Membership in small groups fulfills some of these needs. There are such a multitude of groups from which each of us can choose that there are four questions one needs to ask oneself and answer in evaluating his decisions about joining and remaining active in a group. First, one needs to know what it is he wants and needs from a small group interaction and the ways in which a given group will satisfy these needs. Second, one needs to know the purpose of the group and how it is compatible with his needs. Third, one needs to ask what will be demanded of him by his membership in that group. Finally, one needs to weigh all these things in relation to joining one group as opposed to seeking a different group to join.

Deciding to join and participate in a small group is a process of evaluation. One evaluates himself, the group, and the potential relationship between the two. Communication experience 13.5 describes a way you can evaluate your participation in a group.

Communication Experience 13.5

Principle

Everyone is a member of small groups. A person's participation in these groups can only be evaluated after learning to observe himself and his interactions.

Procedure

1. Work in even-numbered groups.
2. Tape-record a real discussion taking place between participants, or create a discussion that can be taped.
3. Divide the groups into dyads. It is preferable for dyads to be composed of people who feel they can be open with each other.
4. Each dyad listens to the tape and analyzes their individual participation in that discussion.
5. Analysis is to be based on each individual's disclosure of what he meant to be contributing and the dyad's evaluation of his effectiveness.
6. As part of the analysis, keep a tally of the number of contributions made by the individual and the total number of remarks made by the group during the discussion.

Discussion

During the discussion, how did the participants feel about having their conversations taped? How did this affect the individual's behavior? How open were the dyads in their analysis of their individual behaviors? Did each individual observe things that he did not want to discuss, but were nonetheless helpful to him in evaluating his own participation? Were there any differences in what an individual heard in listening to the tape from what he had expected to hear; from what he originally thought the discussion was like? What are the implications for interacting in groups? Was the discussion group and the dyad a "group" within this chapter's definition of groups?

As illustrated by communication experience 13.5, the first step in improving one's participation in a group is observation. After one has observed oneself, one can then evaluate. How effectively one has participated is a matter of interpretation. The interpretation that counts is the individual's. A person who asks questions in a group that other members don't want to hear might seem annoying to them.

Participation in a group and effective decision-making contributions are complex and necessary skills. Chart 13.1 summarizes some guidelines for effective participation. The person who has mastered his interpersonal communication skills, understands the nature of decision-making groups and follows these guidelines, can work effectively in the small group.

Chart 13.1   Guidelines for Participating in Decision-Making Groups

1. Share thoughts aloud with the group. Decision making involves exploration of all ideas: those that are rejected and modified as well as those accepted by the group.
2. Pay attention to group processes. Understand the nature of groups, the dimensions on which they operate, and the membership and leadership functions that are vital to the group's processes.
3. Accept the slow nature of group decision making, realizing that in exchange one gains the resources of others' ideas, efforts, and companionship.
4. Be aware of the communication processes at work, and evaluate the effectiveness of the patterns of communication in the group.
5. Encourage others to participate.
6. Continually evaluate how the group is processing in its task accomplishment and what, if anything, in its interpersonal dimension impedes its task orientation.
7. Share any insights or questions regarding what can be done to facilitate the decision-making process.

An analysis of the guidelines for effective participation in the decision-making group is based on two underlying principles. First, the participant must be aware of the nature of the small group and the decision-making process. This kind of awareness allows him to contribute more successfully because he understands what is called for in the situation. The second basis for the guidelines is that communication in the small group is interpersonal communication in a given context. All that one knows about message making and the sending and receiving functions of interpersonal communicators need to be used in the small group context. The participant in the small group is communicating interpersonally. The context adds certain constraints on how and why he does what he does. But even within the context, the effective participant makes use of his understanding of interpersonal communicators as mutually controlling interactants, who have reasons for talking and listening to one another, who do so within all the dynamics that affect any interpersonal situation, and who need to use the interpersonal skills they have mastered.

Interference with Intentional Communication

The small group provides a context in which interpersonal communication takes place. One cannot communicate as he intends if he does not understand that context. A lack of understanding about what a given group is and why one has chosen to join it makes it difficult for him to participate in it effectively. Effective participation is also difficult if there is a lack of awareness about how groups function and what is demanded of the individual member.

Communication in the small group has to do with reality construction and with message-related behaviors. Interference with intentional communication is any inability or unwillingness on the part of the individual to see things as the group does or to behave in relation to the group in accordance with group norms. If the individual does not choose to remain in the group this is no problem. If on the other hand he values membership in that group, it is a problem. One of the reasons that individuals join together is to support one another in their perceptions of reality. The individual who wants to be a member but sees things differently interferes with the group's intended ways of seeing things.

Communication in the small group is also related to the ways in which group members communicate with one another verbally and nonverbally. The individual who cannot or does not want to conform to the norms of the group cannot communicate with them as he intends, unless his intention is nonconformity. A group that values formal ways of talking to one another will not understand the messages of a member who uses profanity so naturally that he is unaware of it. If he uses it to shock them, then he is communicating as he intends. If he is unaware that his mode of expression differs from the group's, he cannot communicate as he means to.

A group functions because it has a purpose. Its effectiveness in accomplishing its purpose is measured in part by the cohesiveness or "we" feeling among members of that group. A group that is filled with antigroup feeling cannot function in an effective way. Those people or attitudes that work against cohesion in a group are an interference with small group communication.

In this chapter, we have been concerned with communication in the small group. These are the important points to remember:

Summary

1. A small group is defined as two or more people in a face-to-face communication situation. The number of people must be few enough so that they can communicate directly over a span of time.
2. A group is defined as people in an interdependent relationship with some commonality of purpose.
3. Dynamics of small groups include group climate; group pressures and standards; individual motives and group goals; leadership and membership functions; the structural properties of the group; and the task and social dimensions on which the group operates.
4. An individual joins a group because he believes that it will fulfill some need and/or is a better way of accomplishing some purpose than individual activity. Three factors affecting one's choice to join a group are its attraction; its potential for need satisfaction; and group identification.
5. Group membership affects the individual in terms of socialization and reality construction.
6. Communication in the small group encompasses all of the message-related behaviors of group members, including reality construction and patterns of verbal and nonverbal interaction.
7. Within the broad category of small groups there are several types, none of which are mutually exclusive: primary groups; casual groups; therapeutic groups; educational groups; and problem-solving or decision-making groups.
8. Participation in the decision-making group involves one's fulfillment of the membership and leadership functions of the group.
9. All the dynamics related to small groups come into play in participating in the decision-making group.
10. Effective participation in the decision-making group requires that one share thoughts verbally; attend to and evaluate group processes; accept the nature of group work; be sensitive to communication processes and patterns; encourage others to participate; evaluate the functioning of the group and share any insights.

11. Interference with intentional communication in the small group occurs when people prefer to work as individuals and thereby do not contribute to successful group efforts.

Questions for Discussion

1. Is a communication class a small group?
2. What effects does cohesiveness have on the group's task performance?
3. Discuss the differences between leadership as a function of a group and leadership as an individual characteristic.
4. Discuss the ways in which membership in a group affects one's reality construction.
5. How can one determine the membership functions a person plays in a group?
6. Discuss the difference between the individual satisfying his own needs and behaving in ways that are counter productive to the group.
7. In what ways does communication in a dyad differ from communication in other small groups?
8. Why do groups exist?
9. Is there such a thing as "group" aside from the total of individuals within the group?
10. Why are decisions made by groups?
11. What is the value of group problem solving as opposed to individual problem solving? Group versus individual decision making?

Notes

1. George C. Homans, *The Human Group* (New York: Harcourt Brace, and World, 1950), p. 1.

2. Dorwin Cartwright, and Alvin Zander, *Group Dynamics: Research and Theory,* 2d. ed. (Evanston, Ill.: Row, Peterson and Company, 1960), pp. 74–75.

3. Elliot Aronson, and J. Mills, "The Effect of Severity of Initiation on Liking for a Group," *Journal of Abnormal and Social Psychology* 59 (1959): 172–81.

4. B. Aubrey Fisher, *Small Group Decision Making* (New York: McGraw-Hill Book Company, 1974), p. 152.

5. Fisher, *Decision Making,* p. 145.

6. A good deal of small group literature has discussed problem solving in terms of Dewey's five steps in reflexive thinking. This view has become less popular as we understand the less than rational ways in which people work in groups.

Cartwright, Dorwin, and Alvin Zander. *Group Dynamics: Research and Theory.* 2d. ed. Evanston, Ill.: Row, Peterson and Company, 1960. A comprehensive anthology of research into the different aspects of group dynamics, the study of small groups.

Fisher, B. Aubrey. *Small Group Decision Making.* New York: McGraw-Hill Book Company, 1974. Recommended for those students who wish to have a more in-depth understanding of decision making in the small group.

Haiman, Franklyn. *Group Leadership and Democratic Action.* Cambridge, Mass.: Houghton Mifflin, 1951. A good basic introduction to communication in the small group.

Harper, Nancy. *Human Communication: Core Readings.* New York: MSS Information Corporation, 1974. The section of small groups selects some important research in the area.

Wilmot, William. *Dyadic Communication: A Transactional Perspective.* Reading, Mass.: Addison-Wesley Publishing Company, 1975. The small group of two is explored. Emphasis is on communication in dyads.

Selected Bibliography

Public Communication: Speaking in Public

Introduction

Any human communication, interpersonal or public, involves people and their message-related behaviors. **Public communication** is that kind of human communication that occurs between large numbers of people in relatively formal situations. Like interpersonal communication, public communication occurs between people and involves those conventions established for the exchange of the ideas incorporated in their messages. It is these **situational conventions,**[1] the rules and structures shaping the message-making behaviors, rather than the basic communication processes themselves that change from interpersonal to public communication.

As early as the fifth century B.C. people were studying **oratory,** the means of expressing oneself in oral words, and **rhetoric,** the entire process of communication that included oratory. The courts of law required that a person speak in his own defense. So too was the political system based on a person's ability to speak on his own behalf to audiences of his fellow citizens.

While today we live in a legal system that permits one to hire a lawyer to speak in his defense, and our political system allows one to use speech writers to compose public addresses, the study of public address continues to flourish. There are many reasons to study speaking in public today: (1) to understand public speaking as a communication transaction between speaker and audience, similar to interpersonal communication, while differing in some important aspects; (2) to use

one's knowledge of the similarities and differences from other kinds of human communication to increase one's competence as a communicator; and (3) to learn how to prepare and deliver messages suitable to the public speaking situation.

This chapter focuses on the public speaking situation as a communication event. It addresses each of the reasons for studying public speaking discussed above.

Communication Goals

This chapter uses the theoretical and experiential approach to discuss public speaking. It is written to enable you to:

1. Compare and contrast public and interpersonal communication situations.
2. Understand public speaking as a transaction between the speaker and the audience.
3. Understand the four elements of the public speaking situation: speech, speaker, audience, and occasion.
4. Grasp the effects of the other elements on the speech itself.
5. Understand the public speaker as an oral communicator who affects his message and how the audience receives it.
6. See the importance to the speaker of audience analysis.
7. Analyze the content and delivery aspects of a speech.
8. Develop and apply guidelines for content and delivery skills in public speaking.

Public Speaking: A Transaction Between Speaker and Audience

Whenever a person attempts to express himself to others, publicly or interpersonally, the process involves people, messages, and the rules governing the interaction. Messages are the symbolic actions of speakers and listeners about their feelings toward one another and each other's ideas. This leads to several understandings of all interactions in which public speakers and listeners participate.

First, speakers and listeners are "knowingly" engaged in a mutual, ongoing relationship.[2] The speaker presents his speech to an audience who is there to listen. Each is aware of the other and the rights and responsibilities each bears in the interaction. The speaker who abuses his audience by talking "at" them rather than "to" them loses the interest and/or attention of the audience. The audience that cannot settle down and pay attention may find itself without a speaker willing to put up with their behavior.

Second, both speaker and listeners enter the public communication situation for some purpose. On the most overt level, the speaker's purpose is to express himself; the audience's is to listen. But the reasons why any speaker wishes to speak are as varied as the speakers themselves. So too, are the reasons for audiences attending the speech. Communicators, be they senders or receivers, engaging in personal or public exchanges, participate if they have some need to do so and refuse if they do not. Each has a purpose. His willingness to participate depends on whether or not his needs are met.

Finally, the speaker and listener are knowingly engaged in a relationship in which the listeners' perceptions of the speaker's evidence are the "coin of exchange."[3] The basis on which the listeners accept the speaker may be emotional, logical, or any combination. The speaker presents himself and his ideas. The audience perceives him and his ideas through its own set of intellectual and emotional filters. If they judge him "worth listening to," they participate. If not, they dismiss him and his ideas. All participants, speakers and listeners, know that this is what occurs. It is in this sense that they are engaged in an interaction. To have a complete understanding of the public speaking situation one needs to be aware of the four elements of that situation. One also needs to understand the roles and relationships of the speakers and listeners in those circumstances. These understandings are the foundation on which one prepares to plan and deliver any public speech.

Public Speaking Situation: Speech, Speaker, Audience, and Occasion

A public speaking situation has four elements: *speaker, speech, audience,* and the *occasion.* Each of these elements has its counterpart in interpersonal communication situations. The *speech* is the verbal message and corresponds in part to what is called the "message" in interpersonal communication. The *speaker* in interpersonal terms is the "sender." In the public communication setting the speaker refers to two things: the person giving the speech and all of the ways he goes about presenting his message. Aristotle referred to the impact of the speaker on his message as the speaker's **ethos.** In contemporary terms it is also called the speaker's credibility. The *audience* for a speech has its interpersonal counterpart in the receiver of the message. The *occasion* is similar to the communication environment, the physical and psychological environment and relationships in which the communication occurs.

In analyzing a speech, each of these elements needs to be addressed. John Kennedy's inaugural address, for example, suited the occasion, speaker and audiences (those present and the American public at large) well enough to become almost a classic in its time. Phrases from it such as "Ask not what your country can do for you—ask what you can do for your country" were so often repeated in the 1960s that they became somewhat trite. Martin Luther King's address to those marching on Washington is another example. His "I have a dream" theme which originated in that speech became as overused as the phrases from Kennedy's address. Communication experience 14.1 is designed to illustrate the interplay between the four elements of the speaking situation being discussed.

Communication Experience 14.1

Principle

Any public speech is affected by the other elements of the public communication situation: the audience, speaker, and occasion. These shape the message contained in the speech.

Procedure

1. Work individually.
2. Read and analyze Lincoln's Gettysburg Address which appears on the next page. Decide on its message and the way it is developed.
3. Select someone else to give the speech. The person selected might be a well-known public figure, popular professor, or fellow student.
4. Select an occasion on which that person could hypothetically deliver the speech.
5. Rewrite the Gettysburg Address for the selected speaker to present on the given occasion.
6. Deliver the speech to the class as the imaginary speaker would.
7. Discuss who the speaker was supposed to be, and the effect on the speech's content and delivery.

Discussion

Would it be possible for any living person to give the Gettysburg Address as it is? Who? Why or why not? What effects does the occasion have on the rewrite of the speech? What effects does the speaker have? What kinds of differences in the American culture today as opposed to nineteenth-century culture explain the kinds of changes that would be made in the address? What were the differences between versions composed by different class members?

Fourscore and seven years ago

★ ★
★ ★

As illustrated in communication experience 14.1, the speaker, audience, and occasion all affect how one composes a speech. Before one can attempt to write a speech, he needs to analyze each of the other three elements. This helps him make decisions about his subject matter and how to deal with it.

Effects of Speaker, Audience, and Occasion on the Speech

Speaker: Oral Communicator Who Shapes the Message

The speaker affects the speech both by his *ethos* (who he is) and what he does in creating and delivering the speech. The speaker's ethos has to do with the audience's perception of him and acceptance or rejection of him in terms of his message. The speaker who has or gains his audience's confidence and/or respect is viewed by them as more believable than a speaker who has not. It is in this sense that he has high credibility or positive ethos. Ethos is probably the single most important factor in public message making. The speaker who achieves good ethos is far more capable of being listened to and accepted than one who has not.

The speaker's creation and deliverance of his speech are rooted in his own perception of himself, the others to whom he speaks, and the situation. Every human being has his own set of speaking skills: vocabulary, reasoning, humor, resourcefulness, etc. While the topic of two speeches might be the same, the messages can differ as much as the two different people who have to compose them. Furthermore, people vary in terms of their levels of self-confidence, attitude toward expressing themselves orally, and their perceptions of how they will be received by others. Each of these factors affects how the speaker creates and delivers his address. His creativity and delivery affect the speech and its reception by the audience.

The public speaker conveys his message in verbal (words) and the nonverbal codes accompanying those words. Communication experience 14.2 is designed to illustrate the interplay between the verbal and nonverbal messages in the public speaking situation.

our fathers brought forth on this continent, a new nation, conceived in Liberty, and dedicated to the proposition that all men are created equal.

Now we are engaged in a great civil war, testing whether that nation or any nation so conceived and so dedicated can long endure. We are met on a great battlefield of that war. We have come to dedicate a portion of that field, as a final resting place for those who here gave their lives that that nation might live. It is altogether fitting and proper that we should do this.

But, in a larger sense, we cannot dedicate — we cannot consecrate — we cannot hallow — this ground. The brave men, living and dead, who struggled here, have consecrated it far above our poor power to add or detract. The world will little note nor long remember what we say here, but it can never forget what they did here. It is for us, the living, rather to be dedicated here to the unfinished work which they who fought here have thus far so nobly advanced. It is rather for us to be here dedicated to the great task remaining before us — that from these honored dead we take increased devotion to that cause for which they gave the last full measure of devotion; that we here highly resolve that these dead shall not have died in vain; that this nation, under God, shall have a new birth of freedom; and that government of the people, by the people, for the people, shall not perish from the earth.

Address at Gettysburg
November 19, 1863

SUPERSTAR

Everytime I look at you, I don't understand
Why you let the things you do get so out of hand
You'd have managed better if you'd had it
  planned
Why'd you choose such a backward time and
  such a strange land?
If you'd come today you would have reached a
  whole nation
Israel in 4 B.C. had no mass communication
Don't you get me wrong—I only want to know

Jesus Christ, Jesus Christ
Who are you? What have you sacrificed?
Jesus Christ Superstar
Do you think you're what they say you are?

Tell me what you think about your friends at the
  top
Who'd you think besides yourselves the pick of the
  crop?
Buddah was he where it's at? Is he where you
  are?
Could Mahomet move a mountain or was that
  just PR?
Did you mean to die like that? Was that a
  mistake or
Did you know your messy death would be a
  record-breaker?
Don't you get me wrong—I only want to know

Jesus Christ, Jesus Christ
Who are you? What have you sacrificed?
Jesus Christ Superstar
Do you think you're what they say you are?

Communication Experience 14.2

Principle

Public speaking is message-making behavior. Messages are carried in the speaker's verbal and nonverbal codes as interpreted by the receivers of those messages. The verbal and nonverbal codes affect one another.

Procedure

1. Work in groups of eight-to-ten students.
2. The group selects a speech for which they can get a written copy and also a filmed or videotaped version. (Important contemporary addresses are often taped; the text for them also appears in newspapers like the *New York Times* on the day after the speech is delivered.)
3. The speech can either be that of a contemporary public figure or something composed by a student. In the latter case the written version must be available before the oral presentation is made. Students must also be able to go to the oral presentation.
4. Read and analyze the written version of the speech.
5. Decide as a group on the main point of the speech, the ideas that develop that main point, and supporting material. Determine the group's prediction about the effectiveness of such a speech.
6. Attend the live version of the speech or a presentation of the tape/film of that presentation.
7. Compare and contrast the message and its effectiveness to the group's analysis of the written version.

Discussion

In what ways did the oral presentation differ from the written? What did the speaker do that differed from what the group expected? What was done as had been expected? What was the effect of the audience on the speech? What was the effect of the audience on the speech's oral presentation?

As illustrated in communication experience 14.2 the nonverbal behaviors of the speaker carry messages that affect the verbal message. In public as well as in personal communication situations, the verbal and nonverbal codes carry messages. The meaning of those messages lies in people, not in the codes.

Audience: Auditors Who Bring Meaning to Messages

The speaker means something by his words and actions. The receivers decode some meaning from those words and actions. These meanings are not always the same, especially in the case of nonverbal codes. A speaker's appearance and its meaning to the audience is a result of how they perceive him. The speaker dresses in whatever way he thinks is appropriate to give his speech. His audience is made up of people who have their own standards of what constitutes appropriate dress. He uses gestures and tones that he believes convey the meaning he wishes to convey. His audience decodes whatever meaning they believe to be in those gestures and tones. Because meanings are in people and not in words or actions themselves, the audience becomes a crucial element in the speaking situation. It decides whether or not a speaker has credibility and the meaning of the message as delivered by the speaker.

In classical times Aristotle emphasized that it is one's hearers who determine the meaning of what one says.[4] The audience acts as the judge or evaluator. It is the audience that gives meanings to the verbal and nonverbal codes used by the speaker. If the speaker wishes the audience to decode his messages in ways that are similar to his intent in encoding them he must understand his audience well enough to address himself to them in the ways in which they are most likely to understand him as he wishes to be understood. This concern for the audience on the part of the speaker is called **audience analysis.** Audience analysis is the attempt to understand the potential receivers of a message so as to make that message most clearly understood by them.

Any public communicator has a large anonymous audience with whom he tries to communicate. "Anonymous" is the key word. It is what distinguishes a public audience from personally known receivers. Interpersonally and publicly, there are people anonymous to us to whom we speak. When, for example, the letter carrier comes to deliver the mail, she may be anonymous to the homeowner. If the homeowner wishes to make a request, she makes certain assumptions about how to do so. So too must the public communicator.

Audience analysis is based on assumption making. The speaker does not know the audience before he speaks to them; he is not even sure who will be there to hear him. The speaker's audience analysis is based on his attempts to make the most accurate assumptions he can about whom his audience will be. This accomplishes two things for the speaker. First, it allows him to have some idea about how to compose his message. Second, it prepares him to change his plan of action if he finds his audience different in any significant ways from what he has assumed they would be.

An example of contrasting audience analysis occurred at a fund-raising dinner for a national political party. After a long and elaborate meal, the first political candidate rose to speak. The speaker assumed that the audience was there because they were interested in the party and its candidates. He forgot that they had just spent several hours eating and drinking. The speaker talked "at" them for almost two hours. The audience grew more and more restless. Many people left their seats and wandered to other tables to whisper to their friends. The speaker continued on. Although he was a popular candidate, the applause he received when he finally finished was lukewarm. The next speaker was introduced. He spoke for exactly four minutes. When he finished he received a standing ovation that lasted longer than his speech. It was apparent to those present that the applause was as much an expression of annoyance at the long-winded speaker as a reward for the second speaker. The first speaker had not effectively analyzed his audience and their needs on the given occasion. The second speaker had.

Occasion: Communication Environment Shaping the Exchange

The third element of the public speaking situation that affects the speech itself is the occasion. The same speaker with the same subject and essentially the same audience might give different versions of his speech depending on the occasion. A speech on the economy given at a businesspersons' luncheon would differ from a speech to the Congress of the United States. A funeral elegy differs from a speech of introduction. Both have the same subject matter; the topic is about a person. But the occasion, the reason for the gathering, affects how that person is spoken of.

The speaker needs to consider the occasion in the process of analyzing the audience and the speaking situation. The audience is there for a reason. One of the reasons for any individual member of the audience's attendance is the occasion. Considering the occasion is one more way for the speaker to have a full understanding of the speaking situation and its given environment before specifically beginning to prepare the speech he is to deliver.

The Speech: Public Message

In public communication, the speech is often in written form. As such the content can be analyzed separately and apart from its delivery. The best way of organizing a discussion of the content and delivery of a speech is to use the classical concept of the **five canons of oratory.**[5]

The Five Canons

The five canons encompass all of the elements of content and delivery in the speech. They are: *invention, arrangement, style, delivery,* and *memory.* The analysis of each provides the public speaker with guidelines for the preparation and delivery of his speech.

Invention in contemporary terms is the discovery or creation of the thoughts and ideas of which the speech is composed. It is the interface between the person who is going to give a speech and the knowledge available to him from which to create his composition. A speaker may be given a topic or he may have to select one. In either case his task is to work out what needs to be included in the treatment of the topic to handle it appropriately for himself, his audience, and the occasion. The canon of invention, therefore, has to do with the raw data of which the speech is to be made. It encompasses all the thinking and researching the speaker must do in amassing the content for his speech. This includes his main ideas, support, and evidence.

Arrangement refers to the ways in which the ideas are ordered. Any speech has three basic parts: the *introduction,* the *body,* and the *conclusion.* In the *introduction,* the speaker gets the audience's attention and lets them know what it is that the speech is to be about. The *body* of the speech is that section in which the speaker develops his main points and supplies the supporting ideas and evidence. In the *conclusion,* the speech is summarized or somehow tied together and ended. Arrangement, then, is the sequencing of the speaker's materials in each of these three parts of the speech.

A speech has a *thesis* or purpose statement, which is incorporated in the introduction or body of the speech, depending on the arrangement choices made by the speaker. There are several ways in which a speaker can go about organizing his material. The ways in which he organizes himself are primarily concerned with the body of the speech in which most central points and supporting materials are presented. Patterns of arrangement include chronological (beginning to end), cause-effect (conditions and results), topical (main ideas), problem solution (existent conditions—ways to change conditions). In arranging the materials of his speech, the speaker is trying to organize himself and make his ideas as clearly understood as possible. Any choices he makes in arranging his materials that accomplish that end for himself and his intended audience are effective ways of organizing his materials.

Style, the third canon, also has to do with the ways in which the speaker puts his ideas together. It is the unique way in which any speaker develops his ideas. His use of language (vocabulary, analogy, story, expression) is an element of style. So too, the specific manner of expression that is becoming to him. All of the choices the speaker makes in his selection and use of the verbal code are elements of style.

Delivery and **memory** have to do with the presentation of the speech. Once the speaker has created, organized, and styled his message, his task is to present it to an audience. Delivery and memory, then, have to do with his manner of speaking, his bodily actions, etc., and whether or not his speech is delivered from memory, a manuscript, or an outline.

The speech itself is the product. It is what the speaker presents to his audience. The ways in which he makes all of his decisions regarding that product are the result of his understanding of all of the elements of the speaking situation.

Speaking in Public: Guidelines for Content Development

The content skills of the public communicator have to do with the canons of invention, arrangement, and style. They are a formalization of what any person does in less formal communication situations. Invention, arrangement, and styling of ideas so as to be clear and understandable to one's listeners are skills that people perfect in daily interpersonal communication. Public communication differs in that the speech is given in its entirety to the audience. The speaker therefore bears the burden of clarity more than in the interpersonal situation. When a friend instructs his neighbor on using new ski equipment, the neighbor can ask for clarification when he needs it. If one reads about ski equipment in a book, he can stop and reread or think about what he's read where necessary. In the public speaking situation, the speaker needs to make allowances for the audience's thinking processes. She can do this in two ways. First, in the preparation of the speech, knowing that it is difficult to absorb too much information at once, the speaker must find ways to repeat herself; repetition is a valuable part of a speech. Those supporting materials that explain a main point are a form of repetition. Others are statements like, "As I have said," etc. While these are unnecessary in other forms of communication, they are vital in public speaking.

The second way that a public speaker allows for the audience to digest her thoughts, is by paying attention to them as she speaks. While it is not possible to read the audience's minds, a speaker can practice reading their behaviors. The body language and broken silences of an audience can help the speaker evaluate her pacing and the audience's ability to digest her thoughts.

The content skills of any communicator encompass his ability to think, reason, and express his thoughts and feelings in words. The public communicator must be as aware of his use of words as an interpersonal communicator. The understanding of language as a symbolic form of expression is as significant to the public communicator as to the person engaged in interpersonal communication. In addition, the public communicator bears the responsibility for organizing and arranging his

★ ★

My Fellow Citizens: We observe today not a victory of party but a celebration of freedom — symbolizing an end as well as a beginning — signifying renewal as well as change. For I have sworn before you and almighty God the same solemn oath our forebears prescribed nearly a century and three-quarters ago.

The world is very different now. For man holds in his mortal hands the power to abolish all forms of human poverty and all forms of human life. And yet the same revolutionary beliefs for which our forebears fought are still at issue around the globe — the belief that the rights of man come not from the generosity of the state but from the hand of God.

We dare not forget today that we are the heirs of that first revolution. Let the word go forth from this time and place, to friend and foe alike, that the torch has been passed to a new generation of Americans — born in this century, tempered by war, disciplined by a hard and bitter peace, proud of our ancient heritage — and unwilling to witness or permit the slow undoing of those human rights to which this nation has always been committed, and to which we are committed today at home and around the world.

Let every nation know, whether it wishes us well or ill, that we shall pay any price, bear any burden, meet any hardship, support any friend, oppose any foe in order to assure the survival and success of liberty.

This much we pledge — and more.

To those old allies whose cultural and spiritual origins we share, we pledge the loyalty of faithful friends. United, there is little we cannot do in a host of cooperative ventures. Divided, there is little we can do — for we dare not meet a powerful challenge at odds and split asunder.

To those new states whom we welcome to the ranks of the free, we pledge our word that one form of colonial control shall not have passed away merely to be replaced by a far more iron tyranny. We shall not always expect to find them supporting our view. But we shall always hope to find them strongly supporting their own freedon — and to remember that, in the past, those who foolishly sought power by riding the back of the tiger ended up inside.

To those peoples in the huts and villages of half the globe struggling to break the bonds of mass misery, we pledge our best efforts to help them help themselves, for whatever period is required — not because the communists may be doing it, not because we seek their votes, but because it is right. If a free society cannot help the many who are poor, it cannot save the few who are rich.

To our sister republics south of our border, we offer a special pledge — to convert our good words into good deeds — in a new alliance for progress — to assist free men and free governments in casting off the chains of poverty. But this peaceful revolution of hope cannot become the prey of hostile powers. Let all our neighbors know that we shall join with them to oppose aggression or subversion anywhere in the Americas. And let every other power know that this Hemisphere intends to remain the master of its own house.

To that world assembly of sovereign states, the United Nations, our last best hope in an age where the instruments of war have far outpaced the instruments of peace, we renew our pledge of support — to prevent it from becoming merely a forum for invective — to strengthen its shield of the new and the weak — and to enlarge the area in which its writ may run.

Finally, to those nations who would make themselves our adversary, we offer not a pledge but a request: that both sides begin anew the quest for peace, before the dark powers of destruction unleashed by science engulf all humanity in planned or accidental self-destruction.

We dare not tempt them with weakness. For only when our arms are sufficient beyond doubt can we be certain beyond

★ ★

doubt that they will never be employed.

But neither can two great and powerful groups of nations take comfort from our present course — both sides overburdened by the cost of modern weapons, both rightly alarmed by the steady spread of the deadly atom, yet both racing to alter that uncertain balance of terror that stays the hand of mankind's final war.

So let us begin anew — remembering on both sides that civility is not a sign of weakness, and sincerity is always subject to proof. Let us never negotiate out of fear. But let us never fear to negotiate.

Let both sides explore what problems unite us instead of belaboring those problems which divide us.

Let both sides, for the first time, formulate serious and precise proposals for the inspection and control of arms — and bring the absolute power to destroy other nations under the absolute control of all nations.

Let both sides join to invoke the wonders of science instead of its terrors. Together let us explore the stars, conquer the deserts, eradicate disease, tap the ocean depths, and encourage the arts and commerce.

Let both sides unite to heed in all corners of the earth the command of Isaiah — to "undo the heavy burdens . . . [and] let the oppressed go free."

And if a beach-head of cooperation may push back the jungles of suspicion, let both sides join in creating a new endeavor, not a new balance of power, but a new world of law, where the strong are just and the weak secure and the peace preserved.

All this will not be finished in the first one hundred days. Nor will it be finished in the first one thousand days, nor in the life of this Administration, nor even perhaps in our lifetime on this planet. But let us begin.

In your hands, my fellow citizens, more than mine, will rest the final success or failure of our course. Since this country

was founded, each generation of Americans has been summoned to give testimony to its national loyalty. The graves of young Americans who answered the call to service surround the globe.

Now the trumpet summons us again — not as a call to bear arms, tho arms we need — not as a call to battle, tho embattled we are — but a call to bear the burden of a long twilight struggle, year in and year out "rejoicing in hope, patient in tribulation" — a struggle against the common enemies of man: tyranny, poverty, disease, and war itself.

Can we forge against these enemies a grand and global alliance, North and South, East and West, that can assure a more fruitful life for all mankind? Will you join in that historic effort?

In the long history of the world, only a few generations have been granted the role of defending freedom in its hour of maximum danger. I do not shrink from this responsibility — I welcome it. I do not believe that any of us would exchange places with any other people or any other generation. The energy, the faith, and the devotion which we bring to this endeavor will light our country and all who serve it — and the glow from that fire can truly light the world.

And so, my fellow Americans: ask not what your country can do for you — ask what you can do for your country.

My fellow citizens of the world: ask not what America will do for you, but what together we can do for the freedom of man.

Finally, whether you are citizens of America or citizens of the world, ask of us here the same high standards of strength and sacrifice which we ask of you. With a good conscience our only sure reward, with history the final judge of our deeds, let us go forth to lead the land we love, asking His blessing and His help, but knowing that here on earth God's work must truly be our own.

ideas so that they are understandable within the format of the public speaking situation. The basic processes between personal and public communication are as similar as the physical skills necessary to an athlete be he a hockey player or soccer star. The situation and rules governing it change as do the rules of an individual sport. To be effective, one need have the basic understanding of the processes, and learn the rules governing the individual game. Communication experience 14.3 is designed for you to develop your content skills.

Communication Experience 14.3

Principle

All message making is communicative behavior. Messages in the public speaking situation differ in some ways from interpersonal messages. But, in many ways, they share common elements.

Procedure

1. Work individually.
2. Clip a news item from a campus newspaper.
3. Using the guidelines for the content skills at the end of the chapter, prepare a three-minute speech on the item.
4. Use your knowledge of interpersonal communication to prepare to tell a group of five classmates about the contents of the same item.
5. Write an analysis of the differences in content and delivery between the two kinds of presentations of the information.

Discussion

In what ways did the language of the two messages differ? In what ways did the delivery of the two messages differ? In what ways does knowing about interpersonal communication help in preparing a public message? In what ways must an interpersonal message be changed to suit a public audience? In what ways does one's knowledge of nonverbal interpersonal communication affect his preparation and presentation of a public message? Are interpersonal messages and public messages more alike or unlike one another?

As illustrated by communication experience 14.3, public message making is not unlike interpersonal message making. Both involve verbal and nonverbal codes. Both involve message makers and intended receivers. Both occur on some sort of occasion or in some sort of context.

To prepare a speech a speaker must analyze the audience and occasion, and then follow some guidelines for composing a speech.

To analyze a potential audience, a speaker must gather as much information as she can. Sometimes this is specifically available. A speaker invited to speak somewhere can question those inviting her about the audience. A student speaking in class can herself informally poll her potential audience to find out its interest in the topic. Where specific information is limited, the speaker needs to ask herself a series of questions on which to base her assumptions about the audience. The four essential questions for a speaker to answer before composing her speech are: (1) who is the audience (age, sex, education, occupation, economic status, religion, politics, interest groups, etc.); (2) why are they here (voluntarily or as a requirement; to be entertained, educated, or provoked; because of the speakers, occasion, or both); (3) what do they want to know (their interests, prejudices, prior knowledge of the subject, ability to handle new or controversial information); and (4) what is the attitude of the audience toward the speaker (friendly, hostile, neutral).

When the speaker has completed as effectively as possible the task of gathering information about the audience, she can then begin to organize and prepare ideas for the speech. Chart 14.1 summarizes the essential steps in content preparation.

Chart 14.1   Steps in Content Preparation

In developing the content of any speech (except one that is impromptu) it is important to think about a subject; do whatever research is necessary to know it thoroughly, and select the ways in which the materials can be organized so as to be clear and interesting to an audience. This involves seven steps.

1. Selection of a subject and research on it.
2. Adjustment of the subject to fit the speaker, audience, and occasion.
3. Composition of a thesis statement and the main points necessary in the development of the topic.
4. Selection of the supporting materials (evidence, supporting ideas, etc.).
5. Selection of an order for the main ideas and supporting materials (Choice of pattern of arrangement: Chronological, cause-effect, problem solution, etc.).
6. Composition of an introduction and conclusion.
7. Determination of delivery style (memory, manuscript, or outline) and rehearsal.

Let us take a hypothetical situation and apply each of the steps presented in chart 14.1. Jane, a junior in college, is enrolled in a public speaking course. She is interested in sports and decides to make a speech on that subject. After researching the topic, she narrows it down to intercollegiate sports. This too she decides is too vast a subject for a ten-minute speech. She limits herself to the subject of sports at the university she attends, with specific attention to attitudes toward athletes by other undergraduates at the university.

At this point Jane has a subject that is narrow enough to handle in a short speech. In deciding how to handle the topic, she considers her own attitudes; how she believes she is perceived by her fellow classmates; and her classmates' attitude toward campus sports. Having gone through the process of analyzing herself and her audience, she reviews her research materials and decides which are pertinent to her topic as it now stands. She frames a thesis or purpose statement—the central thought of her speech. Next, she determines the main points she wants to make. For each of these she decides on supporting material and evidence. Each of these decisions is based on her topic, her purpose, and her analysis of herself and her audience.

Having decided on the ideas for the body of her speech, she determines the pattern of arrangement of ideas most suitable to her topic. Jane then decides what to use to introduce her speech, and what she wants to say to conclude it. She then decides how to deliver it; whether to use a manuscript outline, or to deliver the speech from memory. She then practices giving the speech aloud to friends who are willing to act as her audience.

Delivery Skills: Guidelines for Delivering the Message

The delivery skills of the public speaker encompass the canons for delivery and memory. The similarities and differences between the content skills of the personal and public communicator are parallel to the comparisons between interpersonal and public delivery skills. Any communicator needs to be able to speak clearly, loud enough to be heard, and at a pace at which he can be understood. Whether one communicates with one other human being or one thousand, he needs to use his ability to express himself in such a way as to make others want to listen to him. Furthermore, he needs to be aware of himself and all of his nonverbal behaviors as he speaks. When we talk of *delivery* in public communication, we are speaking of all the communicative behaviors accompanying the speaker's words. To deliver a speech effectively is the same as delivering any message in a way that one's listeners hear and understand him. The public communicator's delivery skills differ from the interpersonal communicator's skills only in degree. Since he attempts to communicate to large numbers of people, his voice and bodily actions need to be loud and/or large enough to help him express himself. As in other communication situations, the speaker's involvement with his message and with making himself understood as he wishes to be understood are the essential delivery skills.

The public speaker's delivery skills have to do with his nonverbal behaviors. His delivery skills center on the ways in which he uses his verbal code and any other accompanying nonverbal behaviors. His nonverbal behaviors include his: *performance, artifactual,* and *contextual* codes.

Performance codes are all of the gestures, body language, and physical movements of the speaker. These codes, therefore, include how the speaker stands or sits, his use of gestures, his facial expressions, his eye contact, his conscious and unconscious bodily actions, and his *paralanguage,* tone of voice and verbal utterances other than words themselves. The choices the speaker makes about delivery of speech (memory, manuscript, outline) are also part of his performance code.

As a person speaks the audience listens; and also watches. Intentionally or not his performance codes "say" something. The speaker may mean to convey his sincerity, but his facial expression may be read as phony by the audience. He may talk of caring about people but convey a different message because he never looks the audience in the eye. He may say how glad he is to have the chance to speak but appear much too nervous to be happy. Messages are carried in the performance codes. Their meanings are interpreted by those observing the speaker. The effective speaker is conscious of all of his performance codes.

The **artifactual codes** are those nonverbal behaviors that are related to object associated with the speaker or present in the speaking situation. The artifactual codes relate to what the speaker looks like in terms of his clothing, hairstyle, and any other objects that accompany him. The effective speaker uses all of these cues to add to his message. A speaker would not wear a pair of pajamas while delivering a speech, even though audiences know that many people do wear pajamas. He might drink beer, but would not have a can of beer beside him as he spoke. A glass of water, however, is acceptable even in the most formal public-speaking situations. The effective speaker makes sure his artifactual codes enhance his verbal message.

The **contextual codes** have to do with the ways in which the speaker uses time and space. How and when he begins his speech, how long he takes to say what he has to say, the pacing of his words, and where he stands or sits in relation to his audience are part of the contextual codes.

Communication experience 14.4 is designed to illustrate the effect of delivery skills.

Communication Experience 14.4

Principle

Delivery skills in public communication involve mastery of nonverbal codes.

Procedure

1. Work in pairs.
2. The dyad attends an on-campus speech.
3. During the speech, the dyad takes notes regarding the speaker's use of performance, artifactual, and contextual codes.
4. Each person rates the effectiveness of the speaker in terms of his use of these codes.
5. Compare and discuss ratings and the bases for ratings.

Discussion

Who was the speaker? Was he known to either partner beforehand? Would this make a difference? In what ways did ratings differ and why? What is the advantage of having two people rate the speaker? Did the nonverbal behaviors affect the verbal message? How and in what ways?

As illustrated by communication experience 14.4, delivery skills encompass the nonverbal codes. The effective speaker must use all of his performance codes to highlight his message. Any gestures, body Three simple rules to follow can help him. First, the speaker must use his performance codes to highlight his message. Any gestures, body postures, vocal inflection that he can comfortably use to make the listener pay attention and understand his speech are effective use of performance codes. Second, the speaker must use the artifactual codes to reinforce his message. His attire, the notes, and the artifacts in the communication setting must be suitable to himself as a speaker and the message he tries to convey. Third, the speaker must use the contextual codes. Anything in the environment that can or may affect his message must be noted and used to his advantage. The speaker is well on the way to mastering his delivery skills if he remembers what he has learned to express himself interpersonally and changes it only as the situational conventions of the public situation necessitate. The delivery skills are summarized in chart 14.2.

Chart 14.2   Delivery Skills

1. Performance code checklist:
    Gestures
    Bodily movement
    Eye contact
    Paralanguage: pitch, rate, intensity, duration, emphasis
2. Artifactual code checklist:
    Attire
    Use of objects
    Visual aids
    Notes
    Media usage
3. Contextual code checklist:
    Physical environment
    Use of space
    Use of time
    Use of social/psychological context

Interference with Intentional Communication

The ability to speak in public like any other communication involves complex processes. Any failure on the part of the speaker to understand those processes can interfere with his ability to communicate as he intends. The speaker who fails to analyze his audience or occasion is in danger of ineffective preparation for the speaking situation. So too is the speaker who has not evaluated his own speaking skills. Evaluation is the first step before he can decide what he needs to do to improve his ability to communicate as he intends.

A communicator cannot be successful if he does not invest the necessary time and energy in researching his materials and in putting them together in a way that is clear and interesting to his audience. The fact that the speaker understands what he means does not insure that his audience will also understand him. Inadequate planning, preparation, and rehearsal of the finished speech are sources of interference with effective public speaking.

Finally, and most basically, interference exists when the person does not understand the nature of the interaction in which he presents his speech. If he is unaware of his rights and responsibilities to the audience as well as theirs to him, he is not prepared to communicate effectively. Interference with effective, intentional communication exists wherever the speaker has not invested the necessary thought and analysis of the situation and those entering it. In public as well as interpersonal communication, intentional communication does not exist unless the speaker does whatever is necessary to foster it.

Summary   In this chapter we have begun an investigation of the process of public communication by exploring the speech-making aspects of the public address. The most important points to remember are:

1. Public communication is similar to interpersonal communication in its processes and different in certain situational conventions.
2. Public speaking is one form of public communication.
3. A public speaking situation has four elements:
   a. *Speech.*
   b. *Speaker.*
   c. *Audience.*
   d. *Occasion.*
4. The speech is the verbal message. Its content and delivery can be analyzed by dividing it into the five cannons of oratory:
   a. *Invention.*
   b. *Arrangement.*
   c. *Style.*
   d. *Delivery.*
   e. *Memory.*
5. The speaker is the sender, the one who delivers the speech.
6. The audience is made up of receivers of the message, or speech.
7. Public speaking is a transaction between speaker and audience, in which both knowingly engage for their own given purposes.
8. Audience analysis is a necessary part of the preplanning stage for any public speaker.
9. Guidelines for effective public speaking include understanding the speaking situation and preparing for it.
10. Speaking in public involves research and preparation. A speaker needs to do seven things in preparing himself for the speaking situation. (Refer to chart 14.1 on p. 347.)
11. Although the public speaking situation necessitates some differences in the handling of content and delivery than the interpersonal encounter, but the speaker can build on his interpersonal skills for the public speaking situation
12. A failure to understand the complex processes in which people are involved in public communication interferes with the speaker's ability to communicate intentionally.

1. In what ways would an effective interpersonal communicator be likely to be an effective public speaker?
2. Why learn to make a speech?
3. In what ways is a speaker affected by different audiences for his speech?
4. Describe the effects of the occasion of the speech and the speaker.

Notes

1. Harry Hollingsworth, *The Psychology of the Audience* (New York: American Book Company, 1935), p. 22.

2. This discussion is a simplification of Carroll Arnold's treatment of the issue in his article, "Oral Rhetoric, Rhetoric and Literature," in *Human Communication: Core Readings,* ed. Nancy Harper (New York: MSS Information Company, 1974), pp. 377–93.

3. Arnold, "Oral Rhetoric," p. 390.

4. Aristotle, *The Rhetoric and the Poetics,* trans. W. Rhys Roberts and Ingram Bywater (New York: The Modern Library, 1954), pp. 31, 32.

5. The Canons of Oratory are derived from Aristotle's *Rhetoric.* It was in Roman times that Cicero crystallized the concepts into five canons.

**Selected
Bibliography**

Andersch, Elizabeth; Irwin Staats; and R. Bostrom. *Communication in Everyday Use.* 3d ed. New York: Holt, Rinehart and Winston, 1969. A practical approach to the processes of communicating.

Arnold, Carroll. "Oral Rhetoric, Rhetoric, and Literature." In *Human Communication: Core Readings.* Edited by Nancy Harper. New York: MSS Information Company, 1974. A theoretical analysis of the nature of oral and written speech. A discussion of the comparative values of oral and written, spoken and undelivered speeches.

Henning, James H. *Improving Oral Communication.* New York: McGraw-Hill Book Company, 1966. Especially recommended for a more in-depth discussion of public performance and the thinking processes necessary for preparation for that performance.

Marrau, H. I. *A History of Education in Antiquity.* New York: Mentor Books, 1964. Includes an informative discussion of the place of rhetoric and oratory in classical education.

Monroe, Alan, and Douglas Ehninger. *Principles of Speech Communication.* 6th Brit. ed. Glenview, Ill.: Scott, Foresman and Company, 1969. An up-to-date and one of the most often used public-speaking textbooks. It pays special attention to Monroe's system of problem solving within the framework of the speech.

Audiencing: Listening in Public

15

Introduction

All of us at times are members of public audiences addressed by speakers. To analyze public communication from the perspective of the audience serves two functions. First, it supplies a theoretic framework in which to understand more globally the interaction that we call the "public speaking situation." Second, it adds insight that the student can use as a potential member of an audience. The audience is affected by the speaker. It also affects the speaker. The audience member who understands the ways in which the audience and speaker affect one another is a more knowledgeable participant in the process.

The focus of this chapter is on the audience. Our concern is the specific kinds of communication behaviors known as *audiencing* in the public-speaking situation. This chapter addresses itself to the audience as people with a purpose for being in the public communication setting. It analyzes their motives for attending and participating, and discusses the communication behaviors available to them. The audience is viewed as an active participant in the process of communication. Its role, function, and behavior are therefore important to the student of human communication.

Communication Goals

The focus of this chapter is on the audience. It is written so that you can understand the nature of the relationship between the audience and the speaker, and also be a more effective audience member by:

1. Understanding the ways in which audiences determine the meaning of messages.
2. Knowing that each individual as well as the total assemblage is an audience unto itself, affecting the communication process.
3. Defining the reasons for attending a speech and attitudes toward the speaking situation.
4. Distinguishing between attending and audiencing.
5. Understanding the nature of the speaker-audience and audience-audience relationships.
6. Learning some guidelines for improving one's audiencing skills.

Communication Concepts and Experiences

A public speaker considers the audience in preparing a speech. She tailors her speech to fit the audience and presents it in the ways in which she believes will get its attention and win its acceptance of her and her ideas. When discussing the concept of the "audience" in the public-speaking situation, therefore, it is usually addressed from the point of view of the speaker. One discusses the audience in terms of what the speaker should do to get the audience to respond in the ways in which she wants them to respond.

Human communication, however, occurs between people, each of whom affects the process. It is never unidirectional. It always has a quality of mutuality. Communication involves the active participation of all of those in the interaction. From the perspective of human communication theory, then, the audience cannot be viewed only as those whom the speaker affects; the audience must be looked at as people, the ones who determine the meaning of any given message. Speakers and audiences bring meanings to the messages that pass between them publicly, just as they do in the interpersonal situation. This is what makes their interaction a mutually causal activity.

The Audience Defined

A public audience is composed of the **specific** or **immediate audience,** and the **general, larger audience** eventually affected by the speech. When the governor of a state speaks at a college graduation, the information she presents on the state of the state's economy is addressed to the immediate audience; it is also a message that affects the general audience of those who reside in and pay taxes in that state. In our system of government, in fact, it is common practice for an office holder or political candidate to use a specific speaking situation as the forum for presenting information that is addressed to the larger audience. They hear about it through the public media or by word-of-mouth from those who were a part of the immediate audience.

In preparing to make a speech, the speaker gives some thought to whom his audience is. His analysis is on a level of abstraction that allows him to make some generalizations about the kinds of people who will come to hear him and the ways in which they will be most receptive to what he wishes to say. To the speaker, then, the *audience* means the group of people to whom he addresses himself. He does not know all of them individually. To him, they represent a unit. If his assumptions are accurate, he can account for enough of those present in that unit to get some general understanding of them.

One definition of the audience, then, is the people to whom the speech is addressed, taken as a whole. This way of looking at an audience is useful to a speaker. Another definition of *audience* is the "individual" attending and participating in the public-speaking interaction. Individually, each person listening to a speech is an audience. Each is a separate world affected or unaffected by the speaker, understanding or not understanding, agreeing or disagreeing with what the speaker has to say. While a speaker cannot analyze an audience in this way, the student of human communication must. It is understanding each individual as an audience unto himself that explains three things. First, why people sitting side-by-side can "hear" different things. One says how interesting the speaker is; the other how dull. Both have been listening to the same person and the same message. Second, it is the individual in the audience who gives meaning to the message. Each individual's experience is unique. And third, the interaction in the public-speaking situation has a great deal in common with an interpersonal interaction. For purposes of clarity, we will distinguish between the entire group attending the speech and the individual by referring to the former as the "audience" and the latter as a "member of the audience." Each time we speak of a "member of the audience," however, we are speaking of an audience unto itself.

The audience to a public speech is composed of individuals, each of whom is an audience unto himself, and groups that form as audiences within the larger group are usually identified as the audience. Individuals in a large group (audience) tend to affect one another. They affect how one another react to the given event. LeBon's[1] work on *contagion,* behavior changes in people in the crowd situation, indicates that crowds, a kind of audience, affect the individual's behaviors. Everyday experiences provide illustrations. One example is people gathered at a sports or political rally. Another is attendance at a cultural event: opera, play, or film. Theatre owners have long understood that seating audiences close to one another affects their responses to the performance. Communication experience 15.1 is designed to provide some evidence about the nature of the audience at a public-speaking event.

Communication Experience 15.1

Principle

The audience at a public-speaking situation is composed of individuals who are audiences in themselves. It is the individual audience member who decodes the meaning in the message of any public speaker.

Procedure

1. Work in groups of five-to-seven people.
2. Design a brief questionnaire regarding a speaker's message, delivery, effectiveness. It must be composed so that an audience member could fill it out in less than five minutes.
3. Select and attend a speech delivered by a speaker who is controversial or on a topic that is controversial.
4. After the speech distribute the questionnaires to as many audience members as possible.
5. Each group member also fills out a questionnaire. Analyze the results.
6. Compare and contrast results with those obtained by other groups.

Discussion

What amount of agreement was there on the items listed in the questionnaire? What conclusions could be drawn from the differences? From the similarities? How did those who filled out the forms answer the questions differently than did members of the group? What are the implications about the individual in the audience?

As illustrated by communication experience 15.1, there are many "audiences" present in a given audience. Our higher educational system is based on lectures in which students are the "audiences"; our political system involves candidates who use us as audiences; cultural and business communities relate to the "public"; we are individuals whom the message makers seek to have as their audiences.

This chapter is specifically concerned with the audiences in attendance at a public-speaking performance and for such purposes as gaining information on current events or new discoveries in science, or are interested in educating themselves. Students of art may eagerly go to hear a lecture on an artist they like. Others attend because friends with whom they want to spend time are going and it will be worthwhile to join them. A member of an audience who attends voluntarily does so because he supplies himself with a purpose or reason for going. His satisfaction with the event is related to his purpose for being there. If it is to learn, he requires that the speaker teach him; if it is to be entertained, he requires the speaker to be entertaining; if it is to be social (to join friends) his requirements of the speaker may be no more than that he show up and speak.

Mandatory attendance at a speech refers to a situation in which an audience member is required to attend. Common situations in which audience members are required to attend are those in which one's teacher, employer, or friend require that he do so. A professor might require that students attend a lecture given by a speaker she deems important. An employer might give her employee the responsibility of hearing a speaker whom she thinks will add to her employee's knowledge or about whom she herself wants to know. A friend may be giving a speech or sponsoring the speaker and thereby exert pressure on her friend to attend. The audience required to attend satisfies its purposes in the public-speaking setting by being there and fulfilling the requirement. Its satisfaction can also be measured by what happens to it while it is there.

A second way of classifying audiences is in terms of attitudes about the speaking situation. In this scheme the audience is analyzed in terms of its reactions to the speaker and/or situation in general. Classifying audiences in terms of attitudes, audience members are labeled *friendly, neutral,* or *hostile.*

A **friendly audience** is one that is sympathetic to the speaker and/or subject matter. It likes her or is interested enough in the subject matter of the occasion to be receptive to the experience. Voluntary attendance at a speech cannot necessarily be assumed to constitute a friendly audience. If he goes, for example, because he wants to get new information and the speaker rehashes things the person has already heard, his attitude will be one of frustration, disappointment, or anger, rather than receptiveness toward the speaker. Furthermore, one can voluntarily attend the speech of someone whose views he opposes. An antiabortion advocate might go to hear a speaker who is proabortion for the sole purpose of countering his arguments. On the other hand one can be required to attend a speech that happens to be of interest to him. He is thereby receptive to the experience despite the fact that his attendance has been required. The friendly audience is one that is open and receptive to the speaker. This attitude is not related to whether or not the audience is there voluntarily or as a requirement. The only way in which a relationship can be drawn is if an audience's attitude has been affected just because it has been required to attend.

A **neutral audience** is one that is open to the speaker and the situation, uncommitted in their attitudes pro or con. They have some reason for attending, but no strong feelings for or against the speaker or his views. People may enter neutral and be swayed to one side or the other by the speaker. Or they may leave as neutral as when they entered. It is not uncommon for voters to go to hear local candidates speak on candidates' night. A voter may not have made up her mind on how to vote before hearing the speakers. She enters the situation as neutral. She may leave having made up her mind or remain as uncommitted, neutral, as when she attended the speeches.

The **hostile audience** is one that is negative because of the speaker, message, or its reasons for attendance. A controversial speaker may attract as many people who oppose his views as those who support them. A speaker may alienate his audience by what he says in his speech, turning a friendly or neutral audience hostile. An audience may be there for some purpose that is not satisfied and turn hostile to the speaker. An audience required to attend a speech may feel captive and react with hostility toward the speaker.

Each audience is composed of people assembled for a variety of reasons. The attitude of each of these people is shaped by his own reasons for attendance and attitudes toward being there. These affect the individual as much as the others with whom he participates in the speaking situation. Both the individual and the group are important sources of motives for attending the speech and attitudes toward being there.

When one speaks of attending a speech, all one says is that someone has entered the speaking situation physically. *Attending* the speech is being physically present. *Audiencing* refers to participating in the situation. While one can attend to participate, the two do not necessarily go hand-in-hand. In interpersonal communication, being quiet while a speaker talks does not necessarily mean one is listening. In public communication the same distinction holds. One's physical presence is a necessary condition; it is not all that is required to consider the person as actually audiencing the speech.

Participating in the Speaking Situation: Audiencing

Audiences create the occasion at which speakers address them, make meanings for themselves out of what those speakers say, and participate by listening and responding. **Audiencing** is processing the speaker's message. It involves the processes of listening, decoding, and responding. A speaker addressing a collection of people who are attending the event physically but not audiencing cannot communicate as intended. Communication experience 15.2 is designed to illustrate audiencing behaviors of those attending a speech.

Communication Experience 15.2

Principle

The audience presents a speaker with a whole range of nonverbal behaviors while she is speaking. Reading and understanding is part of the interpretation of feedback that a speaker makes.

Procedure

1. Work in dyads.
2. Each dyad selects a speech or lecture (formal class lecture or campus lecture series) to attend.
3. The dyad composes a list of nonverbal behaviors: facial expressions, gestures, body posture, applause, laughter, hissing, etc., that it believes are acceptable audience behaviors.
4. The dyad selects two or three audience members to observe during the speech.
5. Each member of the dyad records any behavior of the person being observed. Using these, it decides whether or not the person observed liked the speech and/or the speaker. Each individual writes down his conclusions.
6. After the speech the dyad seeks out the people they have observed, asking them about their reactions to the speaker.

Discussion

Did the dyad both observe the same things? Did they interpret them the same way? Did they arrive at the same conclusions? How did the conclusions compare to the observed person's statements of opinion? Are these statements to be believed? Why or why not?

As illustrated in communication experience 15.2, an audience exhibits a range of nonverbal behaviors in audiencing even when they do not participate verbally. These behaviors reflect the three aspects of the process of audiencing: listening, decoding, responding.

Listening is defined as hearing and comprehending. It is more than the physical act of receiving the noises produced by the speaker. It is the active attempt at making sense of them. Listening involves the process of **decoding**—translating the sounds one hears into the referents for which they stand. It is the reverse of the process of *encoding* in which the speaker engages. In listening to and decoding the message of the speaker, the audience is actively involved in supplying meaning to the verbal symbols presented by the speaker. The audience also decodes all of the nonverbal behaviors of the speaker. **Responding** to the speaker refers to all of the audience's reactions, expressed and unexpressed, to the speaker's message making.

In public communication, listening is an even more demanding task than in interpersonal communication. Interpersonally one can stop the speaker and question him, thereby calling for clarification as necessary. In the public situation, a formal speech is given in its entirety before the audience has the opportunity to ask those clarifying kinds of questions. This means that the receiver is required to do two things at once. He must listen and try to comprehend what the speaker is saying. At the same time he must make mental note of those points of clarification he needs. The problem that arises is that it is difficult to do both at the same time. The speaker makes a complicated point and the listener tries to understand what he hears. While the listener thinks about it, the speaker has moved on to another point. Speakers try to allow for this by the use of repetition in public speeches. But the speaker does not really have control over what is complicated to a member of the audience. For what is complex to one member of the audience may be quite clear to another. What is simple to some, needs clarification for others.

Understanding the complexities of audiencing the public speech is crucial to the audience. The audience at all times is in the position of choice. When one chooses to audience the speech, he is entering into a transaction with the speaker. Communication experience 15.3 is designed to illustrate the audience's message-making behaviors in response to the speaker.

Communication Experience 15.3

Principle

The audience is in a continual state of responding to a speaker. These responses are not always displayed. When displayed, they serve to guide the speaker in his communication attempts.

Procedure

1. Work individually.
2. For one week keep a diary of the events to which you are part of a public audience.
3. During each of these events observe yourself and your behavior in relation to the speaker.
4. Analyze what you feel about the speaker and/or the message. At the same time try to determine in what ways if any you show this to the speaker: body language, overt response, facial expression, etc.
5. Compare your experiences with those of others in class.

Discussion

Was this difficult to do? Why? Did it provide the individual with any new information about himself? Did his behaviors affect the speakers? How? What was the relationship between what he thought or felt and his behaviors?

As illustrated by communication experience 15.3, audiences are in a continual state of responding to the speaker in a public communication situation. Silence, applause, vocal communication (whistles, hisses, yeas, boos, etc.), bodily action, eye engagement are among the ways in which the audience reacts to the speaker and his message in a public communication situation. Because public audiences are often constituted by large numbers of people, a member of the audience may lose sight of how significant his response is.

Public Communication Relationships

As individuals we are in a constant process of affecting others and being affected by them. What we know comes from others and our processing of that which they offer us. What they know comes from us. This is true when we speak of getting information, such as news items, movies to see, religious events, political happenings. It is equally true in terms of our attitudes and behaviors. We learn how to look at something and value it from our interactions with others in our culture. We learn how to behave toward one another in the process of our socialization. In our culture, for example, men learn to greet one another with handshakes rather than kisses. We learn to say good-bye with hand gestures rather than by raising and shaking our feet.

Just as we learn the ways in which to communicate with one another interpersonally as part of our process of socialization, so too do we learn the ways in which to behave in public communication from socialization into our culture. There is nothing innately right or wrong about a speaker standing while an audience sits. It is social convention that we learn in the process of going to speaking events. There is nothing in the clapping together of one's hands to signify what must be done to show our response. Applause is a cultural invention. It is an action to which we attach the meaning of "appreciation." In some public performance situations, for example, audiences snap their fingers, rattle spoons and glasses, or light pocket lighters or candles to "say" the same thing as does an applauding audience.

In the public-speaking situation, the ways in which the speaker fulfills his role affects the audience's perceptions of his performance. The way the audience receives the speaker and his message affects the speaker. In any public-speaking situation, there are two kinds of relationships: speaker-audience, audience-audience.

Speaker-Audience Relationships

The **speaker-audience relationship** is marked by the speaker as the sender of the message and the audience as its recipient. Although the relationship is formalized by what we have called *situational conventions,*[2] social and environmental conditions dictating behaviors, it is an interaction just as in interpersonal communication. The conventions prescribe the ways in which the participants interact. They do not change the basic process in which individuals relate to one another by means of their verbal and nonverbal communication behavior.

From the perspective of the audience the interaction can be measured in terms of what the individuals get from the speaker. From the perspective of the speaker, the event and his experience of it are shaped by the audience and their responses to him and his message.

The relationship between the audience and the speaker is one of a series of behaviors, perceptions, and interpretations. The meaning of any message is the product of each individual perceiving and interpreting it. What is universal is that the speaker's verbal and nonverbal behavior is perceived and interpreted by the audience and the audience's behavior is perceived and interpreted by the speaker. The effects of the speaker on the audience and vice versa result from these perceptions and interpretations. It is not that the speaker controls an audience or that an audience controls a speaker. Each acts in prescribed ways toward the other. Each interprets the other's verbal and nonverbal behavior. The meanings that each carries out of the situation are the products of his own interpretations. The relationship between the speaker and the audience is an interaction in which each is interpreting the other.

Audience-Audience Relationships

Each person enters the audience as an individual audience for a speaking event. He does not remain in isolation, but is affected and affects others who have assembled to hear the speaker. This is the **audience-audience relationship.** The individual processing the speaker's messages is only one of the many people doing the same thing at the same time. The individual's responses affect fellow members of the audience. When a speaker says something that strikes a member of the audience as extremely funny, he does not stop to think about it but bursts out laughing. If no one else has seen the humor or laughed, the person laughing is bound to become self-conscious. In fact, the next time something strikes him as funny he may be more restrained. The opposite can also occur; one member of the audience begins to laugh and it becomes contagious.

These kinds of influences of the spectators on one another mark the audience-audience relationship. Responses made by others to the speaker's message affect the perception and response of any individual audience member. While not all are affected in the same way, all are affected; and so is the message. The ways in which the speaker and audience react and relate to one another affect the delivery, understanding, and acceptance of the message contained in the speech as well as the ways in which the audience members interact with one another. It is because of these effects that one cannot study public communication by analyzing the formal message alone. One needs to look also at the speaker, the audience, and the occasion.

Guidelines for Improvement of Audiencing Skills

Having an intellectual understanding of what is expected of her, a person enters the public-speaking situation with some preparation for participating effectively. Whether or not she needs to improve her audiencing skills depends on her evaluation of her skills. Communication experience 15.4 is designed to illustrate how you go about evaluating your audiencing skills.

Communication Experience 15.4

Principle

Audiencing involves active participation in the communication process. Skill at audiencing can be evaluated only after observing the ways in which you behave as an audience.

Procedure

1. Work in groups of five-to-six students.
2. Each person writes a phrase on a piece of paper. The phrase should be one that can easily be used by someone making a public presentation.
3. Collect the papers with the phrases and place them in a hat or dish.
4. Select one person in the group to describe to the group some experience that she has recently had.
5. In her description she must do three things:
   a. Speak without verbal interruption until she has completed her story.
   b. Incorporate in her story three phrases from the hat or dish.
   c. Watch group members to see if their behaviors indicate whose phrase she has used.
6. The speaker may take notes while speaking to the group. She may also refer to the slips of paper, if necessary.
7. After she finishes, each person in the group must repeat what the speaker has said. This is done privately with the speaker.
8. The speaker then tells the group two things:
   a. Whose phrases she thinks she used and why she thinks so.
   b. How accurate each was in repeating the story back to her.

Discussion

What does the speaker's ability to know whose phrases she used have to do with audiencing? Is this kind of audiencing similar to public audiencing? How? In what ways does it differ? What does the listener's ability to repeat the speaker's story have to do with audiencing? Is this similar to public audiencing? What effects did listening to hear if the speaker used one's phrase have on the listener? What are the implications for evaluating one's skills as an audience interpersonally and publicly?

As illustrated in communication experience 15.4, audiencing skills involve one's ability to comprehend what the public speaker is attempting to say. Most basically, the effective audience member is that person who successfully attempts to understand the speaker as the speaker wishes to be understood rather than to understand him as the audience member would like him to have expressed himself. For example, a chain smoker goes to hear a doctor lecture on the effects of smoking. The smoker only wants to hear things that will assure him that he doesn't have to worry about his smoking. He makes note of everything the speaker says that he can use in that way and either dismisses or ignores evidence to the contrary. While he satisfies his own needs, he has not been an effective participant in the process. He could have as easily satisfied his needs by staying at home and talking to himself.

There is a temptation to ignore information which is not compatible with our stated hypothesis.

Nobody can be totally objective; it is possible however to know oneself and one's biases enough to separate them as much as possible from what one perceives in another who is speaking. The goal of audiencing is to get something from the speaker. Audiencing effectively means understanding and then evaluating (agreeing or disagreeing with) the speaker. This is very different from evaluating before one understands. The first skill for the audience member to perfect is his listening.

Listening Skills for the Audience Member

Effective listening involves hearing, understanding, and evaluating, in that order. To accomplish these things, the audience member needs to do three things. First, he must know himself well enough to be able to put his judgments aside temporarily to work at listening with an open mind. An open mind is an attitude approaching objectivity. The listener is not totally objective. He has his own thoughts, feelings, and ideas on a subject. Openness means being able to hold these aside while giving the speaker his chance to say what he has to say. Keeping an open mind involves monitoring one's responses—continually checking oneself and one's responses. A listener has to be motivated to stay open to the speaker. One way of motivating oneself is to keep in mind one's purposes for listening to the speaker.

The second thing an effective listener needs to do is evaluate what it is that is useful to him in listening to the speaker. In finding its usefulness he supplies himself with the motivation necessary to listen carefully. There are reasons why something is interesting or not to any given individual. These reasons tell a person something about himself. They tell him about his interests, needs, and what satisfies them. Lack of interest is a measure of a lack of satisfaction. Thus, the most interesting or uninteresting speaker can provide the listener with room for speculation about himself: what it is that makes him interested or not in what is being said or done in his presence. Before one can raise and answer these questions, he has to listen. Noting his response as he does so gives him food-for-thought after the speaker has completed his thoughts. The listener can only evaluate why something was or was not interesting to her if she has listened to hear what was said. Her interest or lack thereof is related to the external stimuli presented by the speaker, speech, and speaking situation itself.

The third aspect of effective listening involves listening to the speech's content. It means being able to digest the main points the speaker is trying to make. This is a two-part step. First, the listener must separate content from delivery. If he has not distinguished between the ideas and the way they are expressed or the person expressing them, the listener cannot evaluate if he is reacting to the ideas or to the person expressing them. An effective listener perfects his ability to respond to the ideas rather than to the speaker as a person or his manner of speaking. It is all too easy to do otherwise. A popular person makes a statement and listeners say it makes sense. The same statement made by a person unknown or of low appeal goes unheard. Any idea that has merit to a listener is something he should want to have. To miss it because of who says it is a loss. To accept something that is really not of value because one likes the speaker is to be shortchanged. In either case the listener has not gotten the message accurately from the speaker.

The other aspect of listening for content is to listen for the speaker's main ideas. Effective listeners learn to recognize the speaker's attempts at highlighting their main points.[3] They learn to outline mentally what the speaker considers a main idea, and the evidence or examples used as its support. Such mental outlining reinforces the listener's ability to separate himself and his own ideas from the speaker's. It helps her distinguish between what she would say or like to hear said from what she has indeed heard. In so doing she comes as close as one human being can to understanding that which another human being says in the ways in which he wants to be understood.

Communication experience 15.5 is designed to illustrate the complexities of listening actively in the public-speaking situation.

Communication Experience 15.5

Principle

Audiencing involves active listening to a speaker and processing his message.

Procedure

1. The class works as a unit.
2. Brainstorm to compose a list of those things that encourage listening and those things that interfere. One of the students in the class is assigned to record the list.
3. Classify items as applying to interpersonal listening, public listening, and both.
4. Divide into groups of six-to-eight people.
5. Each group member writes a list that he thinks is the one the class arrived at.
6. The group compares lists. They make up a group list.
7. Compare group lists with those recorded during the time the discussion took place.

Discussion

Did people listen as the class discussed listening? How can one determine if people did or did not? Why did they? Why did they not? Is this kind of listening comparable to listening in public? In what ways? How does it differ? What are the implications for the individual regarding his audiencing?

As illustrated in communication experience 15.5, listening is an active process. It is closely related to decoding, the second audiencing skill.

Decoding Skills: Listening with One's Eyes and Ears

In the process of listening to that other person to try to understand what he is saying, the listener is acting as the decoder or translator of that other person. In any kind of human communication, it is in the process of decoding that the ability for two or more people to share a common meaning exists or is lost. Shared meaning can only exist when decoding results in meanings similar to those of the encoder. It exists only when the decoder works at trying to understand what the encoder means by his use of word symbols. Decoding, then, is part of the listening process and central to the exchange of ideas in the public communication situation. Effective verbal decoding hinges on a central question: what does the speaker mean by his use of those words? This is very different from the question, what would I mean by that? The difference is that what the speaker means and what the listener might mean were he the speaker are not necessarily one-and-the-same. Each time we change someone's ideas into our own words, we may be changing his ideas. The symbolic nature of language is such that words carry only those meanings as interpreted by the people using them. In attempting to understand another person, one need work to stay as close to what he is attempting to say as possible.

While most literally listening means attending to the verbal symbols used by the speaker, decoding involves translating the verbal and nonverbal codes. In decoding the nonverbal behaviors of the speaker, the receiver must distinguish between the behavior and his interpretation. The central question of decoding nonverbal behaviors is for the receiver to be able to know the difference between what he sees and what he thinks it means. For example, the speaker scratches her head while speaking. The receiver says, "she is confused." His statement is his interpretation. What he does not know is that what he saw was head scratching; what it meant to him was "confusion." If he separates this reaction into two steps, he is able to realize that there is an important missing link: what did it mean to the speaker. The speaker may, in fact, have dandruff and she scratches her head to relieve the itch. In decoding the nonverbal behaviors, then, the effective audience member makes a distinction between his observations and his interpretations. In so doing, she is open to changing her interpretation if further observations lead to different conclusions. All nonverbal behavior has some meaning, but the meaning is open to question and interpretation.

Chart 15.1 Effective Audiencing

To evaluate your audiencing behavior, you must be able to answer these questions:

1. What reason is there for attending this speech and what can be gained from listening to it?
2. How open is the receiver to the speaker?
3. What are the speaker's purposes and the main points he makes in developing them?
4. What does he mean by his use of verbal and nonverbal codes?
5. What are the acceptable ways of showing one's reactions to the speech and speaker.

Responding Skills: Reacting to the Speaker

Responding is reacting to the speaker, speech, and occasion. The audience has a range of permissible behaviors for responding. These are the product of the culture and the time. In our society, for example, the public speaker completes his address before he is questioned. For a member of the audience to stand and raise a question while the speaker is talking violates the custom, unless the speaker has explicitly stated that he wants audience members to do so. But even as there are cultural taboos against interrupting the speaker with questions as he speaks, there are norms encouraging nonverbal behaviors such as laughter, applause, facial expressions, and bodily gestures. Even some verbalization is permitted in particular kinds of public-speaking situations. A speaker at a political rally would not be adverse to supporters who yell out "right on," "victory," or some other supportive phrase. In fact, the absence of response may be upsetting to a speaker. He tells a joke and no one laughs. He makes a surprising disclosure and no one seems to notice. He finishes his speech and the audience sits there without applauding until the silence is broken by scattered hand clapping.

The speaker relies on the audience to respond to him. By their response he can tell whether or not he has succeeded in making himself understood. Effective response skills include the audience's awareness that it is important for them to react, and learning the customs that govern appropriate reaction patterns in the given communication situation.

The audience member enters the speaking situation with some purpose, and participates in order to gain something from the experience. Her participation affects the speaker and the ways in which he gives his speech. Guidelines for effective audiencing have been summarized in Chart 15.1.

Interference with Intentional Communication

In this chapter the focus has been on the audience and its part in the communication process. Interference with communication from this perspective has to do with anything that interferes with or distorts the meaning of the messages passing between speakers and audiences.

The member of the audience who does not know why she is there or what she wants out of the communication situation may present the speaker with an unreachable auditor. So, too, the receiver who cannot separate her own values, attitudes, and code usage from that of the speaker cannot effectively receive what the speaker is trying to convey. The receiver who is busy reacting to the speaker rather than to his message cannot effectively analyze and evaluate his ideas. Her reaction can be one of awe or hatred. In either case her involvement is with her feelings toward that human being rather than her objective attempt at deciphering his message and then reacting to it.

Public communication is also interfered with by the audience who fails to respond or responds inappropriately to the conventions of the given communication situation. The speaker relies on his audience's reactions. If he gets none, he has no way of evaluating his performance. If what he gets is not an accurate reflection of their feelings, they mislead him. In either case, there is interference with his attempt to communicate intentionally and/or the audience's. Clapping enthusiastically after a boring, worthless speech is like thanking someone for a slap in the face.

People attend a speech to get something from it. Anything that interferes with their ability to accomplish their purposes hampers the kind of communication they seek. The person who has not learned to analyze the speaker's tactics and is therefore manipulated by him does not participate in communication intentionally, unless what she has come for is to be manipulated.

Public communication is a two-way process in which speaker and audience relate to one another through the medium of their message-making behaviors. Anything that works against these ends is interference with intentional communication.

Summary   In this chapter we have been concerned with the public-speaking situation from the point of view of the audience. The most important points to remember are:

1. The audience and the speaker bring meanings to the messages that pass between them, making their interaction a mutually causal activity.
2. The audience can be defined in two ways: first, as the group of people en masse, who attend the speech; second, as the individual himself, each individual being his own unique audience.
3. People attend a speech either voluntarily or because they are required to do so; in either case the audience is there for a reason.
4. The attitudes of those attending can be classified as friendly, hostile, or neutral. The attitude is not necessarily related to why the person has come, although it may be.
5. Attending a speech is not the same as audiencing. Audiencing is participating in the communication exchange.
6. Audiencing involves listening, decoding, and responding. It is the audience's processing of the message.
7. The speaker and the audience engage in an interaction with one another in the public-speaking situation. A relationship also exists between audience and audience.
8. Guidelines for improvement of audiencing skills can be determined once one has a basic understanding of the processes and relationships involved in the public-speaking situation.
9. These guidelines are related to the receiver's listening, decoding, and responding skills.
10. The guidelines are summarized by relating to five questions:
    a. What reason is there for attending and what can be gained from listening?
    b. How open is the receiver to the speaker?
    c. What are the speaker's purposes and the main points he makes in developing them?
    d. What does he mean by his use of verbal and nonverbal codes?
    e. What are the acceptable ways of showing one's reactions to the speech and speaker?

Questions for Discussion

1. What are the differences between audiencing behaviors at a baseball game and at a graduation ceremony?
2. Compare and contrast listening skills and decoding skills.
3. Compare and contrast listening publicly and interpersonally.
4. What are the ways in which a member of an audience can show his disapproval of a speaker?
5. What effects does mandatory attendance have on the audience's response to the public-speaking situation?

6. Who is a great contemporary speaker? Why? How is the person's greatness measured?

7. Why try to separate the speaker from the speech?

8. What is the difference between observation and interpretation? Why does it matter?

9. How does an audience's silence affect a speaker?

Notes

1. Gustave Le Bon, *The Crowd* (New York: The Viking Press, 1960).

2. Harry Hollingsworth, *The Psychology of the Audience* (New York: American Book Company, 1935).

3. Ralph G. Nichols and Leonard A. Stevens, *Are You Listening?* (New York: McGraw-Hill Book Company, 1957), for an in-depth treatment of listening skills.

Selected Bibliography

Arnold, Carroll. "Oral Rhetoric, Rhetoric, and Literature." In *Human Communication: Core Readings.* Edited by Nancy Harper. New York: MSS Information Company, 1974. A theoretical analysis of the nature of oral and written speeches. Arnold presents an excellent discussion of the relationship between the audience and the speaker.

Bakan, Paul, ed. *Attention: An Enduring Problem in Psychology.* Princeton, N.J.: D. Van Nostrand and Company, 1966. While this book is not explicitly concerned with listening in public, it is a good treatment of theories about attention and human behavior.

Hollingsworth, Harry. *The Psychology of the Audience.* New York: American Book Company, 1935. A theoretical treatment of all kinds of public audiences. It is especially valuable to the student who is concerned with audiencing as communication behavior. This is not a specific treatment of the public-speaking audience. The principles discussed however are of value to someone who wants an in-depth understanding of the underlying processes involved in the audience experience.

Nichols, Ralph, and Leonard Stevens. *Are You Listening?* New York: McGraw-Hill Book Company, 1957. A basic book and a must for anyone concerned with listening processes. The context is not specifically the public context, but the in-depth treatment of listening is an excellent basis on which to understand listening processes in any context.

Public Communication: Media and Messages

16

Introduction

The medium for a message is the channel or pathway through which that message travels from its initiator to its receiver. **Media** can therefore be defined in two ways. In the broadest sense a medium is defined as any means of storing and/or transporting messages. In a narrower and more traditional sense, the media for public messages are thought of as the print and electronic channels: radio, television, newspapers and magazines, books, and films. Public communication relies on media. Public communication is affected by the media. A thorough understanding of public communication involves understanding public media. This chapter focuses on media and messages. It concerns itself with describing media, their functions, their uses, and their influences on public messages and on people, the message makers.

Communication Goals

In this chapter we will explore the media and their part in the process of public communication. The chapter is written so that you:

1. Understand the public media as extensions of the senses.
2. See the media as the channels through which humans communicate publicly.
3. Know the meaning of "media" in the broadest sense; understand it more narrowly as limited to print and electronic technologies.
4. Understand the effect of the medium on the message.
5. Know the difference between public and interpersonal messages.
6. Can analyze the uses to which people put the media, and their fare.
7. See the effects of media on users.
8. Understand the people using the media as influencers of themselves and others.

Communication Concepts and Experiences

All human communication relies on channels for gathering, storing, and transmitting messages. In interpersonal communication, the senses are the channels. Communicators use their senses of hearing, seeing, touching, smelling, and tasting as pathways for messages. One can look at an object and know something about it. Based on what her eyes tell her, she can explore it further by touching, smelling, and in many cases, tasting it. In these ways the senses are the pathways through which messages are sent and received. They are the media.

In public communication, the media extend our senses. We use our senses for gathering messages in public communication. But often those messages are framed by communicators not within our immediate presence. A newspaper carries a story about an event in Israel. A television program covers the opening of a performance in New York. A book describes the way of life of people about whom we would never know in our daily living experiences. It is in this sense that electronic media (radio, television, tape recorders, phonographs) and print media (newspapers, magazines, books, leaflets) extend our senses, bringing within range of our senses messages created at some distance from us.

Communication and the Media

In public communication the media are the channels or pathways through which public messages travel. They can be referred to as **public** or **mass media.** The adjective *public* or *mass* before the word *media* is used to indicate those pathways used in communication between large numbers of people. It is to distinguish them from interpersonal uses of media for communication. Public communication and public media are synonyms for **mass communication** and **mass media.** We choose the former terms because of undesirable connotations of the word *mass.* Mass means a largeness in terms of numbers of people. However, it also implies a wholeness or unity. A mass is a block, a solid unity; in terms of people, a mob or crowd. While there are masses who are communicated with publicly, the audience is made up of individuals. Therefore our preference is for the adjective "public" in reference to communication and media. A public is a people, populace, society. It indicates that one refers to large numbers of people without implying that when people are in large groups they become a block or solid entity.

Public communication and public media are related to one another. They are not one and the same. **Public communication** refers to the processes involved in the communication transactions between large numbers of people. It includes people and all of their message making, transmitting, and receiving behaviors. It includes the **public media,** the pathways or channels through which those transactions take place. While public communication could not take place without public media, the former refers to the processes involved in the interaction; the latter to the pathways and technologies available to assist in those processes. The more advanced our technology becomes, the more capable we are of communicating publicly. When Abraham Lincoln was assassinated, it took days before word reached the entire populace. A century later John F. Kennedy was assassinated. Because of technological advancement, millions of Americans knew about the event within minutes or hours; many of them witnessed the assassination of his alleged assassinator as a Dallas policehouse was televised.

Our use of technologies and our ability to communicate with one another also depend on our understanding of the processes involved in public communication. Because someone has a public medium available does not necessarily mean that he knows how to reach his audience. Understandings of the symbolic nature of language and the ways in which people interact verbally and nonverbally are vital to the improvement of public communication. Friends, relatives, and business associates learn ways of improving their interpersonal communication skills. So, too, public communicators need to understand the processes and skills involved in making and conveying messages. Studies after the debates between John F. Kennedy and Richard M. Nixon in 1960, for example, revealed that what the men looked like on the televised version of their debate affected viewers' reactions to them. Nixon's scowl hurt him more than his words. In

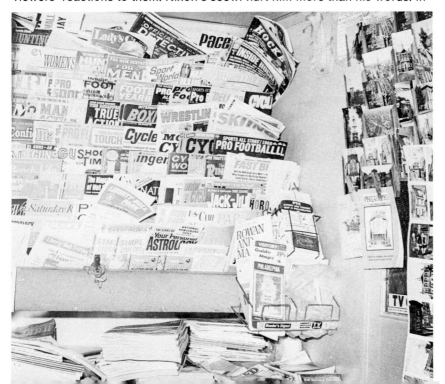

Every individual biography is an episode within the history of society, which both precedes and survives it. Society was there before the individual was born and it will be there after he has died. What is more, it is within society, and as a result of social processes, that the individual becomes a person, that he attains and holds onto an identity, and that he carries out the various projects that constitute his life. Man cannot exist apart from society. The two statements, that society is the product of man and that man is the product of society, are not contradictory. They rather reflect the inherently dialectic character of the societal phenomenon. Only if this character is recognized will society be understood in terms that are adequate to its empirical reality.

Peter Berger

one sense this is added information about the use of technology—the effects of a television camera on a person's appearance. In a more important way it reveals that one's nonverbal communication, his performance codes, affect his message publicly as much as interpersonally.

Public media and their usage, then, are an important facet of the process of public communication. The first thing to do in exploring them is to define what is meant by the term public media. A medium is a channel for a message. In defining public media, our concern is in explaining the kinds of things that can be considered channels for messages.

Public Media Defined

The ways in which we define what we mean by the word *media* determine what our focus is in talking about media in public communication.

A Medium Broadly Defined

Thayer defines a **medium** as anything capable of gathering, storing, and transmitting messages.[1] With this very broad definition, a restaurant, museum, church, or theatre is as much a medium for public communication as a radio, television, newspaper, or book. The physical design of a building, and its contents and arrangement convey the purpose for its existence and how it is to be used. Places of worship, such as churches and synagogues, are for religious activities. Their size and decor are designed so that people know to use them for certain kinds of activities and not for others. An audience can gather in a church to hear a speaker (minister, rabbi, or priest). They do not clap when he delivers his message (the sermon). In an auditorium they would applaud a speaker. In an arena, they would yell and scream. The physical setting and its use is learned by people in the process of their socialization. Messages as to the use of the environment are carried in its design as well as in the message makers using them.

The same holds true for a museum, restaurant, or highway. The architecture of the museum, the decor, and the ways in which its contents are organized and displayed are channels through which the user of the museum is "told" how to behave. Restaurants provide the most clear example of public institutions inviting usage and defining who will use them and in what ways. A national chain of fast-service restaurants not only bear the same name, but the same building design, food, interior decor, and packaging of products for sale. Consumers come to know the products they sell, the prices, and what kinds of people they attract. A

You, you're the one.

We do it all for you.

family with an infant and small children who want to go out to eat would not hesitate to go to that kind of restaurant. Someone who desires a romantic atmosphere for having a night out with a special date would choose a different kind of restaurant. Communication experience 16.1 is designed to illustrate that such public institutions are the sources of public messages.

Communication Experience 16.1

Principle

Messages addressed to members of the public are carried in a variety of everyday institutions. These as well as the print and electronic media are definable as media if we use the word in its broadest sense.

Procedure

1. Work in groups of five-to-seven people.
2. The groups compete to design a restaurant that will be successful near the college campus.
3. Each group must select a name for its restaurant; design a building and its interior decoration; and create a menu.
4. Groups compare the results, and the rationales behind their decisions.
5. Select the group's design that would be the most successful and tell why.

Discussion

What kinds of restaurants were designed? What were the reasons behind the kind of food to be served, the atmosphere created, and the price range decided upon? Are these the kinds of considerations that are in reality used for designing a restaurant? Should they be? How does this process illustrate the restaurant as a public medium?

As illustrated by communication experience 16.1, public institutions are media for mass messages. They are channels storing messages for consumers about how they are to be used. This is media defined in the broadest sense.[2] A more narrow way of defining public media and one that is more traditional than the above definition is that public media are those electronic and print devices that permit a message maker to have access to large anonymous audiences. In defining mass media in this way, the focus is on radio, television, film, newspapers, magazines, books, and similar channels for communicating with the public.

Print and Electronic Media: Effects on Message Making

The two categories into which one can divide the traditional public media listed above are print and electronic media. **Print media** refers to those channels in which messages are encoded into words and pictures to be read by the public audience. In this category are books, newspapers, magazines, newsletters, leaflets, brochures, billboards, public signs, and any other written form of a message composed for large anonymous audiences. **Electronic** or **broadcast media** are television, radio, motion, pictures, phonographs and tape recorders. They are those devices for message storage and transmission that function by use of electric power. The medium selected for the transmission of the message affects that message. Communication experience 16.2 is designed to illustrate the ways in which the medium affects the message.

Communication Experience 16.2

Principle

The medium in which the message is displayed affects that message. All public messages must be encoded in ways that suit transmission in a given medium.

Procedure

1. Work individually.
2. Select two public events such as a sports or political happening.
3. Attend one event in person.
4. Read about that event in the newspapers and listen to reports about it on radio and television after it has occurred.
5. Compare the differences in the encoding of messages and the experience of personal attendance with learning about an event from a report.
6. Use the second event for a comparison between televised versions and newspaper reports.
7. Discuss the conclusions with other class members.

Discussion

How does the experience of attending an event differ from reading about it or seeing it televised? Which is a better way to get information about the event? Why? How does the information one gets in print differ from televised information? How do each differ from information received on the radio? Which is the best medium for information? Why? Which is the best medium for enjoying the experience? Why? What are the implications of the effects of the medium on the message? What effects are there on the audience?

As illustrated by communication experience 16.2, the medium affects the message that it transmits. The effects can be divided into two categories: *packaging* and *reception.*

The ideas of which a message are composed are put into some symbol system in order to be transmitted to one's intended receiver. The medium available to the message maker influences his choices about symbolizing the message. Once he has thought of the message, it is then resymbolized in a form suitable to the given medium. This is **packaging,** the symbolization of the message and the ways in which it is displayed. Let us take for example the student who decides to run for a student government office at a large university. His message is that he is available and that he wants other students to vote for him. There are many ways that he can "say" this. Interpersonally, he can spread the word that he is a candidate to friends and acquaintances. Publicly, he can attend student functions and make speeches to student groups asking them to support him as a candidate. Furthermore, given that it is a large university and that time may be short in the time before election, he might use some other public channels for advertising himself. The choices are ads in the university newspaper, on its radio station or its television channels. He can also choose to use posters and printed handouts. There are many bases on which the office seeker makes his decision: (1) what is allowed in accordance with university rules governing election practices, (2) how much money he has to spend, (3) the relative costs of the different media, and (4) finally, the medium that seems most suited to helping him get votes.

The candidate might decide to use all the media. Or, he might use those that he can afford or that he thinks will give him the most publicity for his money. Whichever he chooses, however, the ways of symbolizing and organizing his message change. An effective poster has fewer words than a leaflet. A radio broadcast supplies listeners with words but no pictures. A television announcement is more visual, so what the candidate and his surroundings look like outweigh his words. In each instance the basic message is to get the students to vote for the candidate. The choice of the medium alters the message to make it fit the pathway it travels.

The second way in which the medium affects the message is the reception of the message by the receiver. The receivers decode what they are given. Print media requires reading; electronic media requires hearing and seeing as well as some possible reading. Seeing or hearing a message rather than reading it affects the receiver's experience of that message. To see and hear a speaker on television gives the receiver more of a sense of being there than to read the message in a handout or on a poster.

The medium affects the public message, how the message is packaged for the receiver's use, the ways in which the receiver gets the message, and who the receivers of a given message will be. The same people who are readers are not necessarily television viewers. Those who watch television do not necessarily listen to radio. Those who read newspapers do not necessarily read magazines.

There are three things distinguishing communication that relies on public media from other kinds of human communication. First, messages traveling via public media are *mediated.* Second, the audience to the public media are *anonymous.* Third, public messages themselves differ from other communication messages because they are *anonymous.*

Public Messages Are Mediated

In public communication in which electronic and/or print media are the channels for message storage and transmission, messages are mediated. In interpersonal communication, one of the codes of nonverbal communication is the **mediational code,** the selection and arrangement of objects or messages in relation to one another. In public communication, **mediated messages** refer to a similar process. It is that process whereby the message goes from the message maker *through the hands of all those who are responsible for shaping it so that it is able to be transported by the public medium* to the receiver. The message is not directly sent from sender to receiver. It travels through a chain of people and devices to get to the receiver. This is what mediates the message.

Any message received from a newspaper, book, radio, or television is mediated. A reporter covers a story. The newspaper reader reads about the event. Between these two occurrences is the mediational system. The reporter presents his story to the editor, who accepts or rejects it. If accepted, he edits it. The story is then passed through the hands of those who decide if it is to be included in that day's newspaper, where it will be included, how much space will be allotted for it, what its headlines will be, and the items it will be spaced near. This is the mediation of the message. A television news report goes through much the same process. Since different technologies are involved, some different kinds of experts and technicians work with the story before it gets to the home viewer. They make whatever decisions are necessary so that that story can be carried and transmitted electronically. When the story appears on a newscast, how much time it is given, the pictures accompanying it, etc., are all part of the mediational system.

Two models of public communication illustrate visually the mediational processes we are describing: first, a version of the Westley-MacLean model, presented in figure 16.1;[3] second, the Shannon-Weaver model presented in figure 16.2.[4]

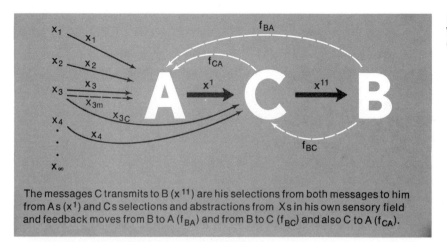

Figure 16.1
Westley-MacLean
Communication Model.

The messages C transmits to B (x^{11}) are his selections from both messages to him from As (x^1) and Cs selections and abstractions from Xs in his own sensory field and feedback moves from B to A (f_{BA}) and from B to C (f_{BC}) and also C to A (f_{CA}).

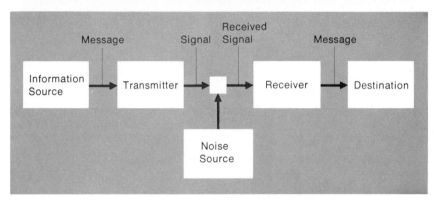

Figure 16.2
Shannon-Weaver
Communication Model.

In this version of the Westley-MacLean model, Letter C stands for the entire mediational system that comes between the message sender (A) and the audience or receiver (B). The X's and X_i's are the raw data out of which the message maker selects, responds to, and makes his message. The nature of mediational systems depends on the particular medium through which the message is transmitted. A message to be televised goes through different transformations than a message to appear in a newspaper. First, the technologies differ and therefore the ways in which the message is symbolized differ. In the former instance, it is symbolized visually and vocally. In the latter, it is put into words and static picture forms. Second, the chain of communication experts through whose hands the message travels differ in one medium from the other. The television message is affected by writers, editors, producers, directors, set designers, actors, audiovisual technicians, and others. The newspaper item passes from the reporter to the editor, layout designers, to print and typesetters and finally to the chain of people who make it available for

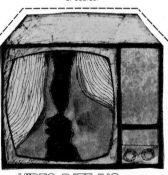

sale. These are but the most important mediators in the processes of a message being transmitted via television or newspaper.

The Shannon-Weaver model, figure 16.2, is important in the study of public communication. Like the Westley-MacLean model, it graphically describes the processes of message transmission. But Shannon and Weaver were electrical engineers who pioneered in research on the use of electronic devices in communications technology. Their model applies specifically to communications systems such as the telephone, radio, and television. The elements of the transmitter and receiver, instruments needed in electronic media, are of significance to the student of human communication. So, too, is the concept of noise. **Noise** in the Shannon-Weaver model means interference, error, or distortion of the message. It is any kind of interference, visual or auditory. Noise is snow on a television receiver, excess sound in the telephone wires, or any unwanted sight or sound that seems as if it is part of the symbol system used by the particular medium. In the Morse Code, then, a "dot" used as a period would be noise, since the entire code uses dots and dashes for letters and numbers.

These models of public communication are introduced to emphasize the nature and effect of the public medium on the message. Messages in the public media are mediated; they do not pass directly from sender to receiver. While this is one difference between public and interpersonal messages, it should be realized that some interpersonal messages are also mediated. An intimate telephone conversation or a love letter mailed from Chicago to Dubuque is mediated. But neither transaction, in any sense, involves a public message. Public media messages are distinguished from interpersonal messages because they travel between anonymous audiences and message makers. And the messages also have an anonymous quality.

The Relationship Between Public Messages, Media, and People

One of the things distinguishing a public message from an interpersonal one is that it is mediated. There are two other important distinctions between public and interpersonal message-related transactions: (1) public messages are anonymous and (2) senders and receivers are in a relationship in which they are often anonymous to one another.

A public message is *anonymous* in that it is not directed to a known, or specific person. Thayer says that the test of an anonymous message is that it reads "to whom it may concern."[5] It is transmitted via the public media to the public-at-large. Those who pay attention to it become its audience. Anyone interested can become part of the audience and receive the message. An exposé on the sex life of a famous athlete can be read by anyone who has the money to buy the newspaper in which it appears, or access to a library or friend having the newspaper. Communication experience 16.3 is designed to illustrate the difference between public and interpersonal messages.

Communication Experience 16.3

Principle

Public messages are mediated, anonymous, and travel between people in an anonymous relationship with one another.

Procedure

1. Work individually or in groups of three-to-five people.
2. Over a two-week period each participant is to keep a record of all the mail she receives.
3. Record how many items are letters, leaflets, public notices, etc.
4. Divide these into interpersonal messages and public messages.
5. Meet with the class and discuss the postal service. Is it a medium for public or interpersonal messages?

Discussion

What are the differences between the public and interpersonal messages one receives in the mail? What characterizes the differences? In what ways are the messages framed differently? Are they addressed differently? What reactions does the recipient have to mail that contains public messages from interpersonal messages? How does the medium affect the message? In what ways are messages public despite the medium?

As illustrated by communication experience **16.3**, **public messages**
are anonymous. They travel through the public media to whomever defines
himself into the audience for that message. This leads to another
distinction between public and interpersonal communication: the
relationship between communicators.

Since anyone can be privy to the public message, the audience is anonymous to the message maker. The reverse is also often true. A news item does not always have a "by-line." Even when it does it is not only the writer of that story who is the communicator. All of those people who are part of the mediational system that decide if the message will be used and how it will be packaged and transmitted are part of a complex organization called "the public communicator." A television show, motion picture, or book is the product of a group of people who create and package the message. Some of the creators are known by name to the audience. Many, however, are behind the scenes. All are anonymous in the sense of not having a personal relationship with the audience.

The audience for the public message is heterogenous, as well as anonymous. Men, women, and children of all races, religions, and economic and educational backgrounds are part of the public toward whom the message is addressed. The message makers try to segment that public. They analyze the total population for those who are the potential audiences, and tailor the product to them. But these analyses are based on assumptions that do not always hold true. A book is written with a certain audience in mind. It may turn out that those who decide to read it are a very different part of the population from those the creator of that book had in mind. Public messages, then, are anonymous, mediated messages transmitted from anonymous message makers to the public at large. Those individuals in the public who pay attention to the messages are the users of the media.

Media Usage: A Functional Analysis

In public communication, the public media are used as extensions of the sender's and receiver's senses through which they can send and receive messages. They are used by communicators with thoughts or feelings they wish to share with a large anonymous audience. A distinction must be made between all the people in the given culture, the *public*, and that part of it that the sender tries to reach, the *audience.* No matter how carefully the sender thinks out and packages his message, the public is not an audience unless it is open to the message. Each of us lives in a culture in which there are thousands of public messages transmitted daily. But each of us is part of the potential audience of only some of those messages. Communication experience 16.4 is designed to illustrate the difference between being a member of the public and a member of a public audience.

Communication Experience 16.4

Principle

We are all the potential audiences for a multitude of public messages in our daily interactions. Whether or not we become part of that audience depends on the message and our interest in that message and access to it.

Procedure

1. Work in groups of four-to-six people.
2. During the course of one week, keep track of all of the federal, state, and campus government people who are mentioned in news stories. (The group must monitor newspapers, news magazines, radio, television, and public discussions.)
3. Make a list of the names of those people. Keep a record of the frequency with which each name appears in any medium during the course of the week.
4. Select ten people for your list and use their names to create a questionnaire. Write each name and place a space next to that name in which can be written the title or position of that person.
5. Have fifty people fill out the questionnaire. Compare results. (Use people on and off campus.)
6. Compare results. Report them to the class.

Discussion

How similar were the names each group selected for its questionnaire? Why? What were the results? Whose names were most commonly known? Were they those that appeared most frequently in the media? What differences were there between on- and off-campus interviewees? What are the implications about public messages?

As illustrated by communication experience 16.4, being a member of the public does not necessarily make a person part of an audience for a public message. Whether one becomes a part of the audience for a public message is dependent upon access to the medium transporting the message and interest in the message being transported. A recipe for chicken in a cookbook is a public message. Those who become the audience for this message are those who read cookbooks and are interested in chicken recipes. A report on ski conditions is also a public message. Those who hate cold weather sports do not make themselves part of the audience for that message. This leads to two important questions about the use of public media: (1) why and in what ways do people use the media, and (2) what is the impact of the medium on the user.

In asking why and in what ways people use media, we are asking what purposes or functions these media serve. This is called a **functional analysis.** It is concerned with the meaning of the media for the person using them. Such an analysis is based on the concepts of audiencing previously discussed. A person becomes part of an audience by choosing to do so. A functional analysis explains what influences that choice.

Two of the theorists who have addressed themselves to the functions served by media use are Thayer[6] and Wiebe.[7] In Thayer's analysis of the uses of the media, he talks about the purposes media use serves for the audience.[8] People use a medium to get information that they can use in the daily interactions with others. One of the reasons for reading a book, therefore, is to have something to discuss with other people. One reads newspapers, magazines, and watches television or listens to radio for news items not only because the news is interesting in itself, but also because it

provides us with something to discuss with other people. This is one use of the media: to provide us with material to talk about with others. Another function of media use is to fill a ritual. Just as we have eating, sleeping, religious, and other rituals, there are rituals for using the media. One woman starts her day by reading the daily newspaper; another wakes to music on the radio; a third cannot enjoy her breakfast coffee without watching a televised morning news program. Other examples of ritualistic use of media are students who study best while listening to music; people who end the day by reading a chapter or two from a book in bed; and the use of magazines to pass the time in a doctor's or dentist's office.

Other more obvious functions of the use of the media and the messages they transmit are to gain information, to be entertained, to escape, or to have something to do. People go to a movie to see the movie; they also go to have somewhere to go. This is one reason why television movies do not totally replace theatre films. Someone who has worked hard all day in the house wants to get out into a different environment. A movie theatre fills that need.

Wiebe,[9] a social psychologist, discusses the function of media use in a slightly different way. According to his ideas, use of a medium such as television allows us to watch the lives of other people without having anything that we must do as a result. For example, one can watch the romantic problems of a couple on a television soap opera for as long as he wishes. He can turn it off when he wants to; he can read a book when it gets boring to him. If the same incident were to occur in his living room between people that he knew, he would have to involve himself.

A functional analysis leads to some conclusions about the effects of the media and messages on the users, the audience.

The Effects of the Media on the Audience

The most traditional measure of the relationship between the media and their users has been to look for the effects of media usage. The Lasswell model of mass communication describes this perspective.[10] Lasswell's model can be stated as "*who* says *what* to *whom* in what *channel* with what *effect*." The *who* is the sender, *what* is the message, *whom* is the receiver, *channel* is the medium, and *effect* is the result. In this paradigm, then, we have a linear model of communication. It describes communication from the perspective of the sender: what he must do to get the receiver to do what he wants him to do.

Our understanding of communication, however, is that it is a transaction between the sender and the receiver. It is not one way. In

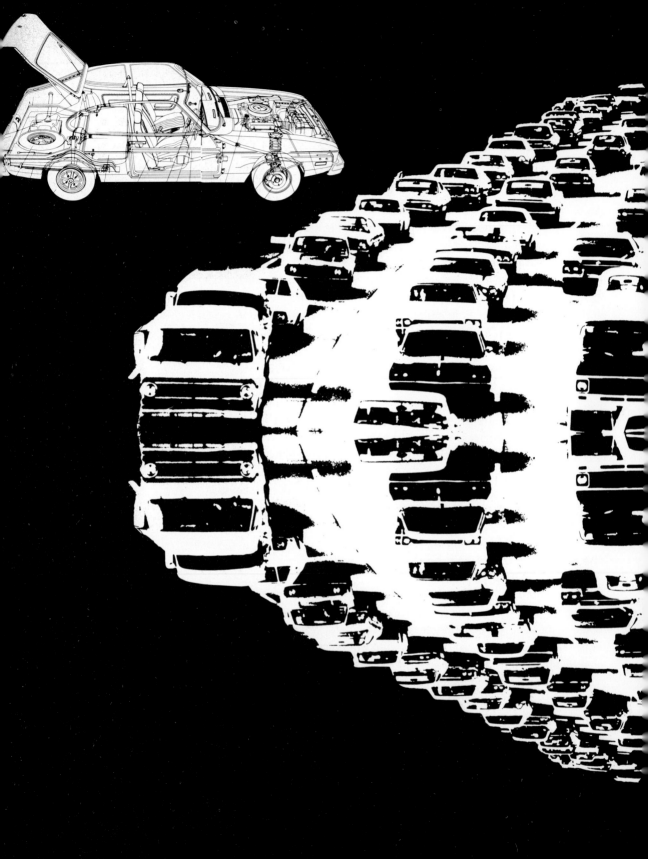

public communication the receiver does two vital things in the communication transaction. First, he elects whether or not to participate. He reads a message or does not; he watches a television show or does not; he buys a newspaper or does not. Second, as in interpersonal communication, it is the receiver who brings the meaning to the message. In the process of his decoding, he decides what that message means to him.

Understanding these two basic functions of the receiver, one sees that whatever the effects that result from media usage, the receiver more than the sender determines them. A boy sees a violent show, and then commits a violent act. One way of analyzing the relationship is to say that his viewing affected his behavior. Another is to ask why did he watch such shows and what did they mean to him? This takes into account his choice to become a member of the audience and how the meaning of the message is a product of his perception as well as the intent of the sender of that message.

A functional analysis is more consistent with a view of communication as mutually causal activity than a cause-effect paradigm. It takes into account the receiver of the message. It addresses the questions of why he was part of the audience of that message and what the message means to him: what uses he has for the message.

A functional analysis leads to some conclusions about the effects of the media and its fare on the public audiences who choose to make themselves receivers of messages. The first conclusion is that we have choices. We are recipients of those messages to which we choose to be recipients. While several people may all read the same newspaper, that does not mean that they pay attention to the same messages. One reader cares about the stock market report and the sports pages; another, current events and latest home fashions; a third buys the paper only for the television page. The messages are there. They do not have meaning unless attended to by a member of the public to whom they are addressed. Even two people reading the same item do not necessarily focus on the same thing.

Secondly, the ritualistic use of a medium makes us accidentally privy to some messages. In passing time in the doctor's office a patient reads magazines. If he's there a long time, he may read things in those magazines he would otherwise find uninteresting.

Third, the media use patterns tell us something about people. A functional analysis clarifies why people use a medium rather than the effects it has on them. People read books, magazines, and newspapers on buses rather than passing the time with television offerings because it is easier to carry the former. People watch television rather than read while they do household chores because television allows a person to do two things at once; books demand more undivided attention. The question is why do people need to fill their time in these ways, rather than what is the effect of a kind of medium or message on a person. One implication is that the more the message maker knows about the uses to which people put the media, and which people have which uses, the more accurately he can judge which messages to use in which media. Another is that the more people know about how and why they use the media, the more they know about themselves.

The fourth conclusion that a functional analysis leads to is that we are all continually in the process of communicating and being communicated with, and that sometimes it is the process rather than the specific content that is meaningful. On vacation, a teacher may read all the mystery novels available to him by way of diversion. He needs to fill his mind with different reading from the more intellectually demanding books he reads during a semester. A domestic worker may have the radio or television on while doing his chores because the sounds make him feel less isolated in his work. A commuter may listen to his car radio to ease the frustration he feels in facing rush-hour traffic on his daily trips to and from the city where he works. Knowing something about people and their uses of the channels of public communication tells the message makers as well as the users something about the human processes involved in media usage. The Westley-MacLean and Shannon-Weaver models of communication discussed earlier in the chapter describe the mediational process through which a message goes. Using them together with a functional analysis gives one a picture of communication from the perspective of the receiver as well as the sender.

The Ways in Which the Audience Influences Itself

Meanings are in people, not in messages. The people making and receiving the message bring meaning to it. This is the way several different people can hear the same message and take it to mean entirely different things. This is as true interpersonally as publicly. Interpersonally, Mary engages in a conversation with Jane, Beth, Jim, and Sue. She says that she went to the movies last night and enjoyed seeing a comedy. Jim had asked Mary out for that night and been told that she planned to go to sleep early. He "hears" rejection of him in her statement about the movie. Beth, Mary's best friend, knows that Mary has been feeling sad lately. She "hears" that Mary went to the movie to try to cheer up. Sue, who is not particularly interested, doesn't really hear what Mary says at all. Each person has been present at the same time and exposed to Mary's message about attending a movie. At least three different messages were decoded in addition to the shared understanding that Mary had gone to a movie.

Publicly, the same process occurs. People attend a political candidate's speech. Each hears what the candidate says and each interprets it to mean what she thinks it means. Each person brings the meaning to the message. At the same time, however, each of us is in the process of becoming the people we are. Each is continually in the process of being socialized and of socializing others. It is in this sense that we are influenced by what we are presented with in our daily interactions with others and in our daily usage of the media. The customs popular in a given culture are learned in our interactions with others. We also learn about them through our media usage. A person living in an urban area may only know about life on a farm from meeting someone who has lived on a farm, or reading about farm life, seeing farmers on television or in films concerning farm life. In this sense what one knows about ways of life different from her own is the product of her usage of mass media.

Behavior, dress, good taste, life-styles, and values are transmitted to us interpersonally and through our use of the media. The viewer watches a television series about a career woman. Her purpose in watching may be to pass the time, to have something to discuss with her friends, or any ritualistic use of the television and its fare. The creators of the show present it for their own purposes: to sell products, to make a statement about a way of life, or to entertain. The viewer learns from it what she needs to learn. It may be that she learns more than anything else is that to lead that kind of life one needs to look a certain way, or that career people live in certain kinds of ways.

What the media present us with most are ways of knowing about ourselves and others. In the process of using the media to serve whatever purposes we use them to serve, we are learning about ourselves and others. This takes us back full cycle to the cencept that introduced this chapter. The public media extend our senses. Our senses serve in exploring the world outside ourselves. We use our senses and the messages we gather to explore our inner selves. The media extend that with which we have contact. They broaden the world that can be explored. In the processes involved in public as well as interpersonal communication, each individual is in the process of exploring self and growing. In this way the user is affected by the medium. It presents her with a range of ideas. Those she pays attention to and what they mean to her are a product of her exposure to them and her individual processing of messages.

Interference with Intentional Communication

The public communicator creates and disseminates those messages that he, for whatever reason, wants others to know about. In order for messages to reach those to whom they are addressed and to convey what the message maker wants them to convey, the message maker must understand the processes involved in public communication. The public communicator who cannot symbolize his message in a way appropriate to the medium in which it will travel cannot communicate as intended. The message maker who does not understand what makes people define themselves into audiences has no way of knowing who, and why or why not, he reaches. And if he does not understand the functions to which they put their media use, he cannot select the best channels for the kinds of messages he wants to reach the kinds of people with whom he wants to communicate.

The audience member, too, can interfere with intentional communication. A person who does not make use of the media is not accessible to the public communicator. If he uses them but pays no attention to the messages, he is not a potential member of the audience.

The media are only the pathways of the messages. They affect the ways in which the messages are shaped, just as gift boxes affect the shape in which one folds a sweater one wishes to wrap in a given box. They affect message reception in that the coding processes workable for a given medium are or are not of interest to a given segment of the audience.

In all other senses, however, the media are instruments. And it is the instrument users and lack of knowledge of them that can interfere with intentional communication.

In this chapter the use of media in public communication has been discussed. The most important points to remember are:

Summary

1. The public media are the pathways, or channels, through which messages travel.
2. Public media are extensions of our senses in that they bring within the range of our perception, data that we would otherwise not know.
3. "Public" and "mass" media are synonymous.
4. One's definition of what "media" means determines which things one classifies as media.
5. In the broadest sense, the media are any means of gathering, storing, and transporting messages. With this as a definition, restaurants, museums, and churches, as well as books, radios, and televisions, are public media.

6. A more traditional and narrower definition of public media are the print and electronic means of transporting messages.
7. The selection of the medium affects the message in two ways:
   a. *Packaging.*
   b. *Audience reception.*
8. Public communication relying on public media are different from other kinds of human communication in three ways:
   a. *Messages are mediated.*
   b. *Messages are anonymous.*
   c. *Senders and receivers of those messages are in anonymous relationship with one another.*
9. An analysis of the ways in which people use the media and their fare is called a functional analysis. It is concerned with the reasons and uses to which people put their media-using activities.
10. The effects of the media are traditionally looked at by what media usage does to the audience.
11. A functional analysis leads to different conclusions. It looks at why people are the way they are and how this is reflected in their media use.
12. Communication is a mutually causal activity. The receiver chooses to enter or not; the receiver brings meanings to the messages.
13. Because the user brings his meanings to a message, he influences himself as much as he is influenced.
14. Any lack of understanding of the processes involved in public communication can lead to interference with intentional communication.

Questions for Discussion

1. Is a stadium a public medium? Explain.
2. What is the difference between the "public" and the "audience"?
3. Are children who are exposed to violence on television likely to become more violent as a result?
4. Is it better to put an ad for cigarettes in a magazine or on the radio?
5. What kinds of messages would be better in neon lights than others?
6. What is a mediated message?
7. Is a television message as mediated as a newspaper article? Which appears or "feels" more mediated?
8. What is the difference between a public and an interpersonal message? Cite examples.
9. Cite and compare ritualistic uses of the campus newspaper.
10. In what ways are the media the carriers of culture and morality?
11. How are the media extensions of the senses?

Notes

1. Lee Thayer, "On the Mass Media and Mass Communication: Notes toward a Theory," in *Mass Communication: Dialogue and Alternatives,* ed. Richard Budd and Brent Ruben (Rochelle Park, N.J.: Hayden Press, in press).

2. Richard Budd and Brent Ruben, *Mass Communication: Dialogue and Alternatives* (Rochelle Park, N.J.: Hayden Press, in press).

3. Bruce Westley and M. MacLean, "A Conceptual Model for Communications Research," in *Journalism Quarterly* 34 (Winter 1957): 31–38.

4. Claude Shannon and Warren Weaver, *A Mathematical Theory of Communication,* 5th ed. (Urbana: University of Illinois Press, 1972), p. 7.

5. Thayer, "Mass Communication," p. 16.

6. The discussion of the uses to which people put the media and their fare is a synthesis of Thayer's article. The student is directed to Thayer for a more comprehensive treatment.

7. Gerhard Wiebe, "The Social Effects of Broadcasting," in *Mass Culture Revisited,* ed. Rosenberg and White (New York: Van Nostrand Reinhold Company, 1971).

8. Thayer, "Mass Communication."

9. Wiebe for a more detailed sociological analysis of the effects of broadcasting, pp. 154–68.

10. Harold Lasswell, "The Structure and Function of Communication in Society," in *The Communication of Ideas,* ed. Bryson Lyman (Institute for Religion and Social Studies, 1948).

Selected Bibliography

Chaffee, Steven, and Michael Petrick. *Using the Mass Media: Communication Problems in American Society.* New York: McGraw-Hill Book Company, 1975. A good basic text for exploring public communication in relation to the media and their uses.

De Fleur, Melvin. *Theories of Mass Communication.* 2d ed. New York: David McKay, 1970. This book is suggested for the four theories it develops regarding the effects of mass media and mass communication. These differ from the point of view of this chapter. Their value lies in rounding out the student's perspective of the ways in which theorists analyze mass communication.

McLuhan, Marshall. *Understanding Media.* New York: McGraw-Hill Book Company, 1964. McLuhan's ideas have had an effect on the thinking about mass media. This is recommended as an introduction to his thinking.

Merrill, John, and Ralph Lowenstein. *Media, Messages, and Men.* New York: David McKay, 1974. Recommended as an introductory text to mass communication.

Thayer, Lee. "On the Mass Media and Mass Communication: Notes toward a Theory." In *Mass Communication: Dialogue and Alternatives,* edited by Richard Budd and Brent Ruben, Rochelle Park, N.Y.: Hayden Press, in press. Thayer's perspectives differ from many others in the field. This article is recommended as an in-depth understanding of the point of view he presents.

Theall, Donald. *The Medium Is the Rear View Mirror.* Montreal: McGill-Queens University Press, 1971. Recommended for the student interested in McLuhan. This book explores McLuhan's ideas, taking them to task.

Bibliography

Abt, Clark C. *Serious Games*. New York: The Viking Press, 1970.

Allport, Gordon W. *Personality and Social Encounter*. Boston: Beacon Press, 1960.

Andersch, Elizabeth; Staats, Irwin; and Bostrom, R. *Communication in Everyday Use*. 3d ed. New York: Holt, Rinehart and Winston, 1969.

Argyle, Michael. *Social Interaction*. New York: Atherton Press, 1969.

Argyris, Chris. *Interpersonal Competence and Organizational Effectiveness*. Homewood, Ill.: Dorsey-Irwin, 1962.

Arnold, Carroll. "Oral Rhetoric, Rhetoric, and Literature." In *Human Communication: Core Readings,* edited by Nancy Harper. New York: MSS Information Company, 1974.

Arnold, Carroll; Ehninger, Douglas; and Gerber, John C., eds. *The Speaker's Resource Book*. Glenview, Ill.: Scott, Foresman and Co., 1961.

Aronson, Elliot. *The Social Animal*. San Francisco: W. H. Freeman and Co., 1972.

Asch, S. E. "Effects of Group Pressure upon the Modification and Distortion of Judgments." In *Dimensions in Communication,* edited by James H. Campbell and Hal W. Hepler. Belmont, Calif.: Wadsworth Publishing Co., 1965.

Bakan, Paul, ed. *Attention: An Enduring Problem in Psychology*. Princeton, N.J.: D. Van Nostrand Co., 1966.

Barbara, Dominick. *The Act of Listening*. Springfield, Ill., Charles C. Thomas, 1958.

Barker, Larry, and Wiseman, Gordon. *Speech—Interpersonal Communication*. San Francisco: Chandler Publishing, 1967.

Barnlund, Dean. *Interpersonal Communication: Survey and Studies*. Boston: Houghton Mifflin Co., 1968.

Bennis, Warren; Schein, E.; Steel, F.; and Berlew, D. *Interpersonal Dynamics*. Homewood, Ill.: Dorsey-Irwin, 1968.

Berger, Peter, and Luckmann, Thomas. *The Social Construction of Reality*. Garden City, N.Y.: Doubleday & Co., 1966.

Berlo, David. *The Process of Communication: An Introduction to Theory and Practice*. New York: Holt, Rinehart, and Winston, 1960.

Birdwhistle, Ray. *Kinesics and Context*. Philadelphia: University of Pennsylvania Press, 1970.

Blumer, Herbert. *Symbolic Interactionism: Perspective and Method*. Englewood Cliffs, N.J.: Prentice-Hall, 1969.

Bois, Samuel. *The Act of Awareness*. 2d ed. Dubuque, Ia.: Wm. C. Brown Co., 1973.

Boocock, Sarane, and Schild, E. O., eds. *Simulation Games in Learning*. Beverly Hills, Calif.: Sage Publications, 1971.

Bosmajian, Haig, ed. *The Rhetoric of Nonverbal Communication*. Glenview, Ill.: Scott, Foresman and Co., 1971.

Boulding, Kenneth. *The Image*. Ann Arbor, Mich.: University of Michigan Press, 1956.

Brooks, William. *Speech Communication*. 2d. ed. Dubuque, Ia.: Wm. C. Brown Co., 1974.

Brown, Roger. *Words and Things*. New York: The Free Press, 1958.

———. *Social Psychology*. New York: The Free Press, 1965.

Bruner, Jerome. *The Process of Education*. Cambridge, Mass.: Harvard University Press, 1961.

———. *Toward a Theory of Instruction*. New York: W. W. Norton & Co., 1966.

Buckley, Walter. *Sociology and Modern Systems Theory.* Englewood Cliffs, N.J.: Prentice-Hall, 1967.

Budd, Richard. "General Semantics: An Approach to Human Communication." In *Approaches to Human Communication,* edited by Richard Budd and Brent Ruben. New York: Spartan Books, 1972.

Budd, Richard, and Ruben, Brent, eds. *Approaches to Human Communication.* New York: Spartan Books, 1972.

———. *Mass Communication: Dialogue and Alternatives.* Rochelle Park, N.J.: Hayden Book Co., in press.

Cartwright, Dorwin, and Zander, Alvin, eds. *Group Dynamics: Research and Theory.* 2d ed. Evanston, Ill.: Row, Peterson, and Co., 1960.

Chase, Stuart. *The Power of Words.* New York: Harcourt Brace and Co., 1953.

Cherry, Colin. *On Human Communication.* New York: John Wiley & Sons, 1957.

Churchman, C. West. *The Systems Approach.* New York: Delacorte Press, 1968.

Condon, John. *Semantics and Communication.* New York: Macmillan, 1966.

Dance, Frank, and Larson, Carl. *Speech Communication: Concepts and Behavior.* New York: Holt, Rinehart and Winston, 1972.

DeFleur, Melvin. *Theories of Mass Communication.* New York: David McKay Co., 1966.

Dewey, John. *Experience and Education.* New York: Collier Books, Collier Macmillan, 1963.

Duncan, Hugh D. *Symbols in Society.* London: Oxford Press, 1968.

Ekman, P.; Friesen, W.; and Ellsworth, P. *Emotion in the Human Face: Guidelines for Research and an Integration of Findings.* Elmsford, N.Y.: Pergamon Press, 1971.

Exline, Ralph. "Psychology: An Approach to Human Communication." In *Approaches to Human Communication,* edited by Richard Budd and Brent Ruben. New York: Spartan Books, 1972.

Fabun, Don. *Communications: The Transfer of Meaning.* Beverly Hills, Calif.: Glencoe Press, 1968.

Fergus, R. H. *Perception.* New York: McGraw-Hill, 1966.

Festinger, Leon. "Informal Social Communication." *Psychological Review* 57 (1950): 271–82.

Fisher, B. Aubrey. *Small Group Decision Making.* New York: McGraw-Hill, 1974.

Frank, Lawrence. "Cultural Organization." In *General Systems Theory and Human Communication,* edited by Brent Ruben and John Kim. Rochelle Park, N.J.: Hayden Book Co., 1975.

Giffin, Kim, and Patton, Bobby. *Fundamentals of Interpersonal Communication.* New York: Harper & Row, 1971.

Goffman, Erving. *The Presentation of Self in Everyday Life.* Garden City, N.Y.: Doubleday & Co., 1959.

———. *Behavior in Public Places.* New York: The Free Press, 1963.

Grinker, Roy, ed. *Toward a Unified Theory of Behavior.* New York: Basic Books, 1956.

Haiman, Franklin. *Group Leadership and Democratic Action.* Boston, Mass.: Houghton Mifflin Co., 1951.

Hall, Edward T. *The Silent Language*. Garden City, N.Y.: Doubleday & Co., 1959.

———. *The Hidden Dimension*. Garden City, N.Y.: Doubleday & Co., 1966.

Hanneman, Gerhard, and McEwen, William. *Communication and Behavior*. Reading, Mass.: Addison-Wesley Publishing Co., 1975.

Harneck, V., and Fest, T. *Group Discussion: Theory and Technique*. New York: Appleton-Century-Crofts, 1964.

Harper, Nancy, ed. *Human Communication: Core Readings*. New York: MSS Information Corp., 1974.

Harrison, Randall. *Beyond Words: An Introduction to Nonverbal Communication*. Englewood Cliffs, N.J.: Prentice-Hall, 1974.

Hayakawa, S. I. *Language in Thought and Action*. 2d ed. New York: Harcourt Brace and World, 1964.

———, ed. *Language, Meaning and Maturity*. New York: Harper & Row, 1954.

Henning, James. *Improving Oral Communication*. New York: McGraw-Hill, 1966.

Hertzler, Joyce. *A Sociology of Language*. New York: Random House, 1965.

Hollingsworth, Harry. *The Psychology of the Audience*. New York: American Book Co., 1935.

Homans, George. *Social Behavior: Its Elementary Forms*. New York: Harcourt Brace and World, 1961.

Hovland, Carl; Janis, Irving; and Kelley, Harold. *Communication and Persuasion*. New Haven, Conn.: Yale University Press, 1953.

Johnson, David. *Reaching Out: Interpersonal Effectiveness and Self-Actualization*. Englewood Cliffs, N.J.: Prentice-Hall, 1972.

Johnson, Wendell. *People in Quandaries*. New York: Harper and Brothers, 1946.

———. *Your Most Enchanted Listener*. New York: Harper and Brothers, 1946.

Johnson, Wendell. *Living with Change: The Semantics of Coping,* edited by Dorothy Moeller. New York: Harper & Row, 1972.

Jourard, Sidney. *The Transparent Self*. Rev. ed. New York: D. Van Nostrand Co., 1971.

Keltner, John. *Interpersonal Speech-Communication: Elements and Structures*. Belmont, Calif.: Wadsworth Publishing Co., 1970.

Knapp, Mark. *Nonverbal Communication in Human Interaction*. New York: Holt, Rinehart and Winston, 1972.

Korzybski, Alfred. *Science and Sanity: An Introduction to Non-Aristotelian Systems and General Semantics*. Lancaster, Pa.: Science Press, 1933.

Lederman, Linda Costigan. "Parallel Evolution in Science: The Historical Roots and Central Concepts of General Systems Theory." Competitive paper presented to the annual conference of the Eastern Communication Association, Philadelphia, 1976.

Lee, Irving. *Language of Wisdom and Folly*. New York: Harper and Brothers, 1949.

Lin, Nan. *The Study of Human Communication*. Indianapolis: Bobbs-Merrill Co., 1973.

Luft, J. *Group Process: An Introduction to Group Dynamics*. Palo Alto, Calif.: National Press, 1963.

McCrosky, James. "Scales for Measurement of Ethos" *Speech Monographs* 33(1966):65–72

McCrosky, James; Larson, Carl; and Knapp, Mark. *An Introduction to Interpersonal Communication.* Englewood Cliffs, N.J.: Prentice-Hall, 1971.

McCrosky, James, and Wheeless, Lawrence. *An Introduction to Human Communication. Boston:* Allyn & Bacon, 1976.

McLuhan, Marshall. *Understanding Media.* New York: McGraw-Hill, 1964.

Marrau, H. I. *A History of Education in Antiquity.* New York: Mentor Books, 1964.

Maruyama, Magorah. "The Second Cybernetics: Deviation Amplifying Mutual Causal Processes." *American Scientist* 51(1963): 164–80.

Maslow, Abraham, ed. *New Knowledge and Human Values.* New York: Harper & Row, 1970.

Mead, George. *Mind, Self, and Society.* Chicago: University of Chicago Press, 1934.

Merrill, John, and Lowenstein, Ralph. *Media, Messages, and Men.* New York: David McKay Co., 1974.

Miller, George A. *Language and Communication.* New York: McGraw-Hill, 1963.

Miller, Gerald. "On Defining Communication: Another Stab." *Journal of Communication* 16(1966): 88–99.

—————. *Speech Communication: A Behavioral Approach.* Indianapolis: Bobbs-Merrill Co., 1966.

Miller, Gerald, and Steinberg, Mark. *Between People.* Chicago: Science Research Associates, 1975.

Miller, James. "Living Systems: Basic Concepts; Structure and Process; Cross-Level Hypotheses." *Behavioral Science* 10(1965):337–79, 380–411.

Monroe, Alan, and Ehninger, Douglas. *Principles of Speech Communication.* 6th ed. Glenview, Ill.: Scott, Foresman and Co., 1969.

Mortensen, C. David. *Communication: The Study of Human Interaction.* New York: McGraw-Hill, 1972.

Murphy, George, ed. *A Synoptic History of Classical Rhetoric.* New York: Random House, 1972.

Nichols, Ralph, and Stevens, Leonard. *Are You Listening?* New York: McGraw-Hill, 1957.

Ogden, Charles, and Richards, I. A. *The Meaning of Meaning.* New York: Harcourt Brace and Co., 1946.

Oliver, Robert. *Culture and Communication.* Springfield, Ill.: Charles C. Thomas, 1962.

Pace, W., and Boren, Robert. *The Human Transaction: Facets, Functions, and Forms of Interpersonal Communication.* Glenview, Ill.: Scott, Foresman and Co., 1973.

Pierce, J. R. *Symbols, Signals, and Noise.* New York: Harper & Row, Torchbooks, 1961.

Postman, Neil; Weingartner, Charles; and Moran, Terence. *Language in America.* New York: Pegasus, 1969.

Prosser, Michael, ed. *Intercommunication Among Nations and Peoples.* New York: Harper & Row, 1973.

Rapoport, Anatole. *Operational Philosophy.* New York: Harper and Brothers, 1953.

Reid, Ronald. *Introduction to the Field of Speech.* Glenview, Ill.: Scott, Foresman and Co., 1965.

Rogers, Carl. *On Becoming a Person.* Boston: Houghton Mifflin Co., 1961.

Rokeach, Milton. *Beliefs, Attitudes, and Values.* San Francisco: Jossey-Bass, 1972.

Ross, W. R. *Aristotle: A Complete Exposition of His Works and Thoughts.* New York: Meridian Books, 1963.

Ruben, Brent. "General Systems: An Approach to Human Communication." In *Approaches to Human Communication,* edited by Richard Budd and Brent Ruben. New York: Spartan Books, 1972.

Ruben, Brent, and Budd, Richard. *Human Communication Handbook: Simulations and Games.* Rochelle Park, N.J.: Hayden Book Co., 1975.

Ruben, Brent, and Kim, John, eds. *General Systems Theory and Human Communication.* Rochelle Park, N.J.: Hayden Book Co., 1975.

Ruesch, Jurgen, and Bateson, Gregory. *Communication: The Social Matrix of Society.* New York: W. W. Norton & Co., 1951.

Sapir, Edward. *Culture, Language and Personality.* Berkeley, Calif.: University of California Press, 1966.

Schein, E., and Bennis, W. *Personal and Organizational Change Through Group Methods.* New York: John Wiley & Sons, 1967.

Schramm, Wilbur, ed. *Mass Communications.* Urbana: University of Illinois Press, 1960.

Shannon, Claude, and Weaver, Warren. *The Mathematical Theory of Communication.* Urbana: University of Illinois Press, 1949.

Smith, Alfred, ed. *Communication and Culture.* New York: Holt, Rinehart and Winston, 1966.

Smith, Henry. *Sensitivity to Others.* New York: McGraw-Hill, 1969.

Thayer, Lee. *Communication and Communication Systems.* Homewood, Ill.: Richard D. Irwin, 1968.

———. "Communication: Sine Qua Non of the Behavioral Sciences." In *Vistas in Science,* edited by D. L. Arm, Albuquerque: University of New Mexico Press, 1968.

———. "On the Mass Media and Mass Communication: Notes Toward a Theory." In *Mass Communication: Dialogue and Alternatives,* edited by Richard Budd and Brent Ruben. Rochelle Park, N.J.: Hayden Book Co., in press.

Theall, Donald. *The Medium Is the Rear View Mirror.* Montreal: McGill-Queens University Press, 1971.

von Bertalanffy, Ludwig. *General Systems Theory.* New York: George Braziller, 1968.

Watzlawick, Paul; Beavin, Janet; and Jackson, Don. *Pragmatics of Human Communication.* New York: W. W. Norton & Co., 1967.

Westley, Bruce, and MacLean, Malcolm. "A Conceptual Model for Communication Research." *Audio-Visual Communication Review* 3 (Winter 1955): 119–37.

Whorf, Benjamin L. *Language, Thought, and Reality.* New York: John Wiley & Sons, and M.I.T. Press, 1956.

Wilmot, William. *Dyadic Communication: A Transactional Perspective.* Reading, Mass.: Addison-Wesley Publishing Co., 1975.

Credits

Cover Photo: David Corona

Chapter 1

2, M. C. Escher's "Relativity" 1953. By permission of the Escher Foundation—Haags Gemeentemuseum—The Hague. 4, Illustrator: Fine Line Illustrations, Inc./N.Y. 5, Photo: Nat Clymer. 7, Illustrator: Fine Line Illustrations, Inc./N.Y. 12, Photos: Emil Fray. 13, Photo: Nat Clymer. 15, Photo: Nat Clymer. 20, From "Made in the U.S.A.—Works Every Time" by George Freeman, 15 January 1976. Copyright © 1976 by the New York Times Company. Reprinted by permission. Photo: David Corona.

Chapter 2

24, Photo: Hal Roach Studios. 26, Illustrator: Fine Line Illustrations, Inc./N.Y. 27, Photo: Hal Roach Studios. 30-31, Photo: Candida Stock Photos, Ltd. 35, "Incident" from On These I Stand by Countee Cullen. Copyright © 1925 by Harper & Row, Publishers, Inc. Renewed 1953 by Ida M. Cullen. Reprinted by permission of Harper & Row, Publishers. Illustrator: Rod Burke. 38, From One Flew Over the Cuckoo's Nest by Ken Kesey. Copyright © 1962 by Ken Kesey. Reprinted by permission of The Viking Press. Illustrator: Fred Womack. 42-43, Photos: Nat Clymer. 44, Cartoon by Saul Steinberg from the New York Times Book Review, 2 November 1975. Copyright © 1975 by the New York Times Company. Reprinted by permission.

Chapter 3

50, Photo: Richard Feiner and Company, Inc. 53, "April 12" by Rod McKuen, copyright © 1969 by Montcalm Productions, Inc., first published in the book In Someone's Shadow, by Random House & Cheval Books. Photo: "The Star Child" from the MGM release 2001: A Space Odyssey. Copyright © 1963 Metro-Goldwyn-Mayer, Inc. 55, Quoted from Walden, p. 251, by Henry David Thoreau. Commentaries by Larzer Ziff. New York: Holt, Rinehart and Winston, Inc., 1961. Illustration: Pablo Picasso's Don Quixote; in public domain. 57, "A Conceptual Model for Communication Research" by Bruce Westley and Malcolm MacLean. In Journalism Quarterly 3-4 (Winter 1957): 31-38; and in Core Readings: Human Communication, pp. 340-41, edited by Nancy Harper. New York: MSS Information Corp., 1975. Used with permission. Illustrator: Fine Line Illustrations, Inc./N.Y. 58, Photo: Bob Coyle (taken two years prior to Watergate). 60-61, Lyin' Eyes by Glenn Frey and Don Henley (Warner Brothers Music Corp./Kicking Bear Music ASCAP, 1975). Photo: Candida Stock Photos, Ltd. 62, Photo: Nat Clymer. 66, "Everybody's Talkin'" by Fred Neil. Copyright © 1967 Third Story Music, Inc. All rights reserved. Illustrator: Rod Burke. 68, Reprinted by permission of the publishers and the Trustees of Amherst College from The Poems of Emily Dickinson, edited by Thomas H. Johnson. Cambridge, Mass.: The Belknap Press of Harvard University Press, © 1951, 1955 by the President and Fellows of Harvard College. 70, Reprinted from Group Processes: An Introduction to Group Dynamics by Joseph Luft, by permission of Mayfield Publishing Company (formerly National Press Books). Copyright © 1963, 1970 Joseph Luft. Illustrator: Fine Line Illustrations, Inc./N.Y. 72-73, Photos: Wide World Photos. 77, Reprinted from Group Processes: An Introduction to Group Dynamics by Joseph Luft, by permission of Mayfield Publishing Company (formerly National Press Books). Copyright © 1963, 1970 Joseph Luft. Illustrator: Fine Line Illustrations, Inc./N.Y.

Chapter 4

78, Photo: Courtesy of CBS. 82, Photo: Nat Clymer. 85, Copyright © Jules Feiffer. 87, From "The Multivalued Choice" by Geoffrey Vickers. In Concepts and Perspectives, p. 272, edited by Lee Thayer. Washington, D.C.: Spartan Books, 1967. Photo: Candida Stock Photos, Ltd. 89, Photo: Brent Rubin. 94, Reprinted by permission of Psychology Today. As a full page advertisement by Psychology Today, appearing in 20 October 1975 issue of the New York Times. Copyright © 1975 by the New York Times Company. Reprinted by permission. 95, Photo: Nat Clymer. 97, Photo: David Attie.

Chapter 5

104, Photo: Candida Stock Photos, Ltd. 108, National Enquirer—Al Johns. 114, Illustrator: Fine Line Illustrations, Inc./N.Y. 116-17, Illustrator: Fred Womack. 118, Photo: Mary Ellen Mark— From Lee Gross. 119, "When You Are Old and Gray" taken from The Tom Lehrer Song Book by Tom Lehrer. Copyright © 1954 by Tom Lehrer. Used by permission of Crown Publishers, Inc. 122, "Richard Cory" is reprinted by permission of Charles Scribner's Sons from The Children of the Night by Edwin Arlington Robinson. Illustrator: Rod Burke.

Chapter 6

129, Photo: The Bettmann Archive, Inc. *132-33,* Excerpted with permission from *Dictionary of CB Lingo,* pp. 43-122. New York: Davis Publications, Inc., 1976. Illustrator: Fred Womack. *137,* From *The Meaning of Meaning* by C. Ogden and I. A. Richards. Reprinted by permission of Harcourt Brace Jovanovich, Inc., and Routledge & Kegan Paul Ltd. Illustrator: Fine Line Illustrations, Inc./N.Y. *139,* Photos: Nat Clymer. *140,* "What All That Carnie Talk Means" by Sheila Anne Webb appearing in the *Des Moines Sunday Register,* 15 August 1976. Copyright © 1976 Des Moines Register & Tribune Company; reprinted by permission. Illustrator: Rod Burke. *144,* By permission. From Webster's New Collegiate Dictionary © 1976 by G & C Merriam Company Publishers of the Merriam-Webster Dictionaries. *146,* Reproduced by special permission of *Playboy* Magazine; copyright © 1975 by Playboy.

Chapter 7

150, Photos: United Press International. *153,* Drawing by Handelsman; © 1975. The New Yorker Magazine, Inc. *156,* By permission of Dead Sea Music, Little David Record Album AM & FM LD 7214. *158,* From *On Edge* by Jim Crane. Copyright © 1965 by M. E. Bratcher. Used by permission of John Knox Press. *161,* Reprinted with permission of Macmillan Publishing Company, Inc., from *Communication: The Transfer of Meaning* by Don Fabun. Copyright © 1968, Kaiser Aluminum and Chemical Corporation. *168,* Reprinted by permission of Grove Press, Inc. and Hutchinson Publishing Group, Ltd. From *The Autobiography of Malcolm X.* Copyright © 1964 by Alex Haley and Malcolm X. Copyright © 1965 by Alex Haley and Betty Shabazz. *169,* State Historical Society of Wisconsin. *171,* Reprinted with permission of the McNaught Syndicate, Inc.

Chapter 8

176, Photo: Candida Stock Photos, Ltd. *179,* From *The New York Times Magazine* of 2 November 1975. Copyright © 1975 by the New York Times Company. Reprinted by permission. *180-81,* Photos: Nat Clymer. *183,* Figure 8.1— "Fig. 1: Schematic Representation of the Process of Abstracting in Man," p. 83, in *Living with Change: The Semantics of Coping* by Wendell Johnson. Selected and edited by Dorothy Moeller. Harper & Row, 1972. Illustrator: Fine Line Illustrations, Inc./N.Y. *185,* "Flubs & Fluffs" by Jerry Robinson. Copyright © 1975 New York News Inc. *186,* Taken from *Fiddler on the Roof* by Joseph Stein. Copyright © 1965 by Joseph Stein. Used by permission of Crown

Publishers, Inc. *190,* Copyright © 1975 Paul Simon. Used with permission of the publisher.

Chapter 9

196, Used with permission of *Communication Arts,* and William Arbogast, photographer. *200,* From Approaches to Human Communication, pp. 1-2, edited by Richard W. Budd and Brent D. Ruben. New Rochelle Park, N.J.: Hayden Press, 1974. *202,* Cartoon by Jerome Martin, Time-Life Picture Agency © Time, Inc. *205,* Words and music by Malvina Reynolds. Copyright © Schroder Music Company (ASCAP) 1962. Used by permission. Photo: Skyviews. *206,* Photo: Nat Clymer. *207,* Photo: Jim Whitmer Photography. *208,* Photo: H. Armstrong Roberts. *211,* From *Word Play: What Happens When People Talk,* by Peter Farb. Reprinted by permission of Alfred A. Knopf, Inc. *214,* Poem: In public domain. Photo: FAO photo by E. Ragazzini.

Chapter 10

218, Photo: United Press International. *221,* "I'm Looking Through You" (John Lennon, Paul McCartney) Copyright © 1965 Northern Songs, Ltd. All rights for the United States, Canada, Mexico and the Philippines controlled by Maclen Music, Inc. Used by permission. All rights reserved. Photo: Rick Smolan. *222,* Photo: Nat Clymer. *223,* From *Are You Listening,* p. 153, by Ralph Nichols and Leonard Stevens. New York: McGraw-Hill, 1957. *225,* Photo: The Bettmann Archive, Inc. *227,* "Figments" by Dale Hale from *The Tretonian,* published 27 February 1976. Copyright © 1976 Manson Western Syndicate. Reprinted with permission. *230,* From *Living with Change: The Semantics of Coping,* p. 157, by Wendell Johnson, and edited by Dorothy Moeller. New York: Harper and Row, 1972. Illustrator: Rod Burke. *234,* From *Catch 22* by Joseph Heller. Copyright © 1955, 1961 by Joseph Heller. Reprinted by permission of Simon & Schuster, Inc. Illustrator: Rod Burke.

Chapter 11

240, Photo: Rick Smolan. *243,* Photo: Nat Clymer. *246,* Copyright © 1975 United Feature Syndicate, Inc. *247,* Copyright © 1975 United Feature Syndicate, Inc. *251,* Lee Thayer quoted in *Interact,* p. 9, by Brent Ruben. Kennybunkport Maine: Mercer House Press, 1973. *254-55,* Photos: Rick Smolan. *257,* Copyright © 1966 Paul Simon. Used with permission of the publisher.

Chapter 12

264, Photo: Rohn Engh. *267*, Photo: David Lukowicz. *270*, "Funky Winkerbean" by Tom Batiuk. Courtesy of Field Newspaper Syndicate. *274*, From *Beyond Words: An Introduction to Nonverbal Communication*, p. 120, by Randall P. Harrison. Copyright © 1974. Reproduced by permission of Prentice-Hall, Inc., Englewood Cliffs, N. J. Illustrator: Fine Line Illustrations, Inc./N.Y. *275*, Photo: United Press International. *277*, Reproduced by special permission of *Playboy* Magazine. Copyright © 1975 by Playboy.

Chapter 13

284, Photo: David Attie. *287*, Photos (left to right): Jan Lukas; Van Cleve Photography; H. Armstrong Roberts. *291*, Reprinted from *The Prophet* by Kahlil Gibran, with permission of the publisher Alfred A. Knopf, Inc. Copyright © 1923 by Kahlil Gibran; renewal copyright © 1951 by Administrators C.T.A. of Kahlil Gibran Estate, and Mary G. Gibran. Photo: Swami Satchidananda attending the International Yoga and Meditation Conference in June 1976, sponsored by the Himalayan International Institute of Yoga Science and Philosophy, Glenview, Illinois. *295*, Photo: Time-Life Picture Agency—Walter Hoving. *298*, Photo: Jon Jacobson. *300*, Illustrator: Fine Line Illustrations, Inc./N.Y. *305*, "Animal Crackers" by Rog Ballen. Courtesy of Chicago Tribune—New York News Syndicate.

Chapter 14

312, Photo: Newsweek—Bernard Gotfryd. *314*, Photo: Jon Jacobson. *318*, "Superstar" from *Jesus Christ Superstar*, A Rock Opera by Andrew Lloyd Webber and Tim Rice. Lyrics by Tim Rice. Music by Andrew Lloyd Webber. Copyright © 1969 by Leeds Music, Ltd. London, England. Sole Selling Agent Leeds Music Corporation, 445 Park Avenue, New York, N.Y. for North, South, and Central America. Used by permission. All rights reserved. Photo: From the motion picture *Jesus Christ Superstar*. Courtesy of Universal Pictures.

Chapter 15

334, Photo: Arthur Witmann—St. Louis Post Dispatch from Black Star. *337*, Photo: Emil Fray. *339*, Photo: Nat Clymer. *343*, Photo: Nat Clymer. *348*, Drawing from *College Professoring* by Oliver P. Kolstoe, illustrated by Don-Paul Benjamin, Southern Illinois University Press, 1975.

Chapter 16

356, Photo: Rick Smolan. *359*, Photo: Ed Carlin. *360*, From *The Sacred Canopy*, pp. 3-4, by Peter Berger, Garden City, N.Y.: Anchor Books, 1961. Photo: Clyde Hare. *362*, Reprinted with permission of McDonald's Corporation. *367*, Figure 16.1—Bruce Westley and Malcolm MacLean, "A Conceptual Model for Communication Research," *Journalism Quarterly* 3-4 (Winter 1957): 31-38; and in *Core Readings: Human Communication,* edited by Nancy Harper, N.Y.: MSS Information Corp., 1975, pp. 340-41. Illustrator: Fine Line Illustrations, Inc./N.Y. Figure 16.2—From the *Mathematical Theory of Communication* by Claude E. Shannon Warren Weaver. Urbana, Ill.: University of Illinois Press, 1972. Copyright © 1949 by the Board of Trustees of the University of Illinois. Reprinted by permission of the University of Illinois Press. Illustrator: Fine Line Illustrations, Inc./N.Y. *368*, By permission of Video-Date, Inc. *369*, Photo: Nat Clymer. *371*, Photos: Nat Clymer. *374*, Photo: David Lukowicz. *376-77*, Quote: Source unknown. Photo: Ewing Galloway. Car diagram: Capri II brochure by Lincoln- Mercury, Division of Ford.

Index

message, 62

    effective, guidelines, 63-64

    skills, field of experience and, 29-31, 43

environment. *See* communication environment

etcetera (etc.), as extensional device, 189

ethos (credibility of sender), 73-75

  in public speaking situation, 315, 317

euphemisms, 154-55, 157-58

  defined, 153, 154

event-data, 57

experience, field of, 26

  as dynamic affecting interpersonal communication, 28-37

    culture, 34

    encoding and decoding skills, 29-31

    interference with intentional communication, 28-37

    perception of self, others, message, 31-34

    social systems, 34, 36-37

  as dynamic affecting listening and meaning, 249-50

  as dynamic of message-making, 80

extensional devices, 188-89, 191

  dates, 189

  etc., 189

  hyphens, 191

  indexing, 189

  quotes, 189, 191

feedback, 109-10

  in communication process cycles, 6

  descriptive, 272

  functions of, 266-73

  as information about code and channel selections, 112-14

  interference with intentional meaning and, 278-80

  mechanisms, 265-66

  as message-making, 273-75

  as self-disclosure, 276-78

  specific, 272

  timeliness of, 272

field of experience. *See* experience, field of

friendly audience, 340

general or larger audience, 336

general semantics, 138

goals, group, 289

group, defined, 287. *See also* public speaking; small group

group identification, as motive for joining group, 293-94

habitual inattention, 236

Hayakawa, S. I., 155, 170

hearing

  listening, perceiving, attending and, 224, 226-28

  physiology of, 228-29

Homans, George C., 288

hostile audience, 341

hyphens, as extensional device, 191

inattention

  habitual, 236

  selective, 236

indexing, as extensional device, 189

individual, and small group, 292-93

  effect of membership on, 294-97

inferences, 163, 165-66

  inaccurate, making, 236

inferential communication, 42

intentional messages, 71

interdependence, 287

interference

  with intentional communication

    audiencing and, 353

    basic elements of communication process and, 17-19

    dynamics affecting interpersonal communication and, 43-45

    effective listening and, 258-59

    media and messages and, 381

    public speaking and, 331-32

    receiver as listener and, 235-37

    sender and, 75

    sender and dynamics of message-making and, 100-101

    sender as receiver and, 121, 123

    small groups and, 308-309

  with intended meaning

    abstracting and, 192-93

    feedback and, 278-80

    message and, 145, 147-48

    language and culture and, 215-16

    types of words and, 173-74

interpersonal communication, dynamics affecting, 25-47

  communication environment, 37, 39

  field of experience, 28-37

  interference with intentional communication, 43-45

  model, 26, 28, 39, 42

interpretation, as active listening, 254-56

intrapersonal communication, 69

invention, as canon of oratory, 322

judgmental language, 158-60

  words with conclusions, 160-62

kinesics, 12, 58

Korzybski, Alfred, 136, 138